THE SCOTTISH INSURRECTION OF 1820

THE SCOTTISH INSURRECTION

OF 1820

by

P. BERRESFORD ELLIS

and

SEUMAS MAC A' GHOBHAINN

Preface by P. Berresford Ellis

Foreword by Hugh MacDiarmid

PLUTO PRESS

This edition first published 1989 by Pluto Press
345 Archway Road, London N6 5AA

Distributed in the USA by Unwin Hyman Inc
8 Winchester Place, Winchester
MA 01890, USA

First published 1970 by Victor Gollancz Ltd

Printed and bound in the United States of America

British Library Cataloguing in Publication Data
Ellis, Peter Berresford, *1943–*
    The Scottish insurrection of 1820.—New ed.
    1. Scotland. Political events, 1820–1830
    I. Title   II. Mac a' Ghobhainn, Seumas.
    1930–1987
    941.107′4
    ISBN 0-7453-0285-8

An Fhirinn an aghaidh an t-Saoghail!
(The Truth against the World!)
                    Scottish saying

CONTENTS

APPENDICES

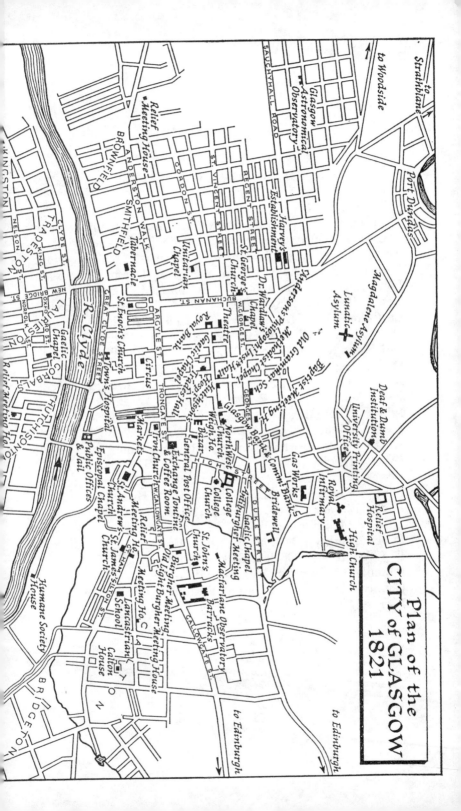

Plan of the
CITY of GLASGOW
1821

ACKNOWLEDGEMENTS

THE AUTHORS WOULD like to offer their deep thanks to those who have helped them in their search for the material for *The Scottish Insurrection of 1820*, particularly the following: Lord Sidmouth, Lady Vivian, A. Landa (Agent General in London for New South Wales, Australia), M. J. Saclier (Archives of Tasmania, Australia), Earl of Wemyss and March, Lt.-Colonel J. F. H. P. Johnson, Lt.-Colonel A. G. M. Urwick, D. W. King (Ministry of Defence Library), Thomas I. Rae and James Ritchie (National Library of Scotland), Miss M. E. Cash (Devon Record Office), H. S. Cobb (House of Lords Record Office), G. R. Barbour (Scottish Record Office), P. A. Penfold (Public Record Office), C. W. Black (Mitchell Library, Glasgow), Margaret H. Martin (Glasgow University Library), John Robertson (Stirling Public Library), Elizabeth A. Liversidge (Stirling County Library), James W. Forsyth (Ayr Carnegie Library), W. M. Martin (Dumbarton Public Library) E. M. Stark (Dumbarton City Library), John B. Purdie (Renfrew County Library), H. I. Hunt (Motherwell Public Library), J. G. Donnan (William Patrick Memorial Library, Kirkintilloch), N. R. McCorkindale (Galashiels Public Library), William Scottie (Airdrie Public Library), P. J. W. Brand (Clydebank Public Library), G. C. Stewart (Hamilton Public Library), W. M'K. Murray (Clackmannan County Library) and Robert M. Strathdee (Midlothian County Library).

PREFACE TO THE 1989 EDITION

P. BERRESFORD ELLIS

When my co-author, the late Seumas Mac a'Ghobhainn, and I wrote our study of the 1820 uprising, first published in April 1970, we knew that we were exploring 'virgin territory'. No full-length study of the uprising had ever been attempted; in fact, hardly anyone in Scotland had even heard of the event. It had been deleted almost entirely from the Scottish historical consciousness. This major radical uprising is still over-shadowed by the lesser affair of the 1819 'Peterloo' massacre in Manchester. One of the reasons that we felt obvious efforts had been made to 'edit' the events from Scottish history was the fact that the rising contained a national content, for it was the intention of the radicals to establish an independent Scottish Parliament – an objective that was unacceptable to the Establishment and its historians. While we realised that we were revealing an important piece of 'hidden history', we were scarcely prepared for the interest which the publication of the book generated. According to the publishers, the book became 'the most reviewed book of 1970' and, at the time of publication, five newspapers, including one London daily and two Scottish dailies, published extracts from it.

Within months the 1820 Commemorative Committee had been formed by prominent Scottish politicians, historians and literary figures. Seumas Mac a' Ghobhainn was elected honorary president of the committee in the following year. The first commemorative gathering in modern times was organised by the committee at the monument in Sighthill Cemetery, Glasgow, to the executed leaders John Baird and Andrew Hardie in September 1970. We were invited to deliver a short address.

The '1820' began to be mentioned in general histories of Scotland, commencing with a reference in John Prebble's *The Lion in the North* (Secker and Warburg, 1971), which made full acknowledgement to our researches. Other books and

1

studies have been less generous in acknowledging our efforts; works such as Tom Steel's 24-episode Scottish Television production 'Scotland's Story', shown on Channel Four in 1984. In programme fourteen, the rise of Scottish republicanism and the 1820 were dealt with. The series was accompanied by a tie-in book of the same name published by William Collins.

In 1973 a play concerning '1820' was produced by the Glasgow Citizen's Theatre which also acknowledged our work, although a video produced by the 'Baird and Hardie Society' in 1986 made no such acknowledgement, presumably because the producers argued that '1820' was a manifestation of 'British' radicalism and failed to mention the nationalist aims of the '1820'.

Within a decade a new primary school at Condorrat, near Cumbernauld, the home of the executed John Baird, was named 'The Baird Memorial School' by the local council, then controlled by the Scottish National Party.

The 1820 Commemorative Committee gave way to the 1820 Society. From 1985 this society became extremely active in seeking to preserve the 1820 monuments, particularly the one at Sighthill Cemetery, in gathering artefacts connected with the uprising and with pursing a campaign urging the Scottish Education Department to revise the teaching of Scottish history in Scottish schools so that children could learn about such events.

The society achieved some astonishing successes. Most notable was the recognition by a Tory Secretary of State for Scotland, George Younger, of the Sighthill monument as an important historical site (*Glasgow Herald*, 3 January 1986) and its listing as a Scottish historical monument. Later that year the monument was restored at a cost of £10,000 and unveiled before 5,000 people on 31 October thanks to a campaign by the society. The actual campaign to raise the money for the restoration proved to be something of a drama in itself. The society had launched an appeal for money at a public rally in July 1985. In November the City of Glasgow District Council offered to put up £5,000 towards the appeal on condition that the 1820 Society were able to raise a similar sum. This provoked a great deal of criticism from Tory politicians and press which receded slightly after the Secretary of State for Scotland announced the listing of the monument.

But, early in 1986, the Council seemed to hesitate.

The monument had been erected by Chartists in 1847 to mark the spot where the remains of Baird and Hardie had been re-interred (described on pp. 290–2). Now the accuracy of the book was called into question when the Parks and Recreation Committee of the Council claimed this was not so: 'Hardie and Baird are not interred there' (Council Minutes, Print 4, 1985/86, page 387, item 14). They based this claim on the fact 'there is no known reference in the cemetery records'. The energetic press officer of the 1820 Society, Councillor James Mitchell, a Scottish National Party representative on Renfrew District Council, said: 'We were shaken to be told by the Council that the working class martyrs we seek to honour are not buried there. We think we have irrefutable evidence to show that Baird and Hardie are indeed interred there ...' (*Glasgow Herald*, November 1985).

The 1820 Society, accepting the evidence presented in this book, called for an official exhumation of the site to ascertain if the remains of Baird and Hardie were there. The call was supported by SOGAT '82, which had been formed out of the Bookbinders Consolidated Union. SOGAT '82 were also concerned to prove that the Glasgow bookbinder, Andrew White, whose death sentence for his part in 1820 had been commuted to transportation, had been buried at the same site when he died on 27 December 1872.

On Monday, 24 March, bowing to pressure caused by the ensuing publicity, Glasgow Council agreed on an exhumation because 'it is considered that the positive identification of the resting place of the 1820 Martyrs is of significant importance in terms of Scottish history, being more important (although much less publicised and known) than the Tolpuddle Maryrs.'

Another Scottish historian entered the argument in support of our contention. Michael Donnelly, the assistant curator of the Glasgow working people's museum, the People's Place, also argued that the evidence that Baird and Hardie were buried at the monument was 'irrefutable'. He pointed to the letter from the Lord Advocate in 1847 (quoted on p. 291 here) and the fact that the latter is also reproduced on the monument itself. Below this is carved the words:

In accordance with these instructions, exhumation took place at an early hour on July 20, 1847 and the remains re-interred in front of this monument on the same day in the presence of a considerable number of friends.

Below this are the words: 'Here they Rest.'

The carvings are on the far side of the monument to the face normally viewed by the public and had not, of course, been examined by representatives of the Council.

On Thursday, 10 April 1986, the exhumation was carried out in the presence of Jack Fuller, chairman of the 1820 Society, Councillor James Mitchell and society members G. Smith and J. Beveridge. The press and media were in attendance but were kept away from the actual exhumation which was covered by tarpaulins. The remains were discovered exactly where this book stated them to be. The following day *The Scotsman* was representative of the reports which appeared in the newspapers and media: 'Doubts concerning the last resting place of two national martyrs who were hanged for leading the Scottish insurrection of 1820 have been dispelled.'

Indeed, initially Glasgow Council admitted 'it is possible to accept the fact that the remains of the coffins found there did contain the remains of Baird and Hardie'. Then, on 4 August 1986, they changed their positive stance to accept the recommendation of the Director of Parks and Recreation for the records to show the wording 'The remains of Baird and Hardie *appear* to have been interred in front of the Martyrs' Monument.'

In subsequent interviews, I felt able to welcome the findings of the exhumation as reported in the press and media as exonerating the accuracy of this book but had to point out that Glasgow Council in their official record, were performing a disservice to future historians and the people of Scotland.

'There has never been any doubt except the doubt created by the "pussyfooting" attitude of Glasgow Council. In view of the overwhelming evidence, the Glasgow City Council owe it to future generations of Scots and Scottish historians to make it clear that the last resting place of Baird and Hardie is in Sighthill Cemetery.'

Glasgow Council, however, kept its promise to meet the £5,000 towards the renovation of the monument and several other councils joined in, such as Strathclyde, which gave £1,500 and Renfrew, which gave £200, a sum strongly protested against by the five Tory councilors who claimed the donation was illegal under the Local Government (Scotland) Act of 1973. The council's legal adviser eventually had to reassure them on this point. Even so, things did not go smoothly with the restoration and on 25 September 1986, the Glasgow *Evening Times* reported that the carving of a head from the monument had been broken off and stolen. It was obviously a piece of political vandalism for which no one claimed responsibility.

The unveiling of the monument on 31 October was followed by a civic reception in the Glasgow City council chamber and the opportunity was taken to launch a campaign pressing the Scottish Education Department for a review of the way Scottish history was taught in schools, particularly for the inclusion of the facts of '1820' in history books.

With Glasgow Council making the decision to re-name George Place after the South African, Nelson Mandela, the 1820 Society began to lobby the council to commemorate Scotland's own political martyrs and rename George Square (named after the profligate George III, monarch in 1820) as '1820 Square'. The Council rejected the suggestion but, once again conceding to pressure brought by the society, decided, on 22 August 1986, 'in principle' to name a street after Baird and Hardie. The society at once pointed out that there were several streets already bearing the names Baird and Hardie, named after people not connected with the leaders of the rising, and suggesting that at least the forenames be added so that, in future, people could recognise the streets as those named after the 1820 leaders. This was also rejected and the Council left it to the planning committee to make suitable proposals. The Glasgow *Evening Times*, 6 October 1986, reported that the planning committee had refused to consult the 1820 Society on suitable streets, those having some connection with the uprising, and, indeed, had proposed Springburn Road as 'Baird and Hardie Way'. Protests were made when it was discovered that Springburn Road would soon be relegated to a slipway for a motorway route. No more progress has been made in the matter.

One point that became obvious not long after the first publication of this book was that much additional material concerning the fate of individuals caught up in the insurrection could be brought to light. We were almost immediately contacted by descendants of those transported to Australia. In 1972 Peter Walker of Kinnoull found a series of letters written by his great-great grand-uncle, Alexander Hart, who had fought at Bonnymuir, was badly wounded, sentenced to death and then had his sentence commuted to transportation. Hart died in Australia at the age of 90. Walker published some of the letters in the *Scots Independent*, May 1972.

The keyed bugle carried by James Black at Bonnymuir came to light in private hands in 1986. Black (mentioned on pp. 174–5) was badly wounded at Bonnymuir but succeeded in making a spectacular escape from a window after being made prisoner. George Wilson, a lecturer at the West of Scotland Agricultural College at Auchencruive, wrote to the 1820 Society to tell how the bugle had been handed down in his family from his ancestor, James Black, together with the story of how it was carried to rally the insurgents during the uprising.

Perhaps the most macabre items to come to light are the cloak and axe of the public executioner who decapitated Baird and Hardie at Stirling Castle. The items are kept at Stirling although, in 1986, they went on exhibition at the City of Edinburgh Arts Centre.

The John Hastie Museum in Strathaven, one of the centres of radicalism and the home of the executed James Wilson, now has an excellent section devoted to the uprising. East Kilbride District Council, in which Strathaven lies, recently issued a pamphlet life of Wilson for distribution at the museum.

Curiously, the 1820 Society were criticised for ignoring James Wilson by concentrating on the Baird and Hardie monument. But, in fact, the society had been active in holding commemorations at the radical memorial in Woodside Cemetery, near where it was thought Wilson had been buried. After Wilson's execution he had been buried in a pauper's grave at Glasgow High Church but his daughter, Mrs Lilias Walters, and his niece, Mrs Ritchie, had the remains dug up and secretly interred in the Strathaven parish church as detailed on p. 275 of this book.

The 1820 Society promised to attempt to track down the exact location of Wilson's last resting place. In November 1986, David Jackson of Rutherglen, a descendant of Wilson's wife's family, began research with the help of the society, who gave him a small grant. He subsequently found an entry in the Avondale Parish Register which referred to the reinterrment of Wilson's body 'in the second breadth of the east length of the cemetery' (*Hamilton Advertiser*, 5 December 1986). The search for the grave continues.

Among other finds which have come to light is the fact that the centenary of the '1820' was commemorated by members of the Independent Labour Party on 5 September 1920, at a ceremony at Sighthill. An added inscription on the sandstone of the monument had been almost obliterated, but the staff of Glasgow's Mitchell Library discovered the text of the inscription and the fact of the gathering in an ILP newssheet of 11 September 1920 (*Glasgow Herald*, 5 June 1986).

Other more important discoveries have come to light. Perhaps one of the most important finds has been that of some of the original treason trial documents. On p. 267 of this book we note that the records for the trials seemed to have disappeared and our extensive searches had proved negative. Curiously, we discovered that all the records apart from one or two items which had, at the time, been lodged in a '*Baga de Secretis*', which we tracked down to the London Public

Records Office (PRO KB 8), had been removed.

In 1983 Dr Athol L. Murray, Keeper of the Records of Scotland, discovered some of the trial documents among a mass of unsorted material which had been transmitted to the Scottish Records Office from the High Court of Judiciary. Writing to inform me of this find, Dr Murray said: 'My impression was that these documents add little to the material already available in the printed reports and your own book.' Dr Murray felt that 'it does not look as though there was any deliberate attempt to suppress these records. The explanation is probably that, because the trials had not taken place under normal Justiciary procedures, the records did not fit into any of the existing series and were put to one side and forgotten. This is quite a common occurrence with records of all types!'

The trials for High Treason were actually held under English Law and not Scottish Law, contravening the Treaty of Union of 1707 AD.

These records are now held by the Scottish Record Office, referenced as 'JC 21'.

However, some new aspects are revealed by this material. It appears that John Walters, James Wilson's son-in-law, husband to Lilias Walters, was imprisoned in June/July 1820, but released after a Writ of Capias issued against him was 'not found'.

The documents also show that Sir William Rae, the Lord Advocate, was somewhat premature in announcing the termination of the High Treason trials in August 1820 (pp. 264–5). In March 1821 there were still several radicals jailed without trial, including George Gillies and Moses Gilfillan of Stirling, against whom true bills had been found in July 1820 (see p. 226). Amongst the prisoners were the Strathaven leader Robert Hamilton and his companion John Morrison, the ex-army veteran. Walter Provan, Matthew Logan, Alexander Cameron and Peter Ferguson, all from Lanark, were also in jail. On 21 March 1821, Writs of Capias were issued against them in a half-hearted attempt to institute new treason trails, but all were returned 'not found'. Had Scottish juries finally grown sick of the 'mummery', the demand for more state victims to strike fear into the people? Certainly, in logical terms, there was more evidence for treasonable intent against Robert Hamilton, who had for a while led his men towards Cathkin armed with a sword, than there was against the executed Wilson, who served under him.

Another interesting sidelight which turned up in the records of 'The Greenock Infirmary' (privately published, no date) pp. 37–8, was a reference to a banquet held in 1832 to celebrate the passing of the Reform Act. A toast was drunk 'to the memory of Alan Ker', a juryman at one of the treason trials, 'who', it was said, 'by his refusal to bring in a verdict of "guilty" despite extreme pressure from the Bench, had saved two of the Paisley radicals on trial for high treason on August 1, 1820'. This was the trial of James Speirs and John Lang, described on pp. 258–62. The same source refers to a riot in Greenock in 1821 which took place on the anniversary of the day in 1820 when regular soldiers opened fire on an unarmed Greenock crowd, killing and wounding many. During the 1821 commemoration of this event it was reported that placards were placed on street corners calling for 'Revenge' and 'Blood for Blood'.

There are still many aspects of the insurrection of 1820 which deserve further research. Such study may be underway, for in 1987 it was announced that Dr John Brims, former research assistant at the National Library of Scotland, had been awarded a three-year Glenfiddich Fellowship at St Andrews University to conduct research into the insurrection.

One intriguing question which long frustrated my co-author and myself was the fate of the members of the 28-man Committee for Organising a Provisional Government, who were arrested in Glasgow on 21 March 1820. The letters by the Glasgow police chief refer to their arrest and imprisonment. The last that is known about them is that they were still being held *incommunicado* in Glasgow jail in November 1820. On pp. 140–1 we asked the obvious question. Why were they not charged with High Treason? We know that some of the committee, such as John King, who left the meeting only minutes before the arrest took place, must have been government *agents provocateur*. But what of the others? What of their fate?

During our researches we fully expected the answer to lay in the *'Baga de Secretis'* where records, reports and letters connected with the affair had been deposited. But, as we discovered, most of the documentation after 1817 had been removed from that repository some time after 1820. One could spend much time speculating on the reason for this removal. No further reference to the committee has, so far, been discovered.

The Scottish poet, Hamish Henderson, commented in *The Scotsman* (11 July 1986): 'These individuals have disappeared, as it were, into a black hole of history, even their identity is uncertain.' Mr Henderson continues:

This is astounding. Prisoners invariably have relatives and friends who try to keep their plight before the public eye. Every last detail relating to the 'Bonnymuir rebels' transported to New South Wales had been ferreted out and put on record by Margaret and Alastair Macfarlane in their book *The Scottish Radicals*. But of the fate of the 'Provisional' Committee nothing, but nothing is known.

Hamish Henderson puts forward his own theory, one I find totally acceptable in the circumstances.

Ever since the time of Sir Francis Walsingham, successive English Governments have paid well-funded attention to the securing of underground political intelligence. When the authorities began to interrogate the arrested Committee members, they may well have discovered a 'Man Who Was Thursday' situation. Did the Committee consist, more or less in its entirety, of members of two or more rival intelligence organisations who were mutually unknown to each other, and had been 'jollying each other along'? If so, the Government would have had no alternative but to allow them to drift discreetly into obscurity.

Nobody reading the account of the antics of the

Government spies King, Turner, Craig and Lees, as described by Messrs Berresford Ellis and Mac a' Ghobhainn in their book on the Rising, will be disposed to dismiss this speculation as totally fantastic or incredible.

One of the greatest research breakthroughs on the '1820' would be the discovery of a solution to the conundrum of the fate of the committee. Neither the Macfarlane book, *The Scottish Radicals* (1982) nor Thomis and Holt's *Threats of Revolution in Britain 1789-1848* (1978), which discussed the '1820' in Chapter 3, have actually come up with any new research material on the subject. Indeed, Thomis and Holt seem to go out of their way to ignore research material already available. Hamish Henderson has observed that Thomis and Holt seem oddly eager to play down the role of *agents provocateur* in the lead-up to the rising. In fact they claim (p. 126) that the charge of infiltration by government agents into the Radicals 'is a piece of nonsense, as far as Scotland is concerned'. Henderson has pointed out: 'Unfortunately they pay scant attention to a good deal of hard evidence, and even make light of such a cool and accurate observer as Cockburn that "there had been the secret agency of some in fomenting the treason".' In fact, they base their argument on the statement (p. 80) that 'Castlereagh denied any Government involvement.' The only intelligent rejoinder to that has to be: he would, wouldn't he? After all, one remembers the part Castlereagh played in trying to provoke a premature rising in Ireland in 1797 by means of *agents provocateur*. How, through a government espionage system, he built up reactionary organisations and merciless *dragonnades* against the Protestant Republicans of Ulster. Castlereagh was, in the words of Lord Byron:

Cold blooded, smooth-faced, placid miscreant!
Dabbling its sleek young hands in Erin's gore -

One can hardly take his word at face value.
Thomis and Holt try to convince their readers that John King was not a government agent. 'Attempts have been made to

argue that the Bonnymuir rebels had within their own number a certain John King who had been retained by the authorities', say Thomis and Holt, 'and who directed the authorities to where the insurgents were resting ... The flight of King before the rebel army marched out to the battle site is no proof of his complicity, but suggests rather that he was by this time a disillusioned conspirator who fled on realising that he had been mislead by false hopes of a mass rising' (p. 81).

Hamish Henderson argues: 'Nobody in a position to evaluate the existing evidence will be inclined to give this "disillusioned conspirator" theory an instant's credence.' Indeed, Thomis and Holt give the impression that they had not read this volume with care or, doing so, they simply chose to ignore the facts presented. Andrew Hardie wrote a letter, while awaiting execution, which gives a detailed account of the events leading up to Bonnymuir. He first met the enigmatic King, who was always out ahead of everyone else, and always promising reinforcements which never turned up, in Condorrat at or near the home of John Baird. 'When we found him [Baird] there was one King had been waiting with him, upon us coming forward. This King belongs to Glasgow, but what he is I do not know, but this I know, that he acted a very unbecoming part with us. King had told Baird that there was a party of two hundred well armed men coming out, and that they were all old soldiers.'

Hardie went on: 'King left us at Condorrat, and went before us on the pretext of getting the Camelon and Falkirk people ready by the time we should be forward.' In his statement, Hardie also makes it plain that King actually selected the site of the battle. '[He] said that we should have to go up on the moor, and wait there until we got a reinforcement from Camelon.'

Hamish Henderson believes that there can be no doubt that, as Andrew Hardie so succinctly put it towards the end of his letter, 'we were outwitted and betrayed'. He says that 'this narrative speaks for itself' but, in addition, in the poem which Hardie wrote in Stirling awaiting death, his suspicion of King is made absolutely explicit. Hamish Henderson adds:

'Revealingly, the poem borrows its measure, and, so to speak, its verbal cue, from the old nursery rhyme:

There was a man of double deed
Who sowed a garden full of seed.'

The poem is given in full in Appendix 3 of this volume.

There is much more work to be done on '1820' in terms of extending our knowledge of the event by the gathering of more information and particularly, as I have already said, tracing the mystery of the fate of the 'Provisional' Committee. However, it is very exciting to look at the developments which have taken place since this book was first published. At that time people were astounded that such an event, resulting in 85 indictments of High Treason, in public executions, in transportations and imprisonments, could have been so effectively eliminated from historical consciousness. It is exciting to see the new awareness, the enthusiasm of the 1820 Society, and the new research endeavours. Although this book remains the only full-length study of the insurrection, it is to be hoped, along with the activities of the 1820 Society, that this new edition will help sustain the attempts to place '1820' firmly in the history books. It provides a very necessary corrective to the Scottish historical mythology manufactured by Sir Walter Scott and it makes historical sense out of the later movements of Scottish nationalism, its republican outlook and of 'Clydeside Socialism'.

Ensuring that people know their history, and can learn from their history so that they are not condemned to perpetuate it, was one of the aspirations of my co-author, the late Seumas Mac a' Ghobhainn. Seumas died aged only 57 years on 21 January 1987. As an historian, an author and journalist, Seumas was firmly dedicated to the Scottish Gaelic language – *Gàidhlig*, as he always insisted in correctly spelling it. He was the leading figure behind the foundation of Comunn na Cànain Albannaich – the Scottish Language Society – formed in 1969. The publication *Rosc* said in 1972: 'If the Scottish Gaelic language survives into the 21st Century it will be mainly thanks to the efforts of this tenacious Scotsman who, over the past ten years, has been a veritable one-man national cultural movement.'

Before his death Seumas expressed the wish that his ashes should be scattered at the 1820 monument in Sighthill. On 11 February 1987, it fell to me to perform that melancholy task. Members of the 1820 Society, Seumas' friends and admirers of his work, gathered as his remains were piped to the monument to the tune of 'The Flowers of the Forest'. Reverend John Prentice of the Martyrs Church of Scotland, Paisley, performed the religious rights. There were several speeches but Councillor James Mitchell summed up the general feeling that it was more than fitting for Seumas' remains to be scattered at the monument which he, more than anyone, had worked so tirelessly to bring to the notice of his fellow countrymen. As the tribute on the wreath from the 1820 Society read: 'His name will ever live in Scottish history as co-discoverer of the facts of 1820. His loss has bereft Scotland of a modest but great man.'

FOREWORD

by Hugh MacDiarmid

THE AUTHORS OF this book have done not only an excellent job but, in view of the escalation of the Scottish National Party and corresponding developments in Wales and even in Cornwall, a very timely one. The book sets out in full detail and with admirable clarity its subject, an insurrection that has up to now only been known to a few specialists. The work must be regarded as a preliminary study into the growth of Scottish national radicalism; the full story of its growth from 1790 onwards must wait the long overdue complete research into the Friends of the People Movement and, in particular, the significance of the relations between the English, Scottish and Irish elements involved.

At the time of the Spanish Civil War, I was expelled from the Communist Party of Great Britain on the grounds of "nationalist deviationism", for asserting that where Scottish and Irish members of the International Brigade were brigaded together all went well, but where English members were brought together with the Scottish and Irish, trouble ensued. Subsequently, I was readmitted to the C.P.G.B. and assured that the Party had learned a great deal about the national question from me. That is as may be, but it has a great deal more to learn, and though the Scottish Secretariat of the Party has now declared itself in favour of Scottish Independence, the English, who of course represent the great majority of the Party, cannot be expected to agree. In this and all other connections R. L. Stevenson's declaration that there are no two adjacent peoples in the world more utterly and unalterably different than the Scots and the English is fully borne out by this book and by all similar studies covering the relations of the two countries.

While it is undoubtedly true that John MacLean was the greatest leader the working class of Scotland has yet had, and that all sorts of living currents in the movement today can be traced back to him, until recently both the Communist Party of Great Britain and the Labour Party have been content to use his name while repudiating his policy.

An element that has militated very largely against Mac-Lean's memory is the idea that towards the end he became mentally affected, as a result of his prison exposures. But I have letters he wrote right up to his death and these are as clear and rational as ever. In my view what finally broke him was less his admittedly great sufferings in prison than his feeling that most of his friends had repudiated his teachings and were committed to courses which must prove disastrous—as indeed they have proved.

That so great a proportion of our people know nothing of MacLean except his name—if that!—is not surprising in Scotland, where owing to the educational system scarcely anything of value in relation to our literature, history, national biography, or economic facts gets through the filter. I bracket with Mac-Lean's name not only the names of the pioneers and martyrs with whom this book deals but the names of John Murdoch (the crofters' leader—MacLean's agrarian counterpart), and John Swinton (who aided the Negroes in South Carolina before the Civil War, became a friend of Walt Whitman and knew Karl Marx) as examples of Scots who are far too little known—and yet in my opinion, of more consequence than most of those who figure prominently either in our history books or in contemporary life.

The sustained vindictiveness meted out by the Establishment to its opponents leads Philip Mairet in his book *Pioneer of Sociology: The Life and Letters of Patrick Geddes*, to say: "The worst enmities were aroused by his achievements when he had failed to move man in a position to do what he proposed, and simply took action himself. Some of them privately hoped his schemes would miscarry, or even sought openly to obstruct them. If, nevertheless, a plan of his achieved conspicuous success, ill wishers sometimes had to bear the reproach of being asked: 'Why did *you* not do this before? You could have done it', and it was this that rankled. Years after, when such resentments might well have been forgotten, they were strong enough to frustrate the efforts in Edinburgh first of a professor and later of the chancellor (Sir J. M. Barrie) to honour Geddes with an Ll.D."

This continued malevolence reminds me that a young historian of my acquaintance, researching into the life and activities of Thomas Muir, found the officials at Registry House, Edinburgh, and at the National Library of Scotland, helpful enough on the surface; but they assured him that there was nothing else in their keeping beyond what was already known and used by such historians as H. W. Meikle and George Pratt Insh. But he persisted and found a lot of material in their repositories casting new light on the whole business. He found boxes of correspondence and other invaluable material in the Kilmarnock Museum and elsewhere that had lain quite unknown to these historians. And incidentally, he found incontestable evidence that Burns, instead of going back on his own principles when he joined the Dumfries Volunteers, when the bogey of a possible French invasion was raised, simply realised that the real object of the Volunteers was to suppress any radical developments and, like other members of the Friends of the People, joined in order to infiltrate the Volunteers and frustrate the intentions of the authorities. Despite the unprecedented adulation of Burns, the devotees of Scotland's national bard are prepared to believe that Burns (admittedly under the stress of economic circumstances) betrayed his Republican principles.

I am sure the same kind of thing is true of many issues in Scottish history. Major M. V. Hay of Seaton, in his book *A Chain of Error in Scottish History*, was only concerned with falsifications made for religious sectarian reasons, but there are many such chains of error still unrevealed and of greater relevance to our affairs today. Material contrary to the official assumptions had been, and still is, carefully concealed, and those who persist in asserting this are stigmatised as of "the lunatic fringe"—or, as John MacLean was and as were Fletcher of Saltoun and Lord Belhaven, opponents of the Union with England, actually "mental cases!"

MacLean came at the end of a long sequence of Scottish Radical and Republican thinkers. That his doctrine is, as Rudolf Bringmann, William Ferris and other writers on the Gaelic Commonwealth show, profoundly related to our hidden

Gaelic traditions, and in coming to it MacLean was not the victim of a mental disequilibrium nor (as Harry Macshane suggested) merely imitative of the Irish Movement, but realising the deepest impulse of his whole nature in their final and highest form, and that so far from indicating any mental breakdown this development is in logical accord with the entire evolution of his political thought, and did not betray but crowned his career. Its relationship to all that had gone before, its consistency with his profound grasp of the whole situation in which Scotland was (and is) involved, and the forthrightness, courage, and firmness with which he crowned his stand for Scotland are in themselves enough to dispose at once of the suggestion that MacLean's brain was in any way impaired.

This book on *The Scottish Insurrection of 1820* has great value in its exposure of the use of spies and agents-provocateur, and of the unbridled unscrupulousness of the Establishment and its readiness to manipulate the law, insisting on English law and sending police and other agents into Scotland heedless of Scottish legal rights, with the hypocritical approval of the magistracy, the landed gentry, the Church, and the other pillars of the status quo. There has been talk recently of the Welsh Republican Army (Free Wales Army) and even of something similar in Scotland, and all who imagine that wrongs can be easily righted and that any attempt to right them either by constitutional or other means will not incur like measures today as obtained in Scotland during the trials described in this book, have the whole history of national movements and the struggles for democratic freedom against them. To be forewarned is to be forearmed, and readers of this book who are in any doubt about what is meant by the phrase "the full force of the law", can hardly escape a very salutary enlightenment which will stand them in good stead if they encounter secret agents, double dealers and spies—creatures who undoubtedly infest the Scottish Movement today just as they did in the time of the Friends of the People and the United Scotsmen.

HUGH MacDIARMID

Biggar, August, 1969.

ONE

INSURRECTION!

TWO ABREAST, THE column of sixty hussars cantered purposefully along the road to Glasgow. Despite the fact that their flamboyant blue, crimson and gold uniforms were coated with dust from a hard ride, the soldiers held themselves upright and alert in their saddles and they rode in impeccable order as if they were on a parade ground. The sun had long since disappeared behind the hills and the road was shrouded in the semi-gloom of early evening, causing the men of the column to cast anxious glances from under their black fur shakos at the wayside bushes and trees. Their fear of an ambush was shared by Major James Douglas, Deputy Quartermaster General of His Majesty King George IV's Army in Scotland, a small, nervous man, riding towards the head of the column. To Douglas, this journey—which he considered a foolhardy plunge into the midst of danger—was almost as incredible as the news which had been brought to Edinburgh earlier that afternoon. Just after luncheon that day, Sunday, April 2, 1820, a despatch rider from Lt.-Colonel Northcott's 1st Battalion of the Rifle Brigade, who were stationed in Glasgow, had arrived at Edinburgh Castle with the astonishing news that all South-West Scotland had risen in arms and that Glasgow itself was beseiged by a rebel army. There had certainly been growing agitation in Scotland during the past five years among those who called themselves "Radical Reformers" and there had even been talk of a general uprising in the industrial belt among the disaffected workers, particularly the weavers; but no one, as Douglas recalled, had taken the matter really seriously. Hearing the news, the Commander-in-Chief of the Army in Scotland, Major-General Sir Thomas Bradford, K.C.B., K.T.S., had shown a great calm, or so it appeared to Douglas. He at once ordered a squadron of the 10th Hussars to saddle and mount as an escort for himself and the entire General Staff to go to

Glasgow, leaving orders with the Lord Provost of Edinburgh to make preparations to secure the city from any attack in his absence.

To rush to Glasgow before ascertaining the exact extent of the uprising was, to Douglas, an enterprise lacking wisdom, and a dangerous one. Douglas was inclined to scrutinise every aspect most carefully before reaching a decision and, in this respect, he considered that the Commander-in-Chief had made a hurried and totally unwise one. The fact that Major-General Bradford and his staff were surrounded by well-trained cavalry soldiers of the line, veterans of the recent European wars, did not ease Douglas's mind from the fear of ambush, nor did the fact that the journey from Edinburgh had revealed little sign of insurgent activity. True, however, in the numerous villages en route, crowds had jeered at the soldiers and, in Airdrie, people had even thrown stones and other missiles at the hussars who, being tough, disciplined troops, had not broken formation but, eyes front, had ridden stoically through the barrage. Just the same, Douglas had reasoned, if the rebels wanted to assassinate the Commander-in-Chief, and there seemed every reason to believe they did, the most likely place would be in the suburbs of Radical Glasgow, where the insurgents could melt away without trace into the protection of the houses.

Apprehensively Douglas peered through the dusk to Bradford's short, thick-set figure riding immediately ahead of him, shrouded in a greatcoat to keep out the April chill. At the age of 42, Major-General Sir Thomas Bradford had managed the military affairs of Scotland since July, 1819—less than one year. It had been a turbulent period, with plots and counter plots for parliamentary reform among the agitators and the large body of disaffected workers, particularly in the South-West. In the North-West, in A' Ghàidhealtachd, the Government's policy of "Clearances" was also sparking off riots and minor insurrections which kept the troops busy. It was because Scotland seemed to be on the very verge of an uprising that Bradford had been appointed to command. In his past service, Bradford had shown a particular flair for police duties rather than military ones. During the Irish uprising of 1798 he had won such a distinction and was appointed brevet lieutenant-colonel, becoming Assistant Adjutant-General in Scotland when an uprising by the republican United Scotsmen organisation was feared. Later, fighting under Wellington, Bradford was severely wounded at the Battle of Bayonne and, in 1814, was again appointed to the staff of the C.-in-C., Scotland. Bradford had then been given command of the 7th Division of the Army of Occupation in France, 1815–17, where he had exploited his talents to the full. He was a blunt, North Country man, a hard-working and proficient commander whose talents lay away from the battlefield and in the administrative side of the army. As an administrator he had, for nearly a year past, been preparing for this moment when he could move against the Radical agitators and "teach them a damned fine lesson".

Riding alongside Bradford, in the reds and golds of the 7th Hussars, was the slim and elegant 44-year-old Major-General Sir Richard Hussey Vivian. Vivian, described as one of the most handsome and best cavalry officers in Europe, had been expressly sent to Scotland by the Duke of York, Commander-in-Chief of the Army, in case of disturbances. Bradford, although two years younger than Vivian, was his senior in rank by one year and Vivian was acting on his staff in an advisory capacity only. Vivian was a direct contrast to Bradford, a spirited, dashing officer—some were inclined to describe him as a "glory seeker"—who had fought at Waterloo, something for which Bradford envied him as his own brother had been killed on the field while he was recovering from his Bayonne wound. Vivian was now acclaimed as the army's leading expert on cavalry tactics and, in 1819, he had been sent to Newcastle to advise the local military on putting down riots there by the use of cavalry. Later in 1819 he had been sent to Scotland where his old regiment, the 7th Hussars, were stationed. The Duke of York felt he had made a wise choice for, while Bradford's administrative abilities were essential in keeping Scotland under control, Vivian's knowledge of battle tactics would be useful in the event of an uprising.

As the column reached the darkened streets of the outlying suburbs of Glasgow, the tension of the Hussars increased; sabres were rattled in scabbards to ensure their looseness and outriders peered cautiously ahead as if expecting to confront the entire rebel army in the darkness. The pace of the column quickened as it clattered through deserted streets to the centre of the city.

All was deathly quiet. Houses were firmly shuttered and no light was visible anywhere. No sentries challenged their app-roach. James Douglas afterwards recalled that he felt that the column and the entire General Staff were riding into a trap.

That Sunday morning the citizens of Glasgow and the sur-rounding countryside had awoken in a tense, excited atmos-phere, the like of which had not been felt since the start of the Rising of 1745. On the walls of houses in the streets of the city, and in the towns and villages of the counties of Dumbarton, Stirling, Renfrew, Lanark and Ayr, proclamations had been posted during the night calling the people of Scotland to rise in arms. The proclamation, signed by "the Committee of Organis-ation for forming a Provisional Government, Glasgow, 1st April, 1820", announced the intention of the insurgents to achieve "Liberty or Death!" The insurgents were going to return home having achieved "freedom, or return home no more".

Just after dawn the drab streets of the suburbs and the more richly endowed squares of central Glasgow began to fill with people. It seemed that the entire 147,000 inhabitants of the city—weavers, mechanics, cotton spinners—hearing the news of the proclamation, had hurried out to read the document for themselves. Those who could not read listened with rapt attention as the more learned members of the crowd read aloud its contents.

FRIENDS AND COUNTRYMEN:—*Roused* from that torpid state in which We have been sunk for so many years, we are, at length, compelled, from the extremity of our sufferings, and the contempt heaped upon our Petitions for redress, to assert our RIGHTS, at the hazard of our lives and proclaim to the world the real motives, which (if not misrepresented by designing men, would have United all ranks) have reduced us to take up ARMS for the redress of our *Common Grievances*.

The numerous Public Meetings held throughout the Country have demonstrated to you that the interest of all Classes are the same. That the production of the Life and Property of the *Rich Man* is the interest of the *Poor Man*, and in return, it is the interest of the Rich to protect the Poor from the iron grip of DESPOTISM, for, when its victims are exhausted in the lower circles, there is no assurance but that its ravages will be continued in the upper. For once set in motion, it will continue to move till a succession of Victims fall.

Our principles are few, and founded on the basis of our *Constitution* which was purchased with the DEAREST BLOOD of our ANCESTORS, and which we swear to transmit to posterity unsullied, or PERISH in the Attempt. Equality of Rights (not of Property) is the object for which we contend, and which we consider as the only security for our LIBERTIES and LIVES.

Let us show to the world that We are not that Lawless sanguinary Rabble which Our Oppressors would persuade the higher circles we are—but a BRAVE and GENEROUS PEOPLE, determined to be FREE. LIBERTY or DEATH is our *Motto*, and We have sworn to return home in *triumph*—or return *no more*!

SOLDIERS: . . . come forward then, at once, and Free your Country . . .

FRIENDS AND COUNTRYMEN: . . . come forward, then, and assist those who have begun the completion of so arduous a task, and support the laudable efforts which we are about to make . . .

Owing to the misrepresentations which have gone abroad with regard to our intentions, we think it indispensably necessary to DECLARE inviolable all Public and Private Property. And, we hereby call upon all JUSTICES of the PEACE, and all others to suppress PILLAGE and PLUNDER, of every description; and to endeavour to secure those Guilty of such offences, that they may receive that Punishment which such violation of Justice demands.

In the present state of affairs, and during the continuation of so momentous a struggle, we earnestly request all to desist from their labour from and after this day, the First of April, and attend wholly to the recovery of their Rights and consider it as the duty of every man not to recommence until he is in possession of those Rights which distinguishes the FREEMEN from the SLAVES: viz: That of giving consent to the laws by which he is governed. We, therefore, recommend to the Proprietors of Public Works, and all others, to Stop the one, and Shut up the other, until order is restored, as We will be accountable for no damages which may be sustained; and which after this Public Intimation, they can have no claim to.

And We hereby give notice to all those who shall be found carrying arms against those who intend to regenerate their Country, and restore its INHABITANTS to their NATIVE DIGNITY; We shall consider them as TRAITORS to their Country, and ENEMIES to their King, and treat them as such.

By order of the Committee of Organisation for forming a PROVISIONAL GOVERNMENT, Glasgow, 1st April, 1820.

A footnote to this rather tedious proclamation added:

The wishes of all good men are with us. Join together and make it one Cause, and the Nations of the Earth shall hail the day when the Standard of Liberty shall be raised on its *Native Soil!*

Groups began to form on street corners, growing into mobs which taunted and jeered at any passing soldier or well-dressed gentleman. Stones and other missiles were thrown and a number of prominent citizens only just managed to escape from the rage of the mobs with cuts and bruises. The Glasgow police force seemed little inclined to try and tackle the mobs roaming the streets. In fact, of all the officials in Glasgow that day, Captain James Mitchell, the police commandant ("the tallest master of police we ever saw"), was the least surprised at the rising. For some days past he had been kept informed by his agents that the proclamation was to be posted. He had risen early that Sunday morning and was engaged in mustering his eighty to ninety strong police force and organising a duty roster. He was little concerned with the antics of the crowd; what concerned him more was the preparation of raids on the homes of leading Radicals.

The military in the city also stood impassively by as the mobs rampaged through the more select quarters of Glasgow. They were acting under direct orders not to attempt to interfere with the people except in self-defence or to save property from destruction. The senior ranking officer in the Glasgow area, Lt.-Colonel Northcott of the 1st Battalion of the Rifle Brigade, was a wary man who had no wish to precipitate another "Peterloo" incident (when the military had fired on unarmed Radicals attending a meeting in 1819 at Manchester), unless acting under orders from his superiors. Northcott's immediate action on seeing the proclamation had been to issue despatches requesting all available troops to converge on Glasgow. He had also sent a despatch rider post haste to Edinburgh bearing the news to Bradford.

Northcott then gave his mind to how best he could secure Glasgow from attack. He had ridden to 44 Bell Street where Samuel Hunter ran Glasgow's Tory newspaper, the *Glasgow Herald*. But it was not as editor of the *Herald* that Northcott sought to consult Hunter, for the 51-year-old, 18 stone, Glasgow dignitary was also the colonel commanding the Glasgow Yeomanry forces. Hunter had long prophesied trouble from the "lower orders" in the city and felt that the disaffection could be laid at the doors of Glasgow's 15,000 Irish inhabitants, most of whom had flooded into Scotland after the abortive risings of 1798 and 1803 when there had been attempts to set up an independent Irish Republic. "Once a rebel, always a rebel", was Hunter's opinion. Hunter had conceived almost a fanatical hatred of the Irish since his service in Ireland in the military during the '98 Rising. It was certainly true that many Irishmen had, in fact, joined Scottish revolutionary movements and the organisation of the republican United Irishmen had been duplicated by the United Scotsmen organisation which was still in existence in 1802 but whose efforts to establish a Scottish Republic had ended with an abortive rising, mainly confined to Perthshire in 1797.

Reading the proclamation, Hunter made a mental note for the editorial leader which he was to write in his newspaper the next day. He noticed that in one paragraph the proclamation referred to Magna Carta and the Bill of Rights, which were not part of Scottish history. To Hunter this seemed to suggest that the author was an Englishman, because a Scot would naturally refer to the Declaration of Arbroath in place of the English Magna Carta. As later events were to show, this was a highly significant fact.

After some discussion Hunter and Northcott agreed that it was not immediately necessary to mobilise the entire force of the Glasgow Yeomanry (which consisted of 1,015 enlisted men, 37 commissioned officers and 78 non-commissioned officers). A current rumour had it that the actual signal for the rising was to be the stopping of the London–Glasgow Royal Mail coach which was due to arrive at Glasgow Post Office in Nelson Street at 5 a.m. the next day. Already, Dugald Bannatyne, the Postmaster of Glasgow, had been to see the Hon. Henry Monteith, Lord Provost of the city, to request that cavalry meet the coach as a means of protection after its three-day journey from London. Hunter decided on the full mobilisation of the Yeomanry forces at 4.30 a.m. the next day and, in the meantime, gave orders to his second-in-command, Robert Douglas Alston, to assemble Captain Smith's company of sharpshooters. These were ordered to take up positions in the Royal Bank, Queen Street. Hunter assumed that the Royal Bank, the city's treasury, would be the first object of a Radical attack on the city. It was generally supposed that the Radicals would try to seize money to pay their men and to buy arms. All the local banks, under the direction of Northcott, immediately sent the money they held to the central Royal Bank for safe-keeping.

James Jones, the Corps Adjutant, was ordered to issue Smith's men with twenty rounds of ball cartridge apiece. Jones, an Argyll man, was eager for action. Formerly a lieutenant in the Royal Marines, he had served aboard the English frigate H.M.S. *Shannon* in its famous battle with the U.S.S. *Chesapeake* and had been the first man to board the *Chesapeake* and take the sword of surrender from her captain. It was this sword which Jones buckled on to his Yeomanry uniform that Sunday morning as he directed the fortification of the Royal Bank.

The barricading of the Royal Bank seemed to strike the reality of the situation into most "well-disposed" citizens, who immediately retired to their homes and barricaded themselves inside. Consternation of an immediate Radical attack began to spread among the authorities. One old magistrate bade farewell to his son, one of Smith's men guarding the bank, with tears in his eyes, crying he would never see his boy again. The Royal Bank, now barricaded and guarded by the Yeomanry in their green and white uniforms, became a central point for the roaming crowds who stood peering through the tall railing which surrounded the grounds of the building, jeering at the soldiers.

Northcott ordered cannons to be set up on every bridge across the Clyde in order to stop any Radical troops moving into the centre of the city. His main concern was to find out the position of the Radical Army, their strength and intentions. A sergeant of the Glasgow Yeomanry, which Hunter called his Glasgow Sharpshooters, wrote afterwards:

I went to the Coffee Room [at Tontine] and found everything in a bustle there. It was concerned that matters were now brought to a crisis and the interesting questions became what was the amount of arms in possession of the rebellious as there would be no doubt in this district of their intentions to obey the appeal.

But the question which was uppermost in the mind of the Rev. Dr Chalmers, conducting the Sunday morning service in his new church of St John's, Gallowgate, was how could a bloody civil war in Scotland be averted. Chalmers was an outspoken Parliamentary Reformer and a frequent contributor to the *Edinburgh Review*, the Whig-Reform journal, but reform by violence was not his creed. Chalmers offered up a prayer for the safety of the city:

O mighty Lord, and Governor of the Universe! preserve this Kingdom, we humbly beseech thee, from the horror of civil war, apparently approaching us in this city. Keep us ever in thy fear; and fit us for all our duties, temporal and eternal.

Prayers were far from the mind of James Hardie, a Glasgow Justice of the Peace, as he walked through the streets that morning carefully noting the location of the proclamations and the crowd's reactions to them. One group that particularly caught his attention was gathered round a watchman's box in Duke Street, where one of the proclamations had been posted. An active anti-reformer, James Hardie began to jostle his way through the crowd to tear down the broadsheet, but three or four men stopped him. One of them was a 26-year-old weaver named Andrew Hardie, who lived with his parents in the High Street, a few streets away. An ex-soldier, and a member of the Castle Street Radical Union Society, Andrew Hardie's passions had been inflamed by the call to arms, as had many others who held Radical convictions. He pushed the officious justice back from the watchman's box so that the man stumbled and almost fell over the curb of the pavement. Recovering his balance, James Hardie ordered the notice to be taken down.

"Where is your authority?" jeered the young weaver.

"There are plenty here who know me for a justice," exclaimed James Hardie. But the crowd, clearly against the authorities, only jeered and catcalled.

"Before I permit you to take down yon notice," said the young weaver, placing himself in the path of the justice, "I will part with the last drop of my blood!" It was a brave speech and the crowd cheered delightedly. But the words were to cost the 26-year-old weaver his life.

Among the crowd who witnessed the incident was John Stirling, a surgeon, also an anti-Radical and known to Andrew Hardie as a friend of the justice. The weaver turned on Stirling and accused him of bringing the justice to the spot and spying on the Radicals. Stirling and the justice retreated before the hostile crowd, who then turned their attention to the proclamation again. The whole scene had been observed by Hugh Macphunn, a clerk to the firm of Messrs. Denniston & Co., Glasgow, who afterwards claimed that he had carefully noted the behaviour of the young Glasgow weaver and his evidence was instrumental in tightening the noose round the young man's neck.

Another young man out in the streets that day and eager for the rising to begin was Robert F. Fulton, an apprentice printer who woke at mid-day, ate a hurried meal and hurried out into the streets in a state of great excitement. For Fulton, Saturday had been a busy day. He had been at work until midnight with his fellow apprentice, John Hutchison, in the shop of their employer, Duncan MacKenzie, at 20 Saltmarket, turning out copies of the Radical proclamation. Just before midnight a man called Lees, who described himself as a representative of the Provisional Government, had called at the shop. It had been Lees who commissioned Fulton, a Radical sympathiser, to print the proclamation of the rising. Lees collected a parcel of proclamations and told Fulton that he would see him later in the Globe Tavern. Half an hour later Fulton had entered the Globe and saw Lees with a woman introduced to him as Mrs Lees, and a man called John Craig, a weaver from Lancefield, Anderston, who was also known to Fulton as a representative of the Provisional Government. They all had a drink together and Fulton received seventeen shillings as the second payment for printing the proclamation. Fulton had then gone home to bed and, tired with the arduous work, had slept in late. Now the day had dawned and Fulton, a Radical idealist, was eager to take his part in the uprising.

But there was to be no Radical uprising in Glasgow that day, for the Radicals were confining their activities to spreading copies of the proclamation in the industrial belt of Scotland. The centre of the Radical activity was the house of a man called John King, who lived in the city's suburbs. King called himself a weaver but did not appear to pursue any particular occupation and always seemed to be in pocket. There had been a meeting of Glasgow Radicals in a house in George Street late on

Saturday night at which Duncan Turner, a tinsmith, who also described himself as an emissary of the Provisional Government, had attended. When the meeting finished, Turner took aside William Robertson and Andrew Wilson, two staunch Radicals, and asked them to accompany him to King's house where, he said, they would receive orders. They reached the house at 1 a.m. To Robertson's surprise, the lights were blazing and the windows were uncovered. The place was visible for miles. Inside were a great many people arranging muskets, pikes and gunpowder. A pile of proclamations lay on a table. King and his wife were plying the company with whisky and talking of the "great and glorious" acts that were soon to take place in the fight for liberty. King told them he had just come from the Provisional Government, "all men of rank and talent". He assured them that he had heard it positively stated that George Kinloch of Kinloch, the Radical leader who had fled abroad the previous year before the authorities could serve a warrant for his arrest on a charge of sedition, had landed with a large force of ex-patriate Scottish troops from France. Also, Marshal MacDonald, one of Napoleon's greatest generals, son of Neil MacEachain of the MacDonald clan, the Jacobite school-teacher who had accompanied Prince Charles Edward on his flight to Skye and eventual exile after the '45 Rising, was also coming to Scotland with 5,000 troops.

Duncan Turner took some of the proclamations to post through the city and left King's house at 2 a.m. But en route he called on a man, also named King, living near Jamaica Street and gave him a copy of the proclamation. King gave Turner a golden guinea. Treachery was at work among the Radical forces, for King, previously an under clerk in the Council Chambers of Glasgow, was now a law agent.

At mid-day on Sunday, a dragoon from Hamilton galloped into the town of Ayr with the news. He brought Northcott's message to the officer commanding, asking for all available troops to be sent to the Glasgow area. The church bells were rung in alarm, drums beat to quarters and congregations spilled from the mid-day services. The two squadrons of dragoons, stationed in Ayr, trotted out of the town at 4 p.m. with drawn swords resting against their shoulders.

The 400 strong 4th Royal Veteran Battalion, stationed

permanently at Ayr Barracks, were called out in marching order and left in wake of the dragoons. Shortly afterwards a troop of the Ayrshire Yeomanry (nicknamed the "Dandies") was ordered to muster in Academy Square. They looked every inch "Dandies", in their blue single breasted coats, white drill trousers and Glengarry bonnets. Their commanding officer, Major Campbell of Thornflat, conferred with the town magistrates. It was decided that the "Dandies" would hold themselves responsible for the peace and fortification of the town.

In the meantime a messenger was sent to Alexander Boswell, the eldest son of the biographer of Dr Johnson, at his house at Auchinleck. Boswell was the colonel commanding the Ayrshire Yeomanry Cavalry, the biggest militia force in Scotland, which consisted of three full regiments. Like James Boswell, his son Alexander was something of a writer and poet but his interests were mainly in politics and, as Tory M.P. for Plympton, he had vowed that he would "ride in Radical blood up to his bridle reins!" As commander of the only military force now left in Ayr, Boswell decided to leave Campbell's men standing under arms in the town and ordered the mobilisation of the entire Ayrshire Yeomanry forces for the next day. He scribbled the following order:

Auchinleck

The commanding officer having received a sudden order to call out the corps under his command, however much he regrets the inconvenient time, he relies on the spirit of all individuals, and that every man will turn out in this emergency to put down those who render property and everything valuable to man, insecure; all that can be wished is, that by one well directed effort, we may be spared further annoyance. The first and third troops will assemble tomorrow at twelve noon o'clock in Ayr, in marching order, with necessaries. The second troop, in like order at the same hour, in Mauchline. The fourth troop, at the same hour, in like order, at Kilmarnock.

Alex Boswell, Lt.-Colonel Commandant

His second-in-command, Major Ferrier Hamilton, issued similar orders to the Second Corps of the regiment and soon the Yeomanry were converging on their rallying points from all over the county.

For John Parkhill of Maxwellton, near Paisley, who had been

appointed Commissary-General of the Paisley Radical Contingent, Sunday passed off in a fairly quiet way. On Saturday evening John Neil, who had been one of the Scottish ambassadors to the English Radical meetings in Nottingham, called on Parkhill and showed him a copy of the proclamation. Parkhill felt the document was "exceedingly well drawn up".

Considerable crowds had started to gather in Paisley at 7 a.m. to view the proclamation. Parkhill, Neil and other Paisley leaders met with Daniel Bell, a five-feet-tall ex-officer's batman, who had been appointed commandant of the Paisley Radicals. They were undecided what to do for no news or orders from the Provisional Government in Glasgow had been received. It was decided to hold a full meeting of the Paisley Radicals the following forenoon at the "Smiddy", a special weaver's shop in Maxwellton Street where the Radicals held their meetings.

At two o'clock on Sunday afternoon, Parkhill went to a public house called The Linn, a Radical rendezvous on the corner of Broomlands and the south-east end of King Street, owned by Granny Rowan. It was called "The Linn" because players of hurling ("Heigh Linn") usually gathered there. There Parkhill met a friend from Dalry, who had served in the Foot Guards, and who was "mad because there was no fighting".

Parkhill wrote in his autobiography:

In the afternoon and evening, a more than usual turnout of the inhabitants might be noticed, together with many from the country. There was little preparation, however, for war, further than a few most sanguine carrying a pistol or a gun or enquiring if there was any news from Glasgow. After nightfall the cavalry and infantry were much engaged in showing themselves in various parts of the town in preparation for tomorrow's struggle.

The cavalry mentioned by Parkhill was a troop of the 10th Hussars who had arrived in the late evening from Irvine and these had been followed by a second troop of the same regiment from Ayrshire.

Early Sunday morning John Fraser, the schoolmaster of Johnstone, near Paisley, walked over the hills to Kilbarchan, bearing with him a copy of the proclamation to show his friend Duncan MacIntyre. The previous day, two men had called to see Fraser. They were John Dunlop, a Collier Street weaver, "a most respectable and intelligent man", and James Speirs, also a weaver, "a quiet, sensible man", who had served in a militia regiment. The two men had called upon the schoolmaster to ask him to copy a letter for them. The letter was addressed to Rev. Alexander Telfer and Rev. Clapperton, local clergymen, informing them of the proposed rising and asking them to warn their congregations to act peacefully and submit to the Radical forces and that no injury would be done to their persons or property.

Fraser, perhaps unwisely, had done this. Later that day, about 11 p.m., while he was standing outside the door of his father's drug shop, Speirs had come by and, in a state of great excitement, had shown Fraser a copy of the proclamation. Fraser had taken this copy and hurried to his friend William Reid, a china merchant who was also a Radical. Finally he had returned home, confided the news to his wife Marjorie and retired to bed in anticipation of the next day's events.

He arrived at his friend MacIntyre's house early, and immediately showed him the proclamation. While they were discussing it a friend, John Lang, called and he, too, was shown the document. Fraser then returned home and went on to attend the mid-morning church service. While he was at church James Speirs called upon his wife and urged her to "put it [the proclamation] out of the way" in case of a raid by the military. But for Fraser, and the rest of the population at Johnstone, the day passed by quietly.

It was much the same story at Strathaven where John Stevenson and Robert Hamilton, who had collected 200 copies of the proclamation from King's house in Glasgow on Saturday night, had been posting up the notices in the village during the early hours of the morning. According to Stevenson, "a considerable deal of bustle and excitement ensued" but nothing untoward happened.

At Girvan, a small village on the Ayrshire coast, reputed to be one of the strongholds of the Radicals, the situation was more electric. Mr Fergusson of Crosshill took immediate charge of matters and ordered all law enforcement officers into the town with their arms. Fergusson then ordered the church bells of the parish to be rung to convene the people of Girvan. The villagers crowded into the church while Fergusson told them the proclamation was an act of rebellion and treason. He declared a curfew starting at 9 p.m.

The law officers were then organised in parties to arrest prominent Radical leaders in Girvan and district. Innkeepers were told to report all strangers entering their hostelries with the warning that if they failed to do so their licences would be taken away from them.

The capital city of Edinburgh was stunned by the news from Glasgow. Although in December, 1819, there had been a stand-to alert in expectation of an insurrection, no one had really thought it would have happened. After all, the military in Scotland were far too strong and would outnumber any force the Radicals could possibly throw against them. But now the news was that a Radical army was laying waste the South-West and marching on the city. Making matters worse in people's minds was the fact that Major-General Bradford had left the capital post haste with his staff and an escort of hussars, in the direction of Glasgow, as soon as the news had arrived. The Lord Advocate, Sir William Rae, had given orders to the military in the area to be mobilised.

Henry Cockburn, a Whig-Reformist lawyer, though inclined to run with the hare and hunt with the hounds, was a captain in the Edinburgh Armed Association commanded by Sir James Fergusson of Kilkerran. Cockburn received orders to report to the Edinburgh Assembly Rooms at 8 p.m. fully equipped and armed. Here he found between 400 and 500 of the militia under arms. They waited until 10 p.m. when the Lord Provost of Edinburgh arrived and told them they could be dismissed as the Yeomanry regiments were now alerted and the line regiments were already mobilised to guard the city from attack.

At the same time as the Edinburgh Armed Association were being dismissed, Major-General Bradford and his escort were entering the suburbs of Glasgow. Unknown to them they were in the gun sights of two score or more muskets held by men of the Rifle Brigade and 13th Regiment of Foot. In the darkness the nervous soldiers had mistaken them for a column of Radicals and an eager young officer was about to give the order to fire when the mistake was realised. The General and his staff were conducted to the Star Hotel, at the top of Glassford Street. The weary soldiers were shown to their rooms by the inn's tenant, Mrs Younghusband, "a small, pretty little lady" with an only daughter but seemingly no husband.

B

Immediately after their arrival Colonel Northcott, Samuel Hunter and the Hon. Henry Monteith, the Lord Provost, called on Bradford to discuss the situation. The Lord Provost, magistrates, town clerk and fiscal, had set up the civil administration headquarters in Peter Jardine's hotel, Buck's Hotel, in Argyll Street, not far away. Between the two hotels was the Black Bull which the Lord Provost had commandeered as a headquarters for the officers of the Yeomanry regiments.

It was felt that any trouble would begin at dawn the next morning and Bradford and Monteith decided to issue a joint proclamation warning the citizens of Glasgow what lay in store for them should they answer the Radical call.

WHEREAS, we have observed with much surprise and concern, a highly SEDITIOUS and TREASONABLE PRINTED PAPER, posted up this morning, not only throughout the City, but in numerous places in the Suburbs . . . which is obviously a declaration of immediately intended hostility to the Government and Constitution of this country; We hereby once more give Notice, that all attempts which shall be made to follow up the inflammatory spirit and treasonable objects of the Address, will be instantly resisted by the Civil Powers, aided by the strong Military Force placed at their disposal, and that all measures by assemblages of people in prosecution of such designs, will be regarded as an insurrection against the Government, and instantly put down by the most prompt Military Execution.

AND WHEREAS: we have been informed that it is the intention of those who have issued the foresaid Address to bring in bodies of Men from the Country in furtherance of their traitorous purposes, We hereby warn all such persons to abstain from being led away to their own hazard, and the imminent danger of their lives. And we again warn the loyal and well disposed Inhabitants of this City and Suburbs, in the event of any Rising, as is threatened, shall take place to keep themselves and their families within doors, and on no account to mingle with those who shall be actually violating the Laws of the Country.

Glasgow 2nd April, 1820

Following the issue of the proclamation there was nothing left for the authorities to do but wait for the morning and the first move of the insurgents.

What the Radical forces, preparing to answer the call of their "Provisional Government", did not know was that the twenty-eight-man Provisional Government were in Glasgow Jail and, in fact, had been there since March 21 when they had all been arrested at a meeting in the Gallowgate; that the proclamation calling for the rising was the work of Government agents who, having infiltrated the Scottish Radical organisation and knowing of its weakness as an armed force, were precipitating the rising in order that superior Government forces could quell the insurrection and that the Radicals could be brought to heel by a lesson underlined with military defeat, trials for high treason and executions.

TWO

THE UNION

THE SCOTTISH INSURRECTION of 1820 was predominantly a gregarian Radical uprising born out of the social evils of the time. The aggravation for such a rising had been fermenting in Scotland since the 1790's when the new socio-political philosophy, which had arisen out of the American War of Independence and the French Revolution, found sympathy and strong advocates in the country. But as well as the Radical reform aspect, there was also a strong Scottish national aspect, for it was the intention of the 1820 Radicals, as well as that of The Friends of the People, in the early 1790's, and their successors, the United Scotsmen Societies, to dissolve the Union of Parliaments between England and Scotland of 1707 and "to set up a Scottish Assembly or Parliament in Edinburgh". It had been the intention of the United Scotsmen to establish a completely independent Scottish Republic, the plan was discovered by the Government in 1798, at the same time as the United Irishmen had risen in arms to establish an Irish Republic. But the United Scotsmen were suppressed before they had time to organise a rising of any effect. There is little evidence, unfortunately, to show what sort of independence was envisaged for Scotland in 1820 except that the Radicals planned "to sever Scotland and restore the ancient independence". If we are to believe the Government spy Richmond, the Radicals were "imbibed" with the republican philosophy of the United Scotsmen. However, in order to understand the nationalist aspect of the rising as well as the social one, the peculiar situation in which Scotland had been placed due to its parliamentary union with England in 1707 must first be understood. Before this can be clearly comprehended it must also be seen how Scotland had allowed itself to become unified with England forming the state of Great Britain and achieving a unique place in history as the first (and only)

European state to "voluntarily surrender" its national sovereignty.

Scotland had, subconsciously, been preparing itself for a take-over, or assimilation into, England since the thirteenth century by the gradual destruction of the Scottish language, culture and institutions and their replacement by English. This erosion of Scottish nationality led to the "Highland" and "Lowland" myth which is still common today. It was in 1018 that Scotland became a unified kingdom and by that year Scottish (Gàidhlig) was spoken over most of its territory with the possible exception of an area round the mouth of the River Tweed which had been a settlement of Angles called Bernica. This little kingdom was conquered by Malcolm (1008–34) and assimilated into Scotland proper. Professor Kenneth Jackson, in *The Celtic Aftermath in the Islands*, writes that "in consequence of this, the whole of Scotland became for a time Gaelic in speech . . .".

There is ample evidence to show that it was not until the thirteenth century that English began to make any headway in Scotland. The tide turned against the Scottish language when the royal family stopped speaking it and English became the vernacular of the court; however, James IV (1488–1513) has the distinction of being the last Scottish-speaking king, and Robert Bruce held the last all Scottish-speaking parliament at Ardchattan in 1308. In the fifteenth century, with the royal court now English speaking and the people in the Lothian area of Scotland monoglot English speakers, the English language became the dominant "Lowland" language. Because of the strained relations with England it was felt unpatriotic to continue to call this language "Inglis" and Gavin Douglas (1475–1522) was the first writer to call the "Inglis" language in Scotland "Scots". The Scottish language was then dismissed as "Ysrisch", "Ersch" or Irish and today as Scots Gaelic.

It is not, of course, within the scope of this book to present a linguistic history of Scotland but the position of the Scottish language is an important factor in showing the state of Scottish nationality. The fact that Scotland was once entirely Scottish (Gàidhlig) speaking is, despite the evidence, not yet generally accepted. The "Highland/Lowland" myth is very well entrenched and it will be many years before it is finally removed from Scottish minds.

The entire south-west of Scotland was still Scottish speaking in the eighteenth century. William Wallace who was born in Elderslie, near Paisley, spoke the language according to Blind Harry, the minstrel. And, Professor D. MacKinnon writes, "in the county of Ayr and in Galloway, the old language was spoken many hundreds of years after the death of Wallace". It is recorded that when Prince Charles Edward's army was passing through Galloway in 1745 "the Hielanman wus able tae converse freely wi' the natives", but both found difficulty speaking with the Irish levies, "for their Gaelic wus that different they cud hardly mak them oot". In fact, in 1762, the parish of Barr, in Carrick, was advertising for a school-teacher who "budst be able to speak Gaelic . . .".

The true linguistic history of Scotland has yet to be written, since confusing facts and prejudice about the Scottish language have been propagated since the Reformation in Scotland when a pro-English language element came to power, based in Edinburgh, whose official policy was the "extirpation" of the Scottish language, culture, and way of life. The Scottish Reformation has been described as an achievement of English foreign policy and certainly the English Government, through their ambassador, Sir Ralph Sadleir (1507–87), exerted great influence in the Scottish court. Thus, culturally, the Scottish administration and Norman-Celtic aristocracy had prepared itself for assimilation into England and the Anglicised Scottish Monarch "Jamie Baggy Breeks" (James VI)—a descendant of the Tudor House—was eagerly ready to seize the throne of England and Ireland, as the nearest claimant, on the death of Elizabeth I.

On the night of Saturday, March 26, 1603, Sir Robert Carey arrived at Holyrood Palace, Edinburgh, after riding three days from London, to tell James VI that Elizabeth of England was dead. Two days later a letter arrived from the English Privy Council inviting James to ascend the throne of England and Ireland as James I. So the Union of the Crowns of Scotland and England took place, but it was to Scotland's disadvantage for James forsook his country, leaving it to make London his capital. Although he promised to return to Scotland frequently he returned there only for a brief three-month visit in 1617.

Immediately the Crowns were united, James started to press

for a unification of the parliaments of both countries but he met strong opposition from the English and Scottish peoples. The English Parliament rejected such a proposal by an overwhelming vote in 1607. However, certain laws were enacted by both parliaments making citizens born in Scotland and England after 1603 citizens of the same country, and trading restrictions were lifted. Scotland soon began to see the disadvantage of the Union of Crowns for, with the Royal Court in London, Edinburgh became a semi-provincial city, trades people lost business, and the nobles and gentry moved to London after their king thus increasing the move towards Anglicisation. Also, when England went to war the Scots had to go to war too, to pay money and levy troops, without the approval of the Scottish Parliament. To all intents and purposes the monarchy had become an English monarchy and Scotland had become a semi-independent province.

Even the ardent Unionist historian, Professor Hume Brown, wrote in *The Union of 1707*:

The Union of Crowns brought many disadvantages to Scotland; but the result of it that most vitally affected her was her severance from the nations (states) at a period when new principles and new ideals were guiding their policy. Throughout the entire century, Scotland was a severed and a withered branch, and her people knew it.

Professor J. MacKinnon in his *The Union Between England and Scotland* sums up the position in these words:

A century of English interference, religious dissension and international friction, had reduced the country to beggary and impotence. Contemporary writers are unanimous in charging the political system established in 1603 as the main cause of the national depression that culminated in the poverty and misery of the last decades of the 17th and the opening years of the 18th Centuries. Misgovernment, with its adjuncts of civil and religious strife, was the fruit of a system which placed the fate of Scotland in the hands of an Anglified Monarch whose Scottish Ministers were more or less the tools of English influence and interests.

The Scottish Parliament was too weak to counteract the growing national depression. The Parliament, consisting of a legislature of Three Estates meeting in a single chamber, remained a feudal assembly practically until the end of its existence. It had little influence on the national history of Scotland and, originally, was little more than a baron's court registering the decrees of whatever party happened to be in power. With the removal of the Stuart family from the throne, Scottish antipathy towards England heightened. The royal family of Stuart had held the two countries together. With its passing, the Scottish peoples' desire for the return of their country's full independence intensified.

The intense dislike of the two countries for each other was revived. King William did little to gain the respect of the Scots. On February 13, 1692, the Massacre of Glencoe took place. Popularly thought to be an incident in an age-long clan feud, it was, in fact, the beginning of the terrible genocidal policy pursued by the English and Anglicised Scots against those who retained their language and traditional way of life. William, though he afterwards tried to deny it, signed the order for the massacre twice: "You are hereby ordered to fall upon the rebels, the MacDonalds of Glencoe and to put all to the sword under seventy." Following the massacre, the Scottish Parliament, which forced a special commission of inquiry to be set up concerning Glencoe, began to strike out on its own.

In 1693 the Scottish Parliament passed an act which led to the establishment, in 1695, of the Company of Scotland Trading to Africa and the Indies. The company was at once denounced by the English Parliament which had passed several acts to exclude Scotland trading to any colonies in India or Africa, as England wished to maintain her trade monopoly. William was asked to stop the formation of the Scottish company. The Scots then decided to form their own colonies and William Paterson of Dumfries launched a scheme for establishing a Scottish colony on the Isthmus of Darien (Panama). On July 21, 1698, three ships sailed to establish the new colony. Illness broke out, the Spaniards attacked them and the English in the West Indies, acting on the express orders of the English Government, refused to give the Scots shelter or assistance. The Darien expedition cost the Scots 2,000 lives and £200,000. The blame was laid at the door of William and the English Government and it seemed a rising was imminent by those who felt that the Scottish monarchy—the Stuarts—should be returned to the Scottish throne and full independence from England be declared. There were several riots, especially in Edinburgh, but these were put down.

In 1703 the Scottish Parliament enraged England further by passing an "Act Anent Peace and War" which stipulated that no sovereign could declare war on Scotland's behalf without the consent of the Scottish Parliament. Also a Scots Wine Act made it legal to import wine into Scotland from anywhere outside the country in direct opposition to English trade regulations.

Finally, the Scottish Parliament made the first move towards a severance from the English monarchy. In 1701, just before Anne came to the throne, the English Parliament had passed an Act of Settlement declaring that the Crown should go to Sophia, Electress of Hanover, on Anne's death so that there would be no chance of the restoration of the Scottish Stuarts. In direct opposition to this the Scottish Parliament passed an Act of Security in 1704 which enforced Scotland's right to choose her own monarch after Anne's death. This greatly alarmed the English Parliament and they—in turn—passed an Alien Act, declaring that if, by December 25, 1705, Scotland did not agree to accept England's choice of a monarch, no Scottish goods would be allowed into England and Scots would be treated as foreigners, no longer enjoying dual citizenship. To emphasise that they "meant business" a Scottish merchant ship was seized in the Thames and, in retaliation, the Scots seized an English ship in the Firth of Forth.

The fact that Scotland was now on the verge of dissolving the Union of Crowns was an intolerable situation to the English who had begun to accept the idea that they were rulers of the British Isles and were planning an empire based on Britain rather than England. The journalist and writer, Daniel Defoe, was sent to Edinburgh, as a Government agent, to investigate the possibility of a union between the Parliaments of the two states. Defoe, at first, did not hold out any hopes for such an event. Writing in his *History of the Union of Great Britain*, Edinburgh, 1709, Defoe says that a Union of Parliaments would be tremendously unpopular to the Scottish people. However, by exercising threats and using liberal bribes on certain members of the Scottish Parliament, the English Government managed to set up a body of commissioners (ten from each country) in order to consider the possibility of a parliamentary union.

The bribes to individual Scots were large. The Under-Secretary for Scotland, writing from Whitehall in September, 1706, says:

My lord Treasurer told me this morning that my lord Marlborough had now got the Duke of Argyll in a very good humour on making him—or promising to make him—a Major-General; upon which his Grace has promised to Parliament and serve the Queen in the affair of the Union; he told me also that, to please the Earl of Stair, his son was made a Brigadier and bid me write so to his lordship.

Even the most ardent of Unionist historians agreed that the Union was carried out by bribery and corruption. Professor Lodge, an English historian and pro-Unionist, admits in *The Union of 1707* that:

They [the English Government] had commercial inducements to offer and the ruin of Scottish agriculture to threaten, and by a judicious combination of bribes and menaces, they succeeded in bringing about the negotiations of 1706.

During the negotiations the English pressed home the fact that the alternative to a direct break with England was the restoration of the Catholic Stuart monarchy . . . republicanism was 100 years away. The rulers of Scotland were strongly Protestant and the special position of the Presbyterian Church in Scotland made the idea of Jacobitism abhorrent to the Scottish Parliament. Even so, there was a strong opposition in the Scottish Parliament against any such union with England. This opposition was led chiefly by Fletcher of Saltoun and Lord Belhaven. The debate on the Union took three months and no reference was made to the Scottish people. Popular opinion was entirely against the Union and on several occasions Edinburgh crowds tried to break into the Estates. Reporters of the debate said that on a number of occasions it looked as though a brawl would break out with drawn swords. The anti-Union faction (the first Scottish national party?) walked out of the debate on several occasions and the Duke of Hamilton (torn between the two parties) pretended he was too ill to attend. On November 2, 1706, Lord Belhaven delivered his famous address against the Union:

When I consider this affair of the Union betwixt the two nations, as it is expressed in the several Articles thereof, and now the subject of our deliberations at this time, I find my mind crowded with variety of melancholy thoughts, and I think it my duty to disburden myself of some of them, by laying them before, and exposing them to the serious consideration of this honourable House.

I think I see a free and independent kingdom delivering up that which all the world hath been fighting for, since the days of Nimrod; yea, that for which most of all the Empires, Kingdoms, States and Principalities and Dukedoms of Europe, are at this time engaged in the most bloody and cruel wars that ever were, to wit, a power to manage their own affairs by themselves without the assistance and counsel of any other.

I think I see a National Church, founded upon a rock, secured by a claim of right, hedged and fenced about by the strictest and pointedest legal sanction that sovereignty could contrive, voluntarily descending into a plain, upon an equal level with Jews, Papists, Arminians, Anabaptists and other Sectaries, etc.

I think I see the noble and honourable peerage of Scotland, whose valiant predecessors led armies against their enemies upon their own proper charges and expenses, now divested of their followers and vassalages, and put upon an equal foot with their vassals, that I think I see a petty English Excise man receive more homage and respect, than what was paid formerly to their quondam Mac-Callanmores.

I think I see the present peers of Scotland, whose Noble ancestors conquered provinces, over-run countries, reduced and subjected towns and fortify'd places, exacted tribute through the greatest part of England, now walking in the court of Requests like so many English Attornies, laying aside their walking swords when in company with English Peers lest their self defence should be found murder.

I think I see the Honourable Estate of Barons, the bold asserters of the nation's rights and liberties in the worst of times, now setting a watch upon their lips and a guard upon their tongues, lest they be found guilty of Scandalum Magnatum.

I think I see the Royal State of Burrows walking their desolate streets, hanging down their heads under disppointments; wormed out of all the branches of their old trade, uncertain what hand to turn to, necessitate to become 'prentices to their unkind neighbours; and yet after all finding their trade so fortified by companies, and secured by prescription, that they despair of any success therein.

I think I see our learned judges laying aside their Practiques and decisions, studying the common law of England, gravelled with Certioraries, Nisi prius's, Writs of Error, Verdicts indovar, Ejectione firmae, Injunctions, Demurrs, etc., and frightened with Appeals and Avocations, because of the new Regulations and Rectifications they may meet with.

I think I see the valiant and gallant soldiery either sent to learn the plantations trade abroad; or at home petitioning for a small subsistance as the reward for their honourable exploits, while their old corps are broken, the common soldiers left to beg, and the youngest English corps kept standing.

I think I see the honest and industrious tradesmen loaded with new taxes, and impositions, disappointed of the Equivalents, drinking water in the place of ale, eating his fatless pottage, petitioning for encouragement to his manufactories and answered by counter petitions.

In short, I think I see the Laborious Plew-man, with his corns spoiling upon his hands for want of sale, cursing the day of his birth, dreading the expense of his burial, and uncertain whether to marry or do worse.

I think I see the incurable difficulties of Landed men fettered under the Golden Chain of Equivalents, their pretty daughters petitioning for want of husbands, and their sons for want of imployments.

I think I see our mariners, delivering up their ships to their Dutch partners; and what through presses and necessity, earning their bread as underlings in the Royal English Navy.

But above all, my lords, I see our ancient mother Caledonia, like Caesar sitting in the midst of our Senate, ruefully looking about her, covering herself with her royal garment, attending the fatal blow, and breathing out her last with a Et tu quoque mi fili . . .

On January 16, 1707, the motion was put to the vote but the conclusion was foregone . . . the Treaty of Union was sanctioned by the Scottish Parliament. The peers had voted 42 in favour and 19 against; the Commissioners for the Shires by 38 to 30; the Commissioners for the Burghs had voted 30 in favour and 20 against; thus an overall majority of 41 votes was achieved for the Union. Immediately there were riots and demonstrations all over Scotland. The anti-Unionists debated whether to ignore the Union and set up their own independent parliament which, had they done so, would have received the popular support of the people. Whether historians are pro-Unionist or anti-Unionists, all agree that the Union of 1707 was achieved against the expressed national will of the people of Scotland. "A fresh election as the Government were well aware would ruin any project of an incorporating union", wrote W. C. MacKenzie in *Andrew Fletcher of Saltoun*. "The Union was achieved by the 'Grace of God' and quite contrary to the wishes of the Scottish people", writes the enthusiastic Unionist Andrew Lang (*The Union of 1707*).

It has often been stated by historians that England generously reimbursed Scotland for the state expenses she incurred through the Union. This idea is totally ridiculous. At the time of the Union Scotland's National Debt was £160,000, or one year's revenue, and the English National Debt was £18 millions, or three year's revenue. As, at the time of the Union, the Scottish population comprised of one seventh of the new British state, Scotland was made to assume one seventh of the combined National Debts, a sum of £2½ millions. The "generous" financial arrangement given by England to offset this £2½ million debt was £398,085 10s. which was not only to offset the National Debt but to offset higher Union taxes, to encourage fisheries and manufactories, as well as to compensate for the loss of £200,000 in the Darien Expedition. This sum, called, ironically, the Equivalent, was not paid to Scotland until six months later and when it did finally arrive in Edinburgh, in twelve wagons under a heavy dragoon guard, the crowds rioted in protest at the "Judas money".

Scotland now sent 45 members and 16 peers to Westminster to sit among the 500 English representatives. From the outset the English attitude to the Union was clear. There had been no democratic merger of two nations but a conquest of Scotland by England through diplomacy . . . a bloodless conquest, but a conquest nevertheless. As Defoe put it: "If ever a Nation gain'd by being Conquer'd it was here. They were subdued first, and then made happy, and Scotland flourished." The conception of England being a predominant partner was totally contrary to the Treaty of Union which specified that both countries were to lose their national identity in one equal sacrifice. There was to be no more England or Scotland but Britain, and the Treaty was to be the legal *written constitution*. But this was ignored, England continued to flourish while Scotland became a province. Because of the few voices Scotland had in the new Parliament no action could be taken to rectify the subservient position in which she found herself. "Scotland, however, is one of the very few instances in history of a nation whose political representation was so grossly ineffective as not merely to distort but absolutely to conceal its opinions", writes Lecky in his *Parliamentary History*.

Because of her predominant position, England soon began breaking clause after clause of the Treaty of Union, and the Scots, with only sixty-one voices in 500, could not use Parliament to nullify the Union. They tried, of course, and in 1714, Lord Seafield, one of the prime movers for the Union, proposed the first Self Government for Scotland Bill, the first of many such Bills. In answer to this the Speaker of the House of Commons put the English view plainly. The English "had catcht Scotland and would keep her fast". He was backed by the Lord Treasurer who said: "Have we not bought the Scots and the right to tax them?" With legislation ineffective, the next step was an obvious one.

Reaction against the Union was immediate and in 1708 an attempt was made to restore the Stuarts to the Scottish throne. During March five battleships, and twenty-one frigates, with 4,000 Jacobites aboard, sailed from France with James VII's son, the Chevalier de St George (The Old Pretender). The plan was to reach Leith and then march to Edinburgh but an English fleet under Admiral Byng encountered them in the Firth of Forth causing the Jacobites to retire. In the meantime, seemingly unaware, or uninterested in the anti-Unionist feeling, Parliament continued to pass legislation in direct violation of the Treaty. In 1712 an Erastian Act imposed upon the Church of Scotland, what was to them, an odious system of lay patronage; another Act gave status to Episcopalians; then, in 1713, a malt tax was passed. In 1714 Queen Anne died and George, son of the dead Electress of Hanover, became sovereign of the United Kingdom. The Scots now resolved to act and re-establish their independence by force, restoring the Stuart monarchy to the Scottish throne.

The Earl of Mar, who had been a prominent advocate of Union, raised the Stuart standard at Castleton in Braemar in 1715. The Scots rallied and met with initial successes. James VIII landed in Scotland but the tide of Scottish fortune had already turned. After the initial successes, the Scottish armies were forced to retreat and, in February, 1716, James and several

Scottish leaders, including Mar, fled to France. Those leaders of the '15 uprising who were captured were brought to trial but, because of the overwhelming public sympathy for them in Scotland, they were taken to Carlisle, in violation of Clause XIX of the Treaty of Union, for trial and execution. Again, in 1719 and 1720, "minor" insurrections took place and were quickly crushed. In 1725 an Act was passed declaring it illegal for the Scottish clans to possess weapons and General Wade was sent from London to ensure the Scots' obedience. The same year further taxation laws against Scottish industry were passed leading to another insurrection in Glasgow . . . again quelled by the troops. Two years later a demonstration in Edinburgh led to troops opening fire on the crowd.

While Scotland was thus suffering, the English and Anglicised Scots were increasing their efforts "to root out" the Scottish language. The Society for the Propagation of Christian Knowledge decided (General Meeting Minutes, June 2, 1716): "Nothing can be more effectual for reducing these counties to order and making them useful to the Commonwealth than teaching them their duty to God, their King and Country, and rooting out their Irish language . . .". Supported by ample financial grants from the Government, S.P.C.K. increased their "English only" schools from 12 in 1711 to 128 in 1742 in A' Ghàidhealtachd (Scottish-speaking areas). It is little wonder that the Scottish-speaking population, with few exceptions, supported the popular Scottish rising of 1745 as a hope to throw off this increasing persecution of their language and culture. Again, as in 1715, the restoration of the Stuart monarchy meant to the average Scot only the dissolution of the Union and no more. Mr Lochart, writing to James in Rome, 1725, urged the Stuarts "That our word be 'the restoration of the National Dynasty and the National Legislative!'" He adds, "aversion to the Union daily increases, and that is the handle by which Scotsmen will be incited to make a general and zealous appearance". Charles Edward was careful to "promise many things agreeable to the Scots, and among these was the dissolution of the Union with England", since, it is added, "the Scots generally, but the Highlanders [i.e. Scottish speakers] in particular, looked upon the Union with England as a slavish subjection". Sir Walter Scott comments: "The words 'Prosperity to Scotland

and no Union' is the favourite inscription to be found on Scottish blades betwixt 1707 and 1746."

The history of the '45 uprising is well known. In July, 1745, Charles Edward landed on the island of Eriskay and, on August 19, he raised the Stuart banner at Glenfinnan. A manifesto of his aims was read in which he promised the Scots a dissolution of the Union with England, the calling of a free Scottish Parliament and the free exercise of religion. In less than three months the Scottish army had pushed the English army as far as Corstorphine, three miles west of Edinburgh. Edinburgh opened its gates to the Stuarts and Prince Charles had his father reaffirmed as James VIII at Holyrood Palace. On September 20, nine miles east of Edinburgh at Prestonpans, the Scottish army completely routed the English army commanded by General Sir John Cope. All Scotland was now in Stuart hands.

It had been many years since a Royal Court was held in Edinburgh and many people attended at Holyrood Palace, where the Prince was working sometimes as long as twenty hours in a day. On October 10 a declaration nullifying the Union was issued, thus winning to the Stuart cause strong support from the Scottish Whigs and Presbyterians, who were declared anti-Unionists. The Scots urged Charles Edward to go further and recall the Estates to declare Scotland separate and independent—its situation prior to 1603. This idea was also supported by the French envoy, Alexandre Jean Baptiste de Boyer, Marquis d'Eguilles, who suggested that France would be more willing to lend aid to a project to detach Scotland from England and to re-establish the "ancienne alliance". France had no wish to see a strong England in command of the British Isles, even with a Stuart on the throne. The Scottish chiefs argued that the Prince, with his rule now firmly established in Scotland, could easily repel any English invasion of the country which was sure to come. They reckoned without the Stuart ambition . . . Charles not only wanted the crown of Scotland but that of England and Ireland as well.

On October 31, in face of strong opposition from his political and military advisers, Charles ordered the invasion of England and the Scottish army marched across the border. Despite the hostility, and indifference, of the population, the Scottish army met with initial success, capturing Carlisle, Preston, Lancaster,

Manchester, Macclesfield and then Derby. The Hanoverian king had his baggage packed and was making ready to flee the country. He had called in an army of 6,000 Dutch troops to try and stop the Scots but, at Derby, it was the Scottish chiefs who finally made the decision. They had seen that the English did not want the Stuarts restored to the throne of England. Voltaire says that the English heartily resented the prospect of having a king foisted upon them by their traditional enemy. This, the Scots decided, was all right by them. Their main aim, to annul the Union and restore Scottish independence, had been achieved. They would return to Scotland and maintain Scottish independence.

The Scottish army was weakened, however, by its sojurn in England and retreat followed retreat. By February, 1746, the Scottish army had retreated as far as Inverness and, on Wednesday, April 16, the Scottish and English armies met on Culloden Moor. The English, led by the Duke of Cumberland, defeated the Scots and began one of the worst persecutions of a nation known to history, earning the title "Butcher" Cumberland for their leader. The Scottish survivors were chased from the field of battle and slaughtered. For two days the wounded and dead of the Scottish army lay where they had fallen, guarded by English soldiers so that no medical or burial parties could get to them. Looting was officially organised and £5 was paid for the head of every "rebel" brought to Major-General John Huske, the English Commander at Fort Augustus. Towns and villages were razed to the ground, people slaughtered wholesale and those that managed to escape massacre were imprisoned, executed or transported. Cumberland, as a "final solution" to the Scottish problem, proposed the wholesale transportation of clans to the colonies which developed into the notorious "Highland Clearances". On May 15, 1746, Parliament decided that all prisoners held in Scotland should be removed to England for trial and execution, as they had been in 1715, again violating Clause XIX; not that Parliament was concerned with breaking the Treaty, all pretensions of a Union had gone and Scotland was militarily annexed to England as Wales had been centuries earlier. From August 1, 1746, the wearing of tartans, plaids, kilts, trews, etc., were banned, thus taking away the Scottish pride and sense of belonging to a unique people. Parliament was determined to destroy Scottish nationalism by destroying Scottish nationality.

For most of the eighteenth century Scottish nationalism manifested itself through Jacobitism, an attempt to re-establish the Scottish monarchy and nullify the Union. Had the Stuarts been content with the crown of Scotland, history might have been different. By the nineteenth century the Stuart cause had become a forlorn one and few Scots supported it, for their allegiance had been transferred to radical, socialist republicanism. After the '45, Stuart plots and intrigues continued and Charles Edward made a number of secret visits to the country between 1750 and 1760 but, following the American War of Independence and the French Revolution, a new political philosophy began to sweep the nations of Europe, taking a firm hold in Ireland and in Scotland. This was the philosophy in which both Irish and Scottish nationalism began to channel itself . . . republicanism.

THREE

SCOTTISH REPUBLICANISM

"ALAS," WROTE THE poet Robert Burns to Mrs Dunlop on April 10, 1790, "have I often said to myself, what are the boasted advantages which my country reaps from the Union that can counterbalance the annihilation of her independence, and even her very name!" The young poet referred to the fact that while England flourished in name, Scotland was now officially called "North Britain" and even the office of Secretary of State for Scotland had ceased to exist after the Rising of 1745. After this abortive rising, Scotland fell into a period of political apathy. Her representatives at Westminster were people who were only interested in their own self-aggrandisement and, in fact, represented nobody but themselves. Patriotic Scots, such as Burns, felt betrayed and helpless. The general feeling of the time was summed up by him in his song "A Parcel of Rogues in a Nation".

> Fareweel to a' our Scottish fame,
>   Fareweel our ancient glory!
> Fareweel ev'n to the Scottish name
>   Sae famed in martial story!
> Now Sark rins over Solway Sands,
>   An' Tweed rins to the ocean,
> To mark where England's province stands—
>   Such a parcel of rogues in a nation!
>
> What force or guile could not subdue,
>   Thro' many warlike ages,
> Is wrought now by a coward few
>   For hireling traitor's wages.
> The English steel we could disdain
>   Secure in valour's station;
> But English gold has been our bane—
>   Such a parcel of rogues in a nation!

> O, would or I had seen the day
>   That Treason thus could sell us,
> My auld grey head had lien in clay
>   Wi' Bruce and loyal Wallace!
> But pith and power, till my last hour,
>   I'll mak this declaration,
> We're bought and sold for English gold—
>   Such a parcel of rogues in a nation!

With some Scots this state of apathy and depression did not last long, however. In 1762 a Poker Club was formed "to stir up the fire and spirit of the nation". George Dempster of Dunnichen wrote to one of the club's founders, Dr Carlyle of Inveresk, stating that the club ought to agitate for a complete reform of the Unionist political system existing in Scotland. But in the meantime events elsewhere, which were to have a far-reaching effect in Scotland, completely overtook the Scottish reform movements.

Social conditions in England's thirteen American colonies became so bad that on September 5, 1775, a Continental Congress met at Philadelphia and resolved to appeal to England for a redress of grievances. The Government's answer to this was to send General Gage with an army to set up military rule in the colonies and to arrest the American leaders—Samuel Adams and John Hancock. They escaped, however, and the War of Independence began. On July 4, 1776, the Congress, now the *de facto* government of the colonies, issued a Declaration of Independence, which was largely written by Thomas Jefferson. The war was a bloody one and in 1778 Lord North sent a peace mission to America but the Americans refused to negotiate anything less than complete independence from England. The struggle continued and resulted in General Cornwallis surrendering the English army in Yorktown, Virginia, on October 19, 1781. A formal Peace Treaty was signed at Paris in September, 1783. In 1789 a republican constitution was endorsed making the thirteen former colonies into a completely independent state with New York as its first temporal capital.

Many Scots had fought for the American separatists, perhaps the most famous being John Paul of Kirkcudbright who entered the American navy as John Paul Jones and who achieved the title of "Father of the American Navy". John Paul made two expeditions to the Scottish coast during the hostilities . . . one to Kirkcudbright in 1778 and one to the Firth of Forth in 1779. Many of these Scots returned to Scotland brimful of American republican revolutionary fervour, such as Dr Robert Watson of Elgin, who was to become president of the revolutionary Corresponding Society. Agitation for a reformation of the political system began to grow and in 1783 meetings in three Scottish counties passed resolutions demanding political reform. A meeting was held in Edinburgh to appoint a committee to take the plea to Westminster. Other Scots saw republicanism not just as a political philosophy through which social and political reform could be obtained, but saw it as a means to regain Scottish independence. Reform and nationalism began to go hand in hand.

Another event, which was to prove even more important to Scottish aspirations, was the French Revolution. On May 5, 1789, the Third Estate demanded that the French Estates (Parliament) should meet as one Parliament of the People. In June the Estates became the National Assembly and a new constitution was ordered. The aristocracy sent in troops to dissolve the French Parliament and the people reacted by forming a National Guard. The Bastille, as symbol of the *aristos*' tyranny, was stormed on July 14 and all political prisoners freed. In that year also, as a preamble to what was to be the new French Constitution of 1791, the Declaration of the Rights of Man and Citizens, proposed by Sieyès, was adopted as the basis of the new government in France. This was based on J. J. Rousseau's theories and the American Declaration of Independence based on the idea of government through the natural rights of man; equality of all men, sovereignty of the people, and the inalienable rights of the individual to liberty, property and security.

In this upheaval in France many Scots were prominent figures. Many expatriate Scots were to be found living in the French capital at this time, mainly because of their political beliefs. There was a Scots College functioning there, and a number of Scots also belonged to the Jacobin Club (extremist republican group) while many more Scots were serving in Scottish regiments in the French Army, such as the Gardes Écossaises (Scots Guards), founded in the 1420's at the time of Jean d'Arc, the regiment was the bodyguard of the French head

of state until the 1830's when it was disbanded. According to
Marshal MacDonald, the regiment was still using Gàidhlig in
its orders up till the time when it was disbanded. These expatriate Scots in Paris kept close links with republican-minded Scots
in Scotland. Such a man was Dr William Maxwell of Kirk-
connel, who enrolled as a member of the French National
Guard and was on the scaffold when Louis XVI was executed.
He soaked his handkerchief in "the tyrant's blood" to send
back to Scotland as a souvenir. Maxwell was a close friend of
Robert Burns who shared his political ideals.

A great many Scottish Catholics were in complete agreement
with the revolution, and Bishop John Geddes recalls that he had
to visit Paris at this time to make sure that Alexander Gordon,
the principal of the Scots College there, was keeping himself out
of politics. While there, Geddes found that some Scots had even
found themselves elevated to positions of authority under the
French Revolutionary regime. As a spectator to a meeting of the
French National Assembly on January 4, 1792, he found a Mr
Rose of Edinburgh acting as "hussier" and keeping order in the
chamber. Geddes' namesake, Dr Alexander Geddes, a priest,
was also active in the Scots republican movement and remains
famous for his ode in praise of the revolution, *Carmen saeculare pro
Gallica gente*. Republican-minded Scots, such as Dugald Stewart,
the Earl of Lauderdale, later named as one of the Provisional
Government of the Scottish Republic, and his friend the Earl of
Buchan, began to visit revolutionary Paris. Lauderdale is
reported to have harangued a Parisian crowd on liberty. Both
Lauderdale and Buchan returned to Scotland and started to set
up clubs, ostensibly for debate, which supported the revolution.
In 1791 a new French National Assembly met in October which
divided into two political parties; these were the Girondists
(moderates) and the Jacobins led by Marat, Robespierre and
Danton. The monarchy was rejected. When Burke wrote his
famous *Reflections on the French Revolution*, Thomas Paine, an
Englishman who had fought for the American separatists, wrote
an equally famous reply to it, *The Rights of Man*, published in
1790. Immediately banned as seditious, it was openly hawked
in Scottish cities and was translated into Gàidhlig and sold in
great numbers throughout A' Ghàidhealtachd.

The revolution stimulated Scottish political awareness and

this awareness was reflected in one way by the growth of the English language Press in Scotland; a growth from eight newspapers in 1782 to twenty-seven newspapers in 1790. The sympathy Scotland felt towards the revolution was also reflected in the poetry of the day, particularly in the work of the nationalist poet Burns, who not only wrote poems but actually shipped guns to France to aid the revolutionary endeavour. It was at this time that Burns wrote the great Scottish patriotic song, "Scots Wha hae wi' Wallace Bled . . ." (which was almost immediately translated into Gàidhlig—Albannaich, thug Brus mu'n cuairt) which has since been adopted as Scotland's national anthem. "The Tree of Liberty" and "A man's a man for a' that . . ." are also famous in this context. Burns appeared to change his politics later by joining the Yeomanry forces but, according to Hugh MacDiarmid (writing in the *Glasgow Herald*, March 14, 1967) Burns joined the Yeomanry as part of an overall plan by the republicans being carried out throughout Scotland to infiltrate the ranks of the soldiery.

The Scottish political writer, John MacKintosh, wrote that he hoped the French Revolution would not only serve as a model for social change but also to "stimulate the spirit of freedom" in Scotland.

Certainly this had been the effect in Ireland where a "reform movement", the United Irishmen societies, had sprung up, the first of which had been formed in Belfast on October 14, 1791. A Dublin society was formed in November. These movements were, at first, middle-class debating societies which strove to mould public opinion. In Ireland a plan of parliamentary reform was suggested in 1794 dividing Ireland into 300 constituencies equal in population and every man given a vote, even women would have equal franchise. The leading light of the United Irishmen was a young Protestant barrister, Theobald Wolfe Tone. Tone's major policy, advocated through the United Irishmen, was . . . "to break the connection with England, the never failing source of all our political evils, and to assert the independence of my country . . .". The United Irishmen were soon advocating that the ideals in Thomas Paine's *Rights of Man* should be made a reality in Ireland and an independent Irish Republic should be set up. Tone wrote: "Our independence must be had at all hazards. If the men of property will not support us, they must fall: we can support ourselves by the aid of that numerous and respectable class, the men of the community—the men of no property."

In Scotland, the move to this way of thinking was a more gradual one. Nevertheless, Lauderdale and Buchan, with Lord Daer, Lord Sempill, the Earl of Selkirk's eldest son, Colonel MacLeod of MacLeod, a Whig M.P. for Inverness, and Lord Kinnaird, succeeded in forming a movement based on the lines of the first United Irishmen societies, called the Friends of the People. This was, at first, a reform movement but its leaders were republican almost to a man. They were quite open in advocating the repeal of the Union with England, which made them "nationalists" as well. Lord Daer, writing to Charles Grey (afterwards Lord Grey, the 1830 Whig prime minister) on January 17, 1793, expressed clearly the opinions of the Friends of the People and their stand as Scottish nationalists rather than just mere reformers.

Scotland has long groaned under the chains of England and knows that its connections there has been the cause of its greatest misfortunes. Perhaps you may shrug your shoulders at this and call it Scot's prejudice, but it is time at moments like these when much may depend on suiting measures to the humour of the people, that you Englishmen should see this rather as it is or at least be aware of how we Scotsmen see it.

We have existed a conquered province these two centuries. We trace our bondage from the Union of the Crowns and find it little alleviated by the Union of Kingdoms. What is it, you say, we have gained by the Union? Commerce, Manufacturers, Agriculture? Without going deep into the principles of political economy or asking how our Government or any country can give these to any nation, it is evident in this case that the last Union (1707) gave us little assistance in these, except removing a part of the obstacles which your greater power had posterior to the first Union (1603) thrown around us. But if it did more, what would that amount to, but to the common saying that we bartered our liberty, and with it our morals, for a little wealth.

You may say we have joined emancipation from feudal tyranny. I would believe most deliberately that had no Union ever taken place we should, in that respect, have been more emancipated than we are. Left to ourselves we should probably have had a progression towards liberty and not less than yours.

Our grievances prior to the accession of the Stewarts to your throne were of a kind which even had that event not taken place, must before this time have been annihilated. Any share of human evil that might awaited us, we are ignorant of, where as we feel that we have under gone. Even to the last of our separate parliaments, they were always making laws for us and now and then one to remedy a grievance. And a people acquiring knowledge must have compelled a separate legislature to more of these.

Since the parliaments were united, scarcely four acts have been passed in as many score of years affecting Scots law or merely the incongruities which must arise betwixt old laws and modern manners.

As our courts of law find something of this to be necessary they, instead of applying to the parliament at London, have taken upon themselves, with a degree of audacity, which can hardly be made credible to a stranger, to make under pretence of regularity of court, little laws (acts of parliament as they call them) materially affecting the liberty of the subject.

Kept out of view by your greater mass so as never to make our conscience be the principle objects even to our own representatives at a distance, so as not to make our cries heard in the capital which alone awes an arbitrary govenment; our laws and customs different so as to make our grievances unintelligible; our law established distant so as to deprive us of the benefit of those constant circuits from the capital which, by rendering the learned and spirited defender of the laws, dwelling at the actual source of actual power, acquainted with the lesser transactions of the remotest corner of the country; provides, perhaps, the greatest remedy to a half free state against some of the bad consequences of extended territory.

Our civil establishment distinct, so as to isolate the petty tyranny of office; even our greed and national unity working to retain still more to leave you (our then only protectors, although oppressors) ignorant of internal situation. We have suffered the misery which is perhaps inevitable to a lesser and remote country in a junction where the Governing powers are united but the Nations are not united.

In short, thinking we have been the worse of every connection hitherto with you, the Friends of Liberty in Scotland have almost universally been enemies to the Union with England. Such is the fact, whether the reasons be good or bad.

The first Friends of the People Society started to function on a proper basis in Edinburgh on July 26, 1792, and another in Glasgow in October of that year. The societies attracted a great number of Catholics, from A' Ghàidhealtachd. This was, in some part, due to the "Clearances" which had begun in 1782 and to Irish immigration. The year the Friends of the People started to function, 1792, has been described in Scottish history as Bliadhna nan Caorach (The Year of the Sheep) when many Scots were forced from their ancestral homesteads and replaced by flocks of sheep. These "Clearances" ensured great support throughout A' Ghàidhealtachd, and among the refugee communities of the displaced Scots in the industrial belt, for the nationalist reformers. Great problems arose for the Catholic Church due to the activities of Dr Alexander Geddes and, more particularly, David Downie, a treasurer of the Friends of the People, as these men were both Catholics. Their activities, and the activities of other Catholics in the revolutionary movement, made the hierarchy fearful that their delicate negotiations with Lord Advocate, Robert Dundas, in order to ensure the passing of the Catholic Relief Bill (which Dundas introduced in Parliament on April 23, 1793) might be irrevocably upset. Because this Bill was eventually passed the Catholic Hierarchy in Scotland were full of praise for the political system of the time. The despotic Dundas and the London Government were "humane and generous" and poor insane George III was "the best of Kings". The Church even tried to get some Scottish Catholics to raise a regiment for the king to which Dundas hastily replied "at present His Majesty has not thought it expedient to accept the offer of the Regiment yet I am happy to find that the loyalty of his Catholic subjects in Scotland has met with His Royal approbation". But all this did not stop the Catholic influx into the reform movement.

The organisation of the Friends of the People was due mainly to the efforts of one man, a young lawyer named Thomas Muir of Huntershill, near Glasgow, who had become a member of the Honourable Faculty of Advocates in 1787 at the age of 22 or 23. In 1792 "he literally became a strong man, clad as it were in bright polished political armour". Muir, who is described as 5 ft. 9 in., chestnut hair and blue eyes, had many contacts with the French revolutionary government and he was a great friend of the Girondist leader, La Fayette, who had gained fame by fighting for the Americans. It was due to Muir that tentative communications were exchanged with the French Government which led to the Committee of Public Safety appointing Citoyen Pétry as "agent de la marine et du commerce" in Scotland in October, 1792, in order to report on conditions there. By December, the French Government decided that France would spare no expense to support a republican insurrection in Scotland and also in Ireland and a resolution was passed to this effect on December 14. Citoyen Armand Kersaint explained the decision to the French National Convention a few days later and his speech was reported in the *Moniteur*, January 3, 1793.

The English people like all conquerors have long oppressed Scotland and Ireland: but it should be noted that these two nations, always restive, and secretly in revolt against the injustices of the dominating race, have acquired at different epochs concessions which have engendered the hope of ultimately regaining their entire independence. . . . Since the Union, Scotland has been represented in Parliament, but out of such proportion to its wealth, its extent and its population, that it does not conceal the fact that it is nothing but a dependent colony of the English Government. Yet the Scots know their rights and their strength: the principles developed by the French nation have there found zealous defenders who have been the first to merit the honour of being persecuted by the British Government: but these persecutions have made proselytes, and no where is more joy caused by your victories than in Scotland, the principle towns of which have been illuminated to honour them.

In December, while the French were considering what action should be taken to aid Scotland, the first General Convention of the Friends of the People was held in Edinburgh. The Convention lasted three days from December 11 to the 13th. There were 140 delegates and a Colonel Dalrymple took the chair aided by Lord Daer. Thomas Muir was elected as vice-president of the movement and William Skirving was appointed secretary. Many resolutions were heard and a Captain Johnston, described as chairman of the General Association—another reform movement—decided he would launch a paper called the *Edinburgh Gazetteer* which would "attach itself to the party of the people".

Among the delegates were two visitors from the United Irishmen societies—Dr Drennan and A. Hamilton Rowan. These Irishmen had brought an address from their movement to the Friends of the People which Muir presented.

We greatly rejoice that the spirit of freedom moves over the face of Scotland—that the light seems to break from the chaos of her internal government and that a country so respectable in her attainments, in science, in arts, and in arms; for men of literary eminence; for the intelligence and morality of her people, now from a conviction of the union between virtue, letters and liberty, and now rises to distinction, not by a calm, contended, secret wish for a reform in Parliament, but by openly, actively and urgently willing it, with the unity and energy of an embodied nation!

Delegates rose from their seats and holding up their right hands swore to "live free or die!" The Convention was adjourned until April of the following year. A few weeks later Muir was arrested in his Edinburgh house and interrogated by the authorities. He was released soon after but warned that the authorities were considering issuing a warrant for his arrest to face a charge of sedition. Unfortunately, events had happened in France which made Muir think it was imperative for him to visit the country. The National Convention had declared France a republic on September 20, 1792, causing the Austrian Empire to declare war upon it. Louis XVI and his family had fled to Varennes trying to join a large German and Austrian army grouped at the frontier. Louis hoped to lead this army in, conquer France and impose his rule again. The royal family had been recaptured and now Louis was on trial for his life. Muir was against regicide and felt that he must join a group of republicans, among them many Americans, who were trying to prevent the National Assembly from pronouncing the death sentence on the royal family. Muir arrived in Paris in the very evening of the day on which the French Government had pronounced its verdict. Danton, amidst the frenzied cheers of the delegates, cried: "The coalised kings threaten us: we hurl at their feet, as gage of battle, the head of a king!"

England, Holland, Spain and Portugal now joined Austria in an attempt to crush the republic and restore the monarchy in France. The execution of Louis XVI also sealed Muir's fate. The Lord Advocate denounced Muir saying that he had fled to France to escape trial. "He was a Commissioner, forsooth, of the Black-nebs and Republicans of Scotland, to hasten on the execution of Louis. . . ." A warrant for his arrest was immediately sworn out on a charge of sedition and he was summoned to appear before the court in Scotland on February 11 or be declared an outlaw.

The war against France turned a lot of the members of the Friends of the People, imbued by a false patriotic pride, to forsake the cause and join the fight against the French. In order to impress on the Scottish people the "evil" of the Friends of the People and what might happen to them if they joined or continued in membership, Henry Erskine had a series of resolutions expressing "the greatest abhorrence of the exertions of evil designing persons" translated into Gàidhlig by the Highland Society in January, 1793, and this, with an English version, was widely distributed throughout Scotland.

Arrests and trials for sedition of some of the prominent members of the Friends of the People soon followed. On January 7, 1793, James Tyler was tried for sedition and the following day John Morton, James Anderson and Malcolm Craig were also tried for the same offence. The crime being that they were members of "a club for equality and freedom". They were all sentenced to nine months' imprisonment and a fine of 1,000 merks, plus three years' security for good behaviour. On January 10, 1793, John Elder and William Stewart were charged with sedition, their crime being that they had a medallion in their possession with the words "A nation is the source of all sovereignty" and "liberty and equality". A few days later James Smith and John Minnon were tried for sedition. Then Captain Johnston, editor of the *Edinburgh Gazetteer*, and Simon Drummond, the paper's publisher, were tried. A few days later William Callendar was arrested for sedition, but escaped and was outlawed. Walter Berry, a bookseller, and James Robertson, were tried for sedition. All were imprisoned, fined or transported. These sedition trials took place from January to March and they seemed to have been a part of a deliberate scheme by the authorities to stamp out the movement by frightening off potential members.

Muir wanted to return to Scotland but found it was not easy. Due to the state of war existing between England and France, travel between the latter and any English dominion was forbidden. However, he was determined to return and from Paris, on February 13, 1793, he wrote to "The Friends of the People in Scotland":

Upon the evening of the 8th of this month I have received letters from my father, and my agent Mr Campbell, informing me that an indictment was served against me in my absence and that the trial was fixed for the 11th inst. The distance and the shortness of time could not permit me to reach Edinburgh that day.

War is declared between England and France, and the formalities requisite to be gone through before I could procure my passport would have at least consumed three days. I will return to Scotland without delay.

To shrink from dangers would be unbecoming to my own character and your confidence.

Learning of his intended return, Government agents began a vigorous effort to obtain incriminating evidence against him. They devoted most of their efforts to Kirkintilloch and received enthusiastic support from the Rev. James Lapslie of Campsie Church. Lapslie, who had joined the Friends of the People, had been financially assisted by Muir's parents on numerous occasions after wangling his way into their confidence, but he was a Government informer. In return he received a Government pension for himself and his descendants. Lapslie was to continue in this role in the tragic events of 1820. This minister-cum-spy vehemently denounced Muir and tried to use "spiritual blackmail" on his flock to make them give incriminating evidence. Lapslie then pointed out, to the agents, that the Rev. William Dunn was Muir's closest friend. Although Dunn was never at any time a member of the Friends of the People, he had delivered a sermon, as Moderator of the Glasgow Presbytery, to the Synod of Glasgow and Ayr, dedicated to the Friends of Constitution in Church and State, which supported reform. On November 3, 1792, Muir, addressing a meeting at Kirkintilloch, had recorded a resolution expressing appreciation and support for Dunn's attitude. Immediately the agents decided to get hold of the minutes of this meeting in order to use the resolution as evidence against Dunn. On Lapslie's information, agents went to the homes of Mr Baird, a High Street merchant, and a Mr Freeland, who was branch secretary at Kirkintilloch. They demanded the minute book but the astute reformists tore out the incriminating pages. Dunn, however, was arrested and taken to Edinburgh on March 11. He was imprisoned in the Tolbooth for three months purely on suspicion of being con-

nected with Muir in a political sense. On his return to Kirkintilloch Rev. Dunn was greeted as a hero.

On April 29, 1793, despite pleas by the authorities that the
wisest course was to remain in France, Muir was issued with a
passport signed by Le Brun, Maille, Gorat and Nicoleau,
Ministers for Foreign Affairs. The young lawyer sailed on the
American ship *Hope*, commanded by Captain George Towers,
bound for Baltimore via Belfast. While waiting in Belfast to
ship for Scotland Muir was made an honorary member of the
United Irishmen. In the meantime, he had been declared an
outlaw in Scotland and his name was removed from the Roll of
the Faculty of Advocates on March 6. He also received letters
from his father urging him to go to America and not to return
home. His father promised to supply letters of introduction to
the American President, George Washington. Muir ignored
these requests and reached Port Patrick in July. From here he
made his way to Stranraer where an inkeeper discovered his
identity and denounced him to the authorities. George William-
son, Messenger of Arms, was given a warrant to conduct Muir
from Stranraer prison to Edinburgh and his trial was fixed for
August 30.

The trial opened presided over by Lord Justice Clerk
McQueen with Lords Henderland, Dunnisinnan, Swinton and
Abercromby. Robert Dundas, the Lord Advocate himself,
appeared for the Crown, and Muir defended himself. The
fifteen members of the jury chosen were either officers of the
Crown, members of the Goldsmith Hall (vehemently opposed
to Muir) or Placemen or Pensioners liable to be removed if they
displeased the Crown. The authorities wanted to ensure a conviction. Captain John Inglis of Auchdinny pointed out that
"Being in His Majesty's service he did not wish to be on this
Jury as he thought it unfair in a case of this nature, to try Muir
by servants of the Crown." McQueen overruled Inglis' scruples
and said he must serve. Muir protested, "shall these men be my
Jurymen who have not merely accused me but likewise judged
and condemned me without knowing me in my vindication".

The main points brought against Muir was that he had circu-
lated a newspaper called *The Patriot* and, at the Edinburgh
Convention, delivered "An Address from the Society of United
Irishmen". It was said that Muir had also made a speech at the

Convention "of a most inflammatory and seditious tendency, falsely and insidiously representing the Irish and Scottish nations as in a state of downright oppression and exciting the people to rise up and oppose the Government".

Muir's speech has become a classic in speeches from the dock and for many years it was studied as part of the curriculum in the schoolrooms of the young American Republic.

Is the time come [demanded Muir] when the mind must be locked up, and fetters imposed on the understanding? And are the people to be precluded from that information and knowledge in which others are so materially concerned?

Oh unhappy country. Miserable people, the rememberance of former liberties will only make you more wretched.

Extinguish then, if you can, the light of heaven, and let us grope, and search for consolation, if it can be found under the darkness which will soon cover us.

Muir continued:

Gentlemen of the jury, this is perhaps the last time I shall address my country. I have explored the tenor of my past life. Nothing shall tear from me the record of my former days.

Gentlemen, from my infancy to this moment I have devoted myself to the cause of the people. It is a good cause—it shall ultimately prevail—it shall finally triumph.

Gentlemen, the time will come when men must stand or fall by their actions—when all human pageantry shall cease—when the hearts of all shall be laid open.

He concluded:

I am careless and indifferent to my fate. I can look danger and I can look death in the face, for I am shielded by the consciousness of my own rectitude. I may be condemned to languish in the recess of a dungeon—I may be doomed to ascend the scaffold. Nothing can deprive me of the past—nothing can destroy my inward peace of mind, arising from the rememberance of having discharged my duty.

Muir was sentenced to fourteen years' transportation and ordered to remain in the Tolbooth in Edinburgh until such time as a ship was ready.

In September another prominent member of the movement, the Rev. Thomas Fyshe Palmer of Dundee, was arrested and charged with writing and printing seditious literature. At his trial part of a pamphlet he wrote was read to the court:

Fellow citizens! the friends of liberty call upon you, by all that is dear and worthy of possessing as men—by your oppression, by the miseries and sorrows of your suffering, brethren, by all that you dread, by the sweet remembrance of your patriotic ancestors, and by all that your prosperity have a right to expect from you—to join is in our exertions for the long preservation of our perishing liberty, and the recovery of our long lost rights.

Palmer was sentenced to seven years' transportation and wrote from his cell to his comrades that the Government's attitude to Scotland would be "the destruction of a whole people merely because they will be free!" It was against this background that Burns wrote, in September, 1793, his Ode for General Washington's Birthday:

> Thee, Caledonia, thy wild heaths among,
> Fam'd for the martial deed, the heaven-taught song,
> To thee I turn with swimming eyes;
> Where is that soul of freedom fled?
> Immingled with the mighty dead,
> Beneath that hallowed turf where Wallace lies!
> Hear it not, Wallace, in thy bed of death?
> Ye Babling winds, in silence weep!
> Disturb not ye the hero's sleep,
> Nor give the coward secret breath!
> Is this the ancient Caledonian form,
> Firm as her rock, resistless as her storm?
> Show me that eye which shot immortal hate,
> Blasting the Despot's proudest bearing!
> Show me that arm which, serv'd with thundering fate,
> Braved usurpation's boldest daring!
> Dark-quenched as yonder sinking star,
> No more that glance lightens afar,
> That palsied arm no more whirls on the waste of war.

On November 15, 1793, Muir and Palmer were put on board the Excise Packet, *Royal George*, and transported to London where they arrived on December 1, in irons. Attempts were made to stop the execution of the sentence and on January 31, 1794, the Earl Stanhope moved that the Lords appeal against Muir's sentence by petitions, this was seconded by the Earl of

c

Stair and defeated by 49 votes to 2. Stanhope bitterly commented, "if this was the law, he would only observe that Scotland had no more liberty . . .". On February 10, Charles James Fox, the Whig leader who had supported the French Revolution, commented: "God help the people who have such judges." On February 24, 1794, Richard Brinsley Sheridan, the playwright, who had entered Parliament in 1780, asked for clemency for Palmer. Henry Dundas and Lord Melville opposed this and the motion was rejected by 171 votes to 32. Lord Colchester observed: "Muir and Palmer were actually removed from Scotland and transported to Botany Bay though there was no statute then in force to warrant it."

Despite these warnings, the remainder of the Friends of the People decided to go ahead with their scheduled Convention for November 19, 1793, in Edinburgh. On November 4, A. Hamilton Rowan and the Hon. Simon Butler arrived in Edinburgh to attend the Convention as envoys from the United Irishmen. Among the other delegates was James Wilson of Strathaven, who was to play a prominent and tragic part in 1820. He had already been in touch with William Skirving by letter, commiserating on the loss of Muir and Palmer to the movement. The Convention met openly and discussed universal suffrage, annual parliaments and a convention "bill". The subject of spreading revolutionary literature through A' Ghàidhealtachd was also discussed. On Thursday, December 5, the Lord Provost of Edinburgh, with thirty constables and the military standing by, broke up the Convention. The same evening it reassembled in secret.

The authorities now made an all-out move to crush the movement. Alexander Scott, who had taken over from the unfortunate Captain Johnston as editor of the *Edinburgh Gazetteer*, was warned that a warrant was out for his arrest on a charge of sedition and he fled the country. When he did not appear in court on February 3, 1794, he was declared an outlaw. William Skirving was next arrested and tried on January 13, for sedition. At his trial it was alleged that Skirving wanted to eliminate the constitution as embodied in the Treaty of Union, and put in its place in Scotland "a republic or democracy". He was sentenced to fourteen years' transportation. Maurice Margarot, tried at the same time, was also sentenced to a similar period of transportation. Writing from his cell after the trial Margarot warned Scotsmen that they must form "armed associations" and, in a handbill, he urged "get arms and learn the use of them".

Charles Sinclair was charged in February, 1794, with sedition but turned Government informer and the case against him was not pressed. From March 3 to March 14, 1794, Joseph Gerrald was tried for sedition. Part of a speech he made was read out in court against him. Gerrald claimed:

... that it was ... soon after the Union of England and Scotland the people were deprived of some of the most valuable privileges. It was from that period that the greatest encroachments began to be made on public liberty. But if that Union has operated to rob us of our rights, let it be the object to regain them.

Sentenced to fourteen years' transportation, Gerrald commented: "My lord, we have the example of our own times also. I need not remind your lordship of 1745 and 1715 when many men, who acted with the best intentions, died the deaths of traitors."

The leaders of the Friends of the People were conveyed in April, 1794, to the six-year-old penal settlement at Botany Bay in New South Wales in the transport ship *Surprise*, commanded by Patrick Campbell. The Governor of the settlement, a man named Hunter, gave the prisoners permission to cultivate land and employ their capital in working it. Gerrald, whose health had been broken in solitary confinement at Newgate, died of consumption soon after his arrival while Skirving did not long survive him. Palmer lived in Sydney until 1799 when he began to make preparations for the journey home. With others, he invested in a small vessel which sailed from Port Jackson on January 20, 1800. The ship was delayed in New Zealand for twenty-six weeks and finally ran for Tonga but was not allowed to land. At Fiji they obtained fruit and yams and narrowly escaped shipwreck on Goraa Reef. Sailing for Macao they had to put into Guam and were seized by the Spanish Governor as prisoners of war. Palmer was seized with dysentery and suffered for eight months before he died in June, 1802, two years after his sentence expired. Only Margarot made his way back to Scotland in 1810 and gave evidence to the First Committee of the House of Commons on Transportation in 1812. In Scotland he was said to have resumed "his old activities" but he died in November, 1816, while subscriptions were being raised to relieve his distressed financial state.

Muir's return was as romantic as all the rest of his life had been. When the news of his transportation reached the Scots-Americans, who had supported the Scottish revolutionaries, strings were pulled to get the American Government to do something. General George Washington, in his seventh year of Presidency, ordered the U.S.S. *Otter*, of New York, to be fitted out under the command of Captain Dawes for the express purpose of rescuing Muir and inviting him to become a member of the American Bar. The *Otter* arrived in Port Jackson, New South Wales, on February 5, 1795, and after a fortnight Dawes managed to locate his man. Muir wrote a hurried note to Hunter, the Governor, and taking his pocket Bible, escaped in the *Otter* under cover of darkness.

After a voyage of four months, *Otter* made Nootka Sound but struck a rock and went to pieces. Only Muir and two other sailors survived. The three were captured by Indians and only Muir managed to escape. Muir made his way to Havana via Panama, where he was helped by the Spanish Governor. He was put on board the Spanish frigate, *Nymph*, disguised as an ordinary sailor. The *Nymph*, with another frigate, set off for Cadiz, but on April 26, 1796, they encountered two ships of Sir John Jervis' English squadron, *Irresistible* and *Emerald*, in Canille Bay. The battle lasted two hours and the Captain of H.M.S. *Irresistible*, lying off Cadiz, said in his report of April 28:

Among the sufferers on the Spanish side is Mr Thomas Muir who made so wonderful escape from Botany Bay to the Havannah. He was one of five killed aboard the *Nymph* by the last shot fired by us. The officer at whose side he fell is at my hand and says he behaved with courage to the last.

But the captain of H.M.S. *Irresistible* was wrong. By an ironic twist of fate the surgeon of the *Irresistible* was a school friend of Muir's and when he was looking over the wounded of the Spanish ship he found Muir still alive, although one of his eyes had been shot out. Removing Muir's identification and pretending that he was an ordinary sailor, the man had Muir put ashore with the rest of the Spanish wounded in Cadiz. Despite the nature of the wound, Muir began to recover, and three months later was able to write to the French Government that he had recovered and was now back in Europe to renew the fight for liberty.

With most of the leaders gone, the remaining Friends of the People decided that a rising must be attempted before the Government suppressed the organisation altogether. Robert Watt instigated the setting up of a Committee of Ways and Means. Aided by the movement's treasurer, David Downie, a Catholic goldsmith from Edinburgh, the Committee formulated a scheme to surprise Edinburgh Castle and hold it as the first step in a general insurrection in Scotland. Halberds and pikes were manufactured and reports were made from the various branches of the movement as to their state of readiness for the rising. The revolutionaries in Paisley reported that they were in "a state of great readiness".

But Downie's activities had not gone unnoticed, especially in the pro-Government Catholic Church. Bishop Geddes wrote to Abbé MacPherson of the Scots College, Rome, in a letter dated Aberdeen, March 13, 1794, concerning the Edinburgh Convention, and commented "on this occasion Downie was busy and I hope he is sufficiently frightened" (by the subsequent arrests). It is probable that this communication helped agents to discover the plans of the proposed rising and Robert Watt and David Downie were tried, convicted and sentenced to death for high treason. It is interesting to note that, as a Catholic, Downie had asked Father Alexander Cameron to hear his confession. The good priest wrote to Bishop Geddes to ask "can he be absolved?" The bishop replied asking Cameron to try and get Downie to "save his life either before or after his trial by offering this declaration [confession] of the whole affair".

Arguments have since been made that Robert Watt was a Government agent but this was rejected by Watt in a statement of his aims to obtain "liberty in Scotland". It also seems unlikely as Watt alone suffered the death penalty while Downie's sentence was commuted to life transportation.

The French Government still showed itself willing to support any uprising in Scotland and on February 8, 1795, Citoyen J. B. André placed a memorandum before the Committee of Public Safety urging action in the matter. "Tout fait presumer qu'elle reprendroit son ancienne indepéndence si l'on aidoit à seccouer le joug." (Everything leads to suppose that she [Scotland] would regain her ancient independence if they were helped to throw off the yoke.)

Here it must be pointed out that while the French Jacobin Government were engaged in helping two Celtic countries (Ireland and Scotland) to re-establish their independence, they were, at the same time, destroying the remaining independence of a third Celtic country—Brittany. Brittany had become an autonomous state within the French kingdom in 1532, not, it must be pointed out of its own volition. During the French Revolution the Breton Parliament was still in existence, having managed to retain its administrative and political autonomy, despite increasing centralisation from Paris. When the revolution broke out Brittany whole-heartedly backed it, seeing it as a means to abolish the 1532 Treaty and restore her independence. The French Government did abolish the 1532 Treaty by merely announcing that Brittany was now to become a part of France. The Breton Parliament refused to accept this decision and on January 18, 1790, de la Houssaye, the President of Brittany, protested at the bar of the French National Assembly. Rebuking the French for calling the Breton nation an establishment of privilege, he cried: "Le Corps out des privilèges! Les Nations out des droits!" (The Estates have privileges! Nations have rights!) On February 13, 1790, M. Le Procurer General Syndic of the Etats de Bretagne raised the same protest in a published manifesto. He repeated his protest every year until his death in exile in London in 1805. In 1793, under the leadership of La Rouerie and Georges Cadoudal, a general uprising took place in resistance to the French take-over and this War of Independence dragged on until 1804 when Cadoudal was finally caught and beheaded in Paris. Still the Bretons fought on in a bloody guerrilla war. The Chouans guerrillas fought in the belief that when the French monarchy was restored the Breton constitution would also be restored, even the Breton republicans believed it. Despite the promises of England that Breton independence would be restored at the termination of the Napoleonic wars, the French monarchy were more than pleased to "inherit" the unifying results of the revolution, which successfully crowned their own three centuries long attempts at abolishing the Breton constitution.

It is ironic to contemplate the political sense of values displayed by the French Government in aiding two Celtic countries to gain independence from England while, at the same time, not tolerating the independence of a third Celtic country "next door" to them. One can be cynical enough to ask that, had Ireland and Scotland gained their independence with French aid, how long would they have kept it before fighting a new imperialist conqueror?

FOUR

THE UNITED SCOTSMEN

THE FAILURE OF Watt and Downie's plans for a general
rising in Scotland and their trial for high treason, coupled with
the sedition trials of twenty prominent leaders of the Friends of
the People organisation, was a severe set-back to the Scottish
republicans. With the loss of their leaders, those who were left
decided that the old structure of the Friends of the People had
to be changed. It was decided that a new republican organisation should be formed and called the United Scotsmen societies,
the first of which had been formed in Glasgow on November 13,
1793, and that they should be modelled upon the militant
United Irishmen societies.

The original United Scotsmen society of Glasgow had been
represented at the Friends of the People conventions in Edinburgh but, in a spy's report of the second General Convention
of the Friends of the People, April 3 to May 3, 1793, there are
twelve United Scotsmen societies from Perth listed as being
represented by Robert Sands, Thomas Smith, David Jack,
William Thomson, Moses Wylkie, Andrew Dott and David
Johnston. However, it can be said that the Glasgow United
Scotsmen society was definitely the first which was run strictly
along Irish republican lines.

Certainly the loss of the Scottish leaders had not curbed the
support of the majority of Scottish people for the ideals of the
Friends of the People. In 1796, prompted by the agitation of the
expatriate Scots in Paris, the Committee of Public Safety sent
Citoyen Mengaud as an emissary to Scotland to look into the
prospects of aiding the Scottish republicans. He reported back
that he found the Scots, particularly in Glasgow, much disposed
to revolution and "this feeling had existed since the Union of
England and Scotland". The United Irishmen leader, Wolfe
Tone, was less hopeful about the prospects for a Scottish rising.
In April, 1796, he told Captain Aherne that "there is something

going on in Scotland", but "my opinion is that nothing will be done there unless we first begin in Ireland."

The French, however, were wavering in their decision to send aid, in the shape of troops and arms, to Ireland and Scotland. The Committee of Public Safety were also being petitioned by a third group of Celtic people, the Welsh, to send aid to them. Surprisingly enough, as there seems little evidence of a well-organised Welsh republican group at that time, General Louis Lazaire Hoche of the French War Ministry decided to give priority to the Welsh and evolved a plan to land a French expeditionary force in Wales, and, aided by Welsh insurgent troops, this force was to capture Bristol, England's second city. The French, despite the evidence presented to them by both the Irish and Scottish leaders, were still under the impression that the English labouring classes would flock to the banner of republicanism if they invaded England. Hoche's plan was simple and daring. The expedition was put in the command of Chef de Brigade William Tate, a 70-year-old American, formerly commander of a South Carolina regiment. The force, 1,500 men, were gathered at the Breton port of Camaret. The French army was still, at this time, in bitter conflict with the Bretons, and as the French troops were embarking gunfire could plainly be heard echoing across Camaret as the Bretons tried, unsuccessfully, to stem the tide of the French invasion of their country.

On February 18, 1797, the expedition set sail under the command of Commodore Jean Joseph Castagnier, and consisted of transports, two frigates, a 14-gun lugger and a 24-gun corvette. At nightfall on February 22 the French troops began to disembark near Fishguard at a rocky bay called Carreg Wastad. Colonel Tate made his headquarters in Trehowel Farm above Carreg Wastad. Welsh emissaries met him and organised the deployment of his troops but there was no sign of the promised Welsh military aid.

Colonel Knox of the Fishguard Fencibles was at a dance when the news of the landing was brought to him. At once he mustered his men and beat a hasty retreat from the area. There was a coast fort in Fishguard covering the entrance to the harbour with eight 9 lb. cannons mounted in it. Its permanent garrison was a bombadier and two gunners from Captain Standish's Invalid Company, Royal Artillery. These men were reinforced by thirty additional gunners commanded by Ensign David Bowen from Knox's Fencible regiment. When Knox decided to evacuate Fishguard he ordered the guns of the fort to be spiked. However, the three Royal Artillery men refused to move from their posts or let their guns be destroyed.

Lord Cawdor of Stackpole Court had been aroused from his bed in the early hours and told the news. At once he mustered his Castlemartin Yeomanry Cavalry and galloped to Carreg Wastad where he met Knox flying in disorder. He ordered the Fencibles to halt and return with him. With about 800 men Cawdor camped on the Goodwick Cliffs and sent a messenger to Tate, the French commander, telling him that reinforcements were arriving and demanded his surrender. Tate was in a dilemma. Firstly, his intelligence had erroneously informed him that the Brigade of Guards were in the area and would be arriving within the next few hours. Secondly, his men were not regular troops but were mostly convicts released on the condition that they undertook the expedition and were therefore lacking in discipline and organisation. Realising that they would probably be slaughtered by regular, well-armed troops, he sent a message to Cawdor saying he wished "to enter into negotiations upon Principles of Humanity". Cawdor demanded immediate unconditional surrender and Tate finally accepted. On the morning of February 24 Cawdor accepted Colonel Tate's unconditional surrender in the parlour of Trehowel farmhouse. At 2 p.m. the French paraded on Goodwick Sand and stacked their arms to the beat of a drum. At 4 p.m. the prisoners were marched seventeen miles to Haverfordwest where they were lodged in the local jail, in warehouses and in three churches.

There had been some skirmishes but few people were wounded or killed. A number of Welshmen were arrested by the authorities and tried for high treason. At Pembroke the Welsh smuggled tools to the French prisoners who dug an escape tunnel. Some thirty prisoners escaped and, with the aid of a number of Welshmen, seized Lord Cawdor's private yacht and sailed back to France in safety.

Colonel Tate was interned on a prison ship in Portsmouth harbour with many of his men. Later he was exchanged for English prisoners held by the French. Back in Paris he took a suite of rooms at the Hotel Boston and lived on half pay there until his 80th year with a lady named Genselle. The police became alarmed, for the Colonel's debts amounted to 8,000 francs. These were paid by the American ambassador and the Colonel then sailed from Dunkirk back to America, but nothing after that date is known about him—whether he arrived in America or died on the voyage.

This futile expedition annoyed the Scots and Irish who felt much more could have been gained if the French had directed the invasion to where it would have been welcomed with open arms. By the spring of 1797 the United Scotsmen had spread rapidly, completely taking over from the Friends of the People. The organisers of the United Scotsmen, obviously advised by delegates, such as A. Hamilton Rowan and the Hon. Simon Butler, from the United Irishmen, did not under-estimate the dangers of their association. The trials of the Friends of the People's leaders were too recent for the lesson to have been forgotten. They therefore organised their societies along strictly secret lines.

No branch of the United Scotsmen was permitted to enrol more than sixteen members and when that number was reached another branch was formed. Each branch met regularly and secretly, and when two or more branches in one parish met it was usually for the purpose of selecting a delegate by ballot for the county meeting. Every possible precaution to safeguard against spies was taken. The members, who had selected by ballot the delegate, knew only the branch secretary and the delegate himself. At the county meeting, delegates to the National Convention were also selected by ballot and the dele-gate elected was not told where the Convention was to be held. He was simply handed a slip of paper from the county secretary bearing the name of a man called the "Intermediary" who would, in due time, call for him and conduct him to the National Convention. Even the National Convention had a seven-man secret committee as a governing body and every member of the United Scotsmen had to subscribe to the following oath:

In the awful presence of God, I . . . do declare that neither hopes, fears, rewards, nor punishments shall ever induce me, directly or indirectly, to inform or give evidence against any member or members of this or similar societies for any act or expression of theirs done or made collectively or individually in or out of this society in pursuance of the spirit of this obligation. So help me God.

Members were also bound by oath to endeavour to "form a brotherhood of affection", and to strive for "equal political franchise" among all men. This oath is extremely similar to the oath of the United Irishmen which replaced an older oath current in 1795.

In the awful presence of God, I . . . do voluntarily declare that I will persevere in endeavouring to form a brotherhood of affection among Irishmen of every religious persuasion, and that I will also persevere in my endeavours to obtain an equal, full, and adequate representation of all the people of Ireland, I do further declare, that neither hopes, fears, rewards or punishments, shall ever induce me, directly or indirectly, to inform on, or give evidence against, any member or members of this or similar societies for any act or expression of theirs done or made collectively or individually in or out of this society, in pursuance of the spirit of this obligation.

Members of the United Scotsmen were charged sixpence entry fee and the monthly subscription was threepence. These sums were spent on travelling propagandists and organisers who went all over Scotland, even into small villages where only three or four members might be found. In some districts, Dundee for example, the entrance fee was only one penny but this seems to have been sufficient to pay the local delegate 1s. 6d. per day, plus his travelling expenses, when away from his work on the society's business. Most elaborate precautions were taken to ensure secrecy. A secret salutation was "I love light", to which a fellow member would reply "I hate light". The two men would then join their hands together, mixing the fingers and turning the palms out. Another secret sign was made by placing one hand on the back of another and mixing the fingers. While this seems melodramatic, the United Scotsmen had good reason to pursue a policy of secrecy to ensure the exclusion of Government agents from their body. The Government spy network was a good one and their infiltration into the Irish republican movement brought about the downfall of the United Irishmen.

The National Convention of the United Scotsmen met every seven weeks, usually in Glasgow or its neighbourhood. These frequent meetings were considered necessary for the United Scotsmen believed that "the emancipation of the country was at no great distance when they should rally round the standard of liberty". With riots and demonstrations in Scotland getting more frequent, with the United Scotsmen leader Angus Cameron of Perth sending a rebel call through A' Ghàidhealtachd, with the desperate misery and hunger of the labouring people, and the law scorning all who could not pay for justice, there seemed every basis for this belief.

A rising was being carefully planned by the United Scotsmen and the first step would be the burning of the houses of prominent Unionists. The enforcement of the Militia (Conscription) Ballot Act triggered off an abortive rising in 1797. Riots, on a scale hitherto unknown, broke out at Kirkintilloch, Freuchie, Strathaven, Galston, Dalry and in several parts of Aberdeenshire. At Carstairs, the schoolhouse was burned and the parish registers—used for conscription—were hidden. Similar demonstrations took place at Prestonpans and Tranent. At Tranent a resolution was sent to the Conscription officers:

Although we may be overpowered . . . and dragged from our parents, to be made soldiers of, you can infer from this what trust can be reposed in us, if ever we are called upon to disperse our fellow countrymen or to oppose a foreign foe.

For taking part in a riot in Eccles, Berwickshire, four men were transported for life to Botany Bay. In Glasgow, six baker boys of good character, for making a disturbance, were actually transported without charge, trial or conviction (*Glasgow Advertiser*). But in Perthshire Angus Cameron, the United Scotsmen leader, a wright from the parish of Weem, decided to give the word for the rising. It is stated that 16,000 rose to his call. Cameron, who is said to have been a great orator, rode on horseback at the head of his men, with James Menzies Jnr., a merchant also from Weem (then still a Scottish—Gàidhlig—speaking area), as his second in command. The first success of Cameron's men was in surrounding and capturing Castle Menzies and forcing Sir John of that Ilk to repudiate the Militia Ballot. Cameron then made prisoner the Duke of Atholl and made him swear he would not operate the Act until the "general sentiments of the country were made known".

Cameron despatched a section of his men to Taymouth Castle to clean out the armoury there. He appears to have made strenuous efforts to equip a cavalry squadron. However, the people were generally without arms or proper organisation and when the Government rushed sufficient troops into Perthshire Cameron's army melted away. It must also be remembered that the people still had vivid memories of the atrocities committed by Government troops when they had been let loose on the Scottish people after the defeat of the Scottish army at Culloden in 1746. Angus Cameron and James Menzies Jnr. were indicted for sedition as a first step but they were never brought to trial as both managed to flee the country.

Undaunted by this miscalculation, the United Scotsmen still continued laying plans and seeking support. Later that year one of the chief organisers, George Mealmaker, a Dundee weaver, published—anonymously—"Resolutions and Constitution of the Society of United Scotsmen" which was distributed in Forfar, Perth and Fife as well as in the industrial counties.

In order to check the growth of the United Scotsmen, and the United Irishmen, an Act of 37th Geo. III, cap. 123 was passed on July 19, 1797, suppressing by name these societies and enacting that anyone belonging to them was liable to transportation not exceeding seven years. The first person to be tried under this Act was George Mealmaker, who was arrested in Dundee in November, 1797. He was charged with being a member of the United Scotsmen, "an association which, under the pretence of reform, aimed at rebellion". Mealmaker was also charged with sedition and described as a leading agitator since the days of the Friends of the People in eastern Scotland who had been hawking seditious literature and administering illegal oaths. The trial took place from January 10 to 12, 1798, and during his trial many of the people brought to testify against him, though harassed and savagely bullied, lied desperately, declaring they did not know him. One witness, David Douglas, a wright from Cupar, went to prison himself rather than give incriminating evidence. The jury was, however, "packed", being composed of landed gentlemen and staunch Unionists (some of whose houses had been marked down for burning at the start of the rising) and Mealmaker was sentenced to fourteen years' transportation.

The Lord Advocate, Braxfield, decided to use harsh methods to put down anything that looked even remotely like rebellion. In the middle of 1797 the Cinque Ports Cavalry charged into a crowd of protesting men and women, attacking innocent by-standers and even chasing people seeking refuge in nearby cornfields. A large number of the people were massacred. Such acts only increased the popularity and strength of the United Scotsmen. The Government, however, managed to get spies into one or two societies and such leaders who did not flee the country were denounced and arrested. But, of course, the policy of keeping the branches segregated and secret, preserved the identity of many thousands of members from the knowledge of the informers and no extensive arrests were made.

The connection between the United Scotsmen and the United Irishmen, coupled with the fact that many Irishmen were arriving in Portpatrick to help the Scots organise and train for the rising, was a constant worry to the Government. The Government decided to bribe the Scottish Catholic hierarchy with a view to influencing the Catholic Church to use its spiritual authority to prevent Scottish Catholics and Irish immigrants from joining the United Scotsmen. These bribes, given in 1798, were £600 down, a promised yearly allowance of £50 to the two Catholic seminaries, as well as a sum sufficient to make up the salaries of the priests to £20; in addition, each of the Vicars-Apostolic were to get £100 a year and their coadjutors were to get £50 a year. "The profoundist secrecy had to be maintained regarding this grant from the public funds and even the Roman Catholic laity were kept in ignorance." However, the bribes did not work.

In Cadiz, Thomas Muir had partially recovered from his wounds. On August 14, 1797, Muir wrote to Thomas Paine saying that he was now fit to carry on the work of liberation again. He left Spain by ship and travelled to Bordeaux where, on December 4, 1797, he was guest of honour at a banquet presided over by the local mayor. He was toasted as "The Brave Scottish Advocate of Liberty!" But Muir was still very much a sick man. Overcome by the banquet, he fainted into the arms of the American Consul. From Bordeaux he continued his journey to Paris and, on arrival, he wrote to the members of the French Directory:

Citizen Directors
February 4, 1798

I arrived two days ago at Paris in a very weak and sickly state. Permit me to express to you the entire devotion and gratitude of my heart. To you I owe my liberty. To you I also owe my life.

It is unnecessary for me to make protestations of my love and veneration for the Republic. To my last breath I will remain faithful to my adopted country.

I shall esteem, Citizen Director, the day on which I shall have the honour to be admitted to your presence, the most precious of my life: and if I have passed through dangers and misfortune, that moment will for ever effect their remembrance and amply compensate them.

I have the honour to be, Citizen Directors, with the most profound respect, your grateful and devoted servant.

Thomas Muir

A few days later a deputation of the highest officers in the French Government called upon Muir and conferred upon him the honorary citizenship of the French Republic. Muir, in fact, was the first foreigner in the history of the French Republics to receive this honour.

Muir was given a house in the village of Chantilly, near Paris, where members of the French Government did everything in their power to restore him to health. Muir devoted himself to agitating for French support for a Scottish uprising and he wrote several articles and pamphlets on the subject as well as a treatise on the failure of the Union. He said that Scotland demanded liberty and justice. While at Chantilly, Muir became a friend of James Napper Tandy, the Irish leader, a founder of the Dublin society of United Irishmen. Muir used his pen to expound the Irish cause as well, but there is evidence that he did not get on well with Wolfe Tone, the Irish leader.

The year 1798 proved a fateful one. It was in January of that year that the Government learnt the truth of what was about to happen in Ireland and Scotland. Their informers told them that the United Irishmen and the United Scotsmen were going to set up separate republics in Ireland and Scotland. The Provisional Government of the Scottish Republic was to comprise Thomas Muir, Lord Hugh Sempill, Angus Cameron, Colonel Norman MacLeod of MacLeod (who had been Member of Parliament for Inverness from 1790 to 1796), the Earl of

Lauderdale, three men named Sinclair, Ferguson, Campbell and a man called Sorbelloni. It was also discovered that there were Englishmen plotting to establish a republican government in England itself.

In February, two delegates from the United Irishmen, Arthur O'Connor and a man named O'Coigley or Quigley, were arrested at Margate, en route for Paris, with a man named John Binns, organiser of the United Englishmen societies. The Government moved quickly to suppress the English republicans. On April 18 the leaders of the United Englishmen societies were arrested. These societies were governed by a body of twelve men headed by Binns and Evans. The following day members of the revolutionary Corresponding Society, whose president was Dr Robert Watson, a native of Elgin, Scotland, who had fought the English in the American War of Independence, were arrested. Watson served two years in Newgate and then left the country for France where he became Napoleon's English tutor and then president of the Scots College in Paris. In 1838 he was strangled to death in a London tavern.

The Government began to move quickly and, in March 1798, the Leinster directory of United Irishmen were all arrested. Lord Edward Fitzgerald, a prominent republican leader, managed to evade arrest for a few days but on May 19 he was mortally wounded and captured. A few days later, realising it was now or never, the United Irishmen rose. Having been deprived of many of their leaders, their efforts were badly co-ordinated and the rising consisted of a series of isolated struggles. In the counties around Dublin, only a series of skirmishes took place, but in Waterford and Wexford, the rising was more widespread and the insurgents managed to drive west and north to New Ross and Arklow. The military finally defeated them at the Battle of Vinegar Hill, near Enniscorthy. In the north there were risings in Antrim and Down.

A few days before the rising Napoleon had sailed for Egypt, committing his forces to this objective and allowing, despite the pleas of Wolfe Tone and Muir, only small expeditions to help the Irish. In August, 1798, General Humbert landed at Killala, in County Mayo on the west coast of Ireland, with 1,000 men, and Matthew Tone (Wolfe Tone's brother). His army was quickly reinforced by many Irishmen. The campaign was

exciting but short and his army was surrounded by Lord Cornwallis, the Viceroy, and compelled to surrender at Ballinamuck,
county Longford, on September 23.

In August another French expedition being prepared at
Texel, in the Netherlands with ships of the Batavian Republic,
was defeated by Admiral Duncan at the Battle of Camperdown.
Finally, another expedition consisting of one sail of the line,
with eight small frigates, commanded by Commodore Bompart,
with 5,000 men commanded by General Hardy, sailed on
September 20. With them went Wolfe Tone. They reached
Lough Swilly in the north-west of Ireland on October 11 only
to be engaged by a superior English battle fleet. Bompart, on
his flagship *Hoche*, advised Wolfe Tone to transfer to a smaller
ship which stood a better chance of escape. Frenchmen would
be made prisoners of war but Tone would be regarded as a rebel.
Tone dismissed the idea. "Shall it be said that I fled while the
French were fighting the battles of my country?"

The battle was won by the English and Tone was taken to
Dublin and tried for high treason. In a speech from the dock,
Wolfe Tone told the court:

I mean not to give you the trouble of bringing judicial proof to
convict me legally of having acted in hostility to the Government
of his Britannic Majesty in Ireland. I admit the fact. From my
earliest youth I have regarded the connection between Great
Britain and Ireland as the curse of the Irish nation, and felt convinced that, whilst it lasted, this country could never be free nor
happy. My mind had been confirmed in this opinion by the experience of every succeeding year and the conclusions which I have drawn
from every facet before my eyes. In consequence, I was determined to
employ all the powers which my individual efforts could move, in
order to separate the two countries. That Ireland was not able of
herself to throw off the yoke, I knew; I therefore sought aid wherever
it was to be found. In honourable poverty I rejected offers which, to
a man in my circumstances, might be considered highly advantage-
ous. I remained faithful to what I thought the cause of my country,
and sought in the French Republic an ally to rescue three millions
of my countrymen from bondage.

Wolfe Tone was sentenced to die "the death of a traitor"
within forty-eight hours. But on the evening of November 12 he
was found wounded in his cell. The general opinion today is
that the wound was inflicted by an English agent, as happened

to the Irish republican prisoners McKee, Clancy and Clune in Dublin Castle in 1920. Tone died on November 19, seven days later.

The rising of the United Irishmen completely overshadowed events in Scotland. The Government, thanks to their spy system, had managed to arrest some of the United Scotsmen leaders. On September 6, 1798, Robert Jaffray was tried, convicted of sedition and transported. On September 20, David Black and James Paterson were sentenced to five years' transportation each for sedition in that they "most traitorously expressed sorrow for the success of His Majesty's arms and joy at the existing rebellion in Ireland". Many more United Scotsmen were also charged with "minor offences" such as illegal possession of arms, stealing arms, illegal assembly, etc. Hundreds fled abroad when the failure of the Irish uprising became known.

The uprising, however, had a very important consequence. William Pitt, the Prime Minister, decided that the "urgent political problem" of Ireland should be solved in the same method as the Scottish problem had been solved . . . the Union of Parliaments. At first the Irish Parliament rejected the Union when it was put to a vote in 1799. Pitt therefore decided that the diplomacy, which had achieved the 1707 Union with Scotland, would be adopted towards Ireland. The Union of the British and Irish Parliaments in 1800 cost the Government of Britain more than a million pounds in bribes. As well as financial bribes, twenty-eight members of the Irish Parliament were given peerages; seventy-two members held positions controlled by Dublin Castle (i.e. the English administration) and were therefore entirely at their mercy, and on these people pressures were brought to bear. Lastly, the proprietors of eighty-four rotten boroughs (boroughs that, until 1832, sent members to Parliament though they had few or no inhabitants) were indemnified. Thus the majority of the 300 members of the Irish Parliament were "persuaded" to vote for the Union either by blackmail, financial gain, or the enticement of higher position. On June 7, 1800, the Act of Union was passed and Ireland sent twenty-eight peers and 100 members to the London Parliament who, like the Scots, were absorbed into the English system.

England's attitude towards the Union with Ireland closely resembled that of the Union with Scotland and was summed up neatly by an Under-Secretary called Cooke writing to Prime Minister Pitt in 1799:

By giving the Irish a hundred members in an Assembly of six hundred and fifty, they will be impotent to operate upon that Assembly, but it will be invested with Irish assent to its authority . . . the Union is the only answer of preventing Ireland becoming too great and powerful.

The last sentence meaning "from preventing Ireland completely cutting the connection with England".

Another, and perhaps more tragic blow, overtook the United Scotsmen in 1799. In January of that year, at the age of 33 years, Thomas Muir died at the village of Chantilly. He had suffered enormously from his wounds and ill health had finally overtaken him. Muir's mother wrote the following lines:

> Doomed from this mansion to a foreign land;
> To waste his days of gay, and sprightly youth;
> And all for sowing with a liberal hand,
> The seeds of that seditious libel—Truth.

The United Scotsmen still lingered on and, on July 12, 1799, another suppressive act was passed against them. According to a report of the House of Commons' committee of secrecy, two United Scotsmen were arrested and charged, Archibald Gray and a man named Dyer. Gray managed to escape to Hamburg and there appears to be no trace as to the fate of Dyer. On June 23, 1800, an organiser of the United Scotsmen, William Maxwell, a former sergeant in the militia, was charged with sedition. Maxwell's particular crime was that he had distributed "a most wicked and seditious poem in your own handwriting entitled A Catch". Maxwell received seven years' transportation.

It seems that the United Scotsmen were still hoping for a rising and, in the French Archives, there is a letter dated "19 brumaire an ix" (November 10, 1800) which proposed that a rising in Scotland could be started with the seizure of Edinburgh Castle. In fact, the letter proposed a similar plan to that worked out by Watt and Downie in 1794.

It would seem, however, that, following the Government's success in Ireland, there was little spirit left for a rising. On September 7, 1802, Thomas Wilson was tried for sedition. He was a Fife weaver and had been a delegate of the United Scotsmen at their National Conventions. Wilson was charged with seeking to "overthrow the British Constitution" and sentenced to one month's imprisonment and banishment for two years. Thomas Wilson was the last known member of the United Scotsmen to have been tried and sentenced.

The United Irishmen organisation lingered on until 1803 when Robert Emmet, younger brother of Thomas Addis Emmet, a leader of the rising in 1798 organised a further insurrection. Emmet was arrested in Dublin on July 23, 1803, was tried and, after a dramatic speech from the dock, executed. The Government made an all-out attempt to stamp out the power of the United Irishmen, especially in the nine counties of Ulster. Large numbers of Irish, mainly artisans of the weaving trade, crossed the water to sell their labour in the dark satanic cotton mills of Glasgow, Lanark, Manchester, Lancashire and Yorkshire. The decay of the Irish textile industry, a direct result of the Union and the penal laws enacted against it by the Government to protect English trade, increased immigration. People such as John Doherty of Buncrana (Donegal) left his employment in a cotton factory in Larne for similar work in England and Scotland. Doherty arrived in Manchester in 1817 and in the space of two years had become leader of the Manchester cotton spinners. In January, 1819, he was sentenced to two years' imprisonment in Lancaster Castle. The structure of Doherty's Union closely resembled the military organisation of the United Irishmen.

This influx of former United Irishmen into western, industrial Scotland helped greatly in the building up of the Scottish Union societies which started to spring up in 1809. These societies were to all intents and purposes the United Scotsmen societies under a new name and the Irish immigrants felt absolutely at home in this organisation, so closely did it resemble the societies of United Irishmen. The growth of the Radical organisation in Scotland was furthered to a great extent by this potent infusion of Irish republican thought and by the revolutionary experience of the Irish immigrants. But it must not be supposed, as Hunter of the *Glasgow Herald* supposed, that it was the Irish immigrants who were the main cause of the rise of Scottish Radicalism. Radicalism, and its bitter climax in 1820, was predominantly a Scottish affair and the rally call can be summed up by the words on one of the Radical banners—"Scotland Free—or a Desert!"

FIVE

THE GROWTH OF RADICALISM

WITH THE MONARCHIES of Europe ranged against her, it is
not to be wondered at that the young French Republic threw up
military leaders, instead of civic leaders, for the sake of her own
self preservation. The Corsican officer, Napoleon Bonaparte,
the First Consul (*de facto* head of state) managed to steer the
French Republic into a position where the monarchies finally
made peace with her. The National Assembly elected Bonaparte
First Consul for life in August, 1802, for his work in bringing
about the Peace of Amiens in March of that year. By this treaty,
France promised to retire from Southern Italy and leave the new
republics she had established in the countries along her border
to govern themselves. In return, England gave up her newly
conquered colonies and promised, with the other European
monarchies, to stop aggressive acts against the Republic. Bonaparte was now in a very strong position in France and he did not
hesitate to use that position for the purposes of his own aggrandisement. He had little respect for the principles of the French
Revolution and by a strong centralisation of Government, the
re-establishment of the Catholic Church, the re-call of the
moneyed and titled exiles, and the removal of the French law
system in favour of his own Code Napoleon, he soon started on a
campaign to change the French Republic into an imperial
power. Two years later he completely did away with the fiction
of republicanism and literally crowned himself as Emperor of
France. All the fine ideals of the Republic were completely
overthrown under the military despotism of Napoleon's empire.

Frightened by France's new aggressive imperialism, England
began her long fruitless war with Napoleon in order to protect
her own imperial interests. Scottish republicans were thrown
into a state of disillusionment at the fate of the country to which
they had long looked at as an example of democratic government. The ideal of a Scottish republic grew less and less bright

and soon even the idea of independence became but a dim thought to all but a few under the flood of patriotic fever against the "French aggressors". It was only the steadily worsening social conditions that kept the ideal of the Rights of Man alive in Scotland.

During the period of the struggle against Napoleon Bonaparte, a profound change took place in the very character of both England and Scotland. Within a relatively few years both countries' economies turned from being based upon agriculture to being solidly based upon manufacturing industry. During the period from 1790 to 1812 fortunate landowners, owning agricultural land, found that they could increase their rents as much as 500 per cent. But if the position of the tenant farmer was bad, due to exhorbitant rents, and heavy taxation, the ordinary working man's lot was infinitely worse. During the reign of George III no less that 3,200 Enclosure Acts were passed and more than six million acres of land were enclosed. Labourers deprived of their little plots of land and their rights to the use of common ground, now had to rely on scanty wages of daily labour from an employer. In some cases doles from private charities or poor rates could be obtained by a lucky few. From 1760 to 1813 wages rose by 60 per cent while the cost of living rose by 130 per cent.

Formerly, labourers were able to buy from farmers, small quantities of foodstuffs for their own domestic use. Under the new system the large farmers took all their produce into town and sold in large amounts, refusing to sell in small quantities even to their own workmen. The labourer, forcibly divorced from his small plot of land, demoralised by doles, crushed by taxation and a cost of living far in excess of his income, began to lose his independence and became mentally subservient to the system. The ordinary working man found himself reduced to a way of life not very much different from that endured by the serfs of the Middle Ages. Both in Scotland and in England the policy of the Government had substituted the sturdy, relatively independent, mainly agricultural worker for a labourer robbed of his status, stripped of his common rights and broken in spirit.

A contemporary picture of the time (given in Hammond's *Village Labourer*) describes one aspect of the situation:

Go to an ale-house kitchen of an old enclosed county, and there you will see the origin of poverty and poor rates. For whom are they to be sober? For whom are they to save? For the parish? If I am diligent shall I have leave to build a cottage? If I am sober, shall I have land for a cow? If I am frugal, shall I have an acre of potatoes? You offer no motives, you have nothing but a parish officer and a work-house! Bring me another pot . . .

The industry replacing agriculture, especially the cotton industry centred round Glasgow, was growing and production increased by leaps and bounds. In 1793 exports were valued at £17 millions and by 1815 had risen to £58 millions. In spite of this prosperity the workers continued to suffer grievously as the bulk of the profits went into the pockets of the employers while the workers were paid less than half of what could be termed a "living wage". Every necessity of life was heavily taxed. The price of wheat had almost trebled in less than twenty years while wages declined. Even so, many manufacturers wanted even cheaper labour and obtained pauper children from the workhouses on the pretext of apprenticing them to a trade. For every twenty children taken, the manufacturer undertook to take one mentally deficient child to boost his labour force. These luckless infants, whose average age was between 8 and 9 years, were subject to an appalling slavery; insufficiently clad, fed irregularly and then only on "left overs", they were employed sixteen hours a day, working day and night in relays, sleeping in filthy beds which were never allowed to cool as one batch succeeded another without interval. Those children who rebelled at this form of treatment and attempted to run away, or were even suspected of rebellious attitudes had irons riveted to their ankles and were compelled to work and sleep in them. Women and girls were treated no differently. It was reported that, in 1820, in the New Lanark area alone, some 16,000 young children were thus employed, many of them aged 5 years.

This "new world" was perhaps even more repugnant to the Scottish people than it was to the working people of England. The early Celtic clan system, which had prevailed over practic-ally the whole country, has been described as a semi-commu-nistic one. Skene recalls: "Yet though the conscious socialist movements be but a century old, the labouring folk all down the ages have clung to communist practices and customs, partly the inheritance and instinct from the group and clan life of our forefathers and partly because these customs were their only barrier to poverty; and because without them social life was impossible." The usurpation of the clan system and, of course, the Scottish language in the south of Scotland started in the thirteenth century with the introduction of feudalism from England. Johnston writes: "for long centuries the common people clung doggedly to the old free institutions of their forefathers, recognising quite clearly that the acceptance of feudalism meant slavery and degradation". From the thirteenth to eighteenth centuries there continued "a struggle between the patriarchal tribe and the feudal baron, between the non chartered, semi communistic Gaels, and the ruthless, remorseless, grasping descendants of the pirates who had followed William the Conqueror to the plunder of England". The south of Scotland did not easily succumb to a change in their social order. Johnston points out, "in Galloway the tongues of the children were torn out so that the accursed clan legends of freedom should not be told to a fresh generation".

The defeat of the Scottish army at Culloden in 1746 dealt the all but final blow to the semi-communist clan system in A' Ghàidhealtachd, a system which nevertheless had been very much eroded and upon which a mediaeval feudalism had been grafted. Even so, Skene says that as late as 1847 there were still places in the Outer Hebrides where the land was tilled, sowed and reaped in common, and the produce divided among the workers in accordance with the old Celtic ways. The old Scottish feast of Nàbachd (Nàbaidheachd = neighbourliness) was still held there when the men drew their pieces of land by lot, the produce of certain lots were set apart for the poor and fines went to a common fund to buy fresh stock. John Rae, writing in the *Fortnightly Review* in 1895, says the system was still current in Islay; in St Kilda "they distributed the fishing rocks among themselves by lot" and in Barra they "cast lots once a year for the several fishing grounds in the deep seas off their shores". Punishment fines went to a common fund.

The introduction, therefore, of an intrinsically alien social system did not make Scottish acceptance of the worsening position any the easier. Indeed, antagonism towards the Union was greatly aggravated and while it had, since the Union, been mainly those from the still Scottish-speaking areas of the country who had risen in arms to protect their nationality and their country's right to independence, it was the industrial workers in the south of Scotland who began to react against this assimilation of their country and the enslavement of its people.

The government of the British Isles was in the hands of the Tory Party whose name derived from the Irish word toiridhe (modern spelling: toraitheoir) meaning a pursuer. The name was first applied to robbers in Ireland but, after 1680, became the name for asserters of the royal prerogative and supporters of James II. The Tories favoured landed aristocracy and fiercely opposed foreign entanglements and those who would not accept the Church of England. They reached their zenith under Queen Anne when they were led by Robert Harley and Henry St John. Soon after George I came to the throne they were discredited because of the Jacobite leanings of their leader Viscount Bolingbroke. They were out of office for fifty years until the younger William Pitt revived the party and the Tories began to gain support by promoting the idea of popular rule. Entering office again, under Pitt, in 1783, the Tories remained in power until 1830, but had gone back on their ideas of popular rule in 1789 following reaction to the French Revolution. During their forty-seven years of power, the Tories held the country subservient to its will by military might and police spies, managing to survive many risings and attempts to overthrow it, not only in Scotland, Ireland and Wales but in England itself.

The opposition to the Tories was a weak one. This was the Whig Party, the name derived from the "Lallans" word "to jog along". In fact, the name suited the Whigs admirably, for it was indeed their policy to "jog along". Originally they had supported the middle-class gentry and trades people, as against the aristocratic Tory Party. In the latter days of the eighteenth century, the party became entirely mercantilist in policy and followed the ideas of John Locke (1632–1704), who believed that "sensation" and "reflection" were the sources of human ideas. After the French Revolution, the Whigs took on a middle class character and began to preach the idea of reform.

The Tory Government had completed its programme of suppression of popular rights by 1799 when a series of combination acts, banning all associations, and trade unions, were passed. Lecture rooms where payment was made for admission were classed as brothels and disorderly houses. Printing presses had to be registered and controlled and no newspaper printed in the state could be sent abroad. Barracks were built all over the country and the soldiery kept separate from the civilians in order "that the soldiery should not be contaminated by the revolutionary ideas and would do their work of keeping order the more effectively".

To the people of both Scotland and England there seemed little to gain through constitutional channels. Of Scotland's population, only 5,000 people could qualify as voters. Charles Phillips, an eloquent barrister from Ireland, showed the farce of the parliamentary system when he told the people: "it is quite impossible things go on unless there be some change, either in the members we return to that House, or in the constitution of the House itself. Are you aware that of what is called the House of Commons, 82 Peers nominate 300, and 123 Commoners nominated 187; and thus you have, out of 659 members, 487 actually nominated by 205 constituents, and this they call the representation of the people!"

The Hampden Club in London had kept alive the idea of Radical reform, which had fallen into disrepute with the failure of the French Revolution. The leading figure at the Hampden Club was Major John Cartwright, who had written *Take Your Choice* in 1776, one of the earliest works on parliamentary reform. Now, at the age of 75 years, Cartwright was touring in England and Scotland founding new Radical reform clubs, supported by a former arch Tory, William Cobbett, whose *Political Register* gave the English Radical movement one of its first journals. Cobbett was soon in prison and remained there from June, 1810 to July, 1812. Once released he returned again to the attack, travelling and preaching Radicalism. He reduced the price of his newspaper from 1s. 0½d. to 2d. and avoided the payment of the Government's new newspaper tax by omitting all news from it and concentrating solely on comment. The circulation achieved 50,000 copies a week. In 1817, beset by creditors, he left for America sending his column to the *Political Register* from there. He returned to England in November, 1819, bearing the remains of Tom Paine for burial in England. The Hampden

Clubs prospered and grew into the Radical movement which spread over England and Scotland . . . the only real opposition to the despotic Tory Government.

In Scotland, Alexander Bailie Richmond, a Glasgow weaver, who had studied the conditions of both the Irish and Scottish manufacturing classes decided to join the societies promoting reform. "I considered it my duty," wrote Richmond, "to preserve them [the Scottish workers] from a fate which appeared to me inevitable. I entered into the measures of the period with avidity and enthusiasm, and with the sanguine hope as to the practicability of the scheme, but, with those who had entertained similar opinions found, in sequel, that we had over rated our powers."

The societies which Richmond joined were weavers' union societies, loosely based on the remains of the United Scotsmen societies. By 1809 "there was scarcely a village in Scotland which did not possess such a society". According to Richmond these weavers' reform societies were active "and the organisation remained almost perfect at the close of 1812 when it was broken by the Government". From 1809 conditions, especially for the weavers, began to grow steadily worse. In 1810 there were an unusual number of bankrupts due, in the main, to the greatly curtailed overseas trade situation. In 1811 there was an unprecedented fall in the price of manufacturing labour and Scotland appealed to the Government for relief; the appeal was rejected! The National Committee of the Scottish union societies, of which the young weaver Richmond was now a prominent member, decided to question the existing laws which empowered magistrates to fix rates of wages. They were heartened by a remark of the Lord Justice Clerk Hope, who, commenting on a case where a Glasgow cotton spinner was found guilty of combination and assault, arising out of a wage dispute, told the workers to take their case before the magistrates as there was a remedy in law. The law would help the workers provided they did not resort to violence.

Despite Hope's statement, when a deputation called on the Lord Provost of Edinburgh, in January, 1812, asking him to call a meeting of magistrates to discuss the situation, he would not even listen. The National Committee threatened a mass demonstration by all their societies and the meeting was eventually held. Two committees, of workers and employers, were set up to discuss in detail the case and Richmond found himself a member of the workers' committee. At the first joint meeting of the two committees Richmond was introduced to the Tory M.P. for Glasgow, Kirkman Finlay, who, at the time, was also the Lord Provost of the city. After the meeting Finlay took Richmond aside and invited him home, saying he was interested "in promoting my [Richmond's] views in life". But, Richmond claims, he rejected Finaly's suggestion and saw no more of him for nine months.

The weavers, having discussed the situation, decided to bring a test case against forty leading Glasgow manufacturers in order that some standard wage scale should be decided on. The case went forward in the names of 1,500 Glasgow weavers and the counsel for these weavers was Francis Jeffrey, a 39-year-old Edinburgh barrister who, along with other liberal reformers, had founded the *Edinburgh Review* in 1802, a Whig Reformist magazine. Jeffrey was a liberal and his friend, Henry Cockburn, wrote: "his opinions were in substance just those of the Whig Party, but with this material qualification, that he was one of those who always thought that even Whigs were disposed to govern too much through the influence of the aristocracy and through a few great aristocratic families, without making the people a direct political element".

Jeffrey was aware "that there is a Radical contest and growing struggle between the aristocracy and democracy of this country". And he was in favour of a moderate reform of the political system; he was also an acceptable figure to the employers and to the workers and so was an obvious choice for their legal counsel. In this case, Jeffrey was successful and the magistrates over-ruled the employers' suggestion that the court was not competent to judge the matter. The employers were ordered to state specifically—in a written document to the court—their objections to the weavers' table of wages. The employers appealed to the Scottish Supreme Court who affirmed the magistrates' decision on June 27, 1812. The weavers drew up a table of wages (see overleaf) which were then proposed as the standard rate of labour at the rate of ten hours' labour per day.

The actual wage rates of the time were considerably below these proposals and, incredible as it may appear, at the end of

	£	s.	d.
Clear weekly average of weavers on all the variety of plain fabrics		11	11½
Ditto on flowered and fancy goods of all kinds		15	7½
General average		13	9½
Minimum of above		8	0
Maximum	1	0	6

1816 the wages scale was still 70 per cent below these proposed rates.

From August 14 to October 20, 120 witnesses were called and examined by the court in order to ascertain whether these proposals were justified. Finally, on November 20, the magistrates found the table "both moderate and reasonable". Two days later the weavers met in Glasgow and the magistrates' decision was endorsed. The National Committee sent deputies to inform each union society in Scotland that no work was to be done without payment of the accepted wages scale. A meeting was held in the presence of the Procurator Fiscal of Renfrew at which delegates from eighty societies decided that the Scottish weavers should stop work until the employers brought the agreed rates into force. The strike was immediate and 20,000 looms were stopped. The employers, however, refused to abide by the court's decision. With the law presumably on their side the weavers decided to hold out. But, Richmond wrote, "all disposable troops in Scotland were ordered to the western counties and cantoned in the various towns and villages; and it was rumoured that the operatives were to be put down by force".

The situation did not improve for the Scots when the English Luddite movement tried to move into the country. This consisted of organised bands of workers who destroyed machinery which they thought was replacing them. Leaders of the bands were called Captain Ludd, presumably after a boy called Ned Ludd of Leicester who was insulted by a mill owner and, in revenge, wrecked the man's stocking frames. The movement was mainly confined to Nottingham, Derby, Yorkshire and Leicester and the attempt to introduce machine wrecking into Scotland was a failure although a few nasty incidents took place which gave the authorities an excuse (under the 1812 Frame

Wrecking Bill which made the offence punishable by death) to use the troops.

Apprehension caused by the worsening situation made the National Committee, which included Richmond, go to see Kirkman Finlay in his capacity as Lord Provost of Glasgow. Finlay assured them that the strikers had nothing to fear from the military. Two days after the meeting, however, the Sheriff of Renfrew raided Richmond's house, seized all his papers and arrested him. Richmond was taken to Paisley Jail and questioned for eight hours. The next morning he was released on bail but arrested shortly after and the strike was declared illegal.

The students of Glasgow University, most of them sons of wealthy fathers many of whom were factory owners, supported the reformers and strikers. They held a protest demonstration and the authorities called out a regiment of dragoons to suppress them. This led to a riot in which the students surrounded the house of Kirkman Finlay, also their Lord Rector at the time, and broke his windows. The dragoons finally managed to clear the students off the streets, somewhat bloodily; troops were also used against the strikers and several weavers in the Calton area of Glasgow were shot dead.

Richmond was again released on bail and the strike was eventually broken in February, 1813, having lasted nine weeks. Kirkman Finlay was, in the meantime, making inquiries about Richmond, and eventually asked Richmond to meet him. He urged the young weaver to withdraw his support for the union societies and, in Richmond's own words, offered "permanent provision should be made for me in any manner I wished or chose to point out". Finlay added that in the forthcoming trials of the strikers, Richmond would be looked upon as the principal leader and "the severest punishment awaited me". Richmond tells us that he refused Finlay's offer and there seems, at this stage, no reason to doubt him.

A few days later the weavers were formally charged with combination and conspiracy. The two foremost Whig lawyers were employed to defend them . . . the first being the natural choice of Francis Jeffrey, who had been the weavers' counsel in the wage rate case; the second, was Jeffrey's friend, Henry Thomas Cockburn. Although Jeffrey, as editor of the *Edinburgh Review*, was a well-known public figure in Scotland, as a lawyer he had little success. Called to the Scottish Bar in 1794, at the age of 21, he had been able to make little progress because of his avowed Whig opinions. Cockburn comments: "Whigs made no secret that their object was to emancipate Scotland." In fact, in his first nine years at the bar he had earnt only £240. Poverty drove him into the army where he took an ensign's commission in the Edinburgh Battalion but, Major David Home, his commanding officer, wrote on January 21, 1804: "I never saw a worse soldier." Leaving the army, shortly after his first wife died in 1805, Jeffrey devoted himself to his magazine which he ran with the aid of his friends Henry Brougham and Francis Horner, two Scottish advocates, and Sydney Smith, an English journalist and clergyman. It was only now that Jeffrey was beginning to return to law, seizing the chance to defend the most difficult cases where the rights of working men were concerned.

His colleague, Cockburn, was six years younger than Jeffrey and was called to the Bar in 1800. Seven years later Lord Melville had given him an advocate deputyship, a non-political post, from which Cockburn had "the honour of being dismissed" on political grounds. Like Jeffrey, Cockburn was a Whig Reformist, and a frequent contributor to the *Edinburgh Review*.

The trials started on March 9, 1813, and Jeffrey opened the case by declaring that the weavers had done no wrong. The defence claimed that the court had previously fixed the wage rate and the weavers were acting in accordance with that ruling. The court dismissed the plea; all the weavers were found guilty and sentences of eighteen months' imprisonment were imposed. Sentences of outlawry were also passed on those who did not attend the court. Richmond was one of these, having fled to Lancashire before the hearing. With a reward now on his head he proceeded to Dublin where he lived until the latter part of 1813. Jeffrey was sickened by the existing order and wrote to his friend Horner that there was a struggle between the aristocracy and democracy of Scotland: " . . . freedom must depend in a good measure on their coalition, I still think that the aristocracy is the weakest and ought to give way, and that the blame of the catastrophe will be heaviest on those who provoke a rupture by maintaining its pretensions." In July, 1813, just after the trials, he left Scotland for America and in November of that year married his second wife there.

In 1812 the United States of America had, frustrated by continued English interference in American affairs, restriction of American trade, interference in American freedom of movement and economic policies, declared war on England. The war ended on January 8, 1815, when the Americans won a decisive victory over the English forces. Scotsmen were still considered *persona grata* with Americans and not really regarded as nationals of the country with which they were at war. Jeffrey, in fact, was received and entertained by Munroe, the Secretary of State, and even lunched with President Madison, with whom he had a number of discussions on Scottish problems.

Jeffrey returned to Scotland the following year and began to work hard at the *Edinburgh Review*, making a name for himself at the Bar and preparing for a political career. On February 24, 1816, he made his political début by addressing an Edinburgh meeting on the abolition of income tax.

In the meantime Richmond had made his way back to Scotland in secret. He approached Finlay and begged him to use his influence to have his sentence removed. Finlay, however, said he had warned Richmond previously and would have nothing more to do with him. Richmond continued to live in hiding but the conditions were so bad that he fell ill and did not recover until the summer of 1814. He then approached the Lord Advocate, Archibald Colquhoun, who said that if Richmond gave himself up voluntarily he would see to it that matters would not be so bad. In March, 1815, Richmond surrendered to the Sheriff of Renfrew and was given bail. His trial opened on June 26 before the Edinburgh High Court of Justiciary. Cockburn, Henry S. Vans and Mr Campbell of Blytheswood defended him but, as Colquhoun promised, the trial was not proceeded with. Richmond was given a month's imprisonment to clear him of outlawry and then freed. Richmond appears to have ingratiated himself with his defenders because Cockburn, Vans and Jeffrey, lent him the sum of £300 to aid him set up in business as a manufacturer. This Richmond did, making a success of his business and becoming accepted in the "well-to-do" manufacturing class circles.

Agitation and unrest was not confined to the Anglicised areas of the country and throughout A' Ghàidhealtachd the "Clearances" were forcing thousands to move south to the industrial belt or, more often as not, to take ship for the New World. This policy of genocide carried out upon those who still retained the old Scottish language and traditional way of life, made ready Radical material of the northerners who settled in the industrial belt. During the first ten years of the nineteenth century, thousands of Scots were forcibly evicted from Sutherland and north of the River Oykel. It must not be supposed that these Scots allowed themselves to be persecuted without fighting back, though the terrible atrocities committed against the people following the defeat of the Scottish army at Culloden and suppression of the old clan way of life, had dealt the Scots a blow from which they never recovered. As well as the overt physical persecution, the enforced eradication of the Scottish language did little to foster a healthy independent spirit in the people. Nevertheless, there were local fights, and guerrilla actions against the local landed gentry. But it was to little avail, the Scots were not only being persecuted by an alien conqueror, they were being betrayed by their own countrymen, and, moreover, those who styled themselves "Clan Chiefs" and demanded the loyalty of the Scots.

Iain Mac Codrum summed up their attitude in his *Seallaibh m 'an cuairt duibh us faicibh na h-uaislean* . . .

> Look around you and see the gentry
> with no pity for the poor creatures,
> with no kindness to their kin.
> They do not think that you belong to the land,
> and although they leave you empty
> they do not see it as a loss.
> They have lost their respect
> for every law and promise
> that was among the men
> who took this land from the fore.

Following the defeat of Napoleon Bonaparte, the Scottish people speedily realised that although the French Revolution had failed, having been betrayed by a military despotism, its original ideals were still as valid as ever, and, in Scotland, even more valid. The people, both in the English-speaking areas and in A' Ghàidhealtachd, were suffering naked persecution by an aristocracy which, although it was by this time native to the country, had now voluntarily alienated itself in language and culture from the great mass of the country's population. In the new industrial areas native magnates worked hand-in-glove with the aristocracy. This unholy alliance against the best interests, and even the very existence of the Scottish people, had only one possible effect—it heightened agitation almost to explosion point.

SIX

RICHMOND—THE SPY

In June, 1816, Alexander B. Richmond was writing letters to the *Glasgow Chronicle* pointing out the necessity for provision being made to relieve the distress of the labouring classes. He had renewed his friendship with Kirkman Finlay, M.P., and was a frequent visitor to his house, and it was through Kirkman Finlay that Richmond was employed as a Government agent. Richmond, in his autobiography, says that Finlay told him that he was aware of "an extensive and widely spread conspiracy for the avowed purpose of overturning the Government". Richmond hastens to point out that while he supported the Reform movement he felt that such an attempt would serve the purposes of those opposed to reform and would also serve as a pretext for throwing discredit on reform advocates. He promised Finlay "I would do everything in my power that I might be able to learn particulars."

Being fairly well known in Reform circles, owing to his letters to the *Glasgow Chronicle*, Richmond was "fully aware of the impropriety of appearing publicly amongst them". He decided to form some sort of spy network and recruited, for this purpose, a weaver called John MacLachlan from the Calton district of Glasgow. MacLachlan confirmed that Workers' Union Societies did exist and that each town and village had a Radical Committee; this was duly reported to Finlay who said it was Richmond's duty to "preserve public peace" by infiltrating the Radical organisation and passing on information. Richmond agreed and says, "the only reward I wished was the approbation of good and upright men". Nevertheless, he received large sums of money from Finlay to "aid his work". Richmond decided to "hold no intercourse with any persons filling an official situation under Government", in order that he would not be suspected of communicating with the Government. He arranged to report in secret either to Finlay direct or to James Reddie, the Town

Clerk of Glasgow. "The magistrates of Glasgow," says Richmond, "were not in the secret, depending wholly upon Messrs. Finlay and Reddie, who assured them they were in correspondence with a person who would apprise them when any serious danger approached."

Richmond started to give sums of money to MacLachlan "regulated so as not to excite suspicion". MacLachlan started to attend the Calton Radical Committee's meetings, although he was not a member. This excited the suspicion of William Wotherspoon, a heddle maker, who was a committee member. His suspicions were allayed somewhat because MacLachlan appeared to be a great friend of another committee member named Campbell, an operative weaver. Campbell, in fact, was another member of Richmond's spy system having been recruited by Richmond through MacLachlan. At this early stage in the formation of the Scottish Radical movement there were no plans for an armed insurrection, or the re-establishment of a Scottish Parliament or, if there were, Richmond could find out nothing except that constitutional Radical Committees were growing up in every area in and around the Scottish industrial belt. The sole purpose of these committees was to raise petitions for reform of parliament and alleviation of the terrible labouring conditions. Richmond, however, with a nice comfortable Government allowance, decided that he ought to do something to justify his existence, and, perhaps, get a better reward. If he could show to the Government some sort of armed uprising was contemplated he would probably get enough money from the Government to extend his business.

He visited an old colleague of his from the 1812 Weavers' Union days, a Pollockshaws weaver named William Mac-Kemmie. Richmond told him that Scotland would get nothing by constitutional methods and that the only sure way of resolving the social injustices was by an armed uprising. Scotland should arm and MacKemmie was just the man to start the operation. Richmond added that money was no problem and he would finance the venture. MacKemmie, although a staunch Radical, managed to see through Richmond's façade and immediately threw him out of his house.

In October, 1816, plans started to go ahead for the first large-scale public Radical meeting in the Glasgow Trade Hall. At once the authorities reacted by trying to suppress the meeting and the Lord Provost of Glasgow, James Black, expressly forbade the meeting to be held. The Radicals tried to organise the meeting in the stable yard of the Eagle Inn, Maxwell Street, which was owned by Daniel Caldwell, a Radical sympathiser, but pressure was brought to bear on him and his permission was withdrawn. James Turner, however, the owner of a little tobacco shop in the High Street, Thrushgrove, near Glasgow, offered the Radicals his fields, at the back of his shop, to hold the meeting in. On October 29, 1816, it was estimated that 40,000 people attended this first massive Scottish Radical demonstration which became known as the Thrushgrove Meeting. The 42nd Regiment stood to arms in Barrack Square, Gallowgate, with twenty rounds of ball cartridge in their cartouches. Dragoon squadrons, with sabres drawn, were stationed in Port Eglington Street ready to charge the meeting if a signal was given from the flagstaff on the top of Glasgow Jail, where the Sheriff and magistrates had gathered. The meeting passed off quietly enough, however, and the state debt, acts of largesse, pensions, sinecures were discussed. It was resolved to send a petition for parliamentary reform to Westminster. An anonymous sergeant of the Glasgow Yeomanry, who wrote a personal account of the rise of Radicalism and the subsequent uprising, noted that if the resolutions which were passed were only conducive to "national freedom" then the Whigs "according to their own principles, were bound to support them". He felt that even "the most moderate Tories" would have supported this cause "when popularity might be gained by it and their own strength after all not very materially impaired". But because the Radicals insisted on universal suffrage and justice for the workers as well as "national freedom", the sergeant felt "these houseless orators soon spoiled the cause for which they might have been useful".

Richmond made himself known to the Radicals during the Thrushgrove Meeting and, after it was over, he asked Robert Craig, a 38-year-old weaver from Parkhead, Glasgow, to join him for a drink in the nearby Elliot Tavern. Richmond told Craig that there were 100,000 Radicals ready to rise in arms and he asked Craig whether he would join and "take a position of responsibility" in the movement. Craig, like MacKemmie before him, made short shrift of Richmond's proposals.

The success of the Thrushgrove Meeting started a spate of public Radical meetings throughout the industrial belt of Scotland. The same month a meeting was held in the West Relief Church, Canal Street, Paisley, "for the purpose of considering the distresses of the country". A Mr Hastie chaired the meeting and a general resolution was passed asking the Prince Regent to restore to the people "their undoubted right of choosing annually their own representatives". Another public Radical meeting was held on Monday, December 30, at the Burgher Meeting House, Tarbolton, Ayr, and a report of the meeting comments:

When meetings of this kind are held in large towns and cities, and petitions for a Reform in representatives agreed upon, it is customary for the apostles of corruption to insinuate that such petitions are not to be regarded as expressing the will of the people but merely that of a few powerful party men. Such a remark, however, will but ill apply in the present instance. The men who attended the Tarbolton meeting pretend to no higher rank in society than that of farmers, mechanics and labourers and consequently are too low to be connected with any party, save the party of the oppressed. Their speeches and resolutions, therefore, may justly be regarded as affording a fair specimen of the sentiments which at present actuate the great majority of the nation.

The president of the local Radical Committee, D. Reid, pointed out that "the real and only source of the calamity may be fairly ascribed to the enormous load of taxes with which the country is so unmercifully burdened". Of the recent wars with France, he told the meeting that they were "bloody, expensive, unjust and unnecessary . . .". The wars were totally unpopular with all working classes; the victory was "rotten to the core", and their benefits "a great illusion". Matters would not be remedied by increasing the poor rates. "I would say—Woe, woe to Scotland, when her industrious sons must look to the cold hand of charity for support, and the noble independency of mind compelled to submit to the receiving of alms." Only a complete Radical Reform of a corrupt Government would resolve matters. The chairman of the meeting, William Drinnan, a local merchant, in pointing out the evils of the time, said: "In Scotland, to have the privilege of an elector, a freehold qualification must be purchased and a sum of money given to the amount of £600 and as the money has a dead stock value without interest, of course the elector is likely to give his vote to the man who may pledge himself to do the most for his private interest.''

Another speaker was more nationalist in outlook:

If the calamities of Scotland are not sufficient to wake the people to the need of Reform, let them glance for a moment to those scenes of blood and horror committed in India. There English dominion is founded on tyranny, on violence and terror. To govern these unhappy and unfortunate people, men are sent out, young in years, but still younger in humanity—to be governed at all they must be governed with a rod of iron, and the empire in the East would long since be lost to England if civil skill and military prowess had not united their efforts to support an authority which heaven never gave, by means which it can never sanction. But such deeds are not confined to distant possessions, they are sufficiently gloomy at home. Ireland—that country where nature bestows her blessings in vain, where the kindness of an all bountiful heaven is rendered of no avail by the tyranny and injustice of man, where men of property do as they please without being called to account for their conduct, or if any having the spirit of their ancestory should care to call in question their lord's authority, we all know the consequences. Their spirit is broken down, they are in a worse condition than the slaves of any country, and still they are styled free! Shocking to humanity—they are in one word miserable. And who are the oppressors of Ireland? Even the same detestable faction who now seek our ruin and with rapid stride are now hurling us to the same abyss. Nothing but our united efforts can or will save us. These usurpers must be told that they are the servants of the people—that they have betrayed their trust and that their treachery will no longer be endured.

The meeting sent a petition to George III. Such meetings began to draw large audiences and recruits to the Radical cause, especially in the counties of Dumbarton, Lanark, Renfrew, Stirling and Ayr, the main industrial belt of Scotland. Workers' Union Societies began to grow in strength and, in each town or village, Radical Committees were formed which sent delegates to a Scottish National Committee. The Scottish National Committee sent ambassadors to the English Radicals in order to keep informed of developments there. These Radicals societies were in the main based on the previous Scottish Reform movements and, if Richmond is to be trusted in this, there were a lot of similarities between the United Scotsmen movement and the Scottish Radicals. The swing to Scottish Radicalism was spectacular and Richmond and his fellow agents were busy trying to stir up some form of unconstitutional protest among the Radicals in order to give the Government a legal excuse for the suppression of the movement. The Lord Advocate, Alexander Maconochie, wrote to Lord Melville, on November 15, concerning payment for Richmond and MacLachlan.

I enclose for your lordship's consideration the last of several letters I have received on the subject of the two persons who were employed at Glasgow to obtain information of the designs of the disaffected. Their services were most important and their conduct meritorious and the pledges which were given them ought to be redeemed without delay at least to the extent of giving them the means of subsistence to which your lordship, speaking on the subject to Lord Sidmouth, would at once obtain. They were even employed at a period when there was the strongest reason to believe there was a communication with the disaffected in England to which no trace could be found and we were in total ignorance of the extent of the conspiracy here. Accordingly it was not only with Lord Sidmouth's knowledge that promises were made them but it was at his desire that I prevailed on Reddie to exert every nerve to induce them to take the task which was a service on their part attended with great danger.

Stewart Buchan, a 33-year-old weaver, who had known Richmond from his 1812 days and who lived in the room below him, was the first to fall into Richmond's trap. Buchan was impressed with the way Richmond used to go about the various Radical societies "making inflammatory speeches". Richmond suggested to Buchan that there was now a strong, well-armed, organisation in Glasgow, ready to overthrow the Government. Buchan was, at first, non-committal. Early in January, 1817, Richmond and a man named Ferguson, approached Buchan and asked him to take an oath of allegiance to the Radical physical force wing. Buchan, more gullible than the others, agreed and went to a house in Tureen Street, Glasgow, at an appointed hour to take the oath. Richmond and MacLachlan were there with a weaver named Andrew MacKinlay, who was also taking the oath, which Richmond read to both men.

In the awful presence of God, I ... do solemnly swear that I will persevere in my endeavouring to form a Brotherhood of affection amongst Britons of every description, who are considered worthy of confidence; and that I will persevere in my endeavours to obtain for all the people in Great Britain and Ireland not disqualified by crimes or insanity, the elective franchise at the age of 21, with free and equal representation and annual parliaments; and that I will support the same to the utmost of my power, either by moral or physical strength, or force, as the case may require. And I do solemnly swear that neither hopes, fears, rewards or punishments shall induce me to inform on, or give evidence against any member or members collectively or individually, for any act or expression done or made, in or out, in this or similar societies, under the punishment of death to be inflicted on me by any member or members of such societies. So help me God, and keep me steadfast.

In his biography Richmond shows that he was well acquainted with the organisation of the United Scotsmen and this oath, which he delivered to Buchan and MacKinlay, is modelled on that used by the United Scotsmen societies. It seems obvious that Richmond moulded the former oath to meet his present need. Richmond and his colleagues now began to have success in duping the weavers and other workers into thinking that they were representatives from an "inner committee' of Radicals preparing to rise in arms against their oppressors. It is hard to understand why their activities were not brought to the attention of the Scottish National Radical Committee, or, if they were, why that committee did not act against them. By the end of 1816 Richmond decided to wind up his private business and become a full-time Government agent. Kirkman Finlay "considered it would be proper to have a specific salary agreed upon, sufficient to command the necessary degree of comfort and respectability". The arrangement was made on January 19, 1817, in Finlay's house. It was decided that Richmond would move to New Lanark where he would be given letters of introduction to Robert Owen, the self-made cotton manufacturer who, since 1800, had been hard at work proving that his cotton mills could provide facilities which would mould and improve the character of human beings by the surroundings in which they were placed. In 1813 he had written *New View of Society, Essays on the Principle of the Formation of the Human Character*. He had proved from his New Lanark experiment that it was possible to care for the health, education and financial security of the workers. He had mooted the idea that the workers, through voluntary associations, could control industry and that competition could be supplanted by co-operation. This view, of course, was considered highly dangerous to the Tories and, although there is no mention of it, it seems highly probable that Richmond was sent to New Lanark, with an introduction to Owen, in order to keep a close watch on the activities of this prototype socialist.

From New Lanark, Richmond reported that the Radical societies were being run on the same lines as the United Scotsmen and aimed at the same ends (i.e. the establishment of a Scottish Workers' Republic, which, of course, was not the case). Richmond, MacLachlan and Campbell ingratiated themselves with various Radical societies claiming they were members of a central committee. Richmond says that every second or third night he met either Finlay or Reddie and passed on information. Early in February, 1817, Richmond felt confident enough to supply Finlay with a copy of the "oath" and Finlay immediately set off post-haste to London. During a debate on February 24, Finlay rose in the House of Commons and told the honourable members that "at Glasgow and several other towns in Scotland secret societies also exist". The Commons were shown Richmond's oath causing an upheaval among the members. The Habeas Corpus Suspension Act was immediately passed and the Lord Advocate, Maconochie, was despatched to Glasgow to arrest the ring leaders and prepare their trials. Finlay also hurried back to Scotland and met Richmond. He told Richmond that Sidmouth wanted "to net" as many of the Radical leaders as possible and within a couple of days some twenty people were arrested and taken to Edinburgh.

The first trial for sedition in Scotland for fifteen years was that of Alexander MacLaren, a weaver, and Thomas Baird, a shopkeeper, which took place from March 5 to 7, 1817. MacLaren was accused of making a seditious speech at Kilmarnock which appealed "to the spirit of Bannockburn" (the battle which won Scottish independence from England in 1314). Baird was accused of publishing MacLaren's speech. MacLaren, who told the court that he laboured fifteen hours a day for 5s. a week, said:

We are ruled by men only solicitous for their own aggrandisement; and they care no further for the great body of the people than as they are subservient to their accursed purposes. . . . Shall we, I say, whose forefathers defied the efforts of a foreign tyranny to enslave our beloved country, meanly permit in our day, without a murmur, a base oligarchy to feed their filthy vermin on our vitals and rule us as they will? No, my countrymen! Let us lay our petitions at the foot of the throne where sits our august prince, whose gracious nature will incline his ear to listen to the cries of the people, which he is bound to do by the laws of the country. But should he be so infatuated as to turn a deaf ear to their just petition, he has forfeited their allegiance. Yes, my fellow townsmen, in such a case, to hell with our allegiance!

MacLaren and Baird were brought before Lord Gillies, a Whig judge, who had been a friend of Thomas Muir and had, in fact, been called to the bar at the same time as him. Francis Jeffrey and Henry Cockburn defended Baird and John Shaw Stewart, James Campbell and John Peter Grant defended MacLaren. Jeffrey's speech, commented Cockburn, was said to be the best defence speech given at the Scottish Bar. Despite a plea by the jury for the utmost clemency, Gillies sentenced MacLaren and Baird to six months' imprisonment and to find security for three years.

The second trial for sedition was of a 67-year-old clergyman, the Rev. Neil Douglas, on May 26, 1817. Douglas preached regularly at the Andersonian Institution, in John Street, Glasgow. He was an ardent reformer and had been a delegate to the Convention of the Friends of the People in Edinburgh. A friend of Skirving and Gerrald, Douglas was "a peaceful constitutional reformer" who was now connected with a body known as the Universalists, a Radical reform movement on a more intellectual scale. He was, in the words of J. R. Fraser of Newfield, a "Scottish patriot and a Christian". His sermons, in which he began to advocate political reform, attracted large audiences. Fraser says that Douglas was "so typical in his opinions and pure, high, unselfish character, of the best and most intelligent members of the old Scottish Radical Party". It was Fraser's father, who was tried for high treason in the 1820 uprising, who wrote a biography of Douglas (published in London in 1852) and it was from Douglas that John Fraser learnt the essence of Scottish Radicalism. Douglas often preached in George Street School. He was a fluent Scottish (Gàidhlig) speaker and, as well as English, could speak four other languages. Fraser (in his biography of Douglas) commented that when the people heard of Douglas' political sermons "they came to scoff but remained to pray".

It seemed inevitable that the authorities would act against Douglas, whom Cockburn described as "old, deaf, dogged, honest and respectable". The trial took place at the High Court of Justiciary in Edinburgh before the Lord Justice Clerk, Lord Gillies, Lord Hermond, Lord Pitmilly and Lord Reston. Douglas was defended by Francis Jeffrey, Henry Cockburn, J. P. Grant and J. A. Murray. The Solicitor-General, James Wedderburn, prosecuted. Wedderburn claimed that Douglas, by means of illustrations from the scriptures, had attempted to dishonour George III and the Prince Regent. More particularly, Douglas had compared George III with Nebuchadnezzar and the Prince Regent with Belshazzar. "And, further, the said Niel Douglas did wickedly, slanderously, falsely, and seditiously, assert that His Royal Highness, the Prince Regent, was a poor infatuated devotee of Bacchus, or use expressions of similar import." Niel Douglas had publicly expressed the popular opinion of the working class in Scotland when he said, "we could not deem the battle of Waterloo a subject of congratulation for many reasons". Among the reasons Douglas laid down was that the policy of the Allies was to restore "the idols of Europe and re-establish the tottering thrones and pillars of Antichrist. Time will show whether such measures guarantee peace to the nations or sow the seeds of future fresh wars." Wedderburn pressed the impropriety of ministers of the gospel taking advantage of their pulpit to discuss political questions. It must be pointed out that the authorities had no objection to ministers using their pulpits in order to support the state politics. In fact, in 1820, many ministers, on the advice of the authorities, used their pulpits to threaten their congregations against supporting the Radicals.

Francis Jeffrey made the concluding speech for the defence adding:

And here I must take leave to intimate my dissent from what was said as to the duties of the clergy in this country. It is their first and appropriate office, no doubt, to teach the doctrines of religion and morality; but it is their privilege and function also to allude to our duties to Government, as well as those we owe to our neighbours. In those cases especially in which the hearers are indebted for all the information they receive to their attendance in church, there would be something wanting, if, besides the exhortations and spiritual advice, which are afforded, allusions were not occasionally made to the public duties of the people, as well as to their other moral and religious obligations.

Despite the evidence of informers and police officials, the case against the 67-year-old clergyman was dismissed. Popular public sympathy was clearly on the side of the Radicals and, with each new trial, new members began to join. On June 20, Kirkman Finlay, irritated at the failure of the authorities, attacked Maconochie and accused him of "imbecility in conducting the legal proceedings". The gullibility of the people had been broken, however, and Lord Grey told the House of Lords on June 16, that "Glasgow was one of the places where treasonable practices were said, in the Report of the Secret Committee of both Houses, to prevail to the greatest degree; but there could no longer be any doubt that the alleged treasonable oaths were administered by hired spies and informers."

The authorities pressed on, however, with their cases for high treason based on the evidence that Richmond and his colleagues had fabricated. The first Radical to be brought before the court on a charge of high treason was Andrew MacKinlay, the weaver who had taken the oath at the same time as Buchan, who had been arrested on February 28. MacKinlay's trial came up on June 23 with Francis Jeffrey, Henry Cockburn and J. A. Murray heading a team of defence advocates who were preparing to defend the large number of Radicals awaiting similar charges. Francis Jeffrey was appearing without fee. If MacKinlay was indicted for high treason, there were over twenty other Radicals already imprisoned and Richmond had supplied Maconochie, the Lord Advocate, with the names of a considerable number who could be arrested at a moment's notice. John Keith and William Edgar of Edinburgh, due to be brought up after MacKinlay, were sure that they would be convicted on the fabricated evidence, and they managed to escape and flee the country. James MacEwan, MacDowal Pate and John Connelston, charged with administering illegal oaths, also fled the country and were outlawed.

Lord Hermond was the judge and Henry Home Drummond, the Deputy Lord Advocate, prosecuted. MacKinlay's writer had tried to interview the witnesses before the trial and had demanded to see John Campbell, a friend of MacKinlay, who was going to be a prosecution witness. Campbell was being held incommunicado in Edinburgh Castle and had managed to smuggle a note to MacKinlay saying: "They are wanting to bribe me to swear away your life, but I'm true." MacKinlay showed the note to Jeffrey who immediately raised the matter in the court, pointing a finger towards Drummond, and saying: "My lords, the public prosecutor has been hatching this evidence in the Castle of Edinburgh!" Hermond instantly had Campbell brought to the witness stand and asked if anyone had tampered with his evidence. Campbell replied in the affirmative. Taken aback, Lord Hermond repeated the question and warned Campbell to think carefully about his answer. Again Campbell replied that the Deputy Lord Advocate Drummond, in the presence of the Sheriff of Edinburgh, had tried to bribe him to give incriminating evidence against MacKinlay. He was to get a good permanent Government situation abroad through Lord Sidmouth after he had given evidence for the prosecution.

The case immediately fell through. "The result of that trial protected for a time the liberties of Scotland", commented Cockburn. Richmond says the authorities "appeared like chagrin and mortification personified". Richmond had been in Edinburgh, lurking in the background, in case of trouble MacLachlan, Richmond's colleague, was also listed as a witness for the prosecution. The result of the failure of MacKinlay's trial caused the charges against all the other prisoners to be dropped and they were released.

Throughout the trial verbal rumours of Richmond's activities were being spread about. When the trials failed there was a "general outburst of indignation" against Richmond. Slogans like "Beware of Richmond the Spy" were chalked on walls. The *Glasgow Chronicle* of August 14, 1817, attacked him and Richmond wrote a letter refuting the charges. His name was being linked with Reynolds, the former United Irishman who had betrayed the movement and given evidence which led to the executions of MacCann, Bond, and Byrne. Lord Archibald Hamilton, a noted Whig Reformist, pledged that he would bring forward a charge against Richmond in the House of Commons but when he succeeded in getting a debate on the subject, in February, 1818, the Tories shouted him down. The exposure of Richmond stopped his usefulness as a Government agent. The Lord Advocate, Maconochie, offered Richmond a grant of land at Algoa Bay, Cape of Good Hope, with letters of introduction to the Governor of the Colony. Richmond claimed that from December, 1816, to February, 1817, he had made a deficit of £27 in his spying activities. At the subsequent libel trial in 1834, it was stated that Richmond received £2,000. On October 17, 1817, Richmond wrote to Finlay saying that Lord Sidmouth had agreed to pay him a substantial annuity.

Despite Richmond and his like, freely employed by the Government to infiltrate the various organisations for political reform through the state, the Radical movement began to grow strong, but nowhere did it obtain the strength and organisation that it did in Scotland. The growth of the Scottish Radical Movement was more potent in that it not only had the aim of political reform but, like the Friends of the People and United Scotsmen before it, it was nationally orientated from Scotland. Scotland had once been a relatively prosperous nation-state, after 100 years of union with England (a union which had been absolutely against the will of the people and which had been physically imposed after a number of Scottish uprisings to revoke it) the nation had become a poor and very much exploited province. This is why the speeches of the Scottish Radicals and their banners and slogans not only savoured of Radical Reform but of Scottish nationalism. This was why the Scottish Radicals of 1820 wished to set up a "Scottish Assembly in Edinburgh" once again.

In England Radicalism was also growing and the English developed a Radical Press, consisting of Cobbett's *Register*, Wooler's *Gazette* and *The Black Dwarf*. Following the suspension of Habeas Corpus and the passing of legislation to prevent further Radical meetings, thousands of workmen from northern England, and the Midlands, took part in the "March of the Blanketeers", so called because each man carried a blanket so as to be able to encamp on the march to London. In June, 1817, an abortive rising took place in the Midlands led by a man named Brandeth. He led 500 men on Nottingham but this group was caught by the military and cut to pieces. Brandeth and two other leaders were subsequently executed.

For a time executions and transportations slackened the Radical agitation. The General Election of 1818, however, returned a Tory Government but the Whig Party had gained thirty seats, a sign that people were beginning to see the dangers of outright suppression by the corrupt Tory Government. The Whig reformist, Sir Francis Burdett, urged a reform of Parliament to counteract the growth of Radicalism but the Tories defeated it by 153 votes to 58.

People from A' Ghàidhealtachd moving into the industrial belt in search of work, were enlisting in the Radical ranks almost to a man. In 1813 the evictions in Kildonan, Sutherland, led to the abortive uprising of the Clan Gunn. The following year the "Clearances" in Strathnaver took place with such violence being used against the Scots that 1814 became known as Bliadhna na Losgadh (The Year of the Burnings). Alistair Ranaldson MacDonell of Glengarry, a clan chief who had taken an active and prominent part in clearing his fellow countrymen from their lands, decided to form a society in support of the Scottish language, dress, music and characteristics. He started to have fanciful dreams of a romantic Gaeldom where it was entirely populated by Scottish gentlemen, strictly the duine-uasal and bean-uasal, thoroughly Anglicised but happy to play-act at being their ancestors for a while. Although the society flourished the "Clearances" of A' Ghàidhealtachd continued unabated and Ailean Dall, the blind bard of Glengarry, wrote:

Thainig oirnn do dh'Albainn crois . . .

A cross has been placed upon us in Scotland
Poor men are naked beneath it.
Without food, without money, without pasture,
the North is utterly destroyed.

The final "Clearances" of Strathnaver and Upper Kildonan in 1819, and the evictions in Strathoykel, which started the Culrainn uprising which was quickly suppressed in February, 1820, must have been instrumental in making hundreds more Scotsmen join the Radical movement in the industrial belt. Unfortunately many more thousands left Scotland for good, emigrating to the colonies or America. The Scottish Radicals were also reinforced by the Irish immigrants. Johnston says that the Irish were in the "troubles" and "the advanced left of them almost to a man". The fact gave the Government some concern since it bribed the Catholic hierarchy in Scotland with a view of keeping the influence of the Church as a weapon to prevent the Irish from identifying themselves with the Scottish struggle.

Following the quiet growth of the Radicals in 1818 and constitutional reform having been rejected in Parliament, the idea of an armed uprising was beginning to grow in the minds of the more advanced Radical circles. Like the United Scotsmen and the Friends of the People before them, the Scottish Radicals felt that two things must be achieved; a complete reform of the existing social system based on the equality of rights and the destruction of corrupt officialdom, and the re-establishment of Scotland's independence as a nation-state . . . and like the United Scotsmen and the Friends of the People, the Radicals came to the conclusion that the only means of obtaining these aims was by an armed insurrection.

SEVEN

THE PAISLEY RIOTS

About the year 1819 [wrote John Fraser of Johnstone] reform movements were in a state of great activity throughout the country. The feeling against the Government was intense. In return, Government treated the people with contempt. "The rabble", "the swinish multitude" (improved during the Chartist agitation to "the great unwashed") were terms repeatedly applied to the Radicals in Parliament. The infectious spirit of the French Revolution, though it lightly touched our shores, did not pass freely over them. Many great and excellent men—Robert Burns amongst the number— cordially sympathised with the great uprising of a long outraged nation; and the principles of a Democracy gradually began to gain ground.

Three causes, perhaps, tended to prevent a rapid spread of Republicanism principles in our midst. The many wars engaged in by our Government against the French during upwards of a quarter of a century, diverted public attention from home matters, while the brilliant success of our arms naturally tended to gratify national pride, and to exalt the military above the civil spirit—always dangerous to liberty. Again, it was too much the late custom amongst the influential classes during these times on the least symptom of popular clamour to point shudderingly to the excesses of the French Revolution—as if the Reign of Terror were not but a mere drop in the bucket when compared with the ages of oppression and cold, haughty indifference endured by the people of that country from the Bourbons and feudal aristocracy. And lastly, the sunrise of that Revolution which was fondly expected to illuminate all oppressed nations, ultimately sunk into the night of a great military despotism.

AFTER LYING ALMOST dormant for a year following the farcical High Treason trials in 1817, the Scottish Radical movement was growing stronger than ever before. Paisley, the centre of the weaving trade in Scotland, was also the main centre of Radicalism. The Paisley Radical Committee was, perhaps, the strongest in the country with the Paisley workers behind them almost to a man. John Parkhill says that everyone in the streets around his house in Maxwellton were Radicals and Parkhill himself was a leading figure on the Radical Committee. As well as political agitation, Parkhill says that in 1819 military training after nightfall "had become a common thing" for the more militant Radicals. In Paisley the training was carried out under the supervision of an ex-soldier named Daniel Bell who was termed as the Radical "drill sergeant". A Paisley Radical meeting was held on Meikleriggs Muir on Saturday, July 17, 1819, and it was said some 30,000 people attended. With James Allison in the chair, eight speeches were delivered and, following a proposal from John Neil, the Scottish Radical "ambassador" to the English Radicals, it was resolved to issue an address to the Scottish nation. It was reported that this meeting passed off quietly and each "division" marched away to the sound of a bugle. The meeting, however, was just one of the numerous Radical meetings that were held throughout the industrial belt of Scotland.

Peterloo, which took place on August 16, 1819, had a far-reaching effect in Scotland. The Lancashire and Cheshire Radicals had planned a great demonstration at St Peter's Fields, Manchester, for that day and it is reported that the demonstrators exceeded 60,000. The Radical orator, Henry Hunt, chaired the meeting but, as soon as the meeting began, the Manchester magistrates ordered the local Yeomanry to charge the crowd with drawn swords, ostensibly with the object of arresting Hunt and his followers on the platform. Several people were trampled or sabred to death and many hundreds were injured, the mêlée becoming known as the "Peterloo Massacre". Although the Regent and the Government endorsed the actions of the magistrates and Yeomanry, demonstrations were held all over England and Scotland to protest. Even the Common Council of London, by 71 votes to 45, affirmed "the undoubted right of Englishmen to assemble together for the purpose of deliberating upon public grievances" and expressed their abhorrence of the massacre. The poet Shelley, then in Italy, was moved to write *Masque of Anarchy*:

> Rise like lions after slumber
> In unvanquishable number

Shake your chains to earth, like dew,
Which in sleep have fallen on you:
Ye are many, they are few.

According to Parkhill, the reaction upon the Paisley Radicals was that "drilling got brisker than ever" and the Radicals were organised in squads of thirty men. The idea of the inevitability of a general rising was accepted now by the majority of Radicals and the Paisley Radical Committee compiled a list of the names and addresses of members of the local Yeomanry corps with the idea of seizing their arms and ammunition when the time came. Parkhill claims that surgeons and medical staff were enlisted under the Radical banner and that "even women were employed to prepare dressings for the hospitals". The feeling that a general rising in Scotland was imminent did not escape the authorities. Major-General John Hope, the commander-in-chief of the army, wrote to Lord Melville on August 10:

I wished to have called your lordship's attention for the possibility of some general plans being at agitation for a general rising, of which some rumour is abroad, how true I know not, in which case it may be one of the measures of the disaffected to endeavour to seize upon, and possess themselves of arms and strike at those of the regular militia, deposited in stores; it would therefore be highly advisable that the Lords Lieutenant, and Magistrates of Counties, were prepared against such attack and means devised to protect their arms and prevent them being taken by the mob.

Melville, however, replying the next day, dismissed the idea:

Though I have no doubt that there are persons at Glasgow and the other manufacturing districts in the West of Scotland whose political views are as mischievous as any of those in Lancashire and elsewhere in England, and though it maybe proper and necessary to take all due precautions to frustrate their designs (particularly such precautions as are alluded to in your letter) I have no apprehension of any general disturbance either in this Country or in England.

Melville was, of course, well informed as to the state of the Radical movement through the activities of his spies in Glasgow. In this letter Melville told Major-General Hope, that he had been promoted and this would "have the effect of depriving us of your services on the staff of this country". However, the new commander-in-chief, Major-General Sir Thomas Bradford, had experience in dealing with civil unrest and disorders, in fact, this was the very reason why he had been appointed to the Scottish command. At the same time, Sir William Rae was appointed Lord Advocate of Scotland causing some tension between Rae and the Solicitor General, James Wedderburn. Rae was junior to Wedderburn who had taken for granted that he would naturally fill this role. However, the Lord Chief Justice Clerk, Hope, wrote to Melville on May 23, 1819:

He appears to us to have every qualification which Wedderburn has and several which Wedderburn has not. We think that he will tell his story better in the House of Commons and that by his conciliatory manner and frank and open temper, he will render himself much more acceptable to the Scots members of both Houses and to the country at large.

Protest meetings about Peterloo were being organised all over Scotland and the Radicals decided to hold a mass rally at Paisley on September 4 but, because of bad weather, this was adjourned to September 11. In the meantime the authorities decided to try to suppress the meeting and Sheriff Campbell of Paisley issued a proclamation banning the carrying of flags on September 8. However, on the morning of Saturday, September 11, large bodies of Radicals began to pour into Paisley from Kilbarchan, Johnstone, Dalry, Kilmarnock, Ayr, Galston, and Glasgow, all carried flags which remained furled until they reached the meeting place on the outskirts of the town. A column of 300 men from Glasgow, carrying eight flags, had these flags edged in black in token gesture to the dead of Peterloo. Before the meeting, the Paisley Radical Committee met in the Unitarian Church, in Paisley High Street, to discuss how the proceedings should take place. Mr William Lang, a Bell Street, Glasgow, printer, attended and offered his services in printing a Scottish Radical newspaper. Lang told the meeting "to have a newspaper to advocate the cause" was "absolutely necessary". John Wilson, one of the committee, supported Lang. The committee, who were all dressed in mourning black, then went on to the meeting.

The meeting started with the band from Neilston playing what is now generally accepted as the Scottish national anthem

. . . "Scots Wha Hae . . .". Alexander Taylor, a local school-master, "a man of excellent character and gentle in his disposition", chaired the meeting. Passionately denouncing Peterloo, Taylor told the crowd (which was estimated at being between 14,000 to 18,000 strong): "Oh, I would rather see the bones of all my kindred whiten in the sun, and have my carcass thrown to the dogs, than that such an event should pass without a proper inquiry and punishment upon the guilty perpetrators." He then urged the Radicals "to obtain a proper share in the legislation of Scotland". He also condemned the *Glasgow Chronicle* for attacking the Manchester Radicals. Another speaker urged more militant action. "Sooner shall the loch wash Ben Lomond from its elevated site than the sons of Caledonia shall be silent!"

Yet another speaker added: "The pious Sidmouth has sent his Reynolds, his Richmonds, and his Olivers through the country to ensnare the people and excite them into acts of treason and rebellion. They have suspended the constitution in the foolish hope of putting an end to public meetings; but the sus-pension has not answered the purpose of the miscreant authors. Sooner shall the waves which wash our western shore cease to roll, then we shall forego the right of assembling together." A collection was then made for the relief of the relatives of the Peterloo victims.

In the meantime, under the command of James Brown, the Paisley police superintendent, special constables had gathered in the Court Hall, at 1 p.m. The meeting of the Radicals had started at 2 p.m. and finished in the early evening, but before the meeting was due to end the constables were placed along the High Street as far as the Saracen's Head Inn. When the meeting began to break up, the Neilston contingent, with their band playing, were the first to leave the area but, seeing the position-ing of the police and sensing trouble, they side tracked down Storie Street and managed to get out of Paisley without any trouble. The Glasgow contingent were not so circumspect and began to march down the High Street with their banners waving. As they reached the Cross, the Lord Provost, Oliver Jamieson, stepped forward and tried to seize a Radical flag. A scuffle took place resulting in missiles and stones being hurled at the police. Between 7 p.m. and 8 p.m., a Mr Burns of Gateside told the police chief, James Brown, that he had been knocked down on the street and robbed of his gold watch, chain and seals. The crowd had begun to attack the Council Chambers and Paisley found itself entirely given over to riot. Whether or not the authorities deliberately provoked the riot is not clear, but it certainly seems that their actions were such as to make this theory plausible. The result of the day's proceedings was that at 10 p.m. the Riot Act was read and, as the streets had still not cleared, cavalry were ordered into the town from Glasgow. At 1 a.m., troops of the 10th Hussars galloped into the town and by 3 a.m. an uneasy quiet had descended on the town.

The following day, Sunday, crowds began to gather again and the magistrates and police were hissed and booed whenever they appeared. George Ritchie, a police sergeant, little loved by the Radicals, was badly beaten by a mob. He managed to escape from them and hide for three hours in the house of William Strang, a vintner. As the magistrates, and other dignitaries, made their way to divine service that morning, they were greeted with angry shouts by the people. One man was seized by Bailie Bowie and escorted to jail. Crowds milled through the Town Hall all day and others collected at the Cross. The Sheriff-Deputy, 22-year-old William Motherwell, who had embarked on his poetical career that year by publishing his first work, *Minstrelsy, Ancient and Modern*, was assaulted and knocked unconscious. Between 7 p.m. and 8 p.m. a shower of stones were suddenly aimed at the Coffee Room, beside the Cross. Suddenly, the crowd set off down Causeyside Street, smashing lamps and windows, and passed down Canal Street, George Street and Broomlands. Many stopped at the Methodist Church in George Street and armed themselves by tearing up the railings from its façade. The cavalry were again sent for and dispersed the crowd by repeatedly charging them.

On Monday the crowds were again out in strength and, at 12.45 p.m., the cavalry were brought to the Cross and more military reinforcements were sent for. Lt. Ellis Hodgson of the 10th Hussars and Lt. Strangeways of the 7th Hussars managed to keep the crowd in check until the arrival, between 4 p.m. and 5 p.m., of Major Kingdom and two companies of the 80th Regiment of Foot. Provost Jamieson told the military that there was a meeting of 4 to 5,000 Radicals being held in St James Street and Major Kingdom's men immediately set off down Moss Street towards the reported meeting place. As they marched down the streets they were suddenly charged by "a great crowd" who showered the soldiers with stones before retiring. The cavalry were ordered to charge and eventually cleared the street. Sporadic outbursts of violence continued all day Tuesday and during the evening large crowds were out again and planks were laid across the street to impede the progress of cavalry. Wednesday was fairly quiet until 7 p.m. when a crowd appeared at the Cross. At 9.30 p.m. the military were called out and promptly attacked them. Later, the civic authorities met in Paisley Council Chamber and drew up a proclamation ordering a curfew:

The Sheriff of the County, and the Provost and Magistrates of Paisley, require all parents and masters in the town and suburbs to keep their children and servants within doors as much as possible during the day, while the present riotous disposition continues in Paisley. But it is expected and particularly enjoined that all the well disposed inhabitants will keep themselves and their whole household within doors after eight o'clock in the evening. Council Chamber. Paisley 15th September, 1819.

A reward of 30 guineas was offered for information leading to the arrest of the ringleaders of the rioters. On Thursday the crowds came out in strength again and 258 street lamps were broken, 37 houses were attacked, and large quantities of arms and ammunition were carried off from gun shops. The agitation now began to die down, however, and on Friday a small crowd gathered at the Cross but were cleared by military at 10 p.m. By Saturday, September 18, an uneasy quiet had returned to Paisley and warrants were drawn up for the arrest of suspected Radical leaders. A warrant was made out for the schoolmaster Alexander Taylor, who had been the chairman at the Radical meeting, but Taylor by this time had fled the country and taken a ship for Canada. In Montreal he opened a public stall where he sold all his books, which he had managed to take with him. Afterwards he took a job teaching in a government school in Quebec. Staying one night in the town of Prince William Henry, Taylor fell in with an English soldier whose regiment was quartered in Montreal, and spent the evening with him. Next morning Taylor's dead body was found on the banks of the river. He had been murdered and robbed. The soldier was tried for the crime, but was convicted only of robbery and served two years' imprisonment.

At the end of January, 1820, three young men, Daniel Jamieson, Matthew Adam and Adam MacArthur, were tried in Paisley for their part in the riots. Jamieson pleaded Guilty and was sentenced to four months' imprisonment, providing security to keep the peace for two years. Adam pleaded Not Guilty but was sentenced, after an eight-hour trial, to nine months' imprisonment, providing security for two years. The case against MacArthur was dropped.

On September 20, the Paisley Council met and, in view of the disturbances, it was requested that the Vice Lord Lieutenant of the county should contact the Home Secretary for permission to establish a permanent barracks in the town. This resulted in the Williamsburgh Barracks being erected in 1822. At this same meeting, a vote of thanks was recorded for the actions of Lt. Hodgson, Lt. Strangeways and Major Kingdom in the recent riots. A rifle corps was also raised in the town consisting of two companies of 120 men each. Captain MacAlpine, commandant of this body, commanded the first company, and Captain Stewart commanded the second company. It was decided that in case of a rising the High Church Bell would sound the alarm and the men would be called to arms immediately.

Checking on the police organisation in Scotland, in case of an uprising, the new Lord Advocate, Sir William Rae, found that the police system in Glasgow was so defective that, on September 19, he sent Captain Brown of the Edinburgh force to reorganise things. Brown appointed Captain James Mitchell as "master of police" and the strength of the force was immediately brought up to sixty men . . . a few months later the force was eighty to ninety men strong. At the same time, Brown set about organising a more proficient spy system using money donated for that purpose by the Lord Advocate. It was probably Brown who enlisted the aid of the spies King, Turner, Craig and Lees, who were active in 1820. The last reference to the Government spies was made in a letter to the Lord Advocate from a man named Ball, writing from Edinburgh on September 8, 1820, who asks about the expenses incurred for the informers and shows that Richmond was still a leading figure in the Government spy network.

I wish that Lord Sidmouth would permit me to apply £500, placed in my hands for behalf of Richmond, in extension of the debt thus much more usefully incurred by Captain Brown in procuring secret information as to the state of Glasgow and its vicinity in those late perilous times.

Captain Brown, in fact, wrote to the Lord Advocate in September, 1819, that he had definite information that an uprising was being planned. '. . . there might be a bit of a brush—rather desirable than otherwise—it could not continue long or be on a very extensive scale."

The fear of an imminent uprising caused Samuel Hunter, the editor of the *Glasgow Herald*, to ask permission to raise a Glasgow Yeomanry regiment. Hunter, an 18 stone, 51-year-old son of a Wigton minister, who had been a surgeon with the North Lothian Fencibles and had seen considerable service during the Irish uprising in 1798, soon recruited over 1,000 men to his Yeomanry force which he designated The Glasgow Sharpshooters. Using his considerable influence in Tory circles, Hunter soon had them properly equipped and uniformed in green wool jackets, fringed with silk and cotton tambour (a rich gold and silver embroidery), three rows of dark covered buttons, a white vest, green trousers and polished Wellington boots. Hunter, himself, dressed in a kilt when on military duties and appears to have spoken some Gàidhlig, though he detested those Scots who clung to the old language.

In October the first Scottish Radical newspaper had been launched by Gilbert MacLeod, with the help of William Lang. This was called *The Spirit of Union*, the union referring to the Radical Union Societies. *The Spirit of Union* revealed the extent of the Radical activities reporting the large-scale demonstrations at Ayr, Kilsyth, Paisley, Clayknowes, Glasgow and Neilston. At Airdrie a band was arrested for playing "Scots Wha Hae . . ." and Rodger and Miller, officials of the Airdrie Radical Committee, were arrested but were later released on bail to a great reception by the townspeople. A meeting at Broxbrae, Stirling, was attended by 2,000 people and a newsvendor in Glasgow was sentenced to transportation for circulating "seditious literature". The parish minister at Newmiln refused to baptise children who bore the name of prominent reformers or Radicals.

The Spirit of Union was doomed from the start. After eleven issues, the last being dated January 8, 1820, the authorities suppressed the newspaper and MacLeod, the editor, was arrested. In the last issue there was a brief announcement that the editor lay in jail and that a new newspaper would be started by his friends entitled *The Scottish Patriot*. MacLeod was charged with publishing articles "from an intense and contemptuous Gallowgate orator in which appeared the statement 'that the people's only prospect of relief lay in correcting their own wrongs' " and declaring that people should refuse to pay taxes and that those who joined the Yeomanry should be publicly named and watched. The trial came up on February 14–21, 1820, and the sentence of five years' transportation to the penal colony at Botany Bay was read on March 6. Poor MacLeod died long before his sentence had expired.

On November 1, 1819, the Radicals demonstrated against the Government at Johnstone. Gathering at 1 p.m., the meeting was attended by a number of bands and one newspaper observer counted 32 flags. The observer listed a number of their mottos: For a nation to be free, it is sufficient that it wills it; Let all who love liberty rally round the standards; A day, an hour, of victorious liberty is worth an eternity of bondage; Liberty the object, reason our guide; Against tyranny and oppression our lives we'll spend our rights to gain. One banner had a portrait of Sir William Wallace on it with the inscription: Sir William Wallace, like our ancestors, we'll defend our liberty and laws. A banner with a thistle proclaimed—We are the descendants of Wallace and Bruce. Another banner, showing the strong Irish influence in Scotland, showed a thistle and harp, and the words —May our union be firm. The demonstrators went to Elderslie, where Wallace the hero of the Scottish War of Independence was born, and here they halted beneath "Wallace's Tree" and the bands played the Scottish national anthem. Three cheers were given and a number of pistols were fired in the air. The Radicals then began to march back to Paisley armed, it is said, "with two great battle-axes in front". The authorities in Paisley, however, were lying in wait for the Radical procession and troops of cavalry had been positioned all day, with sabres drawn, outside the Tontine and Saracen Inns. News of this reached the Radical leaders and, instead of marching into the High Street and into the trap set for them, they side tracked down Storie Street and dispersed before the cavalry could be brought into action against them.

Another great Radical meeting of 5 to 6,000 people, was held at Linktown of Kirkcaldy on November 3 "for the purpose of expressing their opinions relative to the attack made on their friends at Manchester by the Magistrates and Yeomanry of that place; and likewise to state their sentiments on the subject of Parliamentary Reform". The meeting began at twelve noon with the band playing the Scottish national anthem. Mr Robert Ramsay took the chair and exhorted the Radicals to behave calmly. "Our enemies have insinuated that no such meeting as this can take place without riot or tumult; but I hope that this day we shall give the lie to such insinuations, and show that they are the insinuations of ignorant and foolish men; I say more, they are the insinuations of base and designing men, who want to deprive us of the liberty of meeting together lest we should unveil to each other their delinquencies." Mr A. Mitchell then read to the meeting fourteen resolutions which he asked them to pass.

1. That according to the spirit of the Constitution, the people have an undoubted right to meet and consult together for the purpose of having their grievances removed; consequently any interruption offered by those in power to the exercise of such, is illegal, and may be considered a dangerous approach towards establishing despotism; resistance to which is the duty of everyone who is not willing to become a slave.

2. That the outrage committed at Manchester on the ever to be lamented 16th of August, by the Magistrates and Yeomanry of that town, upon the unoffending assemblage of its inhabitants and others, who were drawn into a fatal security that their meeting might proceed undisturbed, was at once cowardly, treacherous, and attended with circumstances of cruelty which were manifested by indiscriminate killing, maiming and wounding of men, women and children, even while supplicating forebearence on their part of their murderous pursuers.

3. That the blood shed upon this occasion calls loudly for justice;

and that those who may obstruct justice, identify themselves with the perpetrators of that inhuman transaction.

4. That this meeting views with indignation the advisers of the Crown supporting the offenders by not only applauding them but also seeming to throw every possible obstacle in the way of their being brought to condign punishment.

5. That it is the opinion of this meeting, ministers have shown themselves, alike, unworthy of the confidence of the Sovereign or the people.

6. That nothing is so likely to prevent the recurrence of such base and cruel transactions as those exhibited at Manchester, or to enable us to recover our rights wrested from us by an Oligarchy, as that of obtaining full, free and equal representation in Parliament, by the adoption of Major Cartwright's Bill of Rights.

7. That it appears, from Ministers having advised the Regent to approve the ruthless deeds done at Manchester, that nothing less than a military despotism seems aimed at, and consequently the destruction of our liberties.

8. That the different societies or committees shall continue to exist as organised bodies, to unite and act in concert with similar establishments throughout the kingdoms until that grand object Radical Reform be obtained.

9. That it appears to this meeting that nothing at present seems more likely to frustrate the designs of our oppressors than a firm determination to abstain as much as possible from the use of Excised Articles by which safe and easy method we will also secure the means of our own defence.

10. That a subscription be opened for the purpose of bringing to justice the inhuman perpetrators of the deeds done at Manchester; and that the sum so subscribed be put under the management of a Select Committee who shall, after defraying the expenses of the meeting, transmit the balance to Major Cartwright by him to be applied in such a way as may fulfil the intentions of the meeting.

11. That the thanks of the meeting to be voted to that venerable friend, Major Cartwright, Sir Francis Burdett, Sir Charles Wolesly, Henry Hunt, Messrs. Wooler, Pearson, Harmer and Dennistoun, for the manly manner they have come forward in support of the cause of Liberty, Humanity and Justice; and to all other friends of Radical Reform.

12. That highly as we value the doctrines and many of the ministers of the Established religion of our country, we nevertheless feel ourselves called upon to express our indignation at the false and unfounded assertion of the Synod of Fife. viz. that the lower orders

of the people were instigated to tumult by the circulation of blasphemous and seditious pamphlets.

13. That if by tumult and insurrection the reverend gentlemen
alluded to the late unhappy events at Manchester, they certainly
identify themselves with the approvers of that horried massacre and
seem to breathe the same spirit of their clerical brethren at that
unfortunate place.

14. That the excessive weight of taxation and the lavish expendi-
ture of the public money, with the destructive operation of the corn
laws upon the commerce of the country is sufficient to stimulate the
people to complaint without the aid of blasphemy and sedition.

Having read the resolutions, Mitchell asked the meeting to
show "that the weapons which you wield are truth and reason,
and not the sword and bayonet". Mr Lockhart addressed the
meeting briefly, saying that he disapproved of it being convened
and it was a time for moderation and to be circumspect. The
next speaker, Mr Lindsay, compared Peterloo "with the horrible
massacre of Glencoe", and said "some talk of moderation, we
love moderation as well as any, but why talk of it? Is there any
moderation in taxes? Is there any moderation in the standing
army? Is there any moderation in the sinecures and pensions?
And, I dare say, my countrymen, you will allow there was little
moderation shown at Manchester on the memorable 16th of
August." He ended: "Let us always bear in mind that we are the
lineal descendants of those who fought under the banners of
Wallace, when unfurled in the cause of liberty, and also of those
who bled at Bannockburn, and never so far forget the ashes of
our brave and noble progenitors as tamely to submit to slavery.
No, my countrymen, the patient and brave sons of Caledonia
shall never suffer those rights to be torn from them which they
inherited from their ancestors, obtained by their courage and
sealed with their blood."

Again, Mitchell addressed the crowd, summing up the debate
on the resolutions. This time he made a more direct and passion-
ate nationalist appeal when he asked the audience what Scotland had achieved from rule from England: ". . . the massacre of
our people—the debasement of our national character—the
accumulation of a debt beyond all spend-thrift precedent—
famine in our streets and fever in our houses. The
establishment in Europe of a military despotism which

leaves the very name of freedom a mockery—the payment of war taxes in the time of peace, scarcely leaving
it doubtful whether the burdens were imposed to commence the
war or the war commenced to justify the taxes. The suspension
of our constitution if we offer to remonstrate. This has been our
dearly bought indemnity!" After his speech, the resolutions
were read one by one and adopted unanimously. Votes of thanks
were recorded and the band again played the Scottish national
anthem before the meeting finally closed without disturbance.
Two days later, on November 5, the Paisley Radicals held yet
another protest meeting against the suggestion of the Lord
Lieutenant of Renfrew to raise a Yeomanry corps in the county.

Following the Radical meetings, the Lord President of the
Court of Session, Hope, wrote to Lord Melville on November 9,
that "all disguise is now thrown off—even the flimsy pretence of
Radical Reform is laid aside—a complete revolution and plunder is avowed their object". Hope was satisfied "that it will
come to blows and that speedily". He said that Lord Archibald
Hamilton had been seized with panic "which seems to have
deprived him of all judgement and energy [if he had any] and
which seems to be producing consequences almost as pernicious
as his former Radical folly". Hamilton was one of the more
active Whig Reformists who, that year, had managed to get the
Commons to set up an inquiry into the state of the Scottish
burghs but which had been rejected by the Lord Advocate.

Hope told Melville that the volunteer and Yeomanry corps
were not able to recruit men as the people were afraid to join.
He, himself, was trying to raise the Royal Edinburgh Volunteers and "we may be certain of 6 to 700 recruits in a few days".
He asked Melville whether it would be possible to attach some
of the Chelsea Pensioners "as orderly sergeants and drummers"
in order to make up for the sad lack in volunteers. Hope then
recounted how he was sitting in Hill Street when Lord Alloway
and Roger Aytoun, the Duke of Hamilton's agent, had accosted
him and urged him to take measures "to rouse the country's
spirit". Aytoun said that matters were worse than Hope had
heard and Hamilton "was almost beside himself, but would
gladly now do whatever was thought right". Hope replied that
soon Edinburgh and the eastern counties would be in arms.
"This greatly relieved Alloway's mind, who is in a horrible

funk, which I fancy will keep down his Whigism for some time to come." The same day, at 4 p.m., a Radical meeting was held in Edinburgh at the Hallowfair. It was "a shabby meeting", commented Hope, but was held with the aim of giving an impression that the Radicals had command in Edinburgh. Another Radical meeting was held in Kilmarnock on November 20 and Lord Eglington turned out the 1st regiment of Alexander Boswell's Ayrshire Yeomanry, but there was no disturbance.

Towards the end of November, the military started to conduct numerous arms raids throughout the country, having received instructions from Lord Sidmouth, dated November 6, via the Lord Lieutenants of the counties. Sidmouth was particularly worried about the numbers of field pieces unaccounted for in the country.

Having been informed that there are, laying about throughout the kingdom, especially in the maritime parts of it, a great number of cannon which are private property, a considerable part of which were formerly used in merchant ships; I beg leave to call your lordship's attention to this subject; and to request that you will direct the magistrates of the county under your lordship's charge to make the necessary inquiries within their respective districts and if any guns as this description should be found therein, that they will cause immediate steps to be taken with the consent of their owners for rendering them useless, or for removing them to a place of security.

Resulting from a ministerial meeting on November 23, the Government, in spite of strong opposition from Lord Grey and the Whig Party, pushed through the legislation known as the Six Acts. The object of these pieces of legislation was to crush the Radicals. Briefly, they can be summed up as follows: 1. To accelerate "the administration of justice in case of misdemeanour" and to alter the procedure in such cases. 2. "To prevent the training of persons in the use of arms and the practice of military evolutions." 3. To prevent and punish "blasphemous and seditious libels" (a second conviction for libel punishable by transportation). 4. "To authorise Justices of the Peace in certain disturbed counties to seize and detail arms." 5. "To subject certain publications to the duties of stamps upon newspapers, and to make other regulations for restraining the abuses arising from the publication of blasphemous and seditious libels." 6. to prevent more effectually "seditious meetings and assemblies".

E

An anonymous sergeant of the Glasgow Yeomanry, writing his memoirs of the 1820 rising, recalled that "the 13th December [1819] had been for some time anticipated as the day on which an attempt was to be made on Glasgow". Sir Thomas Bradford and his staff set off for Glasgow at 11 a.m. on December 12 from Edinburgh. However, writing to Lord Melville on the same day, Lord President Hope commented: "the letters from Glasgow this morning say that the report is that the insurrection will not take place tomorrow. This is all good, if it is not to take place. But it is very vexatious if it is to take place at last—for the troops will be harassed to death on the one hand, while every attempt will be made to reduce them on the other—and while the troops are absent from this place [Edinburgh], I think it extremely probable that attempts will be made to incite a rising here." Hope described how Sir John Hope and his Yeomanry corps, marching through Edinburgh's Grass Market at 8 a.m. that day, were attacked by a mob.

On December 13, the Glasgow Yeomanry were called out at 10 a.m. and paraded in greatcoats in South Frederick Street. "A vast number of idle people and mostly strangers among them perambulated the street." The early part of the morning showed the roads leading into Glasgow to be crowded with people heading in the direction of the city. The Mid Lothian Yeomanry, the 7th Hussars, the 13th Regiment of Foot and the Glasgow Yeomanry, plus two field pieces, stood ready in the city but "the day went off quietly". A regular turn out of troops was made every morning for two weeks before the scare of a Radical rising had passed.

Lord Hope, writing again to Melville on December 14, put it down to the fact that "the imposing appearance of the troops, on which the Radicals had not at all calculated, disconcerted and overawed them and the rising was countermanded". But, Hope pointed out, that 300 men had marched into Kilsyth fully armed, en route for Glasgow, but hearing all was quiet there, had disbanded. Hope commented: "If a rising at Glasgow is totally abandoned, good and well, but if it be only delayed, it is conclusive as a tendency to harass the troops and put the Yeomanry to much inconvenience." He continued: "I have written to the Solicitor [General] at Glasgow to urge strongly the propriety of making a thorough search for arms, before the troops are drawn off—and to call on the people by a strong proclamation to bring in and surrender their arms [as was done in Ireland] and to warn them that if arms were found concealed by them after such notice, they would be prosecuted with the utmost vigour of the laws." Two days later Hope reported that "the preparations made have defeated their projects for the present—but unless their means are destroyed, by seizing their arms, and breaking up their Etat Major—for they have the facility of circulating orders as regularly and as rapidly as from the Adjutant General's Office—they will retain the power of meeting on a few hours notice, whenever they see a favourable moment". On December 17 Hope told Melville that "the people are rife for rebellion as ever, and only in sullen and sultry silence waiting for a more convenient opportunity".

When the Anglicised feudal chiefs and aristocracy in A' Ghàidhealtachd, learned of the threat to the system, they immediately banded together and passed various resolutions of loyalty to the Crown and constitution. The *Inverness Courier* carried the following advertisement:

LOYAL HIGHLANDERS!
the present crisis calls upon all LOYAL SUBJECTS to rally round the CONSTITUTION of our country. Highlanders from 18 to 40 years of age are invited to attend a MEETING of the
SUTHERLAND AND TRANSATLANTIC
FRIENDLY ASSOCIATION
which is appointed to hold at GOLSPIE in Sutherlandshire, on Tuesday, the 4th of January, at 10 o'clock a.m. for the purposes of envincing their firm attachment to His Majesty's present Government by an offer of their service in a Military capacity.
                                   Thomas Dudgeon, Secretary.
Fearn, December 20, 1819.

It will be wondered how many "Highlanders" will have been able to read this advertisement in English only. Surprisingly, the authorities immediately banned Dudgeon's meeting because they felt that Dudgeon was doing a "double cross' and, in fact, raising men for the Radical cause.

With the country on the brink of revolution, the authorities arrested one of the principal Radical leaders in Scotland, George Kinloch of Kinloch, who is described as a gentleman with considerable estates in Forfar. He was charged with sedition and the date of his trial was fixed for December 22. Kinloch immediately employed Francis Jeffrey, Henry Cockburn and James Moncrieff as his defence advocates and they managed to achieve his release on bail. Cockburn recalls, in his memoirs, that "having laid our views of his risks before him we left him to follow his own counsel and he withdrew. With Botany Bay before him and money enough to make himself comfortable in Paris, he would have been an idiot if he had stayed." Kinloch of Kinloch fled the country and was declared an outlaw, thus depriving the Scottish Radical movement of a leader of standing and influence. Following the Government's pardon of all the 1820 Radicals, in 1832, Kinloch returned to Scotland and was elected Member of Parliament for Dundee in that year. He died of "excess of duty in Parliament".

With the arrest of Kinloch and MacLeod, two of the prominent Scottish Radical leaders, the rest of the Radicals in Scotland grew firm in their resolve that the Radical Reform must be precipitated by a general rising in Scotland.

EIGHT

PLANS FOR THE RISING

O N J A N U A R Y 2 9, 1 8 2 0, the mad king, George III, died at Windsor aged 81 years and 239 days. His son, 58-year-old George Augustus Frederick, who had assumed the Regency on February 5, 1811, when his father became totally and irremediably mad, became George IV. There was certainly no joy among the people at this event, Whig, Tory and Radical alike not only did not respect the monarchy but utterly disliked it. The poet Shelley summed up the general opinion when he wrote:

> An old, mad, despised and dying King,
> Princes, the dregs of their dull race, who flow
> Through public scorn—mud from a muddy spring—
> Rulers who neither see nor feel nor know
> But leech-like to their fainting country cling.

From the time of the Regency, the royal family had been held in universal contempt; the Regent and his brothers gambled with a wanton profusion, piled themselves high with debts which they cheerfully expected the state to meet while hunger and strife were rampant in the realm. They showed little taste in their selection of friends or choice of mistresses; crooks, thieves, etc., were to be found at their table in assorted profusion. "Few monarchies," comments J. H. Plumb, in *The First Four Georges*, "have struggled under the weight of such a burden of self-indulgent vulgarity." George IV was totally opposed to any form of political emancipation of the people. A torrent of incoherent arguments, tears, hysteria, half insane and grotesque exhibitions drove him further away from not only his subjects but from the successive governments during his reign. His reckless debts, and the fortunes he squandered on private amusement at a time of acute social distress, made the people bitterly resent his behaviour and even hate him personally.

This hatred led to an attempt on his life in 1817 . . . the first attempt to kill an English monarch since the assassination plot of 1696. With Radical feeling widespread throughout England, Scotland and Ireland, and George IV held in contempt, the Duke of Bedford wrote with conviction that he thought "the days of the monarchy are numbered".

A few weeks after the accession of George IV, a plot was discovered in London for a general uprising which was to be triggered off by the assassination of the entire Government whilst they were having dinner at Lord Harrowby's house in Grosvenor Square, London, on February 23, 1820. The Bank area of the City was to be seized and cannons, which were emplaced there, were to be carried off by the insurgents. Buildings were to be set alight in several different parts of London in order to cause the maximum amount of confusion. The Mansion House was to be seized and used as the seat of the Provisional Government. The plot was organised by Arthur Thistlewood, a 50-year-old prominent member of the Spencean Philanthropists, followers of the teaching of Thomas Spence, a London bookseller who died in 1813 who believed in communities holding land in common. Thistlewood, who came of a "well-to-do" family, spent several years in France after the revolution. He had organised a protest meeting of workmen at Spa Fields, Bermondsey, on November 15, 1816, and was arrested. He was released in August, 1819, and immediately began to make plans for an insurrection. With Ings, a butcher, Tidd and Brunt, shoemakers, and Davidson, "a man of colour", the conspirators hired a room near Gray's Inn Lane and began to make preparations. The Government agents, Edwards and Hidon, managed to infiltrate the organisation and the plot was betrayed. On the evening of Wednesday, February 23, 1820, the day fixed for the rising, twenty-five of Thistlewood's men gathered at a house in Cato Street. A Bow Street officer named Birnie and his men, with an officer called Smithers and troops of the Coldstream Guards, surrounded the house and after a struggle nine people were arrested. Thistlewood managed to escape but was arrested the next day. Thistlewood, Ings, Brunt, Tidd and Davidson were duly executed and five others were transported for life. This abortive English uprising became known as the Cato Street Conspiracy.

In Scotland Radical meetings were still being organised and in the early part of February there was a great county Radical meeting in Ayr and hustings were put up in a field belonging to the Crosskeys Hostelry, between Wallace Street and Limmon's Wynd, bordering George Street. Large groups of Radicals from Kilmarnock, Tarbolton, Mauchline, Stewarton and other parts of the county arrived at the meeting place. James Howie recalls that there were many bands and all the Radical contingents had patriotic flags, and several revolutionary ones. "The party from Kilmarnock had a pole on which was elevated a cap, styled the cap of liberty—a device borrowed probably from the French revolutionary mobs." The pole was borne by a young woman, supported left and right by two others. The republican attitude, especially of the "Ayrshire lassies", comments Howie, was very prominent. The meeting began and many resolutions were passed "all of a revolutionary tendency; but, it was remarked, that all the speakers kept on the safe side of the law. There was nothing brilliant in the addresses, only the commonplace sentiments and platitudes about liberty and people's rights; good enough in their way, but hardly fitted to convince and convert antagonists." Throughout the meeting the Ayrshire Yeomanry were drawn up a short distance away with swords unsheathed.

During the meeting, Colonel Alexander Boswell, who combined the offices of commander of the Ayrshire Yeomanry, Vice-Lord Lieutenant of the County and Tory M.P. for Plympton, in Devon, rode up with several friends and fellow Yeomanry officers. Boswell, born in 1775, was the eldest son of James Boswell, the famed biographer of Dr Samuel Johnson, and was a poet in his own right. Even today his songs, "Jenny dang the weaver", and "Good night and joy be wi' ye a'", are still well known. He is described as "upwards of six feet with broad chest, head well set on shoulders, very noble carriage and a presence producing a voluntary deference and respect, without any supercilious and offensive haughtiness. His arms were long and powerful, his limbs formed for ability and strength. On horseback he was particularly attractive. Whether as an officer of the Yeomanry Cavalry, or as a private gentleman riding for his enjoyment, his style and management were admirable. His splendid grey was very high, with great action, and uncommonly showing; to see him ride up the steep village of Ochiltree on the gallant grey, at a proud canter, was a sight not easily forgotten.'' Despite this pleasing description and the humanity shown in his poems, Boswell was a rabid anti-Radical who had no time for the pleas of the working people. While Boswell sat astride his horse listening to the meeting, the Ayr delegate, William Adam, a shoemaker of George Street, Wallaceton, gave his address. Boswell heard the address in silence and then loudly remarked that Adam was a fit subject for hanging. That night Adam took the wise precaution of leaving his home and going into hiding. A few days later a warrant was made out for his arrest and his house was watched day and night. Adam did not return to his family until well over a year later.

As soon as the business of the meeting was over [says Howie] the different parties left the ground and took their way homewards in a quiet, orderly and peaceable manner. The military, though held in readiness to cut down the people should the least opportunity be given to attack them were disappointed in their expectations, and (Sir) Alexander Boswell, did not enjoy the pleasure he is said to have promised himself a day or two before the meeting was held, of riding in Radical blood up to his bridle reins.

Boswell regularly reported on Radical activities to the Home Secretary, and later that month he wrote to Sidmouth:

The most contaminated villages in this county are Newmiln, in the parish of Loudoun, and Galston. In the former there are a number of disbanded soldiers who have been weavers and who have returned with irregular habits and cannot obtain employment, or at very low wages. These two villages have been poisoned since the year 1794 and the evil has festered ever since, but these together could not produce 500 men. In all the villages where there are weavers of cotton goods a large proportion are Radicals, but these seem in fifties and seldom a hundred, in any one place excepting Kilmarnock and Beith and perhaps Stewarton.

By March the spy system which Sidmouth had instigated in Scotland began to swing into operation. On Saturday, March 4, Peter Gibson, who lived near the Aqueduct, Glasgow, was arrested and charged with making pikes. Gibson was a "prime suspect" and had already been imprisoned in Edinburgh Castle during the "Richmond trials" in 1817 to answer charges of high treason. After MacKinlay's acquittal the authorities had no option but to release him. In Ayr, James Logan, "a notorious rascal and spy", became the local police informant. He managed to get himself elected as secretary of the Ayr Radical Committee and was often arrested by the military and always released. Every time he was arrested he was certain to have some document relating to the work of the Radicals in his possession. Howie recalls:

Every means was adopted and every plan tried by the authorities and their spies to entrap the simple and unwary, that they might obtain commitals on the great charge of High Treason, but happily they succeeded in none of their attempts.

One case Howie recounts was when a barrel of gunpowder was placed outside the door of a man called Campbell of Townhead. Campbell was a leading local Radical. He had the good sense to completely ignore the barrel and it was eventually removed. Pikes and other weapons were left near the houses of other Radicals and the authorities set a watch to see who would take the bait; most of the Radicals were wise and ignored the "plants". The extent to which the authorities went to get incriminating evidence against the Radicals can be seen from the fact that the Sheriff of Hamilton himself tried to induce Alexander Ross, then a blacksmith at Sandford, near Strathaven, to start manufacturing pikes. After the Reform Bill was passed, and the threat of persecution eliminated, Ross made a statement on May 16, 1832, concerning the affair:

I hereby declare, and am ready to make oath, if required, that on an evening in the month of March, 1820, two gentlemen came riding to my shop at Sandford and on asking for me, I went out to see them. This would be about seven o'clock. One of them asked me if I was throng. I said I was: and after a few other questions, he put this question to me, whether I would agree to make a number or quantity of pikes for him? I instantly said I would not—on which he made answer that I would be well paid for my trouble if I would engage to take the job. But I still decline. On this, the other gentleman on horseback asked me if I knew this man, i.e. the person who was asking me to make the pikes? On which I said I did not. But then I recognised the person who put this last question to me to be Mr Dugald M'Callum, one of the Procurator Fiscals of the County of Lanark at Hamilton. I walked with them by their desire, a few yards—to the top of Sandford Bridge, when they alighted from their horses and Mr M'Callum then told me that this was Mr Aiton (the Sheriff of Hamilton) who was with him and wished to employ me to make the pikes; and they begged me not to mention their visit, or the object of it, to anyone, and requested me to go with them to Strathaven where they would treat me with a bowl of toddy. But I declined to go with them and returned to my own shop. I afterwards stated these facts to some of my acquaintances and now again here solemnly repeat this as true.

During March the unrest started breaking out into violence and on March 13, disaffected workmen set fire to the mills at Milngaff, Portpatrick and Ballantrae. Such incidents occurred through the month, including a fire at Paisley on March 25 when a large crowd attacked the military with stones. The Government had managed, by this time, to infiltrate four agents into the Glasgow Radical circles. John King, of Anderston, who called himself a weaver, but did not apparently follow any particular calling and always seemed to be in funds, emerges as the chief of these agents. The others were Duncan Turner, a tinsmith, John Craig, a weaver, and Robert or Thomas Lees, an agent who, it was noted, "spoke with an English accent".

There was, in fact, no doubt that the Scottish Radicals were preparing for an armed uprising in Scotland. A twenty-eight-man Committee for Organising a Provisional Government had been formed and orders had been issued to the numerous Radical Committees throughout Scotland to appoint officers and embark on military training courses. In Glasgow, Dougald Smith had been elected "Commandant of the Glasgow Area". In Paisley, Daniel Bell, was elected. "He had been our drill sergeant, and an excellent one he was; and we therefore appointed him our captain by a unanimous vote", wrote John Parkhill, who was, at the same time, elected commissary-general of the Paisley Radicals. Robert Hamilton was elected in Strathaven and John Baird in Condorrat.

Little is known about the twenty-eight-man committee, except that it seemed to be composed of delegates appointed by the various Radical Committees. It would also seem that the system of electing this committee was carried out in the same way as the election of the National Committee of the United

Scotsmen had been. It was to this committee that John King managed to get himself elected and found that the plans for a rising were afoot but the actual rising was not to take place for at least another year, by which time the Radicals felt they would be trained and equipped and able to give a good account of themselves. This, King reported to the authorities in Glasgow who, in turn, communicated the information to Sidmouth. Writing to Lord Sidmouth on March 18, J. Mitchell, the Glasgow police commander wrote:

The Scottish Radicals have been making preparation for some little time now for a general rising in Scotland and to this end they have kept in close communication with the disaffected in England. Their plan is to set up a Scottish Assembly or Parliament in Edinburgh, likewise similar assemblies are to be set up by the disaffected in England and Ireland. As far as can be gathered by our informants they are imbibed with the republican ideals that were preached by that odious band of disaffected called United Scotsmen who, after their abortive attempt to overthrow Government in '97, it was generally accepted, had disappeared at the beginning of the century, but whose aim was also the destruction of the unity of our kingdoms. The bearer will present you with more detailed intelligence, especially in connection with a meeting of the organising committee of the rabble which is due to this vicinity in a few days hence.

On March 21 the committee met in the house of a man named Marshall, a Gallowgate vintner. King was there and told the meeting he would have to leave at 9 p.m. because he had some business to attend to across the city. The Paisley delegate apparently objected saying that they should all leave together, a clear sign that one of the committee, at least, suspected King of being an informer. The delegate was overruled and King left at 9 p.m. A few minutes later Bailie Hunter, a Glasgow magistrate, with a strong force of police and soldiers, burst in and the entire Radical committee were arrested. It was not until March 29 that Mitchell again reported to Sidmouth.

I have been informed of your opinions by our intermediary on the matters of the disaffected of this place. My lord, it is my earnest desire to serve Government to the extremes of my humble ability. I would strongly urge that action must be taken immediately to quench the treasonable ardours of the disaffected before they grow too strong. A week passed, we apprehended their committee of organisation, due solely to the efforts of an informant who has served his Government well and whom I shall give more intelligence about anon. The man who styles himself prese [president] of this rabble has confessed their audacious plot to sever the kingdom of Scotland from that of England and restore the ancient Scottish Parliament. We know many of the vipers involved in this treasonable plot but I would say, indeed, I would stake all on such a hazard that the disaffected are too weak and unorganised at this date to carry out their wicked intent. Thus, my lord, if some plan were conceived by which the disaffected could be lured out of their lairs—being made to think that the day of "liberty" had come— we would catch them abroad and undefended. The military in North Britain is more than adequate to round up such vermin. Our intelligence leads us to believe that few know of the apprehension of the leaders in this odious treasonable plot and so no suspicion would attach itself to the plan at all. I have given instructions to our informants on these lines—all good men, and true to our principles, who, at tremendous hazard to their life and limb, have infiltrated the disaffected's committees and organisation, and in a few days shall you judge the results. It would, by the severity of their punishment, which must be harsh—quench all thought of patriotic pride and Radical feeling among the disaffected.

Thus, the intention to restore parliamentary independence by the Scottish Radicals is made clear, but the form of Scottish independence is left to conjecture. Republicanism was still a strong force in Ireland, Scotland and England, and the Scottish Radicals would be the direct inheritors of the Scottish Republic ideal of the United Scotsmen and the Friends of the People. Therefore, the type of independent Scottish Government sought by the Radicals would seem more of a socialist republic than simply a return to the Scottish Estates system. The actual details, it seems, will never be known as despite careful research no other information about the twenty-eight-man committee of the Radicals can be traced. Who they were and, indeed, what became of them, is not entirely certain. They were still being held incommunicado in Glasgow Jail in November, 1820. Why were they not charged with high treason, along with the other Radicals that took up arms? Could it be that they would have revealed that the 1820 uprising was instigated by Government agents? Why did they not tell their story on their release; were they, in fact, released? Or were they quietly shipped off to some penal settlement without even a trial? The fate of the Committee of Organising a Provisional Government will probably remain a historical mystery.

John Parkhill does, in fact, mention the arrest of the committee and says that a number of documents were seized at the meeting as well as the committee itself. Parkhill claims that news of the arrest of the committee arrived at Paisley two hours afterwards and the Paisley Radical Committee at once held a meeting in the Smiddy. It was decided that the entire Paisley contingent should be marched off to Gleniffer and to disperse and hide in the hills because it was felt that the papers seized would give the Radicals away. Parkhill says that after they had been at Gleniffer some time it was learnt that the documents were only scraps of notes "being somewhat hieroglyphical would not be very easily understood". The Radicals returned to Paisley and men were sent to Glasgow the next morning to discover what had happened. Parkhill, however, does not amplify on this matter any more and, again, we are left to conjecture.

The day following the arrest of the committee, John King, obviously acting on the instructions outlined by Mitchell, gathered his fellow agents Turner, Craig and Lees, and together they rounded up fifteen to twenty prominent Glasgow Radicals in the house of Robert MacKenzie of Bishop Street, Anderston. At this meeting King claimed that he was a representative of the Provisional Government, "all men of rank and talent", and that the rising was imminent. A provisional draft of the proclamation calling for the rising would be shown for their approval at a meeting which would take place the following night and King hoped that the Radical delegates would support this. The following day there was a public meeting of the Glasgow Radical Committee on Glasgow Green and general business was discussed. Duncan Turner attended this meeting and indicated that he had some urgent matter to bring before the Glasgow Radicals. He proposed that the meeting adjourn to Rutherglen, two miles distant. This was done and in the seclusion of Rutherglen Turner told them there was to be a rising in England and a provisional government would be set up in London. Likewise a rising was now being planned in Scotland

and a Provisional Government was being set up in Glasgow. Letters were then read to the meeting by Turner outlining these plans. These were destroyed immediately afterwards but Andrew Wilson of Camlachie, a delegate, assured the historian MacKenzie of their existence. The meeting passed a resolution to "act accordingly" and within a few days it was reported that 500 to 800 men were drilling in the Glasgow district.

The same day Duncan Turner took the rough draft of the proclamation of the "Provisional Government" to John Anderson Jnr., the son of a Glasgow writer. The proclamation, with its references to English, rather than Scottish, history (i.e. Magna Carta and the Bill of Rights instead of the Declaration of Arbroath) was afterwards claimed by the Press to be the work of English Radicals. However, it is more than probable that the proclamation was, in fact, the work of Lees who, from description, was an Englishman and a solicitor to boot. Why Anderson was brought into the picture is not clear. It would seem, however, that he was part of the Government spy ring, for no proceedings were taken against him after the rising and he was sent abroad with a Government job. Anderson wrote the final draft for the printers; Fulton, the printer, comments on the fact that the draft was written on "law paper".

The spies now set about preparing the rising and, at first, it was felt that a prominent Radical should be enticed into naming himself as the commander of the Radical Army. Two men called on Richard Alexander Oswald, of Auchencruive House, near Ayr, "a gentleman of extremely liberal opinions and an unflinching advocate of the people". Apart from this, Oswald had been the commander of the Ayrshire Yeomanry forces until June 16, 1816, when Alexander Boswell had succeeded him to the command. The two men told Oswald that a rising was planned and the Radical army was ready but waiting for a commander they could trust and respect who would take a lead in the affair when the time came. The Radicals wanted not only a man of Oswald's political ideals but a man with Oswald's military experience. Oswald, however, saw through the ruse and indignantly refused. He acused them of being spies or, giving them the benefit of the doubt, dupes of spies. He gave them one hour to escape before riding into Ayr and lodging information with the authorities. James Howie recalls:

Mr Oswald was the more readily incited to the step he took as he had reason to believe that the whole affair was a plot by Government spies to enable them to lodge against him a charge of High Treason, which they would have done had he not acted as he did.

At the end of the hour Oswald rode to Ayr and told the authorities. Angus Gunn, the criminal officer, and the local militia were called out but no arrests were made.

Radical feeling was rising in Scotland as the parliamentary elections had finished on March 25, ensuring a further term of office for the Tory Government. Also the trial of Henry Hunt, J. Saxton, J. Moorhouse, S. Bamford, R. Jones, George Swift, Robert Wild, J. Knight, J. Healy and a man named Johnson, commenced on March 23, arising out of the "Peterloo" massacre. Hunt and his colleagues were charged with conspiracy to alter the government and constitution of the realm and "with meeting tumultuously at Manchester on the 16th of August last, with 60,000 persons, many armed with sticks, which they carried on their shoulders like firearms, and with bearing flags and banners calculated to inflame the minds of His Majesty's subjects against the constituted authorities of the state". The Government agents decided that April 1 would be fixed as the date for issuing the proclamation and they decided to contact an 18-year-old apprentice printer named Robert F. Fulton, who was a known Radical supporter. Fulton was employed by Duncan MacKenzie, a printer at 20 Saltmarket, Glasgow. Writing from the safety of America some years afterwards Fulton said:

The first time I ever heard of this address was on Tuesday, March 28, when I was sent for through the means of a nephew of one of the Provisional Government, whose name was Craig. By him I was introduced to another member of the Provisional Government, whose name was Lees, with whom I made an appointment to meet at the corner of Ingram Street, opposite the Royal Bank; but owing to the Secret Committee taking suspicion that they were being watched by the local authorities, they removed from the house in which they met in the Saltmarket, to Anderston, from thence to Girvan and last of all to Paisley, where they finally resolved on the copy of the address being printed.

Parkhill makes no mention of the Paisley Radical Committee being consulted and it would appear that this was a story given out by Craig and Lees to make them seem more authoritative. On Thursday, March 30, Fulton, having agreed to print the proclamation, met Lees at the Cross at 8.30 p.m. Lees took Fulton to the Globe Tavern, in the Saltmarket, and here Fulton was given £1 3s. to pay for the paper. To add to the drama, perhaps as an added incentive to convince young Fulton that he was a conspirator in deadly earnest, Lees had the draft of the proclamation concealed between his leg and stocking. Surreptitiously, this was handed over. Fulton enlisted the aid of 20-year-old John Hutchison, a fellow apprentice and fellow Radical. Using the types and presses of their unsuspecting employer, they started printing in the early hours of Saturday morning. Fulton says he managed to print the best half of the proclamations by 5 a.m. on Saturday and at 7 a.m. he delivered these to the house of Craig. He and Hutchison began printing the second half at 9 p.m. on Saturday and these were finished by the time Lees called at the printing shop just before midnight. Fulton writes:

I saw him [Lees] about half an hour afterwards in the Globe Tavern, where he was sitting along with Craig and Mrs Lees, when I received seventeen shillings in cash, and here the business closed with us concerning the address." Before Fulton left Lees, however, the Government agent told him that "the Militia were overpowered, that a Manifesto would be published stating the grounds on which the Radicals had taken up arms, and which was to be followed by a paper currency to pay the Radical troops which were collected. That the five counties were to produce upwards of 70,000 effective men. It appears to me that Lees was either a spy or the dupe of a spy."

In the meantime, King and Turner were trying to organise arms and getting Radicals to make pikes. Whenever they were successful in getting a group of Radicals together with arms they would discreetly withdraw and inform the nearest authorities. On Thursday, March 30, the military were informed "by persons unknown" that two smiths in a machine factory at the head of John Smith Street were making pikes. A magistrate with a party of military raided the premises but "the two men, who were the object of the search, made their escape through a window into the Grammar School ground". On entering the factory, the militia were jeered and one workman, bolder than the rest, told them that if they were searching for Radicals they might as well arrest them all. In wonder, the *Glasgow Herald* commented: "the politics of the men employed in this work cannot be ascribed to the pressure of the times, as they have been in constant employment, and at very high wages".

With the proclamation printed and, during the night of April 2, distributed by unsuspecting, enthusiastic Radicals, the Government spies had laid their plot well. All they could hope was that the Radicals would seize the bait and come out into the open, in order that the superior military forces quartered in Scotland, aided by the local Yeomanry corps, could deal the Radicals a smashing blow which would crush them for all time And if the Radicals did not move out of their own accord, then King, Turner, Craig and Lees were prepared—using their disguise as Radical leaders—to entice the more unwary Radicals into committing acts of violence that would incriminate them.

NINE

"LIBERTY OR DEATH!"

On Monday morning, April 3, 1820, the effect of the call for a "Liberty or Death" uprising could be seen across the whole of South-West Scotland. In obedience to the command of the "Provisional Government" almost all the labouring population had abandoned their work and where any remained, agents from the various local Radical Committees compelled them to stop. Even in Glasgow "this was done openly". From Stirling to Girvan, seventy miles from east to west, and from Dumbarton to Lanark, forty miles from north to south, all the weavers, mechanical manufacturing and labouring population became idle and the Radical Committees began to make preparations.

The anonymous author of *The Late Rebellion in the West of Scotland* observed:

The manufacture of arms was continued by night and by day with astonishing celerity and perseverance. Blacksmiths and carpenters shops in the neighbourhood were taken possession of by strangers, and those in the suburbs of the city were literally in a state of requisition, preparing weapons for the approaching combat; files were carried off wherever they could be got at to hammer into pikes; large quantities of lead had for some time previous been stolen from various houses, in order, it is supposed, to be cast into balls. Of these, great quantities were made, and most of their cartridges, since found, were double shotted. In a house in Anderston some cartridges were found with three balls. Pikes were openly sold at from 7d. to 1s. each, according to the quality, and any quantity of powder could be brought at 3d. per lb. Of fire arms they had a considerable number. Besides pikes and pistols they had made a great number of weapons called "clegs" of the nature of a dart, with a considerable weight of lead attached to the end, which could be thrown to a considerable distance with precision and effect. These were intended to annoy the cavalry from closed and narrow lanes or houses. Drilling in large bodies at all hours was open, extensive and undisguised. Parties to the amount of many hundreds drilled during the day time in the Green of Glasgow, at Dalmarnock Ford, at the Point House, at Tollcross, and many other places without interruption.

At dawn on Monday the regular garrison in Glasgow was standing to arms in their respective barracks. The 1st Battalion of the Rifle Brigade were stationed the Infantry Barracks in Gallowgate Street, which had been built in 1795 to house 1,200 men; the Cavalry Barracks in Eglington Street, built for 1,000 men and horses, held only a few troops of the 10th and 7th Hussars. Samuel Hunter's 1,000 strong Glasgow Regiment of Sharpshooters (the yeomanry corps) were paraded in St Enoch's Square with the 500 strong Armed Association (known to the Glaswegians as the "armed assassins"). In Vincent Street the Glasgow Yeomanry Squadron (Light Horse), commanded by Charles Stirling of Cadder and James Oswald of Shieldhall, stood to. The few artillery men with their eight pieces of flying artillery were stationed at vantage points on the bridges over the Clyde. A troop of the Glasgow Yeomanry Cavalry had been despatched to Hamilton the previous evening to escort the London Mail Coach safely to the city, as rumour had it that the signal for the insurrection was to be an attack on the coach. But towards 5 a.m. the coach and its escort arrived safely in the city. After standing to until well past breakfast time an order was given to the Glasgow Yeomanry "to disperse but to remain in half uniform to be ready at a moment's notice". A troop of the Yeomanry were kept on picket duty at the George Inn.

General Sir Thomas Bradford had already sent despatches to London explaining the situation and also a request to Woolwich Arsenal to send immediately by sea to Scotland 1,500 stand of arms, 10,000 flintlocks, and half a million ball cartridges. Colonel the Hon. Keith Elphinstone's 33rd Regiment and Lt.-Colonel Cookson's 80th Regiment, from Edinburgh Castle, were ordered to march immediately to Glasgow, and the main body of the 7th Hussars from Hamilton, and the 10th Hussars from Piershill Barracks were also ordered into the city. To replace these line troops all the Eastern Counties Yeomanry regiments were alerted and ordered to Edinburgh while the Upper and Middle Ward Cavalry assembled at Hamilton and Airdrie.

Samuel Hunter broke the news to the readers of the *Glasgow Herald* in his Monday's edition under the innocuous headline of "A Strike of Work in Glasgow". He began:

We are sorry to state that at no time since the beginning of Radicalism has there been such a general apprehension of danger as within these last ten days in Glasgow and its neighbourhood. It was supposed that the new fangled notions which dazzle some of our people had given way to the thinking sober mindedness of the Scotch character; but if appearances are to be trusted this conclusion has been too hastily withdrawn. There has lately prevailed a system of intimidation not formerly attempted; and many well disposed peaceable people in manufactories and work shops have been obliged to enter the lists of disaffected from terror of their lives.

The order to cease work "has been but too implicitly obeyed", Hunter commented. But it would seem that a number of Radicals doubted the authenticity of the proclamation of the "Provisional Government" for Hunter adds: "At first, those who are lukewarm in the cause of the Government, and who are ever ready to make apologies for the proceeding of the disaffected, pretended it was a Government trick, and quite unauthorised by the Radicals." Finishing his leader, Hunter wrote: "Half past Twelve O'Clock—The crowd is increasing in our streets, but all continues peaceable. We are obliged to go to Press."

Just after the paper had gone to press the Dunbartonshire Yeomanry Cavalry, commanded by Captain Dennistoun, arrived in the city, and a few hours later Major Ferrier Hamilton's two regiments of the Ayrshire Yeomanry arrived. Boswell had been up early that morning parading his men and had sent Major Crawford and his troops to Paisley, Ferrier Hamilton's men to Glasgow and Captain Montgomerie with three troops of the combined regiment were ordered to remain in Ayrshire "for the defence of the county". Boswell decided to ride to Glasgow with Ferrier Hamilton and the route took them through Kilmarnock and Stewarton. Kilmarnock seemed peaceful enough but at Stewarton a man shouted at Boswell as he rode down the street, "Haud up your heid, Soor-Milk Jock!" At this taunt, Boswell displayed his quick temper, which was to lead to his death in a duel just over a year later. Drawing his sword, he leapt from his horse and would have killed the man had he not had the sense to take to his heels.

Ferrier Hamilton's men arrived in the early evening and at the Black Bull Inn they received orders from James Douglas, the quartermaster, to proceed to billets in the Gallowgate. After a consultation with Bradford at the Star Hotel, Boswell and his escort returned to Ayr where rumour had it that the French were landing arms and money to aid the Radicals. The rumour of the return of Kinlock of Kinlock and Marshal MacDonald was still rife.

As the Ayrshire Yeomanry made their way to the Gallowgate, the hostility of the Glaswegians became apparent to the men. At Glasgow Cross a crowd barred their path but Andrew Watt of Tarbolton, "clapped his spurs to his horse, and the animal rearing, threw itself upon the mob, overturning a dozen of them, and effectively clearing the way". The soldiers had to duck as missiles were thrown at them and as they went down one street "a brickbat from a window landed in the holster of a member of the Kilmarnock troop, but before the donor had time to close the windows the recipient, John Boyd, returned the property with compound interest, and it may be said of the unfortunate Glaswegian, the subsequent proceedings interested him no more".

The anonymous Glasgow Yeomanry Sergeant (*Notes on Radicalism in the West of Scotland*) wrote that during the afternoon of Monday he was standing at a gate leading into Miller Street when a crowd of "perhaps 200" came up the street following a uniformed Yeomanry soldier, Thomas Graham, who was walking up the street with his father, Robert Graham, a local writer. The crowd were jeering and catcalling them and the sergeant, thinking "some rascal would induce the crowd to hostility", made to join them. As the Grahams reached the monument commemorating Sir John Moore the crowd began to throw missiles at them. At this moment three more Yeomanry soldiers, William Smith, William Brown and William Black appeared and tried to protect the Grahams, crying, "You are all a pack of cowards!" Stones were thrown and one struck Robert Graham who immediately turned and pointed to a man in the crowd shouting "Catch that fellow!" The Yeomanry sergeant recalled: "I immediately ran after him. Mr. Black had started [after him] from the other side of the street." The two men followed the fugitive until they came to a house owned by a Mr

Kelly in Virginia Street. Here, the fleeing man tripped and fell and his pursuers leaped upon him. They were joined by William Brown and the three men dragged their struggling prisoner to the police office. The Yeomanry sergeant comments: "The man, Charles Fitzpatrick, was sentenced to eighteen months' imprisonment. A punishment, in my opinion, inadequately severe for all he did." As the sergeant walked about the city observing the state of affairs, he recalled seeing parties of Radicals, sometimes ten to twelve strong and sometimes as many as 100 drilling but "these parties were but indifferently armed with few guns and pistols and a considerable number of pikes".

The Lord Provost, the Hon. Henry Monteith, and the Glasgow City magistrates had sat up all night preparing plans for the defence of the city should the insurgent army, whose strength and whereabouts were a source of puzzlement and speculation, attack. They had drafted a proclamation declaring a curfew in the city from 7 p.m. and this was posted in all parts of Glasgow and its environs.

In consequence of the present threatening appearances, the Lord Provost, Magistrates, Sheriffs and Justices, hereby order all shops to be shut this and every following night, until tranquillity is restored, at the hour of six; and hereby enjoin all the inhabitants of the city, to retire to their houses as soon as possible thereafter, and not later than seven o'clock.

All strangers are hereby enjoined to withdraw from the city before seven o'clock at night. Parties or groups of people standing together, or walking the street after the hour of seven, will be deemed disturbers of the peace and will be dealt with accordingly.

If the lamps are put out, the inhabitants are desired immediately to illuminate their windows with as much light as they can conveniently command. God Save The King. Glasgow, 3rd April, 1820.

During the afternoon, the Lord Advocate, Sir William Rae, and his staff—which included John Hope and the Sheriff Deputy, Robert Hamilton—arrived from Edinburgh. They took up residence in the Star Hotel and set to work immediately with police duties. Captain Mitchell and the Procurator Fiscal, Mr Salmond, sought the co-operation of William Reid of the *Glasgow Chronicle*, Robert Chapman, a printer, and James Haldane, an engraver, as typographical experts. They were asked to take a copy of the proclamation of the "Provisional Government" and check its type against the types of every printer in Glasgow in order to ascertain what press the proclamation had been produced on. They were told, in particular, to examine the press of William Lang of Bell Street, a known Radical who had offered to print a Radical Reform newspaper at the Meikleriggs' Muir Radical meeting the previous year. All day Monday the three men were engaged in their search and in the evening reported that Duncan MacKenzie's press at 20 Saltmarket had similar type to that used in the proclamation. Captain Mitchell dismissed the report and insisted that only Lang could have printed the proclamation. The three men assured Mitchell that such was not the case. Mitchell, of course, knew who the real culprit was and had known long before the proclamation was printed. It was clear that Lang was the man on which he wanted to "pin" the printing of the proclamation. The three experts remained firm and this placed Mitchell in a quandary. Perhaps he had not counted on the difference between printing types and had hoped that his "experts" would back him in the arrest of Lang. Ignoring the evidence, Mitchell had Lang arrested a week later but, after some insistence from the three men, and maybe a threat of public exposure, Lang was released and it was not until April 27 that Duncan MacKenzie was arrested and charged with "printing and publishing the treasonable address". He was kept in the Glasgow Tolbooth until May 3 and then released. His arrest was a mere formality and Fulton and Hutchison were given plenty of time to flee the country before a reward was offered for their arrest on April 29.

The only activity in Glasgow that Monday was a clash in Sauchiehall Street. The Government agent John Craig had managed to collect thirty men and march them to Sauchiehall Street, west of Anderston. Craig told these men, who were mainly armed with pikes, that they were to join an insurgent detachment which was to attack the Carron Iron Works. As they started off down the road, one of the pikemen, clumsy and not used to his unwieldy weapon, broke a lamp and the noise attracted a nearby police patrol. The Radicals fled in all directions and only Craig was caught by the policemen and taken to Anderston where he was examined by the local justice of the peace, Mr Houldsworth. Had it not been for the clumsy pikeman, Craig would have led the unsuspecting Radicals along the banks of the canal to the Port Dundas Toll where a full company of Hussars were waiting to intercept them "on information received". Craig—the spy—was leading them into a trap which could have led to their slaughter. To try to preserve Craig's "cover" as a genuine Radical, Houldsworth fined Craig 5s. but as Craig did not have the money on him the justice himself paid the fine. Robert Fulton commented afterwards: "Now it is very strange that a Justice of the Peace would become bail for a prisoner of this description . . ." Knowing that his position was now precarious, Craig disappeared and was never heard of again.

During the afternoon of Monday a large Radical contingent gathered on Sacel Hill, despite the large numbers of military in the area, and proceeded to practise military drill with two flags, one being the pre-Union Scottish flag and the other being a Radical banner, at their head. Later, on Monday night, the Gallowgate Iron Foundry was broken into and a considerable number of files were carried off. The manager had previously ordered the entire stock of rifles to be removed to a place of safety under the supervision of the military. A number of dyeworks were also broken into and poles were carried off to make pike shafts.

After the Ayrshire Yeomanry had passed through Stewarton some 60 Radicals gathered under the direction of the local shoemaker, William Orr, who had been elected Radical commandant of the area. The men paraded in military fashion and Orr, with drawn sword, read the proclamation of the "Provisional Government". The Stewarton Radicals, with Orr at their head, and John Crawford, a local weaver, beating time on a side drum, marched out of the village and spent some time practising military drill. Lt. Gardner, of Captain Montgomerie's command, was immediately despatched with a troop of Ayrshire Yeomanry to engage them but they dispersed before the military arrived. It was more or less the same story in the village of Balfron where some 200 armed Radicals paraded and waited for some time, presumably for a messenger from the "Provisional Government", but after a while, and hearing the military were converging on the village, the Balfron men dispersed.

Paisley was the main centre of the early insurgent activity that Monday. The Paisley men seemed to be well in advance of the rest of the country as it is reported that they had printed their own Provisional Government of Scotland bank notes to exchange for arms and ammunition and the local weavers had provided the entire Paisley Radical contingent with cartridge webs having weaved these on their own looms. At 10 a.m. the Paisley Radical Committee met in the "Smiddy", the weaver's shop in Maxwellton Street. According to the Radical Commissary General, John Parkhill, "the sun was shining in all his majesty" and the "Smiddy" was filled "with anxious patriots". Among these men, however, Parkhill observed a great many "who, I was sure, would never lift a pike in our favour". The first subject on the agenda was the question of obtaining arms and it was decided that the insurgents should conduct an arms raid in the Barony of Stanley that evening. The gun powder problem provided a debate and the Paisley area commandant, Daniel Bell, suggested that each man should secure $2\frac{1}{2}d$. worth of powder. At this, one old man, obviously disgusted by the entire proceedings, stood up and cried: "Behold! The British Government, the strongest on yerth, is to be over turned wi' five bawbees worth o' cheap poother!" The man was shouted down and the meeting broke up, agreeing that the insurgents should meet at the Brae of Maxwellton that evening.

Government troops were being rushed into Paisley all day as General Bradford felt that the town, which had been the centre of a near insurrection in the previous year, was a likely "powder keg". At 6 a.m. the 400 strong Royal Veteran Battalion arrived from Ayr having made a forced march of thirty-six miles in seventeen hours. One soldier had gone lame and fell behind as the Battalion approached the outskirts of Paisley. As soon as the column had marched out of sight, two men sprang from a hedge on the soldier and disarmed him. As soon as the soldier managed to rejoin the Battalion in Paisley and reported what had happened, the military threw a cordon round the Elderslie and Johnstone districts and conducted a house to house search. The soldier's musket was recovered but the culprits were not found. Later that morning the 120 strong Port Glasgow Armed Association, commanded by Colonel John Dunlop, arrived closely followed by the 80 strong

Kilbarchan Armed Association. At 5 p.m. two troops of the 1st Regiment of the Ayrshire Yeomanry, numbering 100 men, commanded by Major Crawford, arrived in the town to the taunts and jeers of the crowd. Many of the troops had expressed their uncertainty at being used against civilians but as they entered Paisley and found themselves attacked with all manner of missiles by the hostile population, their attitude changed. One trooper, who had previously expressed sympathy with the people, told his officer: "I'm no that man noo, for I've got a brick on the side of my head and anither on my shoulder, and ready to gie 'em twa for't." One man threw a cleg at the Yeomanry but was spotted by a sergeant who pursued the man down the narrow passages and across gardens before capturing him and dragging him to the jail. By late afternoon it was estimated, along with the hussars who had arrived the previous day, that there were nearly 1,000 troops in Paisley.

Despite this concentration of troops the rebel spirit of Paisley seemed unperturbed and the Provost of Paisley, Oliver Jamieson, decided to issue a proclamation ordering a curfew in the town.

Information having been recieved which renders it necessary to adopt immediate precautions for preventing and suppressing riot and disturbance in the town of Paisley and neighbourhood, and for bringing to justice the persons who may be concerned therein, the Lord Lieutenant and Magistracy deem it proper to issue the following orders (and in doing so they have to express their anxiety to prevent the sacrifice of innocent lives, while they declare their determination at all hazards to preserve the peace and maintain the authority of the laws):—1st. Upon the alarm bell being struck, all well disposed persons who are not called upon to aid the civil power will retire to their houses, and protect themselves and their property as best they can. 2nd. All persons not called upon as aforesaid shall keep to their houses after seven o'clock in the evening until further notice. 3rd. In case of tumult happening after dark, all well disposed persons will put lights in their upper windows, secure the lower, and retire to the back part of their lodging. 4th. It is earnestly enjoined that all well disposed people will avoid standing in closes, as these, in the event of disturbance will be cleared by military force, without distinction of persons. 5th. In case of injury being offered to the civil or military force from houses or otherwise, warning is hereby given that such injury will be retaliated

on the spot. 6th. Tavern keepers will be careful who they admit into their houses; and in case of tumult will allow no company to remain in their houses, unless such persons as they shall be accountable for; and no person whatever to be harboured by them after seven o'clock in the evening until further notice.
Paisley. 3rd April, 1820.

This was posted through the streets of the town but a great many of them were torn down immediately by the angry townspeople. While the printers were busy printing this official proclamation, one of the Paisley Radical Committee entered the printing shop and commanded the printers to desist printing the proclamation at their peril. He told them that he was an agent of the Provisional Government of Scotland and they must obey. An attempt was made to seize the man but he escaped into the crowds outside. *The Late Rebellion in the West of Scotland* says: "The proclamation of the Authorities in this city were everywhere torn down or defaced with open exultation and contempt; while, if any hand more daring than the rest pulled down the Radical address, it was immediately replaced with vengeance directed against the hand that tore it down."

At 9 p.m. the Paisley insurgents gathered at Maxwellton Hill to the south-west of the town. Led by Daniel Bell they visited the houses of Robert Rowan of Millarstone, George Muir, Craig's of Lownsdale and some houses in Ferguslie and West Toll. In all they collected four muskets and four fowling pieces. Bell then led his men to the houses of Alexander Robertson, the senior, near Machie's Mill, Thomas Robertson at Foxbar and Archibald Fulton at Liechland. These raids greatly improved their growing arsenal with a number of pistols as well as muskets and sporting pieces.

At 11 a.m. Bell and his men arrived at the house of Ross Robertson of Foxbar House and knocked on the door. Robertson, woken from his sleep, peered out of his bedroom window and saw, according to his statement, about forty armed men outside his house. He asked them what they wanted. A voice, presumably Bell's, replied that they were soldiers of the army of the Provisional Government of Scotland and they wanted arms and ammunition. Robertson refused saying he needed his guns to protect himself and family. He also "represented to them the illegality of their proceedings". Bell warned him that if he did not give up his arms voluntarily, they would have to take them by force. At this Robertson said he would go and get them a pistol which was all he had. However, Robertson woke his younger son Matthew and together they armed themselves with pistols, took up positions at the upper windows, and opened fire on the insurgents. Bell and his men immediately returned the fire.

A watchman from a nearby bleachfield saw the firing and ran to the house of Ross Robertson's eldest son, Alexander, whose house was not too great a distance away. Waking Alexander, the watchman cried that the Radicals "were out" and attacking his father's house. Arming himself, Alexander Robertson crept up in the rear of Bell's men and opened fire. Within a few minutes one of the insurgents fell dead. This was young Adam Cochrane, a Paisley weaver. According to Parkhill "it was singular circumstance that the shot which killed Cochrane passed through him and lodged in the elbow of a young lad named MacKechnie who was standing beside him". Parkhill and a number of the insurgents were for breaking into the house but at this moment one of the scouts, sent out by Bell to keep watch for the military, arrived and told Bell that a cavalry patrol was three minutes' ride from Foxbar. Bell and his men retreated leaving behind them the dead man. "This unhappy young man," commented the *Glasgow Herald*, "was the most determined of all Radicals, and was the more dangerous as he had been a soldier, he was fearless of danger and in the prime of his life."

The insurgents made their way back to the "Smiddy" where several of the Radical Committee were waiting for a report. They were under the impression, says Parkhill, that David Wylie, one of the more hot-headed of the Paisley Radicals, was the person who had been shot. Another insurgent "patrol" was still out commanded by John Dickie, who was secretary of the Paisley Radical Committee. They had gone to Pinnel Glen, a mile north of Kilbarchan, to make pikes; as the town was full of military it was impossible to carry out the task in a local blacksmith's shop and the glen was deserted. They carried iron, hammers, and other smithy tools and one man even carried an anvil and bellows. On their return, outside of Millarstone, they heard the sound of approaching cavalry and Dickie ordered a detour to the north, crossing Alt Patrick Burn, a little below Elderslie Bridge, and from there the insurgents made their way to Kilbarchan. When they arrived there the local Radicals refused to join them, and rather low in spirits, the Paisley men returned to the "Smiddy" to report their news. It was later revealed, by Rev. Dr Fleming in March, 1837, that the Kilbarchen Radicals and Neilston Radicals had been threatened with "eternal damnation" by the local clergy if they joined the insurgents.

On Tuesday morning the proclamation of the "Provisional Government" was still posted up all over Paisley and the authorities, now being reinforced with the military, decided it was high time to remove it. At one street corner, however, an officer attempting to remove the proclamation and replace it with the civil authorities' curfew notice, found it impossible because of the hostility of the crowd. He returned with a police officer, a corporal and four troopers, who were promptly pelted with stones. The soldiers, without preamble, opened fire on the crowd and several were wounded including one woman who was shot through the neck and died shortly afterwards.

Later that day the Paisley insurgents gathered openly at Foxbar nearby Ross Robertson's house, despite the fact that a large body of military were now based at the house. One hussar officer estimated the insurgents to number 300 to 400 strong. Messengers were sent to all the mills and factories with an order for them to be closed down immediately or else "the Provisional Government would not make up the loss or damage they might sustain by the ravages of the mob". Although the military, for some reason, did not attack this group, the insurgents eventually dispersed, it being "a rather stormy day, and the rain fell during the great portion of it", according to Parkhill. Another meeting was held in the "Smiddy" and there was talk of Glasgow being in arms but no messengers had arrived from the "Provisional Government" and there was little encouragement for the few hundred Paisley insurgents to act against the strong concentration of troops in the town. The Paisley commandant, Daniel Bell, suggested that they disband and wait for news.

The military and police, however, had already started to

move against the known Radicals and many leaders had narrow escapes. A warrant was issued for the arrest of John Dickie, the secretary of the Paisley Radical Committee, and a troop of military was sent to his house. Mrs Dickie saw them approaching and promptly seized all her husband's papers, thrust them into a kettle and put it on the fire. The soldiers entered but, after a search, could not find Dickie nor any incriminating evidence. After they had left Mrs Dickie burnt the papers and sent word to her husband to escape into the country and "lie low".

During the afternoon the Sheriff Deputy, William Motherwell, with soldiers and police raided Parkhill's house. Parkhill was still at the "Smiddy" and the soldiers contented themselves with ransacking the place but they found nothing. Motherwell, the poet-policeman, asked Mrs Parkhill if she had any pikes or guns hidden. She replied she had nothing but a very long spear. Motherwell, taken aback, demanded to see this and Mrs Parkhill replied it was her maiden name. Motherwell laughed and asked her what had become of her husband and she replied she did not know. Satisfied, the military left. When Parkhill returned a few hours later, his wife told him what had happened and they decided it would be best for Parkhill to go into the country and wait until "the troubles" were over. "For the time being," wrote Parkhill, "I had to sleep where best I could."

Throughout the week in Paisley raids and arrests followed each other. The military and the population were openly hostile to each other and bayonets were indiscriminately used on the crowds. On Friday, a troop of military actually charged with fixed bayonets at the head of Lady Lane and a large number received severe wounds. One old man named Campbell died from his wound shortly afterwards.

At dawn on Tuesday in Glasgow, the military again stood to in anticipation of the signal of an attack on the mail coach; but the mail arrived safely and many of the troops were dismissed. The main body of the 10th Hussars arrived with the 80th Regiment and it was estimated that the total military strength in Glasgow was now around 5,000 men. According to the Yeomanry sergeant "the crowd of idlers had greatly increased. Crowds were roaming the street with their hands in their pockets. Mills and factories had come to a standstill and it was thought that during the whole day in the neighbourhood large bodies were probably drilling." Hunter commented: "Many corps [insurgents] have been observed drilling in this neighbourhood several nights past and some of them even during the day. In some places strangers have taken possession of smiths' shops, who instantly fell to work in manufacturing pikes etc."

Sir William Rae decided that a proclamation offering a £300 reward for information leading to the arrest and conviction of those involved in printing the "Provisional Government" proclamation should be made. This was duly drafted and posted through the streets.

300 POUNDS REWARD

WHEREAS certain Wicked, Evil-disposed, and Traitorous Persons, during the night of the 1st, or on the morning of the 2nd of April instant, did *feloniously*, *traitorously*, and *daringly*, in furtherance of a *conspiracy* to compass or imagine the Death of Our Lord the King, *or to levy war against Our Lord the King* within His Realm, or to commit other Treasons, *publish* and *affix* on the walls and public places in many parts of the City and Suburbs of Glasgow, and other parts of the County of Lanark, a most *wicked*, *revolutionary* and *treasonable address* to the Inhabitants of Great Britain and Ireland dated at Glasgow, April 1, 1820, and bearing to be issued "by order of the Committee of Organisation for forming a Provisional Government" directly and openly *proclaiming* rebellion *against Our Lord the King and the laws and constitution of this realm*, inciting and stimulating the Subjects of Our Lord the King to take up arms for the overthrow of the Government and Constitution as by Law established, and to *levy war against Our Lord the King*, and further endeavouring to Seduce the Soldiers of Our Lord the King to desert their duty and to join in a threatened insurrection, and to intimidate and to overawe all loyal and peaceable Subjects by threats of violence and devastation. The LORD PROVOST and MAGISTRATES of the City of Glasgow, SHERIFF of the County of Lanark, and JUSTICES of the PEACE for the Lower Ward of Lanarkshire, hereby offer a

REWARD OF £300

To any Person or Persons who shall, within Fourteen Days from this date, DISCOVER AND APPREHEND, or cause to be DISCOVERED AND APPREHENDED those guilty of this OVERT ACT of HIGH TREASON, by printing, publishing, and issuing, the said Revolutionary and Treasonable Address, under the said Treasonable designation of the

Committee of Organisation for forming a Provisional Government. Glasgow, 4th April, 1820.

The issue of this proclamation offering a reward was immediately followed by another, and sterner, warning to the population to return to work "before the adoption of the final and decisive measures".

WE, THE LORD PROVOST and MAGISTRATES OF THE CITY OF GLASGOW, SHERIFF of the COUNTY OF LANARK and JUSTICES of the PEACE for the LOWER WARD of LANARKSHIRE, in the present state of the City and the County, wish earnestly and solemnly to make this call on the misguided people, who have been unwarily led into their present state of insubordination, to return to their duty before the adoption of the final and decisive measures which that conduct will render immediately necessary.

An Audacious Address has appeared, which involved the authors in the guilt of HIGH TREASON. It calls upon the people to take certain steps, in obedience to those who have issued it, and to effect their object. viz. REBELLION against the King and the LAWS of the LAND. That Address tries to seduce and withdraw from their work the honest and the industrious, and to intimidate the loyal and well disposed.

WE, THE LORD PROVOST, MAGISTRATES, SHERIFF and JUSTICES, deeply regret this Rebellious Address should have induced any of their fellow subjects to listen to the interested plans of its authors.

We, therefore, do hereby announce to all those who have been so far seduced or intimidated as to Strike Work, that they are thereby assisting in the Rebellious Plans alluded to in this Address:—that they are participators in the guilt and are exposing themselves to the certain punishment of High Treason.

We further deem it right to inform the misguided, that all those who, knowing the projects and designs of the authors of the aforesaid Address, do conceal from the Civil Authorities of the Country what they know respecting these Treasonable plans, are guilty of a heinous crime in the eye of the law, and are liable to severe punishment.

To the numbers of loyal, honest, and peaceable Subjects, whom the audacious threats and menaces of the evil disposed have led against their own inclination, to join in the present strike of work, we do now give the assurance of perfect protection which the great Military strength in this City secures. The disloyal and the seditious cannot carry their purposes or their threats of violence into effect. Every man who thinks must know that if the Military Force is exerted as circumstances may immediately and indispensably require, the consequences must be ruinous and fatal to all who resist. We wish earnestly to separate the innocent from the guilty; but longer continuances in the present State of insubordination makes all guilty and we cannot and will not longer delay the measures necessary for the punishment of the guilty.

We would particularly point out to all Proprietors of Public Works, Manufactories etc. that it is their indispensable duty by the allegiance which they owe their king to use all their exertions and influences with their Workmen to prevent them joining or continuing in the Strike of Work, and to prevent those dependent upon them assisting the purposes of the disloyal of the continuance of the present state of things.

To those who have lent and assisted themselves in prompting that state of things—who have struck Work, and have intimidated the peaceable and well disposed Workmen, and endeavouring by the crowds on the Public streets to create Alarm and Confusion, and to lead to Violence and Outrage, we speak a different language. We command and enjoin all persons, without delay, to return to their lawful occupations. The present Strike of Work is avowed to be for Treasonable purposes and the Crowds parading the streets know well the purposes of such Assemblages. We are determined to enforce this order which the Allegiance and Duty of every man requires him to obey. The contempt and violation of these orders can only be considered, in consequence, of the plans pointed out in the above mentioned Treasonable Address, as a resolution to aid and assist in Rebellion. The whole Military Power of the District will be employed in the most decisive manner to prevent the Laws of the Land being insulted and violated by an audacious display of numbers by the Disloyal. The consequences must be on the heads of those who have seduced and misled the Inhabitants but these consequences will be fatal to all who venture to oppose and resist the overwhelming Power at our disposal.

Glasgow, April 4, 1820.

GOD SAVE THE KING

The only "audacious display" that Tuesday was an attack on Glasgow Yeoman by a "discharged soldier" who attempted to seize the man's musket. The attacker was wounded in the head and dragged off to prison. Perhaps the most important event of the day was that a despatch rider was sent to Perth, where a troop of the 10th Hussars commanded by Lt. Ellis Hodgson were stationed, bearing orders for this troop to ride immediately to Stirling and hold themselves in readiness to ride to the Carron

Iron Works as an attack was expected there on Wednesday. The 80th Regiment, on their march to Glasgow, had already sent a troop of men to take up stations inside the works itself. This was done following a report by the Government agent, John King, to the effect that the Radicals would launch an attack on Carron the following day. King also informed the authorities that a Radical attack against Glasgow could also be expected on Wednesday. Orders were given for the troops to stand to arms all Tuesday night. All the agent provocateur, King, had to do was to organise two groups of Radicals, make them believe the rising had started, and persuade them to attack Carron and Glasgow itself.

The events of Tuesday were recalled in a statement by William Flanagan, a weaver of Dobbie's Loan, Glasgow, some years later, and this statement was corroborated by Robert Walker, a weaver of 76 Rottenrow, Glasgow. Flanagan and a Radical colleague, William Maltman, met King's assistant, Duncan Turner, at Glasgow Green on the Tuesday morning. Turner informed them that there was "news of a disastrous nature" from England. Leeds, Halifax and Huddersfield had refused to take part in an English rising, and Manchester was afraid to act. Only Carlisle had stopped work and were waiting to see what Glasgow would do. Turner assured the Radicals that "if we would strike the first blow, Manchester and Carlisle would begin also. If not, they could not, or durst not attempt any such thing." Turner asked Flanagan and Maltman to return to the Radical Committee and asked them if they would act. They were to return to the same spot with an answer at 4 p.m.

The Radical Committee was meeting at the corner of the High Churchyard, a place called The Alley. William Maltman reported on the meeting with Turner and a debate ensued; this resulted in half the Radical Committee, led by Maltman and John Watson, declaring they had been betrayed and withdrawing their support from the projected rising. The other half, however, elected Arthur Bryant as "delegate to the Provisional Government" in place of Maltman, and Flanagan was elected as a delegate for the Castle Street Radical Union. Flanagan and Bryant met Turner at 4 p.m. and reported that one half of the Glasgow Radicals were prepared to act. "Turner seemed highly pleased and informed us that the Select Committee (the

Provisional Government) had received news more favourable than in the morning." The country was rising and the Radicals in England were coming out in support of their provisional government.

He requested us to return and inform our Unions to hold themselves in readiness at a moment's warning:—to meet him that night at 8 o'clock opposite the Roman Catholic Chapel, Clyde Street, where we would have further information to communicate from the Select Committee.

Flanagan, Bryant and the remaining members of the Glasgow Radical Committee met Turner at the appointed spot and Turner proposed that they retire to a field near Port Eglington to escape the notice of the military patrols.

"The rain was falling in torrents. Turner then informed us that this time a blow was actually struck." The mail coach would not arrive in the morning and this was to be the signal. Turner wanted 100 men from the Glasgow Unions to accompany another 100 from Anderston "to go to Carron, to secure a large quantity of arms and ammunition and two pieces of cannon; that sufficient refreshment would be provided for them by the way and that they might rely they would not see a military man till they returned. He [Turner] then addressed every individual in turn, how many men he thought he could produce? When finding he could rely on about 100 volunteers, he told them to go and inform their Unions or those that would turn out to repair immediately to the Germiston Road where he would meet them and deliver orders."

Flanagan points out that Andrew Hardie, of the Castle Street Union, did not attend this meeting. Turner asked Flanagan if he knew where Dougald Smith, the Radical commandant of the area, could be found. Smith, he said, must lead the Glasgow volunteer column or else resign his commission to someone else. Flanagan went to the Barony Kirk where he informed the Unions, which he represented, of the situation and directed the volunteers to the Germiston Road. Then Flanagan went to Dougald Smith's house and found him in bed, not having been informed what was going on. Smith immediately arose, dressed and joined Flanagan in rounding up some of the Radicals. They called at the house of a Mr Anderson in the High Street and collected Mr Bryson, the Drygate delegate to the Radical Committee. As they were making their way to the Germiston Road they accidentally met with Andrew Hardie who demanded to know what was happening. On hearing what Flanagan had to say Hardie immediately announced he would join them.

At the appointed place they found Turner and the Radical party waiting for them. Turner asked Flanagan if he had found Smith and Flanagan introduced them. Shaking hands with Smith, Turner exclaimed: "Go forward and take command of your party." The party, however, consisted of only 60 Glasgow men and of the men from Anderston there was no sign. According to Flanagan there was a great deal of discontented muttering at this and Turner launched forward into an exposition of the Radical cause. The Provisional Government, he assured them, had positive information that there was an insurrection in England and in other parts of Scotland. The workmen at Carron had struck and would deliver to the Radicals two pieces of cannon and a large quantity of arms and ammunition. The Radicals would return through Kilsyth (the place Hodgson's hussars had been told to go to if the attack on Carron failed!) where they would raise the local Radicals and then continue to Glasgow. "Turner stated that there was no doubt whatever of our success."

Dougald Smith refused to take command saying that the party was far too small to attack the Carron Works. If the Anderston party did not come forward to reinforce the group he, Dougald Smith, would and could not lead the men. A violent argument broke out, some men agreeing with Smith while others said that once the party were on the march they would soon be joined by other insurgents. Turner said that he would lead them himself but he was part of the chain of communication with the Provisional Government and could not be spared.

Andrew Hardie then asked one of the men if he would go and when the man answered in the affirmative Hardie said, "Then so will I." After a while those who were willing to go stood on one side of the road while those who would not crossed to the other. Only thirty men followed Hardie.

Turner requested Hardie to take command of them [recalls Flanagan] and Turner likewise gave Hardie his instructions how to proceed. For I saw Turner take a card, or half a card, from his pocket and give it to Andrew Hardie saying that the other half was before them, and that on their arrival at Condorrat the person would produce their half, and the reading of the two would correspond, and that they were to confide in the person producing the card at Condorrat, as their conductor to Carron. Turner then addressed Hardie and said, I hope Hardie, you will act bravely if necessary. Being chagrined myself at the none arrival of the party from Anderston, that Turner had promised to bring forward, I returned to Glasgow with Dougald Smith and several others, leaving Germiston as far as I recollect about one o'clock in the morning.

This was the last appearance of Duncan Turner who, having despatched the Radicals on the path to imprisonment and death, disappeared like his colleague Craig. In the meantime King, the chief of the four Government agents, had already set off for Condorrat bearing with him the corresponding half of the card which Turner had given to Hardie. To make sure a group of Radicals would appear to attack Glasgow, King had directed the fourth agent Robert or Thomas Lees to send James Shields, an "honest but unsuspecting" Paisley weaver, to raise the Strathaven Radicals. Lees gave Shields "credentials" from the "Provisional Government" to show Robert Hamilton at Strathaven. Shields was to inform Hamilton that Kinloch of Kinloch was now camped with 5,000 men on Cathkin and a strong division was also mustering on Campsie; these would launch an attack on Glasgow from the north at dawn on Wednesday. The Strathaven Radicals were to march up from the south to join the Cathkin division. Lees then organised a meeting of Radicals at Clydebank, near Anderston, on the following morning and tried to get them to march on Kirkintilloch but his proposal was met with scepticism. Lees, "the man with the English accent", realised that he had now become suspect and he also disappeared as completely as Craig and Turner had done; only King was now left to accomplish his task of setting a trap for the Radicals. The traps set by the four Government agents were clever ones and it looked as though the Radicals would fall for them hook, line and sinker.

TEN

THE BATTLE OF BONNYMUIR

At 5 a.m. on Wednesday, April 5, Andrew Hardie with his twenty-five men arrived at Robert Baird's house in Condorrat where he found a man calling himself "John Andrews" waiting for him. Hardie showed "Andrews" the piece of card given him by Duncan Turner and "Andrews" immediately supplied a corresponding piece of card. "Andrews" then introduced Hardie to Robert Baird's brother—30-year-old John Baird who, said "Andrews", would command the expedition against the Carron Iron Works. Baird, a Condorrat weaver, had served seven years in the 95th Regiment of Foot which, at the time of Waterloo, became known as the Rifle Brigade and was, in fact, one of the regiments opposing the Radicals in Glasgow. Hardie and Baird took an immediate liking to one another.

Baird's brother, Robert, however, was sullen and suspicious of the whole proceedings. It had been 11 p.m. the previous night when he, his wife, and John Baird, who had lodged with them since his discharge from the army after Waterloo, had been woken up by the sound of knocking. Their first thought had been that it was a military raid as John was a well-known Radical leader in Condorrat. When Mrs Baird had opened the door a man stood there in the driving rain and introduced himself as "John Andrews", a messenger from the Provisional Government. "John Andrews" was later identified as the Government agent John King. "Andrews", or rather King, asked to see John Baird and, in the cottage kitchen, showed the Bairds his credentials. Robert Baird afterwards recalled that he presented a piece of paper headed "Provisional Government for Scotland in Glasgow" and this was signed with the names of John Cowie, James Murray and someone called Pattison. John Baird accepted King's document as *bona fide* and asked him what he wanted. In the meantime Mrs Baird kindled up the dying fire in order that King might dry out his clothes and then bustled around making refreshment for him. King explained that a troop of Glasgow Radicals would be arriving in Condorrat in the morning en route to attack the Carron Iron Works. He added that the workers at the Carron munition factory had gone on strike and were going to deliver to the Radical forces a large quantity of arms and ammunition plus two pieces of cannon. These arms were to be escorted back to Glasgow via Kilsyth and delivered to the Radical leader George Kinloch of Kinloch who was even now preparing to launch an attack on Glasgow from Cathkin Braes. King said he had come, on behalf of the Provisional Government, to ask Baird to raise the Condorrat Radicals in order to reinforce the Glasgow men. Baird immediately agreed and laughed off his brother's objections to the venture. The Bairds let King sleep in John's bed while he went out into the stormy night to rouse the Condorrat Radicals. Only ten of them, however, arrived at the Baird's cottage before dawn the next day.

The combined forces of Baird and Hardie's men only amounted to thirty-five men. Robert Baird was openly against his brother continuing the venture and told the men they were fools to think they could seize Carron with such a pitifully small army. King, however, said that they would soon be joined by men from Anderston, Camelon and Falkirk. Baird suggested that the Radicals stay in Condorrat until they were reinforced. King opposed this proposition saying that if the party moved on it would give heart to the men from Falkirk to join them. He, as representative of the Provisional Government, would go on in advance of the Radicals and raise new recruits. This was agreed to and John Kean of Glasgow was elected to go as King's escort.

With Baird as the commander of the Radicals and Hardie as the second-in-command, the group left the village of Condorrat —according to one early riser in the village—"in good military order". This villager, letting his imagination run riot, later told the *Glasgow Herald* that the insurgents had occupied the Condorrat blacksmith's shop all night, barricading the windows with sods of turf to drown the noise from passing military patrols, while they made arms, pikes and ball cartridges.

At 6 a.m. the party halted at a tavern at Castlecary Bridge

where Baird ordered a breakfast of porter and a dozen two-penny loaves from the innkeeper, Archibald Buchanan. The bill came to 8s. Later, at the trial, the Lord Advocate, Sir William Rae, claimed that Baird had tried to give Buchanan a bill which, he said, would be redeemed by the Provisional Government for Scotland in six months' time. Buchanan did not support this and said Baird had paid 7s. 6d. out of his own pocket for the refreshments and asked for a receipt which Buchanan had written at Baird's dictation.

The party called, and paid for porter and bread, 7s. 6d. by cash. (signed) Archd. Buchanan.

It is probable that Baird asked for the receipt in the belief that the bill would be repaid by the Provisional Government. The Radicals were not in the inn more than half an hour and Buchanan, an interested spectator, watched them marching off down the road to Falkirk from his window.

Not far from the inn Baird decided to split the party into two groups, one taking the route by road and the other a route along the Glasgow–Edinburgh Canal. Baird had suggested this "less they should miss any of their friends coming to join them". Hardie took charge of the party going along the turnpike road, and decided to call at the toll-keeper's house and a few other houses on the outskirts of Castlecary in order to bolster the Radicals' meagre supply of armaments. James Russell of Long-croft, Denny, was in the kitchen of his house at about 7 a.m. when his children suddenly cried from the door that armed men were coming. Hardie's men entered his house and told him they were requisitioning arms and ammunition. Russell said it was unlawful for them to take his guns . . . the Radicals had taken two muskets hanging on the kitchen wall and a quantity of ammunition. Hardie answered by giving the man a receipt signed on behalf of the Provisional Government.

On the outskirts of the village the party met a traveller on horseback going to Glasgow. The Radicals stopped him and Hardie said that if the man would take their advice he would not go there because "a revolution was taking place in Glasgow". They then let the bewildered man continue his journey. This traveller rode a mile down the road where he met a mounted trooper of the Kilsyth Troop of Stirlingshire Yeomanry,

Private Nicol Hugh Baird, an engineer from Kelvinhead. The traveller, an Englishman, asked Private Baird if he knew what the news was from Glasgow and told him of his encounter on the road. Private Baird was visibly shocked and without answering the traveller's question, turned his horse and spurred it towards Kilsyth. The traveller, even more bewildered, turned his horse and rode back down the road, passing Hardie's marching men. As he passed Hardie he called out that he was following his advice and returning to Stirling. This Englishman returned "to the safer side of the Border" a day or two after this encounter. It was not until twelve years later that the historian, Peter MacKenzie, tracked him down and wrote his account of the affair. Had this man given evidence at the subsequent trial he would have been able to prove that Nicol Baird perjured himself at the trial and swore Hardie's life away on a completely fabricated account of an encounter between Hardie and himself.

Hardie's men continued marching down the Falkirk road when they suddenly encountered another rider on horseback . . . a sergeant of the 10th Hussar regiment. The hussar, Sergeant Thomas Cook, pulled up uncertainly at the sight of the band of armed men. Hardie stepped forward and asked him where he was going. Cook told him that he was on his way to Kilsyth with despatches. Hardie then demanded that the hussar hand over his arms, ammunition and despatches. The hussar replied that he had no ammunition and asked, rather apprehensively, what they were doing. Hardie said that they were seeking their rights and would do Cook no injury. Cook assured them that he was sympathetic to their cause. One of Hardie's men stepped forward and gave the hussar a copy of the proclamation and Hardie told the man he could go. Cook rode post haste to Kilsyth and made his way to the inn where a troop of the 10th Hussars, commanded by Lt. Ellis Hodgson, were resting after a forced march from Perth. Hodgson was in the inn talking to Lt. John James Davidson, a Tory lawyer from South Castle Street, Edinburgh, who was in command of the Kilsyth Troop of Stirlingshire Yeomanry. A few minutes before, Nicol Baird had finished gasping out his incredible tale of how he had encountered a large body of armed insurgents on the road who had fired at him and how he, single-handed, had attacked them, drove them off, and raced back to Kilsyth to report to Lt.

Davidson. The officers were discussing what should be done when they heard the clatter of Cook's horse in the cobbled courtyard. Hodgson leant out of the window and demanded what was wrong. The red-faced sergeant gave him a report and handed him the proclamation. Hodgson gave it a brief glance and returned it to Cook. He knew its contents already as he had seen it the day before at Stirling. He gave immediate orders for his men to mount up and pursue the insurgents.

His men, weary and cursing, obeyed. They had been riding for the past twelve hours. The day before a despatch rider had arrived in Perth from Glasgow. He had brought an order from Lt.-Colonel Taylor, who was in temporary command of the 10th owing to the illness of Sir George Quenton, to the effect that Hodgson's troop, which had been stationed in Perth on a semi-permanent basis, were to ride to Stirling immediately and hold themselves in readiness to ride to the Carron Iron Works. The order had been made following the Government agent King's report that the Radicals would attack the Carron Works on Wednesday. In fact, a troop of the 80th Regiment of Foot were already installed in the Carron Works itself and were standing ready to repulse any attempt to seize the munitions factory. This was revealed by a manager at Carron some years afterwards.

Hodgson mounted sixteen hussars on horses borrowed from the Yeomanry, as their own mounts were blown after the hard ride from Perth, and Davidson mounted a similar number of Yeomanry Cavalry and the troops set off in the direction of Falkirk and Carron in which direction Hardie's men were last seen going.

William Grindlay of Bonnymill, on the outskirts of Bonny-bridge village, saw the Radicals marching down the road towards Falkirk at about 9 a.m. From Grindley's house one enterprising Radical requisitioned a pitchfork. A mile and a half beyond Bonnybridge Hardie and Baird rejoined forces. Here they were also rejoined by King who appeared without John Kean, the Radical elected to accompany this "representative of the Provisional Government". King made an excuse that he and Kean had parted from one another while hiding from military patrols. Kean was never seen again and it is still a matter of conjecture what became of this young Glasgow weaver. King told Baird and Hardie that he had been to Camelon and that the Radicals from there would join them shortly. He advised Baird to take the men off the main highway for safety. He thought it would be wise to march the men on to the bleak waste of Bonnymuir. King would then go down to Camelon and conduct the reinforcements back to the rendezvous on the moor. Baird agreed and marched his men a mile on to the moor and sat them down to rest on a hill top. From the top of the moor, in fine weather, the insurgents could have seen the Firth of Forth, Abbey Craig, the Grampian Hills and Stirling Castle in the distance.

Now Lt. Hodgson and his men, riding towards Falkirk, would have gone straight along the highway without touching the moor. But at or near the village of Bonnybridge Hodgson was told that the insurgents were on the moor and was given directions as to where they could be found. Moreover, he was told that the insurgents were led by a man named Baird. Who gave Hodgson this information? Hodgson did not reveal the source of his information at the subsequent trial, nor did the court pursue the matter. Neither, unfortunately, did the defence. The reason has since been obvious. There was only one person who knew where the insurgents were and the name of their leader. The informant was none other than King, who, instead of going to Camelon to escort the Radical reinforcements to the place, was making haste to Kilsyth to inform the authorities. After informing the military King, alias "Andrews", disappears from history. One can only wonder at the reward which Sidmouth's government paid him for his efforts. Was he, like Richmond, offered lands and letters of introduction to important personages in one of the colonies? Or did he decide to "chance his hand" and settle for a sum of money, changing his name once more, to live on in the guise of an honest weaver somewhere in Scotland or England?

The insurgents had been resting on a hill for about an hour when one of them spotted the column of cavalry in the distance coming directly towards their position. Baird weighed up the situation—a group of half fed, ill-armed weavers, against a troop of well-equipped, battle-hardened cavalry. He made his decision, remembering the words of the proclamation—"Liberty or Death!" Both Baird and Hardie were ex-soldiers and the two conferred quickly as to what should be done to hold their position against the oncoming cavalry. Hardie favoured forming a square but Baird decided to place his men in a position a few yards down the hill, where, from the angle at which the cavalry were approaching, their front would be covered by a five foot high dyke.

Writing in his cell in Stirling Castle, a few days before his execution, Hardie recalled:

We then immediately ran down the hill cheering, and took up our position. There was a slap [gap] in the dyke which we filled with pikemen. The cavalry took a circular course through the moor and came under the cover of a wood at our right flank. As soon as they made their appearance past the end of the wood, firing commenced immediately. I cannot say who commenced firing first. I think the cavalry had fired a shot or two before they came to the wood with the intention probably to frighten us, for they afterwards told us they did not expect us to face them.

Lt. Hodgson rode up within earshot and shouted to the insurgents: "Lay down your arms!" Baird and his men answered with a ragged volley. The hussars and Yeomanry retired a little distance to observe the situation and then Hodgson, raising his sabre, cried "Charge!" He led his men for the gap in the dyke but the fire of the insurgents repulsed them. Then one hussar charged the gap on his own. The insurgents, not used to rapid loading, were mostly relying upon their pikes to repel further attacks. As the hussar reached the gap an insurgent made a stab at him and the hussar fired back. The man fell forward on his face. Hodgson now led a second attack on the gap while the Yeomanry kept up a fire to keep the insurgents down. Again Baird's men managed to fend off the attackers. Hodgson again called to them to surrender and one man threw down his musket and fled into the nearby wood. Hodgson again charged, this time straight at the dyke itself, and his horse managed to clear the dyke landing Hodgson in the midst of the insurgents. At the same time Hodgson's men managed to breach the gap in the dyke.

Mr Baird [wrote Hardie] defended himself in a most gallant manner; after discharging his piece he presented it at the officer [Hodgson] empty, and told him he would do for him if he did not stand off.

The officer presented his pistol at him, but it flashed and did not go off. Mr Baird then took the butt end of his piece and struck a private on the left thigh, where upon the sergeant of hussars [Sergeant Saxelby] fired at him. Mr Baird then threw his musket from him and seized a pike, and while the sergeant was in the act of drawing his sword, wounded him in the right arm and side.

Another insurgent jabbed his pike at Hodgson but missed him and the weapon entered his horse's thigh, went into the beast's bowels and the animal later died. Hodgson received a wound in the right hand. Again Hodgson ordered the insurgents to surrender and Baird, seeing the futility of a prolonged struggle, cried: "Treat!" But Hodgson demanded an unconditional surrender and would not treat with Baird. Baird finally agreed to surrender. But, although Hodgson, a strict disciplinarian, "would not allow one of his men to do us any harm, and actually kept off with his own sword some of the strokes that were aimed at us", the general conduct of these soldiers, after the insurgents had surrendered, was far from exemplary. The Yeomanry troops under Davidson seemed particularly cruel in their treatment of prisoners.

Some of them were wounded in a most shocking manner, and it is truly unbecoming the character of a soldier to wound, or try and kill any man whom he has it in his power to take prisoner, and when they had no arms to make any defence [wrote Hardie]. One of the yeomanry was so inhuman, after he had sabred one of the men, sufficient he thought to deprive him of life, as to try and trample him under his horse's feet; but here, my friends, the horse had more humanity than his master, and would not do as he wished him, but jumped over him, in place of trampling upon his wounded and mangled body; and after he (the yeoman) returned from doing so, he called out (speaking very broad) "that he had left him lying wi' his head cloven like a pot".

The man who was cut down was a man called Alexander Hart, a cabinet-maker from Glasgow, who managed to recover from the wound. A young lad, not yet 15, called Alexander Johnston, a Glasgow weaver, ran off into the morass firing his pistol at the soldiers as fast as he could load. The Yeomanry would have cut him down had not Hodgson shouted to them to take him alive. Two more insurgents ran to a nearby loch but were quickly overtaken and caught by the cavalry troopers.

Another of Baird's men was found wounded, trying to bury his pistol and ammunition in the heather.

Another of the party, a Glasgow printer named Black, also fled from the field but was overtaken by a hussar. Instead of cutting down the fugitive, the hussar merely knocked the pike out of Black's hands and told him to make off quickly. Black had not gone far, however, when three of the Yeomanry overtook him and one of them cried: "Cut the Radical bastard down!" The foremost one swung his sabre and wounded Black dangerously about the head and shoulders, then, thinking Black was dead, the three rode off. Fortunately, the whole of the Bonnymuir affray had been witnessed by a farmer, Alexander Robertson, who ran the Damhead farm whose fields lay close by the moor. Robertson had been tending his fields when the skirmish started and wandering round the battle site afterwards, Robertson found Black and managed to drag him back to his farm where he put him to bed and dressed his wounds. A doctor was called and managed to make Black more comfortable. Robertson and the doctor seem to have been Radical sympathisers. A short while later soldiers, searching the area for Radical fugitives, came to the farmhouse. Someone had informed them that the wounded insurgent had been brought there. However, the doctor told them that he could not give them permission to remove the wounded man as he was in a critical condition. The soldiers said they would return the following day when Black was well enough to travel. That night, having received a message from Robertson, Black's uncle, Allan MacClymont, a Larbert weaver, and his son, James MacClymont, came to the farmhouse at midnight. In case the farmhouse was under observation Black, wearing Robertson's blue bonnet as a disguise, escaped through the back window, and was taken to the MacClymont's house at Larbert. Robertson said, at the trial, that he had no knowledge of the affair and that Black had escaped while he had been asleep.

Soon after the escape, however, news of it was given to the Laird of Carnoch who raced to Larbert with a Yeomanry company . . . too late. Black had fled again. MacClymont's house was ransacked by the company of Yeomanry. At that time an apprentice lad named Craig was lying sick in MacClymont's garret with his head bandaged and, at first sight, the Yeomanry took him for the fugitive and beat him severely. But the mistake was soon discovered and Carnoch made the family take an oath that they knew nothing of Black's whereabouts. Carnoch and his Yeomanry then rode on to Camelon where they arrested three local Radical leaders . . . John MacMillan, a nailer, a man called Dawson and a man called MacIntyre. But Black, after lying low for several days, managed to flee the country to safety.

At Bonnymuir, eighteen of the Radicals had been rounded up by the hussars and Yeomanry. A hussar was despatched to Bonnybridge to requisition transport for the wounded to take them to Stirling Castle. He returned with a man from Denny who offered to loan the military his cart and horses as transport. The man afterwards received a threatening letter from Radical sympathisers. The insurgents were then pushed into the cart.

Mr Baird and I [wrote Hardie] assisted one of the wounded men until we got a cart, and they were put into it; one of them was dreadfully wounded in the head, I think in four places, and shot through the arm. Another old man with a frightful looking wound in his face, so much so that his jawbone was seen perfectly distinct; and a third had a sabre wound in his head, and had been left on the field for dead. . . .

Hardie also comments: "The officer of the hussars asked who was our Captain and if his name was Baird." Such information could only have been given by the agent King and Hardie says: "which made it evident that some person who knew him had given them information". It was not until after their trial that Baird and Hardie began to suspect that King was not what he claimed to be. The wounded prisoners were in such a poor way that Hardie asked Lt. Davidson (as Hodgson had gone to Bonnybridge to get a fresh horse) if water could be given them. The Yeomanry officer refused. Hodgson, in fact, stopped a short while at the inn in Bonnybridge where, having taken back the copy of the proclamation from Cook, he wrote his report of the affair on the back of it, listing the weapons and descriptions of the prisoners taken. When Lt. Hodgson overtook the prisoners on their way to Stirling, Hardie again asked for water for the wounded and Hodgson immediately complied with the Radical's request much to the disapproval of Davidson.

The weapons of the insurgents were also gathered up and on arrival at Stirling Castle these were given to the armourer, James Murray, and the ordnance storekeeper, John Bensom. They consisted of five muskets, two pistols and eighteen pikes with a hundred rounds of ball cartridge. These were placed in two chests and sealed, and put in a room below the staircase of the Castle's ordnance store.

When the prisoners arrived at Stirling they were placed in the charge of Stirling Castle's Fort-Major W. Peddie. When the formalities had been completed, John Baird stepped from amongst the prisoners and addressed Peddie. "Sir, if there is to be any severity exercised towards us, let it be on me. I am their leader, and have caused them being here. I hope that I alone may suffer." Then, looking at the wounded, he added: "They have not had much to eat since they left Glasgow. I beg you will be kind enough to order food for them." Peddie wrote later: "Throughout, he [Baird] never shrunk from the position he then assumed."

Hardie wrote: "After we arrived at Stirling we were all put into one room, and being uncommon tired it was not long before most of us buried all our cares in a sound sleep, having previously obtained some bread and water." But Baird "was taken away from us shortly after and put into a dungeon, and had about four or five stones of iron put on him".

As the Radical prisoners were being escorted to Stirling, Captain Nicholson and a troop of Stirlingshire Yeomanry, scoured the countryside around Bonnymuir for fleeing insurgents. The people in the villages, hearing of the skirmish, were clearly hostile to the Yeomanry and as Nicholson's men entered Falkirk they were greeted with hisses and yells and stones were thrown. Nicholson ordered his men to form a line across the road and, standing up in his stirrups, he called to the crowd that their vaunted Radical army had been defeated. "My friends, you may probably despise the Yeomanry, but now that our country has assumed a warlike attitude we are perfectly ready, like honest men and determined patriots, to stand by the Government and civil institutions of our common country...." He then told them that the Yeomanry were protecting them and they had been misled. Pointing to the line of grim-faced cavalry behind him, he told them that if they did not quietly disperse to their homes he would give the order for the cavalry to charge and clear the streets. Sullen and silently the crowd then dispersed.

When the news of Bonnymuir, in a very exaggerated form, reached Glasgow (Edinburgh newspapers had stated the number of insurgents to be over 100), there was great excitement and the church bells were rung as if another Waterloo had been won. Public meetings were afterwards held by merchants and manufacturers and resolutions adopted congratulating the Government on their success. An account was given to Major-General Bradford at the Star Hotel and he immediately sent an express despatch to the Home Secretary, Lord Sidmouth. Bradford then issued, in his General Orders of the day, a highly colourful account of the affray:

GENERAL ORDERS

Glasgow, April 6, 1820

Two orderlies having been intercepted by a band of armed men between Kilsyth and Stirling, on the morning of the 5th of April, Lieutenant Hodgson, 10th Hussars, and Lieutenant Davidson, of the Kilsyth Troop of Yeomanry, with an equal number of men from each corps, by a rapid and judicious movement of nine miles from Kilsyth, came up with the offenders, and after receiving their fire, cut them down and secured the whole of them, consisting of nineteen armed men.

Sir Thomas Bradford requests Lieuts. Hodgson and Davidson, and the non-commissioned officers and privates employed, will accept his best thanks for the zealous promptitude with which they discharged their duty on this occasion.

The General cannot but notice, as a circumstance highly creditably to the zeal of the Kilsyth troop, that the hussars were mounted for the occasion, on horses lent them by the yeomanry, in consequence of their own having made a forced march—and he will take care that the owner of the horse upon which Lieutenant Hodgson rode, and which was killed, shall be indemnified for his loss.

(signed) James Douglas
D.Q.M.G.

The despatch rider from Major-General Bradford reached London with the news on Friday. With great delight Lord Sidmouth personally took the news of the "defeat of the Radical army" to King George IV at Carlton House. A special edition

of the *London Gazette* was then published giving a lurid account
of Bonnymuir and saying that the treasonable Provisional
Government for Scotland, raising its "Hydra-head" in Glasgow, had been completely and utterly defeated. Sidmouth felt
that an announcement of the Government's victory over the
insurgents should be made in the *London Gazette* to deter any
"of the king's foreign enemies" from coming to the aid of the
Scots. He remembered only too well the landing of a French
army in Wales in 1797 and the two French expeditions which
had been sent over to aid the Irish republicans in 1798. His spies
had kept him informed to the activities of the Scots who had
also sought aid from France to set up an independent Scottish
government. He wanted any European government interested
in aiding the Scots to see that such a policy was futile. Lord
Sidmouth lost no time in sending a letter, through his friend the
Duke of Montrose, thanking the Stirlingshire Yeomanry for
their conduct at the "Battle of Bonnymuir".

ELEVEN

THE RISING AT STRATHAVEN

THE CARRON IRON WORKS "raid", culminating in the "battle" of Bonnymuir, had gone according to King's plan. Only the Radical attack on Glasgow, which King had informed the authorities would take place on Wednesday morning, had yet to materialise. It was not until late on Wednesday afternoon that the unsuspecting Shields dutifully set off with his "credentials" from the Provisional Government, on the order of the agent Lees, to raise the Strathaven Radicals, fully believing that a massed Radical attack on Glasgow was imminent. In the meantime, Lees, "the man with the English accent", fearing that the Glasgow Radicals were now suspicious of him and feeling he had done "all he could", disappeared.

In accordance with the information that King had given them, the military stood to arms in Glasgow all day and, in the early evening, only the Yeomanry were dismissed. The Yeomanry sergeant recalls:

Fatigued with the military duties of the day I was returning to bed at nine o'clock anticipating a comfortable night's sleep, when I heard the assembly sounded again. I immediately redressed and felt assured that soon our service would not long be maintained. The night was dreadfully wet and when I came to the rendezvous in George Square, I found seven of the corps posted there to direct those who came to St. George's Church. This was made our headquarters for the night during the whole of which we waited with impatience till we should be called to do the State some service. When I begged to inquire the music of our alarm I was told that the Radicals had commenced operations in Bridgeton—that they had fifes and drums and were forcibly making people join them, who were inclined to remain at home, the number mentioned I don't recollect but it is probably it was stated at many thousands. The truth, I believe to be nearly as follows—about 300 men, armed in various ways and headed by a drummer, did actually parade for an hour. Finding themselves altogether neglected by the unarmed population and probably getting notice of the sounding of the bugle, they vanished more quickly than they appeared.

The sergeant was disgusted that troops were not immediately sent to Bridgeton to engage the Radicals. Reports and alarms continued most of the night and kept patrols busy in the streets "but no mark of disturbance was noted". About 2 a.m. the sergeant's company were ordered to support a Rifle Brigade company in searching the area but nothing happened except they surprised a man "who ran off up the street". At 1 a.m. a man entered St. George's Church, saying he had been stopped by Radicals near Anderston, at the canal, "but he gave such confusing statements that we could make nothing of his information. He was either a spy or backward and in great agitation . . ."

We were dismissed about five o'clock in the morning to be ready as usual [says the sergeant]. As I was going home I met my friend "T" of the Yeomanry Cavalry who proposed a walk rather than going to bed which we accordingly agreed to, and we went to his father's country house. We were informed that great numbers of people had passed that place for town the preceding days, apparently under arms and even ignorant of what was to be done, still the power of the [Radical] delegates had been sufficient to induce them to quit work and be ready to march had the circumstances been favourable to the endeavour.

The report of a Radical force at Bridgeton had been a true one. In fact conservative reports put the number gathered in the suburbs of Bridgeton and Calton on Wednesday night, at between 400 and 600 armed men. Muskets, pikes and pistol were clearly displayed and a colour party bearing the Saltire flag and a Radical banner, which one observer claimed he had seen at a meeting at Clayknowes on November 1 the previous year, marked the rallying point. A group of these men, with drum and flag, marched to Rutherglen and stood in the village centre with the drum beating to arms while a Radical leader called the villagers to come forward "in the glorious cause". Armed men collected more recruits and two more flags at Dalmarnock and a bugle called the Tradestown Radicals to arms.

The author of *The Late Rebellion in the West of Scotland* recalls:

The Radicals, finding the military prepared at every point, and their own numbers few in comparison of what they expected, abandoned their plan in despair, threw away, or hid, their arms in every corner, and dispersed in every direction; many of their pikes were picked up next morning, strewed about the suburbs and the country; but numbers unscrewed the head, put them in their bosoms, and threw away the shafts; a considerable number were thrown into the canal and river, then considerably swollen; a large quantity of ammunition was found; some ball cartridges were picked up in secret corners, where they had been thrown by the Radicals.

It was reported that a man, who sounds remarkably like Lees, had gone to Tollcross and reported that Government troops had been defeated by a Radical army at Bonnymuir.

At Tollcross, upon hearing this, men, women and children seized arms and weapons of any description that they could lay their hands upon, and marched forth prepared to go wherever fortune called them, and to assail whatever might oppose them. The delusion, however, soon vanished, as the truth became known, and chagrin and dejection took place of their former confidence and exultation.

Elsewhere in Scotland, the Radical activity seemed to be dying down. In Johnstone, near Paisley, "many of the Radicals met on the school green", says the village schoolmaster, John Fraser.

. . . and marched, led by Speirs, to two or three mills to stop them. By afternoon the news of no attempt at rising, as was expected, reached them, and a sense of betrayal and failure spread like lightning. The military, infantry and cavalry, marched and rode in every direction, and a great many leading Radicals fled that night, as the two men named [James Speirs and Duncan MacIntyre] did. In every town many apprehensions were made. Universal fear and consternation existed for many days, even weeks.

Lord Elcho, the 25-year-old heir to the Earl of Wemyss and March, of Longniddry, East Lothian, with troops of the Midlothian Cavalry arrived in Glasgow to reinforce the garrison and the Royal Edinburgh Volunteers and the county Yeomanry were ordered to prepare for a forced march to Glasgow in expectation of the massed Radical attack. Apart from Bonnymuir, the only skirmish that took place that Wednesday was when an attack was made on troops of the Ayrshire Yeomanry with "clegs" but no one was hurt and the assailants disappeared.

At Broomielaw, Radicals went on board the steam ships and ordered the sailors to stop work "which was complied with, and all this was done before hundreds, and still the perpetrators escaped". The Sheriff of Glasgow, and a party of military, found a large Radical arms dump along the banks of the Grand Canal, near Port Dundas. During the night a Radical arms raid was made in New Cathcart where twelve men armed with pikes and pistols took arms from several houses including two taverns.

In the early hours of Thursday morning, the Dumbarton authorities were told that the Duntocher Radicals were planning to march on the town and seize Dumbarton Castle in the Radical cause. At dawn, troops of the Dunbartonshire Fencibles surrounded Duntocher and eight local Radical leaders were seized in their beds. These included Robert and George Munroe, Richard Thompson, William Blair, Patrick MacDevitt and William MacPhie. The other two arrested men turned Government informers and escaped charges. A number of other Radicals in the area, warned of the raid, managed to slip through the military net. The soldiers also seized a large number of pikes from local blacksmiths and two pairs of smith's bellows. The prisoners were bundled into carts and, along with the pikes and bellows, were transported back to Dumbarton and imprisoned in the castle. The people of Duntocher recalled the affair as the "Battle of the Bellows".

Shields reached Strathaven, just over fifteen miles from Glasgow, between 5 and 6 p.m. on Wednesday which was "uncommonly wet and dark", and made his way to William Allan's house in High Bellgreen. Allan immediately sent word to the three leading members of the Strathaven Radical Committee, John Morrison, James Russell and John Stevenson. They arrived as Shields was drying his clothes in front of Allan's fire. Stevenson asked him what the news was from Glasgow and Shields dutifully repeated the story which Lees had told him. Kinloch of Kinloch was now encamped on Cathkin Braes with 5 to 7,000 Radical troops. A division was also mustering on Campsie Braes which would attack Glasgow from the north. The Strathaven contingent were to march from the south, round Glasgow and its environs and join the division on the Campsie Braes in time for the attack on the city. He added that the Glasgow men "confidently expected that the Strathaven Radicals would lend a helping hand to crush the reptiles that had so long oppressed us". Robert Hamilton then arrived at Allan's house and asked Shields for his credentials. Hamilton compared the card that Lees had given Shields with the card King had given him and, of course, they agreed and Hamilton pronounced Shields a genuine representative of the "Provisional Government".

Shields was left at William Allan's house while the Radicals went to see James Wilson. Wilson, who was 63 years old, married with a daughter and grandchildren, was regarded by the Strathaven Radicals as a father figure. Stevenson comments: "At Strathaven, this good old man was revered as the father of reform, and looked up to with respect and esteem by all those who were warmed with zeal for the liberty of their country." Wilson was the "Class Leader" of the Radical Union and had been in politics since 1792 when he joined the Friends of the People movement. He was a man "of much reading and reflection, his natural abilities placed him above mediocrity". He had been born in Strathaven and trained to be a hosier but he had worked as a tin-smith, repaired clocks, and even studied medicine which he practised "sometimes with good effect". Wilson also trained pointer dogs and shot game. He was reputed to be a Free Thinker who "sometimes composed scraps of poetry, chiefly sarcastical, with good effect". He was a staunch reader of *The Black Dwarf* and Cobbett's *Register* and was an admirer of Thomas Paine, whose books he always kept in the house. When Wilson joined the Strathaven branch of the Friends of the People he acquired a reputation as an "extremist". When the society started to function the local aristocracy, led by the Duke of Hamilton and Brandon, started to intimidate its members. This caused the majority of the "middle class" members to withdraw from the society and Wilson began to take over and started to publish resolutions "far more violent and irritating than first adopted". Wilson had corresponded with William Skirving in 1793, commiserating over the fate of Thomas Muir and was the Strathaven delegate to the Friends of the People conventions that year. This was the man, then, to whom the members of the Strathaven Radical Committee turned for advice as to whether they should raise the Strathaven

Radicals to join the Radical Army which they thought was now encamped at Cathkin and Campsie. When Wilson heard the news, his reaction was immediate. "I am glad to hear that my countrymen are resolved to act like men. We are seeking nothing but the rights of our forefathers—liberty is not worth having, if it is not worth fighting for."

The name of liberty [says Stevenson] was not an empty sound to Wilson, but the object of his affections, ever dear and present, and twined round his heart, by all the tenderest ties of nature.

In Wilson's house at the time was "a warm hearted Irishman" named Matthew Rony, who was delighted at the news. According to Stevenson, Rony, who is described as an Irish bowlman, entertained the Radicals for fifteen minutes with an account of the exploits of the United Irishmen during their rising in 1798. Rony returned to his house, a few doors away, and, a little while later at 11 p.m. he set off for Glasgow having been instructed by Wilson to bear a message to the Glasgow Radical Committee informing them that the Strathaven Radicals "would be down by break of day".

Under Wilson's directions, the Strathaven men were called to arms and his house became the centre of activity. It was unanimously resolved that the Radicals would make all the preparations they could during the night and march as early as possible in the morning to join the Cathkin division. While some Radicals sallied out on arms raids, Wilson began to shaft a number of pikes. The news spread rapidly through the town and the local Tories immediately retired to their homes and barricaded themselves in for fear that the Radicals would rob them.

With the exception of guns, powder and flints [says Stevenson] I can defy malice herself to insinuate that we purloined a single article. Those men who have the courage to commit high treason will seldom stoop to commit a base or sinister action.

Stevenson recounts:

The night was wet, dark and comfortless; we, however, succeeded in procuring a number of guns; and there was a good deal of bustle and confusion during the night. Mothers, with maternal solicitude, were inquiring after their sons; wives were exhorting and entreating their husbands to return home. In short, the screams of women might occasionally be heard, mingled with the report of musquetry. Our strength about twelve o'clock [midnight] might be little less than one hundred men. Wilson kept a large fire in his house, and as the night was very wet, we called more than once to warm ourselves. He appeared very anxious to make us comfortable, and said he was satisfied with the exertions we were making.

In one of the arms raids, the Radicals called at the house of James Fallow, who lived with his father. Fallow was a well-known coward and the Radicals, finding him hiding below stairs, brought him out. "He was shaking like an aspen leaf. The party received him with a shout of laughter." One of the party exclaimed, "Let us have a little diversion with him!" The Radicals told Fallow he must join their ranks. "He was fairly stultified when we told him he was a prisoner; and the awkward attempts he made to escape excited a great deal of merriment." Unfortunately, this rough "horse play" on the part of the Radicals proved to be disastrous at the subsequent trials.

If we had known that such an innocent frolic [said Stevenson] would have been the subject of a grave charge from a learned Judge to the jurors of our unfortunate townsman, we would not have brought the sychophant from his cowardly retreat under the stair.

The Radicals then marched to the house of Mr Allan, in Flemington, and requisitioned his gun. From here they proceeded to the house of Thomas Alexander who refused to hand over his gun. The Radicals fired into the air and the gun was duly handed out by Alexander's son. The house of John Cullen was next raided and then the party split into two detachments, one going to High Bellgreen and the other to the house of a Radical, W. Symington, who said he would join them first thing in the morning. It was at this stage that Fallow managed to escape successfully from the Radicals.

The family of William Semple of Easter Overton were notorious Tories, who boasted that all the Radicals in Avondale would not be able to take their guns. Stevenson and his arms raiding party surrounded their house and demanded the handing over of their weapons. The Semples refused and the Radicals fired several shots into the air to frighten them. The door was eventually opened and William Semple's son was seen in the act of raising his gun to fire on the Radicals. One of the party immediately sprang forward and wrested the weapon from him. Stevenson told Semple that he would soon get his weapon back and added that things were better for Semple than the Radicals, for if they did not gain the day on Thursday they would lose their lives and not just their guns.

The Radicals were told that John Cochrane, the local merchant, had a number of guns in his shop and, about midnight, an arms raiding party called there. Cochrane was expecting a raid and was waiting up with his wife and son. He heard the party marching down the street and the command to halt. He turned to his wife and said, "There are the Radicals now." He opened the door and four armed men entered, one of these was Stevenson. Cochrane gave them one gun ("we knew he had more and tried to prevail on him to give them up but he stuck most religiously to his first statement, and as we were not disposed to ill use the gentlemen we preteneded to be satisfied"), 7 lb. of gunpowder and twelve or fourteen flints. Cochrane also showed them some ballshot but the Radicals said they could not use it.

Wilson, during the night, was organising arms, sharpening flints and making pikes. One irate wife or mother, Margaret Young, went to his house and demanded to know what Wilson thought would happen to the Radicals the next day. "I hope they will be successful," he answered. Margaret Young accused him of leading people away to be killed to which Wilson fervently replied: "They could not die in a better cause, they are only endeavouring to obtain the rights of their forefathers and I hope they will get them."

As Thursday morning dawned, the position of the Strathaven Radicals had deteriorated. Stevenson reports:

Although our number at one time amounted to nearly one hundred, by the time the sun rose on the morning of the 6th, we could scarcely muster twenty-five; the wetness of the night, the sagacious advice of friends, and the report that all was quiet in Glasgow, will account for the desertion of three-fourths of our number; the rest of us, however, were firmly resolved to join the division which Shields positively assured us were to rendezvous on Cathkin that morning.

John Morrison, William Steel, Robert Hamilton, Andrew Steel, James Russell, William Robertson, William Howatt and

William Hamilton were sent to the village of Glassford, two miles from Strathaven, but the Glassford Radicals would not contribute a single man to the venture. At 7 a.m. the Strathaven party mustered, and although Wilson was "as affable and good natured as ever", he was visibly shaken by the desertions during the night. The Radicals had counted on at least 200 men marching to Cathkin. William Watson took the flag, one which the Radical Committee had made especially for the occasion, which bore the words "Scotland Free—Or A Desert!" The Radicals formed up outside Wilson's house and, with Watson and the flag at their head, they marched off in the direction of Glasgow. Wilson, wearing a sword in a scabbard, followed in the rear, keeping his eyes open for it was feared that the Tories, seeing the Radical force now reduced to only twenty-five men, might attack them from behind.

As the column reached Coldstream, Wilson halted them and told them he knew Gavin Cooper had some guns, but the old man, seeing the Radicals coming, had hid them and the Radicals could not waste time for a thorough search of Cooper's house. The column had marched seven miles along the road when they met two men in a gig who informed them that the "fighting was over and the Glasgow Radicals had given up the unequal contest". If there was an encampment on Cathkin the two men said they had not heard of it. "This was blighting intelligence," comments Stevenson, "but we had staked so much on the Radical side that nothing short of actual proof would convince us." Wilson, however, felt sure that the Strathaven men had been betrayed. Shields, who had slept the night at William Watson's house and was marching with the Strathaven men with a musket and fifty rounds of ball cartridge, assured them he was not the betrayer. He said he had acted in good faith and if the Strathaven men were to go to Anderston and contact King the "committee" would vouch for his honesty. It still had not occurred to anyone that the "committee" itself was the agent provocateur. "I have not exceeded my instructions," claimed Shields, "and, if you have by acting on these instructions, involved yourselves in difficulties, I am sorry for it, but you must be sensible that I am exactly in the same situation." Stevenson said that the Strathaven men felt convinced he was an honest man and looking back on the affair fifteen years later, Stevenson had heard and seen nothing to change his mind.

The Radical column was now nearing Kilbride, eight miles from Strathaven, and it was learnt that a troop of Yeomanry were waiting in the village to ambush them. The authorities had been well informed of the activities of the Strathaven men. Stevenson says they halted for five minutes, examined their flints, primed their pieces, and cursed the cowardly Radicals who had deserted during the night. John Morrison, who was an ex-army man and a veteran of the Peninsular War, endeavoured to cheer up the spirits of the men by laughing at the idea of the Yeomanry attacking them.

I will wager my head against a rotten apple that twenty-five brave fellows like us would route a whole regiment of such vermin! Wallace and Bruce have often fought and conquered in the glorious cause of liberty, and I am proud to see a few Scotsmen leave their homes to tread in the footsteps of such illustrious men, and if we are to perish, let us do it nobly so that our names will be recorded among Scotland's patriotic sons.

Arms at the ready, the Radical column marched into Kilbride but found that the Kilbride Yeomanry Cavalry, commanded by Captain Graham, had just left for Hamilton. The fact that they had been waiting in Kilbride for the Strathaven men convinced Wilson that they had been betrayed and he said it was futile to continue the venture. He advised the column to return home. The majority, however, elected to continue and Wilson handed his sword over to Robert Hamilton. While wishing the company luck, he said he could no longer continue with them as he felt certain they were betrayed. He went into a friend's house nearby to rest before returning to Strathaven.

The rest of the Radicals formed their column again and continued their march to Cathkin, reaching it at about 6 p.m. It was deserted and the Radicals gazed anxiously round for signs of activity. The Radical flag was planted on the brow of a hill and two men were sent to Rutherglen to purchase some bread and cheese and to see if they could "raise" the Rutherglen Radicals. The remaining Radicals started to cross-question Shields as to who were the people who gave him his credentials and if he knew the names of the Provisional Government. He did not pretend to know any names but said that his father was a prominent member of the Anderston Radical Committee and Lees had been in touch with him. Through this connection Shields had been prevailed upon to act as an emissary as and when the "Provisional Government" required his services. The Radicals, on Shields' insistence, sent a messenger to Anderston to contact the Radical Committee and tell them that the Strathaven men had arrived at Cathkin and where was the Radical Army located.

The Strathaven Radicals waited upon their hill until 9 p.m. The men who had been sent to Rutherglen did not return but sent two Rutherglen Radicals to inform them that "the bubble had burst". The Radicals had been defeated at Bonnymuir and the insurrection was at an end. It was reported that the two men had been given some boiled potatoes in Rutherglen to help "sustain the Radical army". The Rutherglen men also informed the Radicals that a man had left Cathkin House on horseback in the direction of Glasgow and it was supposed that he was going to inform the authorities that a Radical flag was flying at Cathkin. The Radicals decided to leave their hill immediately and disperse. They decided to conceal their weapons on the hill, with the exception of William Howatt, who said he had risked his life in procuring his gun and was determined not to part with it. Stevenson and William MacIntyre went to a plantain tree, a short distance from the hill, and covered their guns and ammunition with bracken at the root of some fir trees. Shields was one of the last to part with his gun and leave Cathkin. He obviously felt that the failure of the expedition was his fault despite the fact that he had been successfully duped by the Government agents.

We left the hill with fearful prognostics of the future [wrote Stevenson]. We knew well the vindictive disposition of the old monarchial governments, and that they rarely forgive those who have the hardihood to rise in arms against their despotic proceedings; and while we were hurrying down the hill I felt a strong presentiment that some of us would expiate this on the scaffold.

In ones and twos, eight of the party went into Rutherglen, meeting in the inn, where they ate a hearty meal. William MacIntyre then announced he would return home, he being married and with a family. Nothing the other Radicals could say would persuade him that it was too dangerous. He was intercepted and arrested by the military three miles from his home.

When the Strathaven Radicals had left that morning, the Tories quickly emerged from their homes and began to organise a defence. Messengers were sent out for the military and several "prominent, well disposed citizens" armed themselves. James Wilson, who had returned home during the early evening, was arrested at his own home. Twelve of the Strathaven party were arrested trying to return to their homes and these, along with Wilson, were taken into Hamilton under escort and interrogated by the Sheriff. The prisoners were left in Hamilton Barracks for some days and then transferred to Glasgow. The remaining Strathaven men fled into the country. The rising at Strathaven was over.

TWELVE

THE GREENOCK AFFAIR

FOLLOWING THE NEWS of the "military victory" at Bonny-muir and the suppression of the Strathaven Rising, the merchants and manufacturers, now feeling more secure, began indignantly to demand the severest punishment for the Radicals. The general impression was that the insurrection was now over. Samuel Hunter wrote, in a *Glasgow Herald* editorial on Friday, April 7, "We believe we may congratulate the public on the prospect of a speedy termination to our revolutionary outrages."

Forty-nine prominent Glasgow citizens wrote a letter to the Lord Provost of Glasgow, the Hon. Henry Monteith, demanding a public meeting be called to discuss the situation.

We request your Lordship will be pleased to call us a PUBLIC MEETING of the MERCHANTS, MANUFACTURERS, and PROPRIETORS of PUBLIC WORKS in this City and Neighbourhood for the purpose of considering what steps it may be proper to take regarding the future employment of those who have obeyed the command of a TREASON-ABLE CONFEDERACY to desist from their ordinary labour.

The Lord Provost replied:

In compliance with the above Requisition, I request a MEETING of the MERCHANTS, MANUFACTURERS, and PROPRIETORS of PUBLIC WORKS, in this City and Neighbourhood, in the TOWN HALL on Tuesday, the 11th inst. at 12 o'clock noon

The feeling of indignation against the Radicals began to spread among the moneyed classes of the city. Thursday, the Spring Sacramental—a religious fast-day—saw the churches crowded and from every Glasgow pulpit a tirade was launched against the Radicals and "the great and bloody battle" at Bonnymuir on the previous day. But this did not stem the insurgent activity in the city. Later that day between forty to fifty insurgents left Glasgow and marched to the canal near

Kirkintilloch where they waited "as if", said an observer, "it were a rendezvous". After a while they hid their arms and dispersed. Shortly after, the military raided the area and picked up arms. Later, members of the Rifle Brigade in a carriage, escorted by a troop of hussars, arrived in Duntocher, nine miles north-west of Glasgow on Dalmuir Burn, and arrested ten men. One Radical attempted to escape and was shot through the leg. Arms and ammunition were also seized.

To underline the all-powerful strength of the military, a large parade of Glasgow Yeomanry, the Rifle Brigade, the Dunbartonshire Yeomanry and artillery gunners were ordered to parade in George Square for a review by Major-General Sir Thomas Bradford. But this large gathering of troops was to serve a practical purpose as well, for it was decided to use the troops in a house to house search for arms and Radicals. The troops marched past Bradford who was seated on horseback in front of the Sir John Moore monument. By his side was Samuel Hunter, his 18 stone girth wrapped in a kilt.

After the march past, Bradford made a few congratulatory remarks to Hunter and then rode off with his staff to the Star Hotel for lunch. Hunter then stepped forward and, pointing his sword towards the Cathkin Braes, said: "I am confident that if any treasonable ragamuffins shall dare to approach this city, you shall give them a warm reception."

The troops marched to the fork of Buchanan Street where they were halted and then counter-marched down Queen Street. They were divided into two columns . . . the left of the force going towards Bridgeton and the right towards Anderston. The anonymous sergeant (who afterwards wrote an account of this operation) was in the Anderston division and wrote that the troops formed in a line from the Anderston foundry to the Dumbarton road and then moved forward through the streets, searching houses, making arrests and seizing arms and ammunition. The sergeant remarked that some good looking women "were at the windows of the houses behind which I was placed, and our conversation, tho' not of the highest order, served to while away the fatigues of the soldier and sever him from his danger. We were withdrawn, I think, about half past three and got home very dirty owing to the road, and wet, owing to the rain, about four o'clock."

Bradford was delighted at the turnout and issued the following General Order:

Major-General Sir Thomas Bradford having this morning inspected the Glasgow Corps of Volunteers as well as Cavalry and Infantry congratulates Lt.-Col. Hunter and Captain Stirling upon the soldier like appearance of their men, and begs to assure them, he has on no occasion seen corps more judiciously, or serviceably appointed or that appear in any respect better qualified for duties for which they have been formed.

By order of the Major-General.

James Douglas, D.Q.M.G.
Glasgow, 6th April, 1820

Among the arrests made on Thursday were those of George Washington, David Graham and William Graham, who were said to be "three of the principal Radical leaders". These, "with a trunk containing papers", were taken to the police offices and after questioning removed to the Tolbooth. Washington was a Radical organiser who had travelled in Argyll disguised as a pedlar since 1818, organising Union societies and Radical meetings. Five weeks before the rising he had ordered the people not to pay any more taxes.

The danger of another attempt on the Carron munitions factory worried Bradford (who appears to have been excluded from the knowledge that Government agents were being extensively used at this time). On his orders, sixty carronades—short barrel, large calibre ships' guns, equally effective as field artillery—and vast quantities of ammunition were brought down from Carron, along the river to Grangemouth and on to Leith where they were safely stored in Leith Fort.

On Friday Captain Brown, of the Edinburgh City Police Force, with fifteen coaches full of his men, arrived to aid Captain Mitchell with his "mopping-up" operations. That day the police decided to arrest John Anderson Jnr., who had prepared the final draft of the proclamation for printing. It is highly probable that they made the arrest in order to stop Anderson revealing the truth about the proclamation. He was arrested on the Sheriff's warrant at the instance of the Fiscal and charged "guilty of circulating, publishing and posting up the above treasonable address". Anderson, from Glasgow Jail wrote a declaration about what had really happened and sent

G

it to Lord Sidmouth. Obviously Anderson could not be brought
to trial otherwise his statements would lead to the uncovering
of Sidmouth's spy system and the plot organised by his agents
against the Radicals. A special warrant was made out on April
21 for Anderson to be detained in custody "till liberated in due
course of the law". It was not until August 4 that Anderson was
liberated "on caution" and escorted directly to a ship on which
he was sent to the East Indies where a Government job awaited
him for the price of his silence. Anderson was still living in the
East Indies, working for the Government, in 1834.

On Saturday the military increased their activity and, in the
morning, troops from the hussars and the Rifle Brigade as well
as the Dunbartonshire Yeomanry went to Milngavie following
a report that 500 Radicals had been drilling for some weeks
past in that area. The military arrested five Radicals and
collected seven muskets, 300 rounds of ball cartridge and
numerous pikes. It was noted that the ball cartridge was
particularly ill made. Later in the day, Sir John Hope's troop
of Midlothian Cavalry arrived in Glasgow to reinforce the
military.

In Edinburgh, fifteen of the Bonnymuir prisoners who were
well enough arrived under the charge of a Macer of the High
Court of Justiciary, who had gone to Stirling the previous day
to take possession of them. Early on Saturday they had been
taken from Stirling Castle and put on board a steamboat for
transportation to the ancient port of Newhaven, now a suburb
of Edinburgh. From there, six carriages took them to the Tolbooth of Edinburgh, where they arrived at 3 p.m. Only Hart,
MacFarlane and Clackson or Clarkson were still suffering from
the wounds they had received and were too ill to be moved.
They remained at Stirling Castle until April 28 when they were
also moved to Edinburgh by steam packet.

Captain Brown and his men, after taking part in several
raids in Glasgow, Airdrie and Kirkintilloch, arrived back in
Edinburgh late on the Saturday night.

The *London Gazette*'s Saturday edition published the offer by
King George IV of a £500 reward for the discovery of the
Radical leaders. The King had been assured by Sidmouth that
the danger of the rising was now over and the leaders were all
but arrested.

By The King

A Proclamation

George R.

Whereas, it hath been represented unto us that, during the Night of the First Day of April Instant, many copies of a Printed Treasonable Paper, entitled An Address to the Inhabitants of Great Britain and Ireland, and purporting to be issued by order of a Committee of Organisation for forming a Provisional Government were affixed on the Walls and other Conspicuous Places in the City and Environs of Glasgow, and in various parts of the Counties of Lanark, Renfrew, Ayr, Dumbarton and Stirling; now We being desirous of bringing to Justice the Authors and Printers of the said Treasonable Paper, do hereby, by and with the advice of our Privy Council, promise our most gracious pardon to any person concerned in the Affixing and Publishing the same, except the Authors and Printers thereof, who shall give such information to one of our Principal Secretaries of State, or to our Advocate of Scotland, or to the Lord Provost of Glasgow, as shall lead to the Detection of the Authors or Printers thereof; and, for further encouragement to make the said Discovery, We do hereby offer a Reward of *Five Hundred Pounds* (except as before excepted) giving such information as aforesaid, composing and printing the said treasonable paper, such Reward to be paid on the conviction of the Offenders by the Lords Commissioners of our Treasury.

Given at Our Court, at Carlton House, the eighth day of April one thousand, eight hundred and twenty, and in the first year of Our Reign.

God Save The King

However, the idea that the rising was all over was ill founded. It was Greenock that "was destined to become a scene of death and blood" that Saturday. All week the town of Greenock, one of the principal ports in Scotland, had been comparatively peaceful as regards Radical activity, but, as the week progressed, more especially after the events at Bonnymuir and at Strathaven, the town began to fill up with people seeking passages to Canada and America. Even so, Greenock itself remained free from riot or demonstration.

In Paisley that Saturday, the 120-strong Port Glasgow Armed Association, commanded by Colonel John Dunlop, were preparing to leave the town. The militia had been stationed in Paisley since Monday and—now that all appeared quiet—

orders were given to Dunlop that the services of the Port Glasgow militia were no longer required. Dunlop planned to leave the town at 4 a.m. and march to Port Glasgow where he would dismiss his men to their homes for a well-earned rest. However, the Lord Provost of Paisley, Oliver Jamieson, called to see Dunlop and explained to him that Paisley Jail was over-crowded and that he had five "prominent Radical leaders" on his hands. These had to be taken to Greenock Jail but it was unfair to ask for line troops to be spared for escort duties. In the meantime Dunlop had also received a message from Brad-ford asking Dunlop to meet him in Paisley later on Saturday morning to discuss military affairs. Dunlop decided he could send a company to Greenock with the Radical prisoners while he, and the rest of the Port Glasgow militia, remained in Paisley until the afternoon. The time could also be utilised in clearing up the corps' financial affairs in the town. Dunlop ordered one of his officers, Carswell, to make ready a company of thirty men for the journey. However, there were numerous rumours that an attempt would be made to rescue the prisoners after they had left Paisley. Being a cautious man, Dunlop decided to make up Carswell's company to eighty men together with another officer named Cleland. The militia and their five prisoners, in a cart, set off from Paisley at 12 noon. Dunlop sent word to the Chief Magistrate at Greenock, James Dennistoun, by the driver of the mail coach to expect the prisoners late in the afternoon. Dennistoun, however, made no special provisions for the recep-tion of the Radical prisoners. A rumour that sixteen Radical prisoners would arrive in Greenock en route to prison soon spread over the town and crowds began to gather in the street about 4 p.m. It was also reported that several strangers arrived in the town during the course of the day.

Carswell sent ahead two outriders from his column to warn Dennistoun of their expected arrival but when these two soldiers arrived at Cartsdyke, the entrance to Greenock, they were pelted with stones and rotten vegetables. Even then Dennistoun made no special arrangements for the prisoners' reception. The Port Glasgow militia, with fifes and drums lead-ing the column, marched into the town. Riding behind the drummers, Carswell and Cleland noticed that the shops were shut and boarded up and crowds of sullen, hostile people hung about the streets. Jeers and taunts followed the militia as they marched through Cartsdyke, fifes and drums playing swaggering martial airs. The column arrived in Greenock at 5 p.m. and started to push through the crowds to the Bridewell. The people were in an ugly mood but did no more than jeer and taunt the soldiers as they marched along. Above the shouts of the crowd Carswell suddenly heard a voice call to the prisoners: "Cheer up! You will soon be released from your situation!" He stood up in his stirrups and peered into the crowd to try and spot the man who had called out—but in the dense mass of people it could have been any one of the hundreds of hostile faces.

The militia managed to escort their prisoners to the jail without serious incident. One troop entered the jail with the prisoners while the other troop formed up outside. Dennistoun, realising that a nasty incident could be sparked off at any moment, tried to address the hostile crowd to try and get them to disperse but he was shouted down. The militia then reformed and, with arms shouldered, began to march back through the town. Taunts and cries of "Traitors!" and "Sour-milk Jocks!" were flung at them and then, as the crowd found taunts non-effective, stones and other missiles flew at the soldiers. At Cathcart Street the discipline of the militia began to fail. Opposite the Tontin Inn, in Cathcart Street, Carswell ordered the soldiers to fire a volley over the heads of the crowd ... two people fell wounded. Enraged, the crowd redoubled its attack on the soldiers and by the time they had reached Rue End, several of the militia had been hurt by flying bric-à-brac. They were soon out of control and were soon firing indiscriminately at the people. Three were killed on the spot, eighteen were seriously wounded and these were later removed to the local infirmary where six died of their wounds. The soldiers had to fight almost a military rear-guard action against the infuriated people all the way to Cartsdyke before the crowd were halted.

For a while the crowd stood undecided. Then a voice called "Away for Port Glasgow!" Iron railings were torn up for use as weapons. Swords and guns appeared in the hands of some people. With a piper leading them, the crowd set off down the Port Glasgow road. When they reached the gate of a Mr Gemnill, a man stepped forward and halted them. He shouted that it was useless attacking Port Glasgow as a messenger had been sent off post haste to warn the military there. But, he added, the crowd could revenge its dead by attacking Greenock Jail and freeing the Radical leaders lodged there.

It was 7 p.m. when Chief Magistrate Dennistoun, learning of the intention of the crowd, gathered his force of special police officers outside the prison. He and his men had barely time to barricade themselves in the prison yard before the infuriated crowd arrived. The battle was a short one. Dusk was casting its grey-blackness everywhere when the defenders of the prison were assailed by a barrage of stones and had to fall back from the yard as the large, wooden prison gates were smashed in. The crowd flooded into the prison and released the five Radical prisoners, leaving all non-political prisoners safely in their cells. By 10 p.m. Greenock was its quiet and stable self again with only its dead and wounded to recall that any disturbance had taken place.

Dennistoun and his officers met in Greenock Council Chambers and issued the following proclamation:

Whereas, in consequence of the outrageous assault made this evening on the Prison of Greenock, and the rescue therefrom of five prisoners confined on a charge of High Treason, the Magistrates have deemed it their duty to call on a strong military force for the security of the town; and they solemnly warn the inhabitants to avoid all breaches of the peace and all molestation or insult of the military, who have positive orders from the highest civil authority in Scotland to act instantly in self defence in case of receiving personal insult: All persons, therefore, who presume to molest the military have themselves alone to blame for the consequences that may ensue. A reward of fifty guineas is hereby offered by the Magistrates of Greenock to any person who will give such information as will lead to the conviction of the persons guilty of the aforesaid assault and rescue.—Council Chambers, Greenock, 8th April, 1820.

At 1 a.m. on the Sunday, a troop of the 10th Hussars and a troop of the 7th Hussars rode into Greenock at full gallop with sabres drawn expecting to meet with a large force of insurgents. They had been informed that the Radicals had captured Greenock and were using it as a base to launch an attack upon Glasgow. They galloped as far as Blackhall Street, on the extreme far side of the town, before they realised the streets were deserted. Shortly afterwards a force of the Renfrewshire Militia arrived and patrols were sent through the streets. However, all was quiet in the town.

At 8 a.m. a company of the Rifle Brigade and a company of the 13th Regiment of Foot arrived by steam packet from Glasgow. With these new troops came the Lord Lieutenant of Renfrewshire, Lord Blantyre, who was to be killed in a rising in Belgium in 1830. He was accompanied by Sir Michael Shaw Stewart (Bart.) of Erskine House who, for many months, had advocated the necessity of having a Yeomanry corps stationed in Greenock as it was a major exit from Scotland to the Americas. Surprised at the peaceful reception, Blantyre made his headquarters in the White Hart Inn and ordered refreshments for his troops. He and Stewart remained in the town all day but the insurgent prisoners—and any comrades that might have come to Greenock to help them—were well away by that time. In fact, only one of the five prisoners was ever recaptured: at Dalry, on Thursday, April 20, and taken to Ayr prison.

To offset any danger that the Port Glasgow Armed Association might be blamed for starting the incident by firing on the people of Greenock, Lord Blantyre sent the following letter to Colonel John Dunlop.

Sir—We, the Lord Lieutenant, Sheriff, and Provost of Paisley, for himself and other Magistrates of Paisley, beg leave, in this manner, to convey to you, and through you, to the very respectable corps of Port Glasgow Armed Association, under your command, our warmest thanks for the patriotic and useful services they have just rendered in this district.

We also beg leave to express our own grateful sense (which accords with that of every respectable person in the town) of the very excellent conduct of all the individuals of the corps while quartered here. We have the honour to be & etc.

Blantyre (Lord Lieutenant)

Blantyre's note was also endorsed by Oliver Jamieson (Provost of Paisley) and another John Dunlop (Sheriff of Paisley). James Dennistoun, on behalf of Greenock, also endorsed the testimonial.

With the exception of the three men who were killed on the spot, a complete list of the Greenock casualties was drawn up and given to Blantyre. The list composed entirely of civilian casualties, no soldiers were seriously hurt. The list of casualties was a mute testimonial of the militia's indiscriminate firing, containing as it did people of every age group. Adam Clephane (48 years old) dead; James Kerr (17) dead; William Lindsay (15) dead; James MacGilp (8) dead; Archibald Drummond (20) dead; John MacWhinnie (65) dead; John Boyce (33) dead. Later, on Sunday, May 5, Archibald MacKinnon (17) also died of his wound. Mrs Catherine Turner (65) leg amputated; Hugh Paterson (14) leg amputated; Peter Cameron (14) flesh wound; John Gunn (24) flesh wound; John Turner (22) flesh wound; Gilbert MacArthur (18) slight wound; Robert Spence (11) slight wound; David MacBride (14) slight wound; John Patrick (30) slight wound; and George Tillery (25) slight wound.

On Wednesday, April 12, Sir Thomas Bradford, the Lord Advocate, Sir William Rae, and the Deputy Lord Advocate, John Hope, arrived at Greenock to join Blantyre in investigating the "Greenock Affair". As the party were walking along Cathcart Street between 2 p.m. and 3 p.m. (the workers' lunch hour in Greenock at that time) the funeral procession of Adam Clephane and John MacWhinnie came down the street bearing the bodies to the cemetery. The *Greenock Advertiser* said that the relatives had been ordered to conduct the funeral while the rest of the town were at lunch so that a crowd would not gather.

The following day, Thursday, John Cameron, a skinner of Cartsdyke, was arrested on the orders of the Lord Advocate, Sir William Rae, as being concerned and connected with the Glasgow Radicals. But the *Greenock Advertiser* said that Cameron was a good neighbour, kept himself to himself, and did not seek to vent his spleen on those of different opinions. "We hope and trust, therefore, he will ultimately be found innocent of any serious breach of the laws." Cameron was, in fact, released from custody a week later on April 20 due to lack of any evidence. However, seven Greenock people were imprisoned in Dumbarton Castle charged with aiding the Radical prisoners to escape. These, inexplicably, were released by the Lord Advocate on July 31.

In the meantime, feeling in Greenock ran high against the

Port Glasgow Armed Association and several threatening letters were sent to Colonel John Dunlop. The very first account of the rising *Detailing the Events of the Late Rebellion in the West of Scotland* . . . written by *a British subject* and published in Glasgow on April 28, 1820, a 62-page pamphlet, states:

Since the affair at Greenock, the town of Port Glasgow has been in a state of anxiety, and alarm. Whenever the military are withdrawn, the inhabitants are forced to arm and stand guard in their own defence for fear of an assault from their neighbours. Threatening letters have been sent to the Commandant of volunteers. Blood for blood is the burthen of their contents. My Lord Duke, if such daring threats escape without investigation and without punishment, we allow the disaffected to strike at the root of that defence on which this country has so much dependence for her peace and her security. It is high time, therefore, that the public voice should fearlessly, and the laws sternly pronounce, that none shall maltreat with impunity, those who are engaged in defending their country under the mandates of lawful authority. The volunteers act under the law, and they must be supported and protected by the law. It is not sufficient that their persons are rendered secure; but, whatever your Grace may think, or the defamers of the Magistrates of Manchester may think, their characters must be also.

This review of the rising, looking into the Greenock skirmish, tries to draw conclusions as to what caused the people of Greenock, previously apathetic to the Radical call, to become so anti-Government to the degree that they did.

It is given out publicly and ostentatiously that the reason of this outrage was, because the volunteers came into town with drums beating and colours flying [the charge with regard to the colours is said to be untrue]. So then the public are to understand that had the party come in with drums muffled, their arms bound with crêpe, and their countenances marked with every symptom of sorrow for the fortune of traitors thus placed in their hands, then the latent spirit of disaffection would have remained asleep and unknown, and the volunteers would have been received as friends. . . .

As a further apology for this lawless transaction, it is said the attack arose from the want of precaution in those authorities who committed the prisoners to the charge of men "of an unimposing aspect, whom, it was well known, certain people in Greenock held in contempt, and, upon these men coming into the town when on military duty with colour clothes, and being jaded and dirty from their march, were fit subjects for the ridicule of the mob" (*London Star*, April 14, 1820)

The pamphlet concludes:

The issue of this affair cannot be too much lamented, and shews more and more the necessity of dragging to light and punishment those men, who, urging on the people to rebellion, lay the country open to such melancholy catastrophes. The innocent sufferers call for justice on their guilty heads; and the survivors of these demand and will obtain the relief of their compassionate countrymen. Scarcely a doubt can remain that the rescue of these prisoners was premeditated and carried into effect by their friends assembled from the country for that special purpose, though, perhaps, increased in numbers by many who were in Greenock endeavouring to escape from this country, and which, doubtless they conceived they could more securely effect in a place where there was no organised military force to disturb them.

Deeply as every feeling bosom must lament the fatal occurrence, still there is some consideration due for the feelings of this country. No language is sufficient strong to reprobate the attempts that are making to load the character and conduct of these volunteers with reproach, obliquy and guilt. None could plead ignorance of the alarming situation of this country. None, and more especially in Greenock, could be ignorant that the standards of rebellion were un-furled in their immediate neighbourhood, and that those conducted to their Jail were men taken under these banners. There was not, and could not be, the shadow of an excuse for insulting and attacking the military while peaceably discharging their duty. If any part of the population in Greenock were tempted to join the ranks of dis-affection and treason, on their heads be, and must be, the shame and guilt.

Greenock as a town, and her respectable population as a body are readily acquitted of such principles or blame. None could be so weak or so wicked as to attempt otherwise. But it is evident that, like their neighbours, they have, to a certain extent, evil amongst them. It is not to be endured that brave men, who, leaving their business, their families and their homes, with such clothing as they had, no matter whether military or not, to defend their country against the worst of foes, and the properties, lives and liberties of the people of Greenock amongst that of others, shall, when in discharge of any lawful duty, but in a more particular manner, when in discharge of a duty, be attacked by Radicals and the coajutors, or well wishers of Radicals, whether of Greenock or

more distant parts—nor is it to be tolerated that they are to be
made responsible for the consequences, or have their characters
torn and their feelings lacerated while represented as shedding
heedlessly and needlessly innocent blood.

Nevertheless, the shooting of a 65-year-old woman and an
8-year-old boy, in fact the firing of the military into the crowd
to excite it to madness, instead of volley fire above their
heads which would have probably cleared the streets, was
hardly the action of disciplined soldiers. And, unfortunately,
this was only Greenock's first taste of bloodletting during the
rising as, on July 30, soldiers of the 13th Regiment of Foot,
"maddened by drink", fired into another Greenock crowd
killing several. This time the authorities could not blame the
behaviour of the townspeople and eventually the regiment had
to pay out compensation. A similar incident, involving members of the same regiment, also took place in Glasgow, but, it is
true to say, such incidents were mainly confined to the Yeomanry regiments and not to the more disciplined line troops.

THIRTEEN

"PERFECT TRANQUILLITY"

A T 5 A.M. ON Sunday, April 9, troops of the 7th and 10th
Hussars and the Rifle Brigade, assembled on the orders of the
Lord Advocate, Sir William Rae, counter-signed by the magistrates and Sheriff of Glasgow, carried out a series of raids in
the city. They arrested over 100 prominent Glasgow citizens
who were suspected of having Radical sympathies and crammed
them into the cells in the police office, Bridewell and Glasgow
Jail. Among the arrested were Alexander (Sandy) Rodger, the
Radical poet from Bridgeton; James Turner of Thrushgrove,
on whose land the first major Radical meeting had been held in
1816; and William Lang, the Bell Street printer on whom the
authorities wished to "pin" the printing of the proclamation
of the "Provisional Government". James Turner wrote a
letter to Joseph Hume, M.P., dated at Glasgow March 1,
1821, recounting what had happened.

I was, on Sunday morning, the 9th of April, 1820, about five
o'clock, awakened from my bed by a tremendous noise, and the bark-
ing of my dogs. I opened my front door and found that my house was
surrounded by military. Mr Salmond, the Procurator Fiscal, and
Calder, the Sheriff's officer, then entered the house. I asked them
what they wanted? They said they were come to seize me. I desired
them to come in and wait till I put my clothes on. Having dressed,
I then asked to see their warrant, when they showed me a paper
which they would not allow me to read, but which they called a
warrant for my apprehension, and the searching of my house for
papers and arms; but at whose instance application was made, or
who granted the warrant, I do not know. They proceeded to search
for papers and found only two, which, upon examination by them,
were deemed worthy of being endorsed, namely a copy of a letter I
had sent to Lord Sidmouth, in 1817, relative to a petition from Glasgow to the Prince Regent, for a redress of grievances; and a letter from
some of the inhabitants of this city, about liberty to meet in my
grounds at Thrushgove anent that petition.

I delivered up my pocket pistols, which I used when travelling, my gun and bayonet, which I purchased from Colonel Cunningham Corbett, when I served as a volunteer under him in 1797; a holster pistol and five ball catridges. These were the mighty store of arms, all of which had been in my possession for more than twenty years. I was first taken to the police office, where I was detained till about 11 o'clock on Sunday night, when I was marched with a guard of horse and foot soldiers to Bridewell and locked up in a solitary cell, as if I had been the worst of criminals. I requested Bailie James Hunter, who accompanied me to Bridewell, that I might be indulged with the use of writing materials, to give directions respecting my business on the following day, but he informed me the magistrates had no power to grant any such thing.

Turner concludes:

But it was not till Friday evening, the 14th, that I was called to be examined on a charge of High Treason! I then answered every question put to me by Mr Hope, the Advocate Depute, and as I thought, to his satisfaction, not withstanding which I was remanded to my cell, where I was detained Saturday, Sunday, Monday and Tuesday; and at six o'clock that Tuesday evening, when I was brought up again for examination, I was informed that I might now probably be liberated on bail.

Bail was, in fact, fixed at £150 which was not returned nor was any redress for wrongful arrest given even though all charges against Turner were dropped. On Monday, April 10, the two justices, James Hardie and Thomas Hopkirk, with a strong body of military, raided William Lang's house in Bell Street. They carried off a number of books and papers and shut up his house, taking away the key. It was later revealed that the Sheriff's officer, Calder, had offered to pay one of Lang's apprentice printers the sum of £300, "to be made a gentleman for life", if he would swear that Lang had printed the proclamation of the "Provisional Government". Despite the evidence of Reid, Chapman and Haldane, the authorities were determined that Lang should appear as the printer of the address.

Arrests were now daily taking place and the *Glasgow Herald* commented that "a number of persons have disappeared not previously suspected of taking part in revolution". The *Herald* goes on to say: "We continue to enjoy perfect tranquillity here, with occasional reports of night drilling in our neighbourhood, which cannot prevail to any extent in the face of the military force stationed here."

At the Ayr Circuit Court, held under the presidency of the Rt. Hon. Lord Meadowbank, two men were charged with stealing guns during Radical arms raids. Joseph MacGheer was charged with stealing a pistol from William Kerr of George Street, Content, and John Forran was charged with stealing a pistol from William Logan, a hardware merchant in Ayr. Both pleaded not guilty and were represented by a Mr Alexander. MacGheer was found not guilty and dismissed simpliciter but Forran was found guilty and sentenced to fourteen years' transportation. Lord Meadowbank, "referring to those recent instances of insurrection", told the court that the military "vengeance would be terrible. Let those misguided men not delude themselves. They have no chance of success."

The public meeting which the Lord Provost of Glasgow, the Hon. Henry Monteith, had promised the prominent citizens "for the purpose of considering what steps it may be proper to take regarding the future employment of those who have obeyed the command of a Treasonable Confederacy to desist from their ordinary labour", began at noon on Tuesday, April 11, at Glasgow Town Hall. The Lord Provost took the chair himself and Kirkman Finlay, M.P., opened the meeting by saying that there was no need to remind people of the current state of affairs. He pointed out that "there existed a large body of armed men" who had formulated a plan to attack Glasgow and this was to have been executed on the previous Wednesday. "There is no doubt the whole strength of the rebel force was then intended to be directed here." According to Finlay it was only the fact that the Radicals were divided in their opinions which prevented "such an assemblage of armed men . . . as could not have been overcome without more bloodshed and more crimes as we have yet witnessed". Large bodies of armed men did, in fact, assemble and he reminded the audience that a drum had called the insurgents to arms in Bridgeton. He then moved that a resolution warning manufacturers to be careful when they employed people in future, especially of their principles and morals, should be passed by the meeting. Accordingly, he proposed:

That in order to perform in the most effectual manner the imperative duty of assisting the Civil Authorities, not merely in putting down, but in extinguishing the seeds of the present desperate reasonable confederacy, this meeting think it necessary to adopt the following declaration:—

We whose names are here unto subscribed, merchants and manufacturers in the City of Glasgow and neighbourhood, are resolved, by every means in our power, to assist in putting down the present Desperate and Unprecedented Resistance to all Lawful Authority by withdrawing our Employment and Support from every person who may have lent, or who shall in future lend, his aid to the purpose of the wicked and treasonable Conspiracy detailed in "Address to the Inhabitants of Great Britain and Ireland" lately published here.

We, therefore, hereby declare our fixed purpose and determination to be, not to employ in future any persons who may have already joined, or who shall hereafter join, the promoters of this treasonable Confederacy, who may have taken up arms, or lent aid and encouragement to it by his presence or his countenance.

We highly disapprove of the conduct of those who have left their work, even when threatened by the menace of the lawless and unprincipled men who conduct the present audacious proceedings, and we are resolved not again to employ any one who has left off working, or who shall in future do so, without a previous minute inquiry into his conduct, and character, and without being satisfied of his innocence, as relates to intention, and of his being the victim of his own groundless fears, not the willing instrument of disaffection and disloyalty.

James Oswald, one of the officers of the Glasgow Yeomanry (Light Horse) referred to the insurgents as a set of misguided men "so desperately wicked and so totally infatuated as to oppose themselves to the lawful authorities of the country". Almost all the "lower classes were contaminated and ready to enter any plan of rebellion". Agreeing with Kirkman Finlay's resolution he added that employers must use firmness and prudence and strike at the roots of the current evil.

Another speaker, James Ewing, said he "perfectly approved" of the resolution and agreed that the Radicals were "full of dark and desperate purpose" but he asked that the employers have sympathy with those who had been seduced, either by threats or bribes, from their work.

Be to their faults a little blind
Be to their virtues very kind.

He urged employers to scrutinise the workers very carefully and added that he deeply regretted the foul stain which had sullied the fame of Glasgow, "once a religious and well disposed city". Radicalism was a cant name for revolution.

Kirkman Finaly interposed to say that he felt the disaffected were mainly confined to the manufacturing class and not so much the agricultural workers. Charles Stirling, another Glasgow Yeomanry officer, rebuked James Ewing and said that people could not be seduced or intimidated into committing acts of treason. All workers who had taken part in the rebellion must suffer alike. He advocated a committee be set up to draw up several "wise and salutary" resolutions with the object of giving the employer an opportunity to know the character of his workmen "by which means the good will be distinguished from the bad". The Hon. Henry Monteith congratulated the meeting on their unanimity and declared it was now time to separate the innocent from the guilty. The resolution was passed unanimously and 155 employers signed it and it was decided to have it published in the next editions of the newspapers. The meeting ended with James Denniston proposing a vote of thanks to Monteith which was seconded by Kirkman Finlay.

Later that day a second meeting was held in the Black Bull Inn, chaired by Robert Thomson Jnr. The meeting unanimously agreed with the resolution passed at the Town Hall but decided to add another paragraph, signed by forty-seven employers, which read:

It was also resolved unanimously

That no person whatever shall be employed by any of the Subscribers who is, or shall become, a Member of any Secret Society, or of any Society to which the Employer shall not be invited to become a Member nor will they employ any person who shall subscribe or contribute money for any secret purpose whatsoever.

On April 14, in accordance with the resolution, a local manufacturer, General Spens, sacked every one in his employ whom he suspected of having Radical sympathies.

Late on Tuesday night Alexander Boswell sat down at his home at Auchinleck and wrote a report to Lord Sidmouth.

The vipers having retired to their retreats disappointed and deceived by their delegates, and Paisley again in quiet, the Yeomanry were ordered home on Saturday. The ferments for two days, I learn, was excessive over the whole manufacturing district, but finding that the rising could not take place and learning that the troops were now determined to act with severity at least, the semblance of a great change has taken place. It is, however, resolved to proceed in apprehending those who were conspicuous on the late occasion and to crush the spirit of the disaffected by enough measures.

I left home on Sunday night at eleven to take command of a small detachment of my Yeomanry near to Galston, a populous village eleven miles from hence, where some culprits were to be seized as a rescue was apprehended. We secured all the avenues leading to the dwelling of those against whom there were warrants, but we only took one man, the Radicals having somehow got notice. I go tonight (or rather tomorrow, at three) to seize the Prese [president], secretary and two delegates of a Union Society and I hope we may succeed as I have taken precautions to prevent alarm.

Acknowledging the letter on April 18, the Home Secretary warned:

The Yeomanry of Ayrshire have had a distinguishing part in crushing the insipient Rebellion but the Civil Authorities must be constantly vigilant and on the alert or tranquillity will not long be preserved.

Despite the "perfect tranquillity", a troop of the 10th Hussars, on patrol near Airdrie, on Wednesday, April 12, were ambushed and several shots were fired at them. The assailants managed to escape in the confusion and a reward of 200 guineas was offered for information leading to the arrest and prosecution of the persons concerned. Later that day a troop of the Ayrshire Yeomanry Cavalry surrounded the town of Mauchline and arrested thirty Radicals, seizing arms and ammunition. The same morning the county's Sheriff Deputy, A. Bell, with members of the 4th Royal Veteran Battalion, left Ayr for Mauchline where they carried out an extensive search for arms. A large number of pikes were found in a field near the town on the following morning. The arrested Radicals were described as the "Radical Committee of Ayr". Another arrest took place that day of a young Ayrshire Yeomanry trooper. The man had deserted his troop while passing

Eaglesham Moor on the previous Monday "thinking it better to be quaffing strong ale at his own fireside in Mill Vennel than fighting the Radicals at Hamilton or Strathaven, and run the risk of getting a hole knocked through his gullet by a Radical pike".

As the military scoured the countryside in search of Radicals, arresting innocent and guilty alike, panic began to seize the people. At Cambuslang the people's fear of the military was so great that the entire inhabitants, men, women and children, left their homes and remained in the fields and glens all night. Tenants on the Duke of Hamilton's lands were forced to take refuge in the neighbouring hills. Irish immigrants, who felt that the military anger would come down heavily against them, "fled this place and neighbourhood, declaring they had seen quite enough of civil war and revolutionary horrors in their own country".

At 11 a.m. on Thursday, April 13, a troop of hussars; Lord Elcho's Midlothian Cavalry; twenty men of the Glasgow Yeomanry and thirty men of the Rifle Brigade, in wagons, together with a piece of flying artillery, set off on the Kilmarnock road. The soldiers went to Kilmarnock and arrested eleven Radicals and from here, detachments raided Newmiln and Galston, where five Radicals were arrested. The military returned to Glasgow on the following day with the exception of Lord Elcho's men who returned to Edinburgh. The *Glasgow Herald* commented that Elcho and his men had made themselves "acceptable" to the Glaswegians and "their non arrival on Friday was the cause of much disappointment and regret in a number of families".

It was felt that the concentration of troops at Hamilton was no longer needed and Lord Belhaven, the Vice Lord Lieutenant of Lanarkshire, decided to decrease their number by 200 men withdrawing the Upper Ward Yeomanry Cavalry, commanded by Sir Charles MacDonald of Lockhart, the Cambuslang Yeomanry Cavalry troop, commanded by Captain Stirling, and the Kilbride troop, commanded by Captain Graham. These troops were thanked in a public testament issued at Hamilton on April 11, in which Lord Belhaven commented: "The whole [troops] indeed deserve the thanks of the county for the zeal and unwearied patience displayed by them in the performance of their arduous and fatiguing duty, during these perilous times."

The withdrawal of these troops left only the Hamilton Volunteers under Captain Stewart and the Royal Lanarkshire Militia under Captain MacLean stationed in the town.

During the week the commander-in-chief, Major-General Bradford and his staff, returned to their headquarters in Edinburgh. With the danger now passed Bradford appointed Major-General Reynell to command the "South Western military district of Scotland". Lt. Meade of the 88th Regiment of Foot was appointed his aide-de-camp and Lt.-Colonel Smith of the Rifle Brigade succeeded Lt.-Colonel Evans as Brigade Major of the Glasgow district.

On returning to his headquarters, Bradford issued the following:

General Order
Adjut. General's Office, Edinburgh.
April 19, 1820.
The Major General commanding the forces in North Britain has great satisfaction in acquainting the troops of the lines, yeomanry and volunteer corps, who were employed on the late occasion, particularly those who repelled an attack of rebels, on the 5th inst. between Kilsyth and Falkirk, and made prisoner a great proportion of the assailants, that His Majesty has been graciously pleased to express his entire approbation of their conduct.

By order of Major General Sir Thomas Bradford KCB, commanding His Majesty's Forces in North Britain.

The raids still continued, however, and about midnight on Monday, April 17, a raid was carried out on a tenement house in Barrowfield, near Glasgow, led by Calder, the Sheriff's officer. The purpose of the raid was to arrest Roger Walsh, a cotton spinner and a known Radical leader. As two officers made their way up the dark passage-way of the tenement building, towards Walsh's room (the tenement block was divided into forty apartments), they were attacked by two men. More officers were called and, after a fierce struggle, these men were arrested and identified as Thomas Connor and Barney MacGarry, two members of the local Radical Committee. Connor, MacGarry and Walsh were brought to Glasgow at 2 a.m. and imprisoned. Later that day a similar raid was made on Milngavie and two prisoners were escorted back to Glasgow.

The hostility of the crowds was increasing as arrest followed arrest. On Wednesday, April 19, Sergeant Murdoch and eight troopers of the Glasgow Yeomanry (Light Horse), Woodall troop, were detailed to escort ammunition from Glasgow to Airdrie, where a Yeomanry troop, commanded by Captain Campbell, were stationed. Before Murdoch and his men left the city, by way of Duke Street, the soldiers were attacked by a large body of men. Murdoch gave the order to charge them and this dispersed them for a while. The crowd, however, reassembled and began to throw stones and other missiles at the military. They followed the soldiers as far as Baillieston, six miles out of the city, and only Murdoch's presence of mind in forming his troopers up and charging them managed to keep the crowd at bay. Murdoch was later commended by Captain Campbell for his "heroic defence of the ammunition".

On April 18 a notice appeared in Carlisle, trying to stir up the Carlisle Radicals to action, and this was claimed to have been printed in Glasgow on April 5, yet the Glasgow Radicals, particularly Fulton, denied all knowledge of it. Taken in context, this would seem to be the work of agent provocateurs employed in the Carlisle area and nothing to do with the Scottish Radicals.

REGENERATION and Liberty!—The Reformers of Scotland, animated with the same untameable spirit of their forefathers, have just exhibited themselves in an arduous struggle against their oppressors, and in a manly vindication of their ursurped rights. The time has arrived when longer acquiesence in Borough mongering is High Treason against the principles of a constitution that authorised resistance to the despotic Stuarts, and transferred the sceptre to worthier hands. The patriots of the North censure the apathy of their brethren of the south, in not making with them common cause in one common and glorious object. Shall the stigma remain? Union is strength and irresistible, and do not let us desert ourselves. If we do, and stand aloof, when the opportunity is afforded of emancipation, then, indeed, shall we deserve to be bound with ten fold chains, and to be crushed with still more intolerable burdens. Glasgow, April 5. Printed at Constitutional Press.

There seemed to have been no reaction whatsoever in Carlisle to this appeal.

In the early hours of Thursday, April 20, the Royal Veteran

Battalion, and a force from Glasgow, surrounded Kilmarnock. This was the second military raid on the area and thirteen suspected Radicals were arrested but, after interrogation, seven were released. A man from Newmiln and two from Galston were also arrested and these were put into a carriage and taken, under escort, to Ayr. It was said that the news of the military raid had been leaked and many Radicals had fled the town before the military surrounded it. Despite this, there was a Radical meeting at the Waterside, Galston, "at which some illegal proceedings took place" but the military again raided the area and arrested a local weaver named John Cuthill. The same day, one of the escaped Greenock prisoners was found hiding in Dalry, arrested and taken to Ayr.

In Edinburgh Captain l'Amy's 120-strong private rifle corps offered to march to Glasgow, or any parts of the country where they might be needed to put down insurrection. As the country was now fairly quiet, the Lord Advocate declined the offer with thanks. Most of the Scottish Members of Parliament, including the Lord Advocate, were now leaving for London to attend the opening of Parliament on Friday, April 21. Before he left, the Lord Advocate received a warm congratulatory letter from Lord Sidmouth, thanking him for restoring Scotland to tranquillity. That Friday, Samuel Hunter could write in the *Glasgow Herald*:

We are now enjoying the most perfect quiet in this part of the country and a great number of those arrested on suspicion of being implicated in the late transactions have been liberated, either simply, or on a bail so trifling as to imply no heavy supposition of guilt. It will be found very difficult, we suspect, to bring home this business to any person of the slightest influence in society, and it was to this circumstance we have all along acknowledged that our safety was owing—the want of leaders, among the ranks of the disaffected.

Of course, the reference to "trifling" bail is grossly inaccurate as can be seen by Turner's £150 bail which was not returned to him when charges were dropped. At the same time, the *Ayr Chronicle* was commenting:

We are glad that the Radicals have made the long threatened attempt at a general rising, because it has taught them several lessons which they could not otherwise learn.

The lessons which the *Ayr Chronicle* pointed out were, that it was hopeless to fight against overwhelming odds; that it had opened the peoples' eyes to the "designs of selfish and designing men in whom they trusted for political views", and, lastly, it had given the Government an opportunity to put down the Radicals severely. "By producing such effects as these, which we hope the late abortive insurrection will do, we entertain little dread of any similar attempts in the future, after the present commotion shall have fully subsided."

The search for Radicals still continued and William Watson, the weaver who had carried the "Scotland Free—Or A Desert" flag for Strathaven men, had a narrow escape from the searching authorities. Watson was reported to have been hiding in Greenock for several days, trying to join a ship sailing for the United States. The *Greenock Advertiser* of April 24 describes Watson, erroneously, as a "Radical leader, one of those who sallied forth from Glasgow on the 5th inst. to make a second Bannockburn of the field of Bonnymuir". Two police agents from Glasgow managed to track him down and raid his lodgings at 6 a.m. on Saturday, April 22. They burst into Watson's bedroom, awakening him and a woman ("supposedly his wife") and arrested them both. As the prisoners and their escort were going down Dalrymple Street, Watson complained that he was thirsty and pointed to the shop of John MacQueen, a spirit dealer, that they were passing. Leaving one man to guard Watson, the other went off to get a drink. Immediately, Watson struck his guard and made off. The two policemen promptly gave chase and MacQueen, thinking it a trick to get off without paying for the drinks, held on to the woman for all he was worth. Watson was soon cornered by the police but a crowd of Greenock workers came to his rescue and began a fight with the policemen. In this mêlée, Watson made his escape. In a fit of temper the policemen arrested MacQueen as an "accessory" but the spirit dealer was eventually released.

The same day, Lt.-Colonel Keith Elphinstone's 33rd Regiment of Foot, left Newcastle, and marched for Glasgow to reinforce the Scottish garrison. The authorities were now concerned with the interrogation of the prisoners they had in custody, in order to organise trials. On Monday, April 24, the Sheriff Deputy of Ayr, A. Bell, wrote to Boswell:

I had before me today your friend Gilchrist from Mauchline. He hesitated some time as to answering the question, and then requested a day or two more to think of it. This hesitation shows more honesty than some of his conspirators, as he might avoid all his confinement by a downright denial, like theirs—I scarcely think, however, that it will be safe to dispense with Paton's evidence, as so doubtful a chance as Mr Gilchrist even if he remains in this country and is forthcoming at the trial. I think Paton gets well off with impunity on condition of giving evidence, after all that he has done. If you believe him likely to abscond, it might be well to commit him like Marshal, but this I leave to your judgement, only if you wish me to grant the warrant, I have no objection to do so.

Your Auchinleck people, I have not yet had time to examine. It might be well worth while to get further evidence.

Bell felt "unfortunately, the most guilty escaped at the beginning" and that the authorities had not sufficiently strong evidence against a number of people. The Sheriff Deputy thought he did not have enough time to collect the necessary evidence as he had to prepare for the Session Courts at Edinburgh which would cause him to leave Ayr. Boswell immediately wrote to Sidmouth saying Bell's duty was in Ayr and "it should be incumbent upon him to abandon all thoughts of the Session" in order to gather evidence for the treason trials. Sidmouth transmitted this request to Sir William Rae.

Monday, April 24, was King George IV's official birthday and the authorities did not lose the opportunity to organise vast military parades, especially in Glasgow, Paisley, Ayr and other "trouble spots". Almost everywhere *feux-de-joie* were fired and bands played while troops executed impressive military drills. In Glasgow, the 7th and 10th Hussars, Glasgow Yeomanry, 13th Regiment of Foot and the newly arrived Horse Artillery gave a display of drill. This was followed in the evening by a "Grand Entertainment" given by the city's magistrates in the Town Hall. Vast crowds thronged the streets and the hussars found it necessary to keep patrols out during the night in case of disturbance.

On April 27, George IV officially opened the new session of Parliament and, although there was no direct reference to the abortive Scottish insurrection made during the official business at Westminster, King George did make reference to the affair in his speech from the throne.

... Deeply as I regret that the machination and designs of the disaffected should have led, in some parts of the country, to acts of open violence and insurrection, I cannot but express my satisfaction at the promptitude with which those attempts have been suppressed, and by the zealous co-operation of all those of my subjects, whose exertions have been called forth to support the authority of the laws.

The wisdom and firmness manifested by the late parliament and the due execution of the laws have greatly contributed to restore confidence throughout the Kingdom: and to discountenance those principles of sedition and irreligion which has been disseminated with such malignant perseverence and had poisoned the minds of the ignorant and unwary.

I rely upon the continued support of parliament in my determination to maintain, by all the means entrusted to my hands, the public safety and tranquillity.

Deploring, as well all must, the distress which still unhappily prevails among many of the labouring classes of the community, and anxiously looking forward to its removal or mitigation, it is, in the meantime, our common duty, effectually to protect the loyal, the peaceable, and the industrious, against those practices of turbulance and intimidation by which the period of relief can only be deferred and by which the pressure of distress has been incalculably aggravated.

I trust that an awakened sense of the dangers which they have incurred, and of the arts which have been employed to seduce them, will bring back by far the great part of those who have been unhappily led astray, and will revive in them that spirit of loyalty, that due submission to the laws, and that attachment to the constitution, which subsists unabated in the hearts of the great body of people, and which, under the blessing of Divine Providence, have secured to the British nation the enjoyment of a large share of practical freedom, as well as of prosperity and happiness, than have fallen to the lot of any nation in the world.

Pressed by Reid, Chapman and Haldane, who had informed them as early as April 3 that the proclamation of the "Provisional Government" had been printed on the presses of Duncan MacKenzie, the authorities decided to act, obviously finding it impossible to charge William Lang with the crime. Following the arrest of Duncan MacKenzie, a reward notice for 18-year-old Fulton and 20-year-old Hutchison was issued on April 29 and circulated.

REWARD OF THREE HUNDRED POUNDS

Whereas Robert Fulton and John Hutchison, Printers, lately employed in the office of Duncan MacKenzie, printer in Glasgow, are charged with High Treason and have absconded

A REWARD OF THREE HUNDRED POUNDS

is hereby offered to any person or persons who will give such information as shall secure the apprehension of Fulton or Hutchison. The foresaid reward to be paid by Mr Salmond, Procurator Fiscal of the County of Lanark, Glasgow, 29 April, 1820.

Fulton and Hutchison, however, had made good their escape to the United States from where Fulton wrote to his friend William Lang with a full account of the printing of the proclamation. Their escape suited the authorities well for it would have been embarrassing had Fulton and Hutchison told the truth in the subsequent trials.

At the end of April the 26-year-old Johnstone schoolmaster, John Fraser, was arrested. In his biography, Fraser gives a detailed account.

It was known that John Dunlop had sailed for America and was safe; but no one knew whither James Speirs had gone. It was concluded he was somewhere out of reach of danger, and no anxiety was felt about him. Three weeks afterwards, a letter, addressed to me, was intercepted in the Johnstone Post Office by Robert Hodgart, writer, son of Mr Hodgart of the Black Bull. It was opened. It was written by James Speirs, in confidence to me, to tell his wife he was safe and to keep herself easy. He had travelled to Ecclefechan, Dumfriesshire, and there begun to weave. Hodgart took the letter to the Sheriff and officers were instantly despatched to apprehend him. By the dawn of daylight, the next morning, a troop of cavalry surrounded my house. Loud knocking at my door aroused me from sleep. I got up and opened the door, Mr Brown, Fiscal, Paisley, and a court official, having a drawn sword in his hand, along with Mr Hodgart of the Black Bull, presented themselves. "We apprehend you," they exclaimed. "For what?" "On a charge of High Treason! Get ready to go with us." Drawers and desks were rifled, and every scrap seized and taken away. In the midst of a troop of Scots Greys I had to walk to Paisley Jail, not understanding the cause of my apprehension.

John Fraser's son, James Roy Fraser, who compiled his father's biography in 1879, recalled:

On this alarming occasion, my mother gave a strong proof of cool self possession which she afterwards manifested at the trial in St George's Church. It appeared that one of the Allans of Kilbarchan had brought my father a copy of the treasonable proclamation that he might keep as a historical curiosity. On the first alarm of the dragoons my mother sprung from bed, looked out of the window, rushed to the desk, seized the proclamation and shoved it in the fire!

John Fraser continues:

The cause of my apprehension was, however, the letter. Because Speirs confided in me, the authorities inferred that I would be connected with the whole rising movement. The suspicion was plausible but utterly untrue. The day after I was imprisoned I was subjected to a searching examination by the Sheriff. I found by his questions that he knew all about my having had the bill [proclamation] I got from Speirs—knew I had read it in Duncan MacIntyre's house. "English" Lang, with many others in Kilbarchan, was apprehended many days before me and examined and he told the Sheriff where he had seen me with the bill. He was only imprisoned a day. It was, therefore, useless for me to deny having the bill. There was Lang to prove I had it. The bill having come into my hand accidentally and implying no complicity on my part with the rising and no criminality, either morally or legally, it only became necessary for me to satisfy the Sheriff how I got it.

Speirs being regarded as safely out of the reach of the authorities, I thought that no injury to him could ensue from my simply telling the truth as to how I got it. Had I not, my having it, unaccounted for, would, in the event of a trial, have been a serious point against me. I was next examined as to having been the writer of the bill. I was not. Some years afterwards, it was proved it came from London, concocted under the auspices of Government by two spies, Oliver and Richmond. The Government wanted to commit the people to overt acts of rebellion to get a few of them hanged, beheaded, and thereby put down the cry for reform. I was next confronted with the two letters to the clergymen, and made to write before them to compare my writing with the letters. I had, however, been sufficiently cautious to alter the usual character of my writing, so that they could not perceive much likeness between the two—none on which to found any charge on me as the writer of the two letters. Of course, I denied knowing anything about them. I had, in writing them, been a mere copyist, had merely done by request a friendly service to the two men who made it, though certainly a very incautious and a very dangerous act.

At the time, a young, inexperienced man, I did not sufficiently realise the incautious and dangerous character of my act. Moreover, the letters, though treasonable, were meant for good to all people. To have confessed being the writer would have been equivalent to putting the suffocating noose around my own neck, and getting my head chopped off at a blow. I was not prepared nor desirous of being thus complimented and distinguished by the polite attentions of the hangman. Being a mere copyist, I felt that, on moral grounds, I ought not to be held as a principal. Who under these circumstances would have told the Sheriff the simple truth?

Three days after this examination an imprisoned debtor told us, through the keyhole of our cell door, that Speirs had been apprehended and was in the next cell to ours. I was painfully astonished. I sent through this same channel my sympathising compliments. He sent me back word that he was the innocent cause of my apprehension by addressing his letter to me, and expressing his deep regret at the circumstance. I saw Speirs' case was a bad one—he having committed himself so openly, in overt acts, on the public streets of Johnstone on the "rising Monday". In a day or two, I wrote the Sheriff, demanding my liberation on the ground that, in point of fact, I had nothing to do with the revolutionary movement. He called on the following Sunday at my cell. "Mr Fraser, I have received a letter from you demanding your liberation and maintaining your innocence. You are the very man we want to make an example of. Your position should have taught you not to mingle yourself up with such political disorderly affairs." "Very well, my lord, I will have to be prepared for the defence when that time comes." Sheriff Campbell delivered himself with a very overawing dignified air. It was all a piece of acting. He told my wife who called on him for the same purpose a few days afterwards, that they had nothing against me, and not to concern herself about public rumours, but come to him and he would tell her how matters stood in relation to my condition. He smilingly told her my imprisonment would do me good in the future.

A very strong feeling grew up in Johnstone in favour of my liberation. William Houston Esq., Johnstone Castle, applied for my liberation to the Sheriff, who regretted he was too long in applying, stating that the cases were then all in the Lord Advocate's hands and that none would be set free until the trials were over. There was no help for it now but submission till the weary time came, nearly four months afterwards. My school was conducted by one of my advanced pupils, Robert Donald, who afterwards became a teacher in Linwood, next to Paisley, where he not long ago died. The political prisoners were now all assorted and classified, preparatory to a long period of bondage.

But the troubles in Scotland were far from being over. At 2.30 a.m. on April 30, a police patrol in a Glasgow suburb was attacked by twenty to thirty armed Radicals. The police patrol had come across the Radicals preparing to attack the house of a cotton spinner employer. There had been a growing number of attacks on employers, particularly those engaged in cotton spinning, who had obeyed the employers' resolution and had sacked those whom they suspected of Radical sympathies.

At the end of April orders came through for the withdrawal of the 10th Hussars from Scotland. They were to leave Piershill Barracks on May 1 and go to London, being replaced by the 7th Dragoon Guards then stationed at Preston. On May 1 it was officially announced that a Special Commission would be set up to consider charges of High Treason against the Radical prisoners. All the lords of the justiciary would serve on the commission which would be headed by Lord President Hope, Lord Justice Clerk Boyle, Lord Chief Baron Sir Samuel Shepherd, and Lord Chief Commissioner of the Jury Court Adam.

The arrests still continued and, on May 3, Sheriff Deputy Bell and a party of military, surrounded a house in Stewarton and arrested three Radicals who were escorted to Ayr. Several others were arrested but released soon afterwards. That day the 8th Royal Veteran Battalion, 860 strong, arrived in Ayr, having arrived back from duties in Ireland, en route for Stirling. At the same time the 7th Dragoon Guards were arriving to replace the 10th Hussars. On May 5 a group of the 7th Hussars raided Eagleston and arrested 11 Radicals whom they escorted to Paisley. On May 12, John Allan of Condorrat was arrested and sent to Stirling Castle. On May 30 a search was made in Bridgeton and a large number of pikes were found in the cellar of a house wrapped up in copies of *The Black Dwarf* . . . "a most appropriate wrapper", commented a justice.

That the "troubles" were not just confined to the industrial belt is clear from the various letters to Lord Sidmouth. D. Dick of Glenshiel, writing on May 19, 1820, commented: "I was in hopes the fate of Thistlewood and others would have had a good effect here in putting an end to the disturbances we have lately experienced. I am, however, sorry to say that is not the case, early this morning my house was fired in and nine shots lodged in the wall." Mr. Dick added that his boat had been "broken into a dozen of pieces" and "I am afraid it is not confined to the lower classes but to the better sort of the old tenants". Three of Dick's horses were also killed.

On June 5, John Hamilton, Factor (Steward) to the Marquis of Hastings, wrote from Loudoun to Alexander Boswell:

Apparently they [the Radicals] are as quiet and humble as possible, and those who have occasional intercourse with them inform me that their expressions are much more guarded than formerly.

In short, that they seem to feel as if they could make nothing of it, and that they may as well not expose themselves to the punishment, which some of their neighbours have experienced. If they continue their reading societies, it must be in the most private manner, and not in the open audacious way formerly adopted. The Manchester Observer and Woolers Publications still come to Newmiln and are read by a few subscribers, but the twopenny pamphlets are exploded and consequently the weekly contributions. One of the Newmiln Baillies told me today that many of his fellows who were most violent in favour of Radicalism actually felt ashamed of their conduct and never now spoke of the subject. None who absconded have yet returned, at least openly. It is reported, but I am inclined to disbelieve it, that some of them lodge in their own houses during the night. Two were recognised in the neighbourhood of Glasgow last Thursday by a person from this neighbourhood. We shall certainly keep a strict watch over them and seize them if possible.

The weavers are all employed and wages improved a little, indeed, for some kind of work, considerably. Meal, cheese and butter are abundant now so that they have not much cause to grumble from want.

Writing from his home in Clifford Street, London, Lord Sidmouth told Boswell: "The rising is certainly smothered; and, I trust, it may 'ere long be extinguished, but we must all be vigilant."

FOURTEEN

"OYER AND TERMINER"

ON FRIDAY, JUNE 9, the *Edinburgh Weekly Chronicle* stated:
A Special Commission of Oyer and Terminer for the trying of all
Treasons and Misprisons of Treasons within the counties of Lanark,
Dumbarton, Renfrew, Stirling and Ayr, have now been received
and we understand it comprehends the heads of all four courts, and
all the Lords Commissioner of Justiciary. The Grand Jury, it is said,
is to be assembled at Stirling on the 23rd and at Glasgow on the 26th
inst. and if true bills are found, the trials will commence early in
July. The brother of the gentleman who officiated in the last trials
for treason in Scotland, is to act as Clerk of the Arraigns, and has
left Edinburgh for Falkirk, to make arrangements for summoning
the Grand Jury.

As the last treason trials in Scotland, those in 1817, had proved
such a fiasco, Lord Sidmouth felt that someone who could be
trusted to push the trials through should be sent to Scotland to
assist the Scottish authorities in conducting the affair and to
make sure there were no slip ups this time. The man he chose
was a London barrister named John Hullock, who was a ser-
geant-at-law, a barrister of the highest rank at the English Bar.
Hullock was well known in professional circles and was the
author of a book entitled *The Law of Costs*, published in 1792
and which had run to a second edition in 1810. Hullock, who
was rewarded for his service to the Crown with a knighthood on
April 21, 1823, was paid the sum of £2,000 to conduct the
prosecution. Sidmouth also sent Sir Samuel Shepherd, the
Lord Chief Baron, to sit on the Special Commission to instruct
the judges in English Law. Shepherd's usual role was at the Court
of the Exchequer in Westminster.

Now, despite the fact that the Treaty of Union of 1707 had
stated "that all Laws in use within the Kingdom of Scotland,
do, after the Union and notwithstanding thereof, remain in the
same force as before", an Act of Queen Anne had dismissed the

Scottish laws appertaining to high treason and the English laws dating back to Edward III (1327–77) were brought into force. Still, however, no English barrister could practise in a Scottish court unless he had a Scottish law degree, and no Scottish advocate could practise in England without an English law degree. This is still in effect today. Despite this, the Scottish authorities accepted Hullock as being qualified to conduct the prosecution in the subsequent trials, entirely contrary to the Treaty of Union.

On June 21 the Bonnymuir prisoners, who had been held in Edinburgh Castle for interrogation, were taken to Stirling Castle by steam boat under a guard commanded by Captain Sibbald. The following day, June 22, the Lords of the Commission arrived by road and were received at St Ninians by Provost Buchan and magistrates Young, Paterson, Aikman and Balfour. A guard of troops of the 13th Regiment and the Glasgow Yeomanry (Light Horse), commanded by Captain Charles Stirling, stood to arms. The Commissioners took up rooms at the Lion Inn where they were welcomed by General Graham, the deputy governor of Stirling Castle. "There was a great influx of visitors to witness the trials, and accommodation for men and horse was difficult to obtain", reported one observer.

The Special Commission opened in the Court House, Broad Street, Stirling, with a prayer from the Rev. Dr Wright, on Friday, June 23. The Commission consisted of Lord President Hope, assisted by Lord Justice Clerk Boyle, Lord Chief Commissioner of the Jury Court, W. Adam, Lord Chief Baron of the Court of the Exchequer, Sir Samuel Shepherd, Lord Hermond and Lord Gillies, who had been called to the Bar with his fellow student Thomas Muir. Mr Thomas G. Knapp was the Clerk of the Arraigns and the Lord Advocate, Sir William Rae, appeared for the prosecution assisted by Mr Serjeant Hullock and Henry Home Drummond, the Adovocate Deputy; in addition, a number of younger Crown advocates were present.

After the Grand Jury were sworn, a proclamation by George IV, against vice, profaneness and immorality was read—this coming from the greatest libertine of all, renowned for all three, must have caused considerable amusement among the people, though they dared not admit to it in public. Mr Knapp announced that one commission had been prepared in Latin and the other in English. The Lords of the Commission decided that the English text should be read. Lord President Hope then addressed the Grand Jury, whose foreman was the Hon. George Abercromby, a fierce anti-Radical, to explain why the trials were being held under English law and not Scottish law.

Trials for high treason, said Hope, were extremely rare in Scotland. Indeed, he thought that the trials of Watt and Downie, in 1794, were the only such trials to be held since the Union of 1707. This, in fact, was almost correct. The trials of 1817 had dissolved in fiasco and the trials of the leaders of the various Scottish uprisings, such as 1715 and 1745, etc., all took place in England, contrary to the Treaty of Union but in order to ensure convictions against the Scots which a Scottish court would probably not have given. Hope explained that the Treaty of Union had preserved Scottish law in all other cases but an Act of Queen Anne determined that in cases of high treason the same course should be followed in Scotland as in England. In "ordinary crimes" Scottish law was more than adequate, but the Scottish law on treason was not well defined. The treason law of England, dating back to Edward III, was clear and by a statute of that reign it was made treason to compass or imagine the death of the King, Queen, his son and heirs, or the Queen and her heirs. The criminal intention was what called for the measure of punishment.

Overt acts of treason varied from providing arms, assembling men to consult for a purpose leading to treason, or instigating others to commit treason. Lord President Hope added that Sir Walter Tyrrel, in killing William Rufus of England, had not committed treason because the statute did not say that the killing of the king was such, but levying war against the king, such as those risings against the English kings Edward II, Richard II, Henry VI and Charles I, were treasonable acts. It was an overt act of treason to enlist men to make war against the monarch to compel the monarch to dismiss the government by force. The statute of Edward III and that of George III (36th), passed in consequence of a daring assassination attempt on him, plus the 57th Statute of George III, made it treason to compass or imagine the death or destruction of the monarch. Lord President Hope pointed out that a statute of Scottish law, passed in the year 1662 "was little different . . .". This slip, in pointing out that there were adequate laws in Scotland, no different from the English law now being imposed on the court, seems to destroy Lord President Hope's entire argument as to why the case should be heard under English law. Probably realising his error in referring to the law of 1662, the Lord President doggedly continued by pointing out that under the 36th Act of George III, it was made treason to levy war against the king within his realm in order to compel him to change his measures or government, or in order to put any force upon him. The legal profession agreed that it was not necessary for troops to be raised in battalions and regularly clothed to establish the crime of levying war. Hope alluded to the start of the 1745 uprising when Prince Charles raised an ill clad and ill armed army. "However ill arraigned, ill disciplined, or ill armed, a body of men may be, when assembled for the purpose of redressing grievances, real or imaginary, it is an act of rebellion, levying war, and compassing the death of the king."

Hope then pointed out the differences between levying war and riot. When a rising was but a "tumult for private purposes" then it was a riot, however numerous the body of people were. The Porteous Riots in this case were not treason, but the breaking into prison and compelling magistrates to liberate prisoners did amount to the crime of treason. Likewise proclamations telling the people to rise, or urging them to rise by the spoken word, also amounted to treason and the authors, printers and publishers were guilty.

In ordinary crimes, many benefits arose from Scottish law. In English law a conviction could follow on the testimony of one credible witness, but in Scottish law there had to be two such witnesses at least. In the present case, under the terms of the English law, it was not necessary for more than one witness to prove each overt act of treason against the accused. The duty of the Grand Jury, at present, was not to infer guilt but to judge whether there were sufficient grounds for bringing charges of high treason against the prisoners.

Following Hope's address, the Grand Jury retired with Lt. Ellis Hodgson and Lt. Davidson, and other eyewitnesses to the Bonnymuir affair. After three hours they returned to the court-room and the Hon. George Abercromby announced that true

H

bills for high treason had been found against John Baird; Andrew Hardie; Thomas MacCulloch, a stocking weaver, Glasgow; John Barr, weaver, Condorrat; William Smith, weaver, Condorrat; Benjamin Moir, labourer, Glasgow; Allan Murchie, blacksmith, Glasgow; Alexander Latimer, weaver, Glasgow; Alexander Johnston, weaver, Glasgow; Andrew White, bookbinder, Glasgow; David Thomson, weaver, Glasgow; William Clackson or Clarkson, shoemaker, Glasgow; Thomas Pike or Pink, muslin slinger, Glasgow; Robert Gray, weaver, Glasgow; James Cleland, blacksmith, Glasgow; Alexander Hart, cabinet-maker, Glasgow; Thomas MacFarlane, weaver, Condorrat and James Wright. These accused were the eighteen "Bonnymuir" prisoners. Following the Grand Jury's findings, the prisoners were brought into the court and served with copies of their indictments and with lists of witnesses. A spokesman for the prisoners, who were not legally represented, then asked the Lord President if Francis Jeffrey and J. P. Grant could be assigned as their advocates and Messrs. David Blackie and William Alexander as their agents. Lord President Hope said that this would be considered and they were informed that the arraigning would take place on July 6 and the trials would probably commence about July 17.

The Commission then adjourned until 9 a.m. the next day when the prisoners from Camelon, Balfron and St Ninians were considered for trial. At 3 p.m. the Grand Jury returned to the court and found true bills against John MacMillan, a nailer, Camelon; James Aitken, grocer, Falkirk; James Burt, nailer, Camelon; Andrew Burt Jnr., nailer, Camelon; James Aitken, wright, Camelon; Daniel Turner, nailer, Camelon; Andrew Dawson, nailer, Camelon, and John Johnstone, a shoemaker, Falkirk. Most of the prisoners asked for Francis Jeffrey and Henry Cockburn to defend them and George Bremner of Stirling to act as their agent.

True bills were also found against James Anderson; James Rait and George Lennox, of St Ninians and William Crawford; George Gillies; Moses Gilfillan; Andrew Reid; Andrew MacFarlane; James Gunn; Robert Drew and Joseph Gettie of Balfron and against Peter MacCullum of Falkirk.

On Monday the Special Commission moved to Glasgow where the justiciary lodged in the George Inn. The same procedure was followed as at Stirling with the Lord President, having sworn in the Grand Jury, explaining the law. Everyone of the Grand Jury, whose foreman was Hugh Boyle of Calderbank, were people with estates and members of the local Yeomanry corps. Having gone through the ritual of retiring with various witnesses the Grand Jury found true bills against James Wilson and William MacIntyre of Strathaven, and also against William Watson and William Robertson, who were not in custody. The two prisoners asked for Francis Jeffrey and James Miller as their advocates and for Mr Fleming to act as their writer.

The Commission again met at Glasgow on Tuesday and more witnesses were examined. At 4 p.m. the Grand Jury returned and found true bills against George Allan; W. Campbell, two Glasgow cotton spinners; John May, a weaver; Alex Graham, a wright and Matthew Bogle, a weaver, all Glasgow men. It is noted that Matthew Bogle was "a man of colour" probably from the West Indies. Alexander Graham asked for Francis Jeffrey and Henry Cockburn to act as his advocates and the rest followed, all naming Messrs. Graham and Mitchell as their agents.

During the holding of these Commissions, the country was far from subdued and quiet. On Saturday, June 21, during the evening, Alexander Dunlop of Clobar, an officer of the Strathblane troop of Yeomanry cavalry, was out with his men on patrol. Suddenly shots were fired at him from behind a nearby dyke, grazing his horse's bridle. He dismounted and returned the fire but his assailant escaped. Later a man was arrested and sent to Stirling on suspicion of being an attacker. A large section of the workers were still out on strike and, at Milngavie, on June 22, a group of Radical strikers fired at the houses of people who were returning to work as a warning for them not to do so. Large-scale military parades and raids for arms were held in order to keep the population in awe of the strength of the authorities. The Glasgow Yeomanry, under Samuel Hunter, were much in evidence on Wednesday, June 28, when the regiment held a spectacular parade which was inspected by the new commanding officer of the area, Major-General Reynell, and his staff, as well as the Commissioners of the court. Following the parade the Commissioners and the justiciary left Glasgow for Dumbarton.

That evening soldiers of the 13th Regiment of Foot rioted against the Glaswegians. The events of the past few months had caused the English soldiers in Scotland to become embittered against the Scots, the feeling being inflamed by the Scottish nationalist attitude, especially towards the English soldiers. Soldiers of the 13th Regiment were drinking in a tavern in the Saltmarket, Glasgow, and the hostility of the ordinary Scottish people had reduced their tempers to breaking point. Between 7 p.m. and 8 p.m., these soldiers left the tavern to return to their barracks. Instead of going there, however, they remained in the street shouting insults about Scotland and Scottish people at passers by. One soldier, arguing with a Scot, became violent and the police were called.

This seemed to incite the soldiers against the "Scotch police" and they drew their bayonets, charging up the street to the Cross, clearing the path before them with vicious jabs. The police managed to arrest one soldier and he was taken, after a fierce struggle, to the police office. The rest of the soldiers took possession of the area from the Trongate to the Exchange. Glaswegians now gathered at the back of the Tontine, their patriotic feelings aroused by the soldiers' insults. The policemen gathered forces and tried to pacify the soldiers but, again wielding their bayonets, the soldiers launched an attack on the crowd. In this running skirmish, which lasted for half an hour, a policeman named Bain, trying to keep off three soldiers who were attacking him, was wounded by bayonet jabs.

"It is wonderful that no person was killed on the spot considering the infuriated state of the military and the manner they dealt out the blows with their bayonets", commented the *Glasgow Herald*, Friday, June 30.

Eventually, the soldiers were overpowered by the police and taken to the police office, but here they managed to break loose and started to smash doors and windows in the office. Reinforcements were called out and a troop of the Rifle Brigade were brought in. These managed to overpower the men of the 13th Regiment. Sixteen of the soldiers were arrested of which four were taken to hospital. On Sunday, July 9, one of them, whose skull was fractured in the disturbance, died in his barracks. Ten policemen received severe bayonet wounds and a large number of civilians were also wounded.

The magistrates arrested a man "trying to inflame the populace". A military and civil inquiry was set up and, despite the evidence that the affair had been instigated by drunken, brawling troopers, the inquiry found that the people of Glasgow (i.e. the police) had made an unprovoked attack on the soldiers. An officer of the regiment, who was not at the scene of the disturbances at all, testified that he was leading his men back to barracks when a group of people attacked them and they had to defend themselves. The fact that the soldiers were drinking in a tavern beforehand was ignored. A letter was then sent to the *Glasgow Herald*, from the regiment, demanding an apology for its "inaccurate report of the proceedings" during the disturbance.

On Thursday, June 29, the Special Commission opened in Dumbarton, the church being adapted as a courtroom for the occasion. The Grand Jury was assembled, again consisting of the local Yeomanry officers and landed gentry, with the Hon. Archibald Fleming as foreman. Again the Lord President gave an address on the law and the jury retired with the various witnesses. True bills were found against Patrick MacDevitt; William Blair; Robert Munroe; George Munroe; Richard Thompson and William MacPhie, all of whom had been seized at Duntocher during the "Battle of the Bellows". Two other prisoners, also from Duntocher, were named in the charge but these turned King's Evidence and their names were struck out. Bills were also found against seven other men who had escaped and presumably fled the country: Robert MacKinlay; William Rowney; Robert Sinclair; John Stewart; Daniel MacNab; Archibald MacLean and Alexander Lindsay, also from Duntocher.

In the afternoon the Commission boarded a steamship and sailed from Dumbarton to Renfrew where the Provost of Paisley, Oliver Jamieson, Sheriff Campbell and local magistrates met them with a detachment of the 7th Hussars. With this escort, the Commission was taken to the Tontine Inn which was surrounded with a troop of the 13th Regiment and the two companies of the Paisley Yeomanry. The authorities were taking no chances with the lives of the Commission in Radical Paisley. It was felt that Radical feeling in Paisley was far from subdued and that the Paisley Radicals might make an attempt on the lives of the Special Commission.

In the meantime, the Johnstone schoolmaster, John Fraser, and his fellow prisoners, John Neil of Paisley, Alexander Thomson and James Speirs, had been confined in a single cell. Fraser recalled:

There was not room for all of us to walk on the stone floor. Two lay on the bed whilst the other two walked. Thus we alternated our exercise. Our small iron grated window faced the High Street. We spent much time, though four or five stories high, in gazing out at the passers by, many an eye being turned up to us.

A Mr Carlyle, a manufacturer, visited the prisoners frequently as a voluntary missionary to give religious advice, as the prisoners had already been condemned by the local clergy who would not visit them. Carlyle and Neil held frequent debates on the credibility of the Bible and the manufacturer supplied the prisoners with books to read such as *The Bishop of Llandaff*, *Age of Reason*, Erskine's *Institutes of the Law of Treason* and Murray's *Grammar*. With the aid of Robin, the assistant jailer, the men managed to get pens, paper and ink as well as candles for the evening. When Robin entered the cell at the time for the daily check, the prisoners managed to secrete letters for him to deliver despite the fact that John Hart, the head jailer, would be standing at the door. The prisoners were allowed two loaves per day and water but permission was given for relatives to bring meals, which were checked by John Hart to make sure nothing else was brought in for the men. A constant communication was set up between the prisoners and George Fowler, a Paisley bookseller, who was another political prisoner confined in the cell below.

We kept up constant correspondence with him, tying our rolled up communications to a bit of thread, and swinging them over the window below, where they were caught and pulled in by George; then he attached his own letters to the thread, which we pulled up. Thus we became so far society to each other. We, in this manner, were constantly posted up with outside news and speculation in reference to ourselves.

The prisoners were not allowed newspapers but managed to get general news occasionally from imprisoned debtors, who were allowed to visit them for general conversation. When news of the Commission came to the prisoners, John Fraser wrote: "We all felt that this Commission smelt of human blood, and that, if it were possible, human blood would be spilt and many of us made to dangle at a rope's end."

The Special Commission opened in Paisley on Saturday, July 1. As there was no Paisley court large enough for the trials, St George's church had been converted for the occasion by Mr Playfair of Edinburgh. The Commissioners and justiciary, wigged and gowned, and guarded by men of the 13th Regiment, Paisley Yeomanry and hussars, left the Tontine Inn. The band of the 13th Regiment led the procession beginning with "God Save the King". In defiance, John Fraser and the Radical prisoners roared out the Scottish national anthem, "Scots Wha Hae".

This we did, shouting at the utmost stretch of our voices. The whole crowd, judges and all, turned their eyes to our open cell windows, our foreheads projecting outwards as far as the iron stanchions would permit. In a little we heard John Hart rattling his keys furiously at the cell door. Opening it, he exclaimed: "Ye're a wheen deevils; I'll put ye in chains, and shut ye up in darkness!" The latter threat he instantly executed. That was the reward we got for our Scottish patriotism.

The same procedure was carried out as at the previous hearings and true bills were found against James Speirs and John Lang. John Fraser, John Neil and Alexander Thomson, were told that they would be brought to trial after Speirs and Lang. True bills were also found against John Smellie, weaver, Elderslie; James Walker, weaver, Johnstone; Robert Parker, shoemaker, Johnstone, and James Nixon, weaver, Elderslie, all of whom had fled the country. A John Young was also named. Speirs and Lang asked for Francis Jeffrey and J. P. Grant to act as their advocates and for P. and J. Jack, Paisley, for their agents.

The Rev. Dr J. Finlay led prayers for the Commission which then left the church to return to the Tontine Inn. As they emerged, angry crowds started to surge round them and the soldiers had to drive them back. A man from Elderslie received a stab wound in the arm and a young man named Logie was cut on the head by a sergeant using a halbert, an axe-like weapon with a hook on the back. Reinforcements were called and Provost Jamieson, observing the crowd to be inflamed by the sergeant's action, ordered the man to go to the police office in order to placate them. The soldiers were told to remove their bayonets to prevent further bloodshed.

Fraser, Neil and Thomson were removed from Speirs' cell and taken to another one where they were locked in with six other prisoners. Although it was a large cell it was

. . . swarming with bugs, innumerable. We were horrified. Every seam in the floor and every crack in the walls was crowded with the vile vermin. We had to lay our mattress on the bare floor. In the morning the mattress, blankets, and our personal apparel were covered with the bloody tribe from which there was no escape. The following night we tried to surround our bed with a rampart of water laid on the floor but the assailants managed to surmount the barricade. There was no hope for us but submission to the conquering enemy; they were too numerous to be exterminated.

Fraser had made himself well acquainted with the treason laws and managed to see Speirs' and Lang's writer, Peter Jack. Fraser put several points to him and the names of those who were to be called as witnesses. John Mitchell, the Radical poet, took the list and travelled the country ascertaining their views and the character of each potential juryman. The names of the more liberal men among them were given to Speirs' and Lang's advocates before the trial.

The Commission opened in Ayr on July 4 and the procedures were again repeated. True bills were found against John Dickie, weaver, Mauchline; Hugh Wallace, weaver, Mauchline; Thomas MacKay, a tailor, Mauchline and Andrew Wyllie, a flesher, Mauchline. True bills were also found against thirteen other men who had managed to flee the country. These were William Orr, shoemaker; John Dunlop, weaver; James Wyllie, weaver; Robert Kerr, slater; James Rayburn, weaver; all from Stewarton; John Goldie, weaver; Joseph Abbott, weaver; Alexander Roxburgh, weaver; George Roxburgh, weaver; James Roxburgh, weaver; Andrew Adamson, weaver and Alexander Wilson, weaver, all from Galston, and, lastly, James Nisbett, weaver from Loudounkirk. The prisoners named Francis Jeffrey and Henry Cockburn as their advocates and Messrs. Morton and Harper of Ayr as their agents.

The business of the Special Commission was now over. The Lord Advocate, Sir William Rae, announced that true bills had been found against eighty-eight persons on a charge of high treason of which thirty-eight had not appeared; some of these had not been discovered, while others had fled to foreign countries. These people would be declared outlaws which, in high treason, had more serious consequences than in ordinary law as it would amount to a record of guilt on the part of those who had fled. Although fifty prisoners were in court to answer charges it was estimated that there were still some 200 suspected Radicals in prison in the five counties under threat of prosecution and the eighty-eight true bills were just a cross-section chosen for the example that the authorities wished to make. Before the trials proper could proceed, the Special Commission, now constituted as the High Court of Justiciary, would have to travel the five counties again for the purposes of arraigning the prisoners—to hear the formal plea of guilty or not guilty.

The court opened at 10 a.m. on July 6, at Stirling, for this purpose, with the same judges and with Lord Advocate, Mr Serjeant Hullock, Henry Home Drummond and James Arnott for the prosecution. Robert Hunter and A. Hope Cullen appeared as advocates for the Bonnymuir prisoners. An attempt had been made to get Francis Jeffrey and Henry Cockburn to act as advocates, in accordance with the wishes of the prisoners, but they had refused, saying they were Scottish advocates who would appear in Scottish courts and had no knowledge of English law and would not appear in an English court.

The first prisoner to be arraigned was the Glasgow stocking weaver, Thomas MacCulloch. Mr Knapp, the Clerk of the Arraigns, read the Bill of Indictment to him and asked him how he wished to plead. At this, Hope Cullen rose and said he wished to make some observations to the court before the prisoners pleaded. Firstly, he objected to the fact that the place where the treason was said to have occurred was not specifically mentioned. The first overt act of treason alleged, was that the prisoners had, on April 1, assembled "with force and arms at the parish of Falkirk aforesaid, in the county of Stirling aforesaid". Hope Cullen argued that the words "at the parish of Falkirk" were too indefinite and that the special vill or hamlet ought to be mentioned. There were several such vills or hamlets in Falkirk and it was impossible, from the indictment, to discover to what place the charges were meant to refer. In support of his argument, Hope Cullen, quoted eight Scottish law references.

At this stage in the trials the authorities showed their hand as to how the trials would be conducted. For the prosecution, Mr Serjeant Hullock stood up and said that it was sufficient in English law to lay the venue of the crime in a county without specifying the parish or vill. The Indictment was certainly good enough in English law, Scottish law notwithstanding. Hullock mentioned, as his references, the trial of Brandeth and Thistlewood in 1817 and Thistlewood and others in 1820. The Lord Chief Baron, Sir Samuel Shepherd, complimented Hope Cullen on the manner he made his pleas but pointed out that the court was not interested in Scottish law. Notwithstanding the authorities from Scottish law, the plea would be overruled in England and it was the duty of the court to overrule it now. Hope Cullen had no option but to withdraw his plea. Mr Knapp then repeated his question.

"Thomas MacCulloch, are you Guilty or Not Guilty?"

"Not Guilty."

"How will you be tried?"

"By God and my country."

"God send you a good deliverance."

The same formula was repeated with each prisoner and the Lord President fixed the trial for July 13 at 9 a.m. The following day the rest of the prisoners were arraigned all pleading Not Guilty. Towards the end of the day the 33rd Regiment of Foot marched into Stirling in preparation to take over from the 13th Regiment, who were to leave Stirling by September for Edinburgh, in preparation to leave for Ireland in October. In the meantime, Francis Jeffrey, Cockburn and Murray, nominated by the prisoners as leading defence advocates, still "positively refused" to attend the trials because they were being conducted under English law. By July 10 they decided they would take part in the defence only if they were assisted by English barristers owing to their "inability in English law" otherwise the "advantage will be with the Crown". Robert Graham of Whitehall and Andrew Mitchell, two of the defence agents, spent £300 out of their own pocket, in order to bring a London solicitor named Harmer to attend the trials and advise the defence on English law.

On Saturday, July 8, the court assembled in Glasgow to hear the pleas of James Wilson and William MacIntyre. Mr Knapp read out the Bill of Indictment, which took one hour to read. Before the pleas were made, A. E. Monteith, the defence advocate, raised an objection "which he did with the utmost humility, confident of his want of a correct knowledge of English law". There was a misnomer in the summons of the Sheriff where a witness named Cuthill was designated as Letham Cuthill when, in fact, the witness was named Lithan Cuthill. He reminded the court that, under Scottish law, Letham could be considered a different person from Lithan. Mr Serjeant Hullock was on his feet immediately sneering at the objection. It was perfectly sufficient he said, both in law and common sense, that if a man was sworn to a name, he answered it. Again Hullock was backed by the Lord Chief Baron, who commented that by the law of England it mattered not how a person spelt his name but that the sound of the name be the same. The Lord President said the objection was without weight. Wilson and MacIntyre then pleaded Not Guilty and the trial was fixed for July 20.

On Monday, July 10, William Campbell and George Allan pleaded Not Guilty. John May, Alexander Graham and Matthew Bogle were brought up and an objection was made to the indictment of Graham. Hullock said it was in his power to correct the mistake and a new indictment was made out. Graham said he pleaded Guilty but was warned by the Lord President not to do so hurriedly. A plea of Guilty was irrevocable. Graham, along with May and Bogle, then pleaded Not Guilty.

Unrest was still continuing, though most of the manufacturing population had now returned to work. On Tuesday, July 11, a patrol of the Rifle Brigade were attacked in the Calton area. Two men were later arrested and fined. The following day the court opened at Dumbarton where, before the arraigning, the advocate for the defence, E. D. Sandford, raised two objections. Firstly, he claimed, that a person on the Grand Jury was not legally qualified to serve. Secondly he claimed that two persons had been in the room with the Grand Jury while they were considering their bills and these had no right to be there. They were "a gentleman connected with the prosecution" and the Clerk of the Arraigns. Sandford also said that the verdict was not in the handwriting of the foreman of the jury.

On the first objection, Sandford refused to verify his charge on affidavit. On the second objection, the court considered the matter as a gross insinuation to the Crown and claimed that the prosecution advocate and the Clerk of the Arraigns could not mix with the Grand Jury after the witnesses had been examined and that the verdict was in the handwriting of the foreman. The Lord President insisted that Sandford make out an affidavit and, seeing the danger, Sandford backed down apologising to the court, agreeing that the jury had not been tampered with and that the information communicated to him was erroneous. All the prisoners pleaded Not Guilty.

The court moved on to Paisley where Speirs and Lang pleaded Not Guilty, and then on to Ayr. At Ayr, James Howie claims

. . . there was not sufficient evidence to prove the charges, and the Commissioners were eager to have a conviction against someone, so as to strike terror to all the country, both presently and respectively, they made a bargain with a young man named MacKay. This young man belonged to Stewarton, it was said, and was advised by the Commissioners, the authorities, and his friends, to plead Guilty to the charge of treason. He, at first, refused to do so, though he was assured of a free and unconditional pardon if he would only act as he was desired to do. By the influence of his father and other relations, who are supposed to have been tampered with by Government, he at last reluctantly consented to plead guilty as the only means of saving his life.

When the court opened, MacKay, Wyllie, Wallace and Dickie were marched under escort from the town jail to the court, in the New Church, Ayr, which had been converted for the occasion. Wyllie, Wallace and Dickie pleaded Not Guilty but MacKay, "to the astonishment of all present pled Guilty".

To none did MacKay's plea cause more surprise than to Mr Grant, the counsel, who had been engaged to defend him and the others. He turned quickly round and looked at the prisoner sternly in the face as if to reproach him for recklessly throwing his life away.

The preliminaries thus gone through, the authorities were all set for the trials proper to begin. The trials would give the legal sanction for the authorities to make examples out of the Radicals whom they had managed to incite, through their agent provocateurs, to take up arms.

FIFTEEN

THE TRIALS

THE TRIALS FOR High Treason opened at Stirling on Thursday, July 13, with the courtroom being "uncommon crowded". Two large boxes of the arms seized at Bonnymuir were carried under military escort from Stirling Castle to the courtroom where 153 gentlemen, who were to form the various juries, were waiting to be assembled. The Lord Advocate, Sir William Rae, Mr Serjeant Hullock and Henry Home Drummond headed a large number of Crown advocates, aided by James Arnott, their agent, who had prepared the case for the Crown. For the defence, Francis Jeffrey, R. Hunter and A. Hope Cullen appeared with Messrs. Blackie and W. Alexander acting as their agents. Jeffrey had been honest with the Radical prisoners and had told them to "prepare for the worst". He had no illusions about a fair trial. The Government were clearly going to make an example of the Bonnymuir men and Jeffrey wrote to his friend, Mrs Morehead, after the trial, "I have made two long speeches, and have not spared or disgraced myself; though success was scarcely possible." It was with this attitude—that "success was scarcely possible"—that Jeffrey prepared to launch into the defence.

Following the entrance of the judges at 9.45 a.m., the eighteen Bonnymuir prisoners were brought into the courtroom. At once Francis Jeffrey was on his feet objecting to the presence of Mr Serjeant Hullock in a Scottish Court of Law. Jeffrey pointed out that Hullock was not entitled to appear in the court because he was an English barrister. He was fully aware that since the laws passed by Queen Anne the treason laws of England were now imposed in Scotland. Nevertheless, he contended that the court was a Scottish one and, meaning no disrespect to Hullock, Jeffrey merely observed that he saw a phalanx of counsel arraigned against the prisoners led by an English barrister. A long, legal argument followed and Hullock seemed to take an exceptional dislike to Jeffrey, taking his arguments as a personal affront. In his arrogance, Hullock began to make slighting remarks about Scotsmen and Scotland. His uncourteous attitude, which was to manifest itself against Jeffrey throughout the trial, provoked even the Scottish Tories in the court to anger. Ranald MacDonald of Staffa, the Sheriff of Stirling, and known as a high Tory, became so incensed with Hullock's remarks about Scotsmen that he wrote a note and flung it across to Jeffrey which read:—"Leave the country —challenge the . . .; and I'll be your second!" Jeffrey leaned over the table and grasped Staffa's hand but Lord President Hope, observing what was taking place, ordered Hullock to apologise to Jeffrey, thus the impending duel was averted. Jeffrey's objection to Hullock's appearance was, of course, over-ruled.

It was decided that Andrew Hardie was to be tried first and the other prisoners were removed. Of the twenty-eight men called to serve on the jury, Hardie challenged sixteen of them. Finally a jury consisting of Andrew Hutton, writer; James Bryce, bookseller; James Wright, writer; Alexander Wilson, carpet manufacturer; William MacFarlane, baker; William Glass, timber merchant; Allan Johnston, architect; Alexander Bowie, mason; James Reid, timber merchant; John Stewart, portioner; John Wilson, carpet manufacturer, and John Baird Esq., of Seafield, were sworn in. Mr Thomas G. Knapp, the Clerk of the Arraigns, then told those who were not sworn in on the Hardie case to leave the court house "as they would do well not to fatigue themselves as they would be wanted tomorrow".

The Lord President, Hope, then made "a curious announcement" even, as one newspaper put it, for those troubled times. "I have to announce to all persons concerned, that no part of the proceedings of this trial (and more especially the speeches of counsel), that no part of the evidence be published till this and all the trials in this and the other countries, included in this Commission, be brought to a conclusion, otherwise the severest punishments that this court can inflict will be pronounced against them." It was essential, said the Lord President, that no one, especially those connected with the trials, should be able to read in a newspaper what was taking place until all the trials had finished. "Therefore, let all persons take care what they are about, for the severest punishments will be inflicted upon them."

The Lord Advocate, Sir William Rae, opened the case for the Crown, listing four counts of High Treason against Hardie, consisting of nineteen overt acts of treason for compassing and imagining the death of King George IV; levying war; compassing and intending to depose the King from the style, honour and kingly name of the Imperial Crown of the realm; and compassing to levy war against the King in order to compel him to change his measures. The Lord Advocate claimed that Hardie was connected with the Radical proclamation and had been seen reading it in Glasgow. He gave a narrative of the events which culminated at Bonnymuir which he described as "a gross and treacherous outrage". Along with the prisoners at Bonnymuir, the military had seized five muskets, two pistols, sixteen pikes, one hay fork, one shaft and a bag of ammunition containing a large quantity of ball cartridge.

Gentlemen, having stated these things to you, I apprehend that having stated without commentary, you will be completely satisfied that this case, if proved—because that remains yet to be done— does amount to an act of levying war against the King, for which I am entitled to ask a verdict at your hands against the prisoner. That there was a levying of war no man can doubt; the troops were attacked; and though the party failed it matters not; if we were to judge on such a question by the adequacy of the means, it is impossible to say in what case treason could be proved . . .

The first witness to be called was John Rennie, a private with the Kilsyth troop of Yeomanry, who gave evidence about the Bonnymuir battle. He said his horse had been wounded by a slug which put him out of action for a while but he particularly remembered seeing Hardie with a pike during the encounter. James Hardie, the Glasgow Justice of the Peace, was the next witness to be called and he told the court how he had seen Hardie reading the Radical proclamation on Sunday, April 2. Hardie, he claimed, "threw him off the pavement" when he tried to tear the proclamation down. The remark made by Hardie, that before he would permit the magistrate to take down the paper, he would part with the last drop of his blood, was particularly damning to the jury. This evidence was corroborated by John Stirling, the Glasgow surgeon, and Hugh MacPhunn. The change keeper at Castlecary, Archibald Buchanan, described how the Radicals had come to his inn and ordered loaves and porter. He described how Hardie had demanded a receipt for the "Provisional Government" and the Lord Advocate emphasised the point to the jury. The Damhead farmer, Alexander Robertson, a rather unwilling witness, said he had seen part of the skirmish and that a wounded person was carried to his house but had "escaped during the night". James Russell of Longcroft, Denny, told the court how the Radicals had entered his house and seized his guns.

At this stage, the Lord President had the boxes of arms opened and the witness immediately identified the guns which the Radicals had appropriated. James Murray and John Bensom, the ordnance store keepers from Stirling Castle, were called to identify the arms as those brought in by Lt. Ellis Hodgson. Then a further witness to the actual skirmish, William Grindlay of Bonnymill, was called. The next witness was Private Nicol Hugh Baird, the trooper who claimed he had been attacked by the Radicals on the road and that he had drawn his pistol and beaten them off, spurring his horse for Kilsyth. Thanks to the ingenuity of "Granny" Duncan, who lived just off the Esplanade, Stirling, leading to Ballangeich, Andrew Hardie's impressions, and letters, written in his death cell, were smuggled out of Stirling Castle for the sake of posterity. "Granny" Duncan attended Baird and Hardie while they were awaiting execution and was in the habit of making porridge for them, which enabled her to carry in letters from friends and smuggle letters out from them. She allowed the porridge to cool, turned it out, laid the letter on the bottom, and replaced the food. "Granny" attended the two men at their execution and died many years later aged 96. It was through this medium that Hardie wrote to a friend that Private Baird should be classed with Sir William Wallace.

The next witness that I will mention is Mr Nicol Hugh Baird, of the Kilsyth Yeomanry Cavalry, who actually swore that he met ten or twelve of us on the road, and that we demanded his arms, and he in return to our demands presented his pistol at us, and said that he would give us the contents of it before he would do so. In the name of common sense what could tempt this coxcomb to swear to such a notorious lie as this, to face and frighten ten or twelve armed men! He is worthy of being classed with Sir William Wallace. I am astonished that after such a feat he did not petition the officer of the Hussars to fight the whole of us on the moor himself. But he had done enough for one day. But the truth of the matter is this . . . we never saw him on the road at all.

Thomas Cook, the sergeant of the 10th Hussars, whom the Radicals had met on the road, told his story simply and without any embellishment. The proclamation which had been given to Cook by one of the Radicals, and on which Hodgson had written down a description of his prisoners and a list of arms taken, was presented as evidence but Cook said he could not be certain who had given it to him. He did, however, remember Hardie and recalled that he had been the man who demanded his arms. Lt. Ellis Hodgson gave a straightforward account of his movements since he was ordered to leave Stirling. The proclamation was again produced and identified by him. He added that he had given it to his commanding officer, Colonel Taylor, for safe keeping. Lt. John J. Davidson, the Edinburgh Tory lawyer and Yeomanry officer, said that all the Radicals had been armed and had attacked the military first. He identified some of the arms and pikes. Concluding the Crown evidence, the Lord Advocate instructed Mr Knapp to read out the Radical proclamation, despite the objections of Jeffrey.

In defence, Jeffrey could offer the court little, except the three statements made by Andrew Hardie to the authorities. The first statement had been taken at Stirling Castle on April 7 by Alexander Dow, a Sheriff Substitute of Stirling, which gave a brief account of the events leading to Bonnymuir. Hardie claimed that he had been told what to do by a man but "he did not know his name or anything about him". He emphasised that the Radicals were not out for plunder but the restoration of the rights of the people of Scotland. He wanted annual parliaments and election by ballot. He also added that a people had the right to obtain what the majority of the Scottish nation applied for, and, he said, it should be the duty of a proper Government to grant whatever the nation applied for. A second statement, taken in Edinburgh jail, before Adam Duff, the Sheriff of Edinburgh, also emphasises the conduct of the unknown man (the Government agent, Turner) who, Hardie said, "was a tall man dressed in a dark coloured surtout [a frocked coat] who, when he gave him cartridges, wished him success and said he would join them soon but never saw him afterwards . . .". Of the agent King, Hardie comments: "This man was little and rather stout made . . . he appeared like a tradesman, was but indifferently dressed and seemed a very active man." A third statement only served to endorse the previous two.

Rising to make his speech for the defence, Jeffrey expressed great anxiety at his task. First, he acknowledged that the Lord Advocate had given a calm, temperate speech, and Jeffrey admitted that his line of defence had devolved on him. He admitted that it was absurd to doubt the facts from the evidence that had been heard, but it was for the jury to decide whether the evidence had been sufficient to leave no doubt that Andrew Hardie had committed an act of levying war against the King . . . an attack on the military by a band of armed men, or skirmishing with the King's troops, was not of sufficient evidence, Jeffrey contended, to prove treasonable intent. Jeffrey also reminded the jury of the conditions of the working classes.

The Solicitor General replied on behalf of the Crown. Unfortunately, the reporter could not take this speech down "there were no lights but those on the bench and table of the court". The Lord President summed up the evidence, pointing out material parts for consideration by the jury. They retired, but returned in ten minutes and found Andrew Hardie not guilty on counts 1 and 3 but guilty on counts 2 and 4. It being 2 a.m., the court adjourned.

Every attention was paid to the prisoners throughout the day consistant with their unhappy situation [reported the *Glasgow Herald*] who conducted themselves with greatest propriety. The dock was not sufficiently roomy to admit all of them sitting at once but they relieved each other. The boy, Johnston, looks extremely young.

The next day the court met at 10 a.m. and was presided over by the Lord Justice Clerk, Boyle, as the Lord President was absent all day. John Baird was brought to the dock and a jury was sworn in with John Smith of St Ninians as its foreman. The evidence was much the same as the previous day with eighteen

witnesses being called and the prosecution closing its case at
6.30 p.m. Again, all Jeffrey could produce in defence was a
statement made before Adam Duff, Sheriff of Edinburgh,
showing how "persons unknown" had led the Radicals into a
trap. "Mr Jeffrey addressed the jury at great length with that
eloquence of which he is master . . ." comments the *Glasgow
Herald*. The Lord Advocate made the final prosecution speech
and the Lord Justice Clerk summed up. The jury retired at
fifteen minutes past midnight and returned two hours later
with their verdict. They found Baird not guilty of counts 1 and
3 but guilty of counts 2 and 4. The court then adjourned until
the next day, when James Cleland was next to be called into
the dock. Jeffrey, however, had seen the futility of proceeding
with a defence on the grounds that the prisoners were not
guilty. He rose and addressed the court:

My lord, as counsel for the unfortunate prisoners, the name of one
of whom has now been called as next in order to take his trial upon
this serious charge, I trust I shall relieve the court and country at
large from some protracted anxiety, and at the same time not neglect
my duty to my clients, which I have endeavoured to discharge
without considering my own insufficiency for the task which was
imposed on me, or exposing myself to remark as having been sparing
of my own toil and labour. My lord, I hope, without departure from
that, I may venture to state now to the court, that after the event
of the trials of the two last days that have gone through with much
deliberation and so great struggle on both sides, I have advised the
unhappy persons at the bar, that if they are conscious of the guilty
charges against them, their wisest course would be to retract their
plea of Not Guilty and acknowledge their guilt openly in court;
and I believe I am now authorised to state, that they are now ready
to withdraw that plea; your lordship, of course, will now give them
an opportunity of correcting any misapprehension on my part, and
allow them to speak for themselves in a matter which they only can
ultimately determine, and where their own consciences must be
the guide of their conduct.

Sir William Rae pointed out: " . . . these prisoners are not to
suppose that, by any confession they may now make, they are to
escape a punishment of a capital nature." Lord President Hope
then asked James Cleland if, understanding that he still might
face a death sentence, he wished to change his plea. Cleland
affirmed that he now wished to plead Guilty. In consequence,

the other fifteen Bonnymuir prisoners all changed their pleas to Guilty. Lord President Hope addressed the court:

My lords, before further procedure is held in this matter, I think your lordships will agree with me in saying that although Mr Jeffrey was well entitled in law to object to the appearance of Mr Serjeant Hullock, or any English counsel in this case against him, yet, in point of fact, there never did exist any necessity for a counsel fearing to meet another counsel at any bar whatever; and, I am sure that the bar of England attended here on behalf of the unhappy men now convicted, it is impossible they could have been better or more ably defended—the point was hit that it was possible to hit for and pleaded in ablest manner; and it must be satisfactory to the country that the result of the trials has been to raise the character of the bar, and to show they are fully competent to conduct any case whatever. With regard to the last proceeding, he has acted with as much jurisprudence as he did with ability in the defence of his clients.

Another of the prisoners, John Anderson, for whom Jeffrey was also appearing, was brought to the dock and Jeffrey again asked the court to accept a change of plea from Not Guilty to Guilty. The Lord Advocate again pointed out "that I can hold out no assurance or expectation that the capital punishment sentence of the law will not be inflicted upon him". William Crawford, another of Jeffrey's clients, was also brought to the dock and the court was asked to accept a change of plea. Jeffrey added that "this is not one of those aggravated cases, which, unfortunately, could not be said of all the others. He was connected with, and misled by persons who involved him in the guilt with which he is charged." The Lord Advocate once again pointed out that "he must plead without any assurance being held out to him of mercy". The Guilty pleas were them accepted by the court and the Lord Advocate rose.

My lords, now that the prisoner [Crawford] has pleaded Guilty, I trust I am not going beyond the proper line of my duty when I state, that as there necessarily must be different shades of criminality attached to the individuals who have this day respectively pleaded Guilty to the high charge exhibited against them, so it is satisfactory to me to have it in my power to say, that the case of this prisoner is not of the most aggravated description, and that I should feel satisfaction, if, on a representation of the circumstances of his case to the proper quarter, a mitigation of his sentence shall be deemed admissable. In closing our sittings in this county at the present time, I trust I may be forgiven for expressing a humble hope that the result of the proceedings of this and the two preceding days will satisfy this court and country that a due attention has been here paid on the part of the public prosecutor to the selection of the individuals fitted to be put upon trial before this high tribunal.

The Lord President Hope, remarking that the conduct of Sir William Rae "has been in all respects most proper upon the present occasion", adjourned the court in Stirling until Monday, July 31.

The court opened in Glasgow on Thursday, July 20, to hear the case of James Wilson of Strathaven. Lord Pitmilly sat with the four law lords and the prosecution consisted of the Lord Advocate, Mr Serjeant Hullock, Henry Home Drummond, the Solicitor General, and J. Hope. For Wilson's defence, J. A. Murray headed a team consisting of E. D. Sandford, Monteith, Graham, Pyper, A. Hope Cullen and Miller, who were assisted by Mr Harmer, an English solicitor, who had been one of the barristers at the trial of the Peterloo men. Mr Knapp, the Clerk of the Arraigns, called a list of 200 names and, after "a very considerable time", twelve men were chosen for the jury whose foreman was James Ewing, a Glasgow merchant. Again, as at Stirling, Lord President Hope "prohibited in the most positive manner the publication of the evidence or the speeches of the counsel in the case of Wilson or any of the trials which are to take place in Glasgow or elsewhere". Again Lord Hope "trusted his prohibition would be attended to, as its violence would bring down on the heads of its violators, the severest penalties of the law".

Mr Knapp read out the indictment and its various counts which occupied two hours and was, in substance, the same charges as those levelled against Baird and Hardie. Mr Hope, on behalf of the prosecution, then explained in detail the various counts to the jury. The Lord Advocate opened the case for the Crown in a speech which lasted an hour and a half, recalling the trial of Thistlewood and referring to the insurrection week in April. As for the Radical proclamation, "this abominable production called on the people to take up arms for the redress of what it denominated the common grievance of the people, and march out against their oppressors, and return in triumph or return no more. According to the dictation of this Address, all the public works were shut up and thousands of the discontented continued to parade the streets for three or four days, creating the utmost alarm in the loyal and well disposed population."

He went on to recall that the Radicals gathered at the house of Wilson and "on the morning of Thursday, a body consisting of fifteen or sixteen armed men sallied forth from the house of the prisoner, and he, with a drawn sword in his hand, proceeded along with them on the road towards Glasgow". The fact that they were armed constituted levying war against the King, argued Rae, but added "to be sure there could be nothing more ridiculous than to expect the puny efforts of a handful of unskilful men could prevail against the Kingly Government and Constitution of our own country, living as it did in the bosoms of nine-tenths of Scotland's population, for I am not to be told, notwithstanding all that has recently taken place, that Scotsmen are otherwise than a more virtuous and a most loyal people".

The first witness to be called was James Thomson, a Strathaven carter, who told the court that he had seen the armed men marching out from Wilson's house. He identified some of the prisoners by name and said that one of them, William Watson, was at their head carrying a flag inscribed "Scotland Free—Or A Desert!" He added that Wilson carried a sword "which he appeared to be wishing to hide; he looked very dull, and as if he were ashamed of his proceedings". Behind Wilson marched his son-in-law, Walters. John Boyd, of Strathaven, was also called and confirmed that the Radicals had left Strathaven marching "in ordinary time and in regular order". He confirmed that Wilson carried a sword but "appeared to be very downcast". Alexander Alston of Strathaven gave evidence to the effect that he had seen the Radicals entering Wilson's house late on Wednesday and heard wood splintering inside. He saw the Radicals march out of Strathaven early on Thursday with Wilson who was carrying a sword. James Fallow, the man with whom the Radicals had some sport by making him a prisoner, gave his evidence, presenting the facts without the boisterous light-hearted atmosphere of the evening in question. It seemed cold and damning evidence to the Radicals. Fallow also gave evidence as to the various raids for arms conducted by the Radicals in the area. A number of witnesses from whom the Radicals had taken fire arms were called, such as John Cochrane Snr. and his son, and William Semple. Their evidence was also most damning.

Jean Hamilton was called and told the court that Wilson had been in charge of the Strathaven men, filing flints and telling his men where they could obtain guns. Margaret Young was also called and reported Wilson's statement that the Radical "could not die in a better cause, they are only endeavouring to obtain the rights of their forefathers, and I hope they get them". William Barry and John Hamilton also gave evidence saying they had seen or heard Wilson giving orders and marching with his men clutching a sword. Robert Steel, a turncoat Radical who used to read the *Spirit of Union* and the *Manchester Observer* in Wilson's house, told the court how pleased Wilson had been on hearing the news from Glasgow concerning the rising. Andrew Shearer, another former Radical, said he had been the president of the Strathaven Radical club where they had read publications like the *Spirit of Union*, the *Black Book* and other reformist works. Shearer said that he was in Wilson's house on the morning of the march and did all he could to persuade Wilson not to go. James Hardie, the Justice of the Peace who had given evidence against Hardie, was called to give evidence about the address though his evidence had no connection with the Strathaven events and seemed entirely irrelevant. The final witness was a clock maker named Archibald Brownlie who, in his spare time, tried his hand at weaving using a frame in Wilson's house. Brownlie was there on Wednesday night and told the court that Wilson had been sharpening his sword to a fine point.

In all twenty-eight witnesses were called for the prosecution and two declarations made by Wilson were read out. Monteith, one of the defence advocates, objected to the first one being read out because the magistrate, before whom it had been taken, had told Wilson to be candid in his statement and said if he were in Wilson's place he would speak out. The court sustained the objection. There was no objection to the second declaration but, as it was "made under undue impression", it was rejected by the court. It was now 10 p.m. and the Lord President indicated that the court should retire for the night. Coaches were ordered to take the jury to a place where they could be kept all together. In the meantime, the Lord President allowed the leading defence advocate, J. A. Murray, to start the address for the defence.

Murray told the jury that he "was well aware of his own inability from want of a proper knowledge of the English law"; and because he was opposed by all the Crown lawyers who had been preparing for the duty they were to perform for months past. Certainly all their efforts and those of the eminent English counsel (Hullock) who was present, would be directed against him, but he had no reason to complain when he was pleading before such a jury. "According to the law of Scotland, an individual accused of any criminal offence has an indictment served upon him making particular mention of the spot where the crime was committed; but here it was different for he believed the prisoner could neither tell what he was accused of nor the place where the unlawful doings charged were said to have been transacted."

"Good God!" interposed Hullock, "was it necessary to make such a dictionary of charges?"

Murray continued, however, saying that evidence had been given that Wilson was a reader of the *Spirit of Union* and the *Black Book* but no evidence had been given "that they were bad, or that any of them ever contained a single paragraph which could be fairly deemed improper". No evidence had been given that Wilson had observed the Radical proclamation, far less been connected in its authorship or circulation. As to the most important charge of manufacturing arms, drilling and levying war on the King, Murray said he would prove that Wilson was, in fact, forced out by the Radicals against his will.

At midnight the court adjourned. The second day of Wilson's trial started at 10 a.m. with Murray calling five witnesses in order to prove that the Strathaven Radicals had compelled Wilson to go with them against his wishes. John Stevenson, in his *Radical Rising at Strathaven*, recalls, "Mr Murray's conduct did not surprise me, it was his duty to urge the best plea he could for the unfortunate prisoner." One of the witnesses for the defence was the Irishman, Matthew Rony, who "when he saw that his old benefactor [Wilson] had fallen into the hands of the Philistines, did not scruple, at the expense of truth, to swear that Wilson was forced out". Bland faced, Rony told the court that a number of Radicals (whom he did not recognise) had forced their way into Wilson's house saying, "Wilson, no excuse will do today, if you do not turn out I will blow out your brains." Next came Mrs Barr who swore that "she heard nothing but swearing, and tearing, and threatening because he refused to go out with them; some were for stabbing, others for shooting him; they threatened to set fire to his house; the persons assembled in his house appeared to be drunk; the prisoner is easily frightened". The important point that was not brought out was that Mrs Barr was Wilson's sister making "an attempt to rescue her unfortunate brother from his perilous situation".

Great stress was laid on the fact that when the Radicals marched out of Strathaven, Wilson marched in the rear of the column, showing, claimed Murray, that he was unwilling to go. When Peter MacKenzie wrote his account of the trial, fifteen years later, he emphasises this point as well, also accepting Mrs Barr and Rony at face value. Stevenson commented: "Mr MacKenzie may manage to write a Gazette well enough, but he knows nothing about military tactics. When we were leaving Strathaven, the town was full of people, and if they had meditated an attack it would have commenced on our rear; we, therefore, naturally enough, put our best men there."

Stevenson had written his account of the Strathaven rising in reply to MacKenzie's version because, "not content with robbing Wilson of his fair reputation, he actually hung the good old man in chains". MacKenzie had made out a case, based on Murray's defence, that Wilson had been forced out by the Radicals and Stevenson was incensed that MacKenzie "was libelling braver and better men than himself". Stevenson goes on to say that "If the reader will compare MacKenzie's account with this narrative, he will see that MacKenzie undertook to write the history of an affair of which he was most deplorably ignorant. Although he had been hired to betray the cause he voluntarily undertook to defend, he could not have done it more effectually. Under the mask of friendship, he has stigmatised and insulted the poor fellows that left Strathaven, along with Wilson, with such virulent perseverance that one would almost think he was actuated by personal motives." Attached to

Stevenson's account is a note from four of the Strathaven party, Andrew Steel, Robert Hamilton, William Steel and William Hamilton, confirming Stevenson's version as a "true and authentic narrative".

Murray, making his final plea, pointed out that in 1708 a Mr Skirling of Keir and a number of other gentlemen, travelled through the country when there was a large French fleet off the coast with James Stuart aboard. Skirling of Keir and the other gentlemen were supporters of the repeal of the Union of 1707, which the old Pretender had promised to enact once back on the throne. No landing took place but Skirling and the others were tried for treason and acquitted. Murray said the case could be compared with Wilson's trial. As for the flag— "Scotland Free—Or A Desert!" . . . was this treason? He, himself, would avow the same sentiment and he was sure that such a sentiment ought to be in the hearts of every honest Scotsman. Reform was no crime and many people in high places had given support to it. Murray contended that conspiracy had not been proved.

According to the *Glasgow Herald* "Serjeant Hullock replied for the Crown in an ingenious and argumentative speech in which he evinced a profound knowledge of the law". The Lord President summed up and pointed out that it did not require great hosts of well disciplined armies to constitute rebellion or High Treason. Prince Charles Edward's original army in 1745 were "half clothed and undisciplined" but it still did not lessen the evil of their intention. In his opinion, Wilson had not proved that he was forced into the commission of the crime by fear. Fallow's evidence was of prime importance and the Lord President emphasising this, said: "It is a melancholy feature in the present case, that the conspirators, when pretending to be in search of their rights, began by forcing people to join them, as they did to the witness James Fallow whom they compelled to go along with them, when they were going from house to house forcing them to give up arms."

The jury retired at 7 p.m. and were out for two hours. On their return they found Wilson guilty of the 4th count only and James Ewing, the foreman, said it was the unanimous wish of the jury to recommend Wilson to the mercy of the Crown.

SIXTEEN

"THIS MUMMERY OF A TRIAL!"

THE COURT ADJOURNED until Monday, July 24, and, in the meantime, the Lord Justice Clerk and Lord Pitmilly took a carriage to Paisley to arraign James Speirs and John Lang and fix their trial for August 1. The court met in Glasgow again at 9 a.m. and William MacIntyre was brought into the dock and a jury was sworn in with Charles Stirling of Cadder, one of the commanders of the Glasgow Yeomanry (Light Horse) as its foreman. The jury was a blatant example of how the juries were "packed" by the authorities. Not only was Stirling, a Yeomanry officer involved in the affair on the Government side, a therefore biased foreman, but Thomas Muir, of Muir Park, who was serving on the jury, had already served on Wilson's jury. However, as circumstances turned out, this jury was not needed.

The Lord Advocate, Sir William Rae, addressed the court, saying that although a true bill had been found against Mac-Intyre, and he had been arraigned with Wilson, who was found guilty on Friday, it did appear to the Crown authorities that MacIntyre had not been so guilty as some others, who had fled the country but would not escape being brought to punishment as soon as they were caught. As the prisoner had not been a conspicuous character in the affair, the Crown was unwilling to lead proof against him and request that the jury find him Not Guilty. "It is the wish of the Crown lawyers to prosecute those only who have been the leaders in the late disturbance." "The real fact," comments Stevenson, "was they had no proof to lead. The reader will easily perceive that the Lord Advocate wished the public to believe that the Crown lawyers were mingling their proceedings with mercy."

Lord President Hope addressed MacIntyre "in very animated style", commenting on the Radicals having been in search of the rights of their forefathers. "What, in the Name of Providence, do you mean by that?" he asked. They enjoyed ten times more liberty than ever their forefathers had done; the trial of Wilson was plain proof, as he had received as impartial a trial as any nobleman had the right to do. The Lord President then dismissed MacIntyre from the court. Matthew Bogle, Alexander Graham and John May were brought into the dock and the Lord Advocate requested that they, also, be dismissed. Lord President Hope begged them to "return to sobriety and honest industry". John May, speaking for his fellow prisoners, thanked the court and they were dismissed. The last two arraigned prisoners, William Campbell and George Allan, were also dismissed from the court. The Lord Advocate, thanking the court for the proceedings, added that he regretted that the Glasgow police had not been sufficient to prevent the strike of work on this occasion but trusted that it would be more efficient in future. The Crown lawyers were well pleased with themselves for Wilson, a reformer since the days of the Friends of the People, was an excellent example to use before the people.

Wilson was brought back into the dock and the Lord President formally addressed him. "James Wilson, you have been indicted of high treason; upon this indictment you have been arraigned and pleaded Not Guilty; and for your trial you have put yourself on God, and your country, which country has found you Guilty. What have you to say for yourself why the Court should not give you judgement to die, according to law?" Wilson, the 63-year-old Radical, sometime poet, doctor, clockmaker, tinsmith, dog trainer and advanced political thinker, began a short speech which, in essence, closely resembles that of Theobald Wolfe Tone of the United Irishmen. We are told that Wilson was an avid reader of reform literature and it is highly likely that he saw a copy of Tone's address to the court and modelled his own speech on it.

My lords and gentlemen, I will not attempt the mockery of a defence. You are about to condemn me for attempting to overthrow the oppressors of my country. You do not know, neither can you appreciate, my motives. I commit my sacred cause, which is that of Freedom, to the vindication of posterity. You may condemn me to immolation on the scaffold, but you cannot degrade me. If I have appeared as a pioneer in the van of freedom's battles—if I have attempted to free my country from political degradation—my conscience tells me that I have only done my duty. Your brief authority will soon cease, but the vindictive proceedings this day shall be recorded in history. The principles for which I have contended are as immutable, as imperishable, as the eternal laws of nature. My gory head may in a few days fall on the scaffold and be exposed as the head of a traitor, but I appeal with confidence to posterity. When my countrymen will have exalted their voices in bold proclamation of the rights and dignity of Humanity, and enforced their claim by the extermination of their oppressors, then, and not till then, will some future historian do my memory justice, then will my name and sufferings be recorded in Scottish history—then will my motives be understood and appreciated; and with the confidence of an honest man, I appeal to posterity for that justice which has in all ages and in all countries been awarded to those who have suffered martyrdom in the glorious cause of liberty.

The Lord President, who had several times tried to interrupt Wilson, warned him about using "expressions which would be detrimental to him" and the newspapers were warned to use their discretion on what they reported. Most newspapers, like the *Glasgow Herald*, commented "he [Wilson] stammered out a few words in an incoherent manner". The Lord President asked Wilson's advocate if he wished to comment and Murray merely pointed out that the jury had unanimously recommended Wilson to the clemency of the Crown. Lord President Hope then addressed Wilson.

James Wilson, you must be convinced of the impartiality and fairness with which the proceedings against you have been conducted. From the exercise of your right of challenge, the jury, by which you have been found guilty, may be considered as chosen by yourself, and the crime they have found you guilty of is the most dreadful that can afflict any nation. All other crimes are trifling compared to it; it strikes at the root of the whole fabric on which our happiness is founded. The horrors of civil war, where citizen is contending against citizen, with deadly malignity, is far more dreaded than the most bloody foreign contest. No doubt, it was never dreamt by any rational being, that the violent people with whom you were connected could be ultimately successful; but the intermediate evils your mischief might have produced are terrible to think of. The rights and liberties of the peaceable and loyal part of the community are to be protected as well as those of the turbulent and disaffected, and when they were pleased with the liberty they enjoyed they were not to be disturbed by the factious proceedings of the evil disposed.

I advise you, most sincerely, to think seriously of your eternal interests, as you are shortly to appear at the mercy seat of Christ, and I beseech you to consider well the errors of your past life, and make good use of the short time allotted to you in this world. Remember that the justice of God is as inflexible as his mercies are infinite; and I trust you have not thrown off all allegiance to your heavenly sovereign, as it appears you have done to your earthly one. The ministers of religion of every sect and persuasion will be ready and willing to assist you in preparing for the concerns of your immortal soul. The recommendation of the jury shall certainly be transmitted to the proper authority and I sincerely hope that mercy will be extended you, but it is often necessary for the Government to consider the expediency of those recommendations and the power vested in the Crown is assuredly not exercised capriciously but for the general safety and prosperity of the State. I advise you, however, to prepare for the utmost extreme; and if mercy be extended to you, you will not be the worse man for the attention which you may give to your religious concerns.

The sentence of the law is—that you be drawn on a hurdle to the place of execution, on the 30th August, and after being hung by the neck till you are dead, that your head be severed from your body, and your body cut in quarters, to be at the disposal of the King; and the Lord have mercy upon your soul.

Wilson, who had stood impassively throughout the speech, now drew himself up. "I am not deceived," he told the Lord President. "You might have condemned me without this mummery of a trial! You want a victim; I will not shrink from the sacrifice. I have neither expected justice nor mercy here. I have done my duty to my country. I have grappled with her oppressors for the last forty years and having no desire to live in slavery, I am ready to lay down my life in support of these principles which must ultimately triumph."

The *Glasgow Herald* commented: "The prisoner was then taken down from the bar without showing any signs of agitation, and confined in one of the iron rooms." The Lord President finished the day's proceedings with a lengthy address in which he expressed the hope that the people of Scotland would be recalled "to their sober sense and to the allegiance which they owe their sovereign; to the obedience which is due to the laws;

and to the attachment which they owe to this glorious consti-tution." He added that the right of representation was the only means of securing liberties "and the right of voting a necessary evil to which we are bound to submit to procure our representa-tion". He spoke of the need for strengthening the police force and for the manufacturers to be "vigorous and strong" in dismissing any of their workmen who they suspected of being "disaffected." He recalled that the court was sitting in a part of Scotland where their forefathers "shed their blood as martyrs—not for the Christian religion alone, but for particular tenets which some men might nowadays think hardly worth defending." He urged the court to endeavour to check "blas-phemy and impiety both in conversations and publications", and aid the law in putting down any disaffection so that they might be proud of their forefathers.

The court proceeded to Dumbarton where, on July 27, the trial of Robert Munroe was the first on the list. E. D. Sandford defended and the Lord Advocate, aided by Mr Serjeant Hullock, prosecuted. The Lord Advocate's arguments were feeble as the Duntocher men, of whom Munro was one, had not turned out in the rising. The only evidence against them was the arms seized in the "Battle of the Bellows". The jury retired at 6 p.m. to consider their verdict and returned twenty-five minutes later to proclaim Munroe Not Guilty. The Lord Advocates decided to admit defeat on the Duntocher cases and asked that Patrick MacDevitt, William Blair, George Munroe, Richard Thompson and William MacPhie be acquitted. "It must be obvious," he said, resignedly, "that I have no proof to offer against them, which has not been adduced against their companion, and as they were all charged with the self same acts I could not expect but a repetition of that evidence to alter the opinion of the Court or the jury."

The prisoners were dismissed. Mr Serjeant Hullock decided to return to England, leaving the direction for the rest of the prosecutions in the hands of the Lord Advocate. His decision to do so can, perhaps, be attributed to vanity, for, seeing that the rest of the high treason trials were founded on such weak evidence which had led to the Dumbarton acquittals, Hullock did not wish to risk his reputation by being associated with failures. In fact, Lord Sidmouth did express his annoyance that the latter trials had failed to get convictions and had not terminated "as prosperously as the early ones". The Lord Advocate, through lack of evidence, found that he had to liberate seven people on July 31 who were being held in Dumbarton Castle on a charge of aiding the prisoners to escape from Greenock Prison on April 8.

The Lord Justice Clerk and Lord Chief Baron held court in Ayr on July 29 to arraign John Dickie, Andrew Wyllie and Thomas MacKay from Mauchline, who pleaded Not Guilty. J. P. Grant and E. D. Sandford were assigned as defence advocates. Two days later, the Lord President and Lord Pitmilly attended at Stirling to arraign John MacMillan, James Aitken, James Burt, James Aitken of Falkirk, Daniel Turner, Andrew Dawson and John Johnstone. All pleaded Not Guilty and J. P. Grant with A. Hope Cullen were appointed counsel in place of Francis Jeffrey who had now washed his hands of the "whole sordid affair".

While the trials were continuing, the country continued to give the authorities trouble. On July 30, James Murray, a young "extremist" Radical, made a spectacular attempt to assassinate the Duke of Atholl at his home in Dunkeld House, near Perth. Murray gained an audience with Atholl and pretended to show him a letter demanding a redress of grievances. Instead of producing the letter from his pocket, Murray drew a pistol but Atholl managed to seize it and the two men struggled together. Atholl called his attendants who dragged Murray away and the Radical was arrested, taken to Perth, and transported for life.

On the same day, between midnight and 1 a.m., the military fired on an unarmed crowd in Greenock. Seven soldiers of the 13th Regiment, "maddened by drink", took guns from their barracks to "teach these Scotch a lesson or two". They opened fire on a group of people and killed two, a policeman was also shot. An officer of the regiment was called out and, unlike the Glasgow affair, the 13th Regiment found they could not exonerate themselves. The culprits were taken away for military punishment but there is no record of what happened to them. The commanding officer of the 13th Regiment, Lt.-Colonel Williams, wrote from the regimental headquarters at Stirling Castle, on August 3, to J. Dennistoun, the Chief Magistrate at Greenock:

I

Having learnt with the most heartfelt sorrow and regret, that two men of the 13th Regiment, forgetful of every principle towards themselves and their corps to which they belong, did, on the morning of the 30th ultimo, as I am informed, in a state of intoxication, fire from their quarters by which proceeding some lives were lost, the officers and commissioned officers and privates, deeply deploring the circumstances, having earnestly requested to subscribe towards the relief of the surviving families of the deceased—I have therefore to transmit to you One Hundred Pounds to be distributed in such manner as you may judge advisable.

I beg to apologise for the trouble I am causing you.

The 13th Regiment was now the most unpopular English regiment quartered in the country and the increasing Scottish hatred of the 13th, following the affairs in Glasgow and Greenock, was a contributory factor to the withdrawal of the regiment to Edinburgh the following month and the final removal, in October, to Ireland.

The court met in the converted George Street church in Paisley on August 1 with the Lord Justice Clerk, Lord Chief Baron and Lord Pitmilly presiding. The Lord Advocate conducted the prosecution and J. P. Grant with E. D. Sandford defended. James Speirs and John Lang were brought from the jail in a coach, guarded by a troop of hussars and manacled to two police officers. The court started the proceedings at 9 a.m. and, after both prisoners were brought into the dock, a jury was chosen out of 160 names called. Sir Michael Shaw Stewart of Greenock and Blackhall was chosen as foreman. Speirs' case was first and Lang was summoned to give evidence for the Crown against his fellow prisoner. Grant immediately objected to this and Lang was removed from the Court while Speirs' case was heard. The charges against Speirs were the usual four counts listing nineteen overt acts of treason, exactly the same as those brought against the previous prisoners. The Solicitor-General opened the case saying that twenty-two witnesses were to be called to prove that Speirs, during the recent rising, was a member of the committee who commanded a mob which went and stopped the cotton works in Johnstone and neighbourhood on April 3. John Fraser, the Johnstone schoolmaster, was summoned as a witness against Speirs. Fraser writes:

On entering the witness box instead of holding up my hand to swear, I addressed the court nearly as follows: "My lords, I have been falsely imprisoned nearly four months on a charge of High Treason—my business ruined, my aged parents and family thrown into trouble and distress; and I want to know the position in which I now stand before giving evidence." This statement created sensation on the Bench, the Bar and the crowded church. The advocates on both sides immediately began to debate the question. The Bench ordered me out of court. After a considerable time, I was recalled, and told by Lord Chief Baron Shepherd that the court had decided —"I stood there only as a witness and would be liberated immediately after giving my evidence; but that it was believed by the Crown I would be able to give very important testimony, and, he trusted I would tell the truth about the matter." I bowed, took the oath and told the history of the bill I had got from Speirs. To every other question I declared utter ignorance, except by report of everything connected with the rising. The court and the Crown badgered me and tried to drive me from this position. They were evidently greatly disappointed with my evidence. The Bench told me I was now free.

In going out I met my wife being brought into the court as a witness. I clasped her in my arms and kissed her, my heart in my lips. I said—I am now free. Be firm, and have no fear. She was detained very shortly. She said that Speirs called one Sabbath forenoon on her and asked that the Radical proclamation be put away or destroyed. The Crown counsel tried to bamboozle her; and she happened to make a witty remark at their expense which created a laugh against them and they thought the better way was to let her go, and ask no more questions. Both my own and her evidence were known to the prisoners' counsel. I told them when they had visited us, and they said, taking the evidence of both together it would do no harm to Speirs. Waiting in a side room for my wife, who soon came, we walked out to the open air and to Johnstone by the canal bank. The crowd recognising me shouted and cheered vociferously.

The court adjourned at midnight and reassembled at 10 a.m. on the following day. Eleven defence witnesses were examined and Grant then addressed the jury in a speech which lasted five hours and five minutes. Grant, in opening his speech, praised the character of English law and pointed out that all insurrections by people were not to be feared unless supported by people of rank and distinction. "In bad times they strengthen the hands of the executive and enable the Government to oppress them still more and more, and in good times they involve their foolish and desperate promoters in certain ruin and destruction. The Lord Advocate summed up for the prosecution and the Lord Justice Clerk gave the final summing up in a speech that lasted four hours. The jury withdrew at 4.10 a.m. on Thursday and returned at 5.20 a.m. The foreman, Sir Michael Shaw Stewart, said: "We find the prisoner guilty of the fifteenth overt act in the first count of the indictment, and unanimously recommend him to mercy on account of his former good conduct." The Lord Justice Clerk stated that if the jury found Speirs guilty of one overt act, they ought to find him guilty upon the whole count.

"We cannot find him guilty upon that," replied the foreman.

The defence advocate, J. P. Grant, said that the jury should return a special verdict.

"We consider this a special verdict," commented the foreman.

On the direction of the Lord Justice Clerk, the jury retired again but, on their return a few minutes later, they adhered to their former finding. The Lord Chief Baron, who had retired to the hotel following the last speech for the prosecution, was sent for and the situation was explained. Shepherd said the jury must return a verdict of guilty on the first count if they had proved one overt act of treason. The Lord Chief Baron started to explain the intricateness of English law but the jury foreman, Sir Michael, interrupted: "But, my lord, permit me to say that this verdict that we have now given in, was a matter of necessity as we do not think we shall ever be unanimous on the general count." The Lord Chief Baron became clearly annoyed. "You have heard positive evidence of the acts that were done by this man, but what was his intentions is still a matter of fact for you to find one way or the other; for instance, a man might embark in a boat and that might be charged as an overt act that the man was adhering to the King's enemies, that is, that he was going to join them, or that he was going to levy war against the King; but the jury merely saying that the man embarked in a boat is finding nothing at all."

"We do not know what the man's intention was, but we thought he might be led into acts from levity of conduct which he ought to be punished for," replied the foreman.

The jury was instructed to retire again at 6.15 a.m. At 6.35 they returned again with a written verdict which stated:

The jury pronounce James Speirs guilty on Monday, the Third day of April last, of striking and giving up his work in a malicious and illegal manner; and that he did not only abstain from work himself, but did compel and oblige others of his fellow subjects to do the same; and maliciously and illegally did hinder and obstruct and prevent divers manufactures of divers liege subjects from being proceeded in, and carried on that day.

The Lord Chief Baron angrily retorted that this "was no verdict at all, as it neither affirmed nor negated the charge of treason". He again forced the jury to retire to consider their verdict and once again they returned endorsing their original view. Finally, the Lord Justice Clerk had to pronounce Speirs Not Guilty as indicted. As soon as the verdict was announced, people in the public galleries started a loud cheering and a young man was arrested by the court officers. After the cheering subsided, the Lord Chief Baron said if anyone else applauded they would be sentenced for contempt of court. Another man was arrested outside the court but his release was ordered as, being outside, he was not disturbing the court proceedings. The Lord Justice Clerk admonished Speirs and discharged him. "On the release of Speirs," said John Fraser, "almost the whole population of Paisley burst out cheering and exulting joy at the fondly desired deliverance."

Despite the all night sitting, a new jury was sworn in at 8.30 a.m. to try John Lang. The Lord Advocate, however, asked for a dismissal saying:

From the proceedings which have taken place in the previous trial, it appeared that while the whole facts charged were admitted to have been proved, yet a jury of this country have, by their verdict, been pleased to find that these did not constitute the crime of treason. I therefore should not feel myself justified in occupying the time of the court by again laying the same evidence in detail before another jury. I do not, therefore, intend to offer any proof against the prisoner Lang but to consent to a verdict of acquittal and I only hope that the result of the last trial might not prove prejudicial to the peace and tranquillity of the district.

Lang, after a short admonishment by the Lord Justice Clerk, was acquitted. As the defence advocates, Grant and Sandford, with P. and J. Jack, the writers, came out of the court, they were

cheered and followed all the way to Jack's offices. Grant and
Sandford had to shake hands with a large number of people.
"The prisoners," says Fraser, "were sent home in a coach. That
night a social meeting rejoicing in the happy escape, took place
in one of the public halls. I was voted to the chair and a joyous
evening was indeed spent—the prisoners, after a terrible ordeal,
being rescued from the jaws of death and the blood seeking
prosecutors defeated." Speirs, however, was to have an unhappy
end. In 1850, while living in the Sneddon district of Paisley, he
fell on hard times. A public fund was raised by "The Friends
and Admirers of James Speirs" and realised about £20, but, in
1852, Speirs died in great destitution.

The *Glasgow Herald* reflected the attitude of the authorities
in not being too pleased with the verdict. The paper commented
that if the April insurrection had been successful, would those
who had been in the employ of the Government have been
charged with treason and, if so, "would they have experienced
from the members of the Provisional Government such patience
and such leniency as were displayed at this trial? The *Herald*
praised the mercy of the jury, in a slighting way, and added that
it hoped Scotland could now "look back on the dark days of
Radicalism".

On August 4, the court was again sitting at Stirling to hear
the trials of the rest of the prisoners kept there. The proceedings
seem highly suspect, for the defence advocate, Grant, submitted
that John MacMillan and Andrew Dawson now wished to
change their pleas to Guilty and this was accepted by the Lord
Advocate who then announced that he would not procced with
the case against their comrades James and Andrew Burt, James
Aitken of Camelon, James Aitken of Falkirk, Daniel Turner
and John Johnstone. It seems highly likely that some mutual
agreement might have been made for the acquittal of some of
the prisoners if the others pleaded Guilty. After some fairly
lengthy discussion the men, with the exception of MacMillan
and Dawson, were dismissed. James Burt, however, was
immediately re-arrested outside the courtroom on another
charge. The eighteen Bonnymuir prisoners were brought into
the dock with MacMillan and Dawson. With the Lord President on the bench were the Lord Chief Baron, Lord Pitmilly
and the Marquis of Graham. the twenty-two convicted men

were asked if they had anything to say, then the Lord President addressed them.

Andrew Hardie, John Baird, James Cleland, Thomas MacCulloch, Benjamin Moir, Allan Murchie, Alexander Latimer, Alexander Johnston, Andrew White, David Thomson, James Wright, William Clackson or Clarkson, Thomas Pike or Pink, Robert Gray, Alexander Hart, John Barr, William Smith, Thomas MacFarlane, John Anderson, William Crawford, John MacMillan and Andrew Dawson.

You present a melancholy spectacle of two and twenty subjects of this country who have forfeited their lives to justice; a spectacle I believe unexampled in the history of this country, such at least I never witnessed and I trust in God never shall witness again. The crime of which you have been convicted is the crime of High Treason, a crime the highest known to law, and the highest I may venture to say, which can be known to a reflecting mind: because in fact whatever the motives which a man has in view who engaged in the crime of High Treason, we all must be aware that the crime, whether ultimately successful or not in its progress, if progress it has, must produce unutterable misery and confusion. It is impossible that treason can make any progress towards success without deluging the country, in which it takes place, in blood and slaughter, plunder and devastation. All countries, therefore, and all laws, have considered the crime of High Treason as the deepest which any subject can possibly commit. At the same time, I am well aware that from the delusion which has been practised against you, and from the principles, perhaps, which some of you have imbibed, you may view this in a different light, and that you may consider yourself not as victims of justice, but as martyrs for liberty. Some of you, for anything I know, may even glory in your suffering; but remember this, that sentence of death is now to be passed on you all; and remember that whatever may be your own opinions as to the moral guilt of the crime of which you have been convicted, remember that you still have the sins that beset human nature to answer for at the throne of God: and I entreat and conjure you all, to look into your own breasts to recall the action of your past lives, and to pray to God to give you that repentance which leadeth unto life and which alas, the best of us have too much occasion for. Remember that repentance alone is not sufficient—remember that you have to appear before God who is not only possessed of infinite mercy but of inflexible justice—that both must be satisfied by us, miserable sinners, before we can hope for mercy at His throne; and as we ourselves have recourse to that Redeemer who stands as Mediator between our God and us, through whom alone we can all hope for mercy. It only remains for me now to pronounce against one and all of you the last awful sentence of the law.

In regard to you Andrew Hardie and John Baird, I can hold out little or no hope of mercy. You were selected for trial as the leaders of that band in which you were associated. You were convicted, after a full and fair trial; and it is utterly impossible to suppose, considering the convulsions into which this country was thrown, that the Crown must not feel a necessity of making some terrible example, and as you were the leaders, I am afraid that example must be given by you. With regard to the rest of you, I hope and trust that mercy may be extended to the most, if not to all of you, but it is not to this court that mercy belongs and we cannot guarantee it. It depends upon the mercy of the Crown alone, a mercy which is never exercised capriciously and ought never to be exercised capriciously. The ministers of the Crown standing in elevated situations which they hold are bound to take into view the interests of the whole community and not to extend mercy to individual cases, merely for the sake of mercy, if the interests of the country should, in fact, demand your punishment. I hope and trust, however, that the contrary may be the case; but let me warn you all, in the meantime, to avail yourselves of the short time that is granted to you, to prepare for the worst. The worst may come upon some of you, and I hope and trust you will be prepared for it, and, at all events, you will not live in future the worse men that you have prepared to die.

The sentence of the law is—that you and each of you be taken to the place from whence you came, and that you be drawn on a hurdle to the place of execution, and there be hung by the neck until you are dead, and afterwards, your head severed from your body, and your body divided into four quarters to be disposed of as His Majesty may direct—and may God, in His infinite goodness, have mercy on your souls.

The twenty-two men were taken from the dock and the Lord President delivered a short homily to the court on "the great and abominable crimes undoubtedly intended" by the Radicals. Whatever "little, petty grievances" the Radicals had, or whatever "trifling alterations" to the constitution that they wanted, the constitution was "the best, the wisest and the freest that the sun ever saw".

The final high treason trials against the Radicals were held in Ayr on Wednesay, August 9, when the Lord Justice Clerk and Lord Pitmilly presided to hear the case against John

Dickie, Hugh Wallace, Andrew Wyllie and Thomas MacKay of Mauchline. Sandford and Grant were appearing for the defence and all the prisoners had entered pleas of Not Guilty. MacKay, however, was the first to be placed in the dock and, as shown in a previous chapter, indicated he wished to change his plea in accordance with the bargain he had made with the authorities. This astonished both Sandford and Grant. The Lord Justice Clerk accepted the plea, and immediately the Lord Advocate announced that it was not his intention to present evidence against the three men who were pleading Not Guilty. He would consent to their acquittal and added that one conviction was enough to restore the county to tranquillity "and to open the eyes of its inhabitants to their real and true situation".

MacKay had been despicably tricked. He was led to believe that by entering a plea of Not Guilty with the other three, he would suffer the extreme penalty of the law, but if he changed the plea to Guilty he would be pardoned. Now he was facing death while the other three were pardoned. The Lord Justice Clerk delivered a short lecture to the three men and advised them "to retire and not again to endanger the ruin of themselves and families by listening to such bad men as he had before alluded to, and trusted that by rectitude, sobriety and religious deportment in their future lives, they would endeavour to make some amends for any share they had in the treasonable proceedings".

The Lord Justice Clerk then addressed Thomas MacKay and said that the sentence of the court was—"That you be taken from thence to the place from whence you came, and that you be drawn on a hurdle to the place of execution, and there be hanged by the neck until you be dead, and that afterwards your head be severed from your body, and your body divided in four quarters to be disposed of as His Majesty shall direct and may the God of all mercy have mercy upon your soul." The last sacrifice had been chosen.

The Lord Advocate, Sir William Rae, rose and informed the court that the trials for high treason were now terminated. True bills had been found against eighty-eight persons in Scotland of which fifty-eight had not appeared, some of them fleeing to foreign countries and others not yet having been discovered.

The Court of Justiciary declared such people as outlaws which, in high treason, amounted to a record of guilt. Two and only two had been acquitted after trial and he entertained considerable doubt how far the verdict rested on sound principles in point of law. There had been twenty-four capital convictions of which the death sentence was to follow. Of the remainder, only twenty-one had received acquittals by the consent of the Crown authorities. He trusted that these proceedings would have a favourable effect in exposing the wickedness and folly of the schemes which had been resorted to and in showing to the people of Scotland the careful way in which the meanest subject's case had been investigated.

The Lord Justice Clerk, thanking the court, added that it must be apparent that there existed in April last a dangerous conspiracy which extended over five Scottish counties at the same time, a thing unparalleled in the manufacturing districts. Under the pretence of reformation and redress of grievances, the April rising was aimed at subverting the constitution and Government of the country by law established. He felt that the evil had, in some measure, been checked but he warned the magistrates of Mauchline, Stewarton and Galston, to "keep a vigilant and attentive eye" on so called reform associations. The court then adjourned indefinitely.

Thomas G. Knapp, the Clerk of the Arraigns, was busy collecting the depositions, court records, statements and preparatory documents normally kept in Edinburgh. On August 4, 1820, however, H. Hobhouse, secretary to Lord Sidmouth, wrote to Knapp:

I have to thank you for your letter of the 15th ultimo from Stirling and of the 24th from Glasgow and am ashamed of having left them unanswered. I am sorry to perceive that the subsequent prosecutions have not terminated so prosperously as the early ones.

I do not see any occasion for you being detained in Scotland for the purpose of making up records. That service may certainly be executed equally well, perhaps better, here [Whitehall] than in Scotland. And if it should finally be determined to deposit them in Scotland rather than in the Baga de Secretis at Westminster, they may easily be returned to Edinburgh after they are completed.

I am etc.

H. Hobhouse

In February, 1821, the notes taken by the shorthand writers at the trials were, indeed, returned from London to the Crown Agent in Edinburgh and it was agreed that an edited version of the trials should be published (H.O. Papers, series 41, volume 6, letters dated February 5 and March 26, 1821). This version of the trials was published in three volumes in 1825 and, with the short and very much abbreviated accounts published in the local newspapers, they formed the basis for Peter MacKenzie's works on the rising. Despite careful research by the authors (including questionnaires to the major libraries and record offices) assurances were given that the 1825 volumes relating to the trials did not exist or were not catalogued. The original records of the trials, the evidence and preparatory statements have completely disappeared. It could be that the records were again returned to London to lodge in the Baga de Secretis, a class of records kept by the Public Record Office. Examination of the Baga de Secretis shows that all records supposedly lodged there after 1817 have been removed. An extensive search of the Scottish Record Office and other likely places have proved negative, showing it is extremely likely that the original records were destroyed, perhaps by the authorities following the startling revaluation of the use of Government spies, published in 1832, when the Government had to give a free pardon to all the 1820 Radicals then living.

The volumes—*A Complete Collection of State Trials and Proceedings for High Treason*, volume 33, covering the years 1817–20, omits all references to the 1820 treason trials, while carrying the less important trials of MacKinlay, Edgar, etc., and MacLaren and Neil Douglas (for sedition) in 1817. The work does point out that some trials had been omitted as they "did not appear to be of sufficient importance". It seems most unlikely that the author should consider Neil Douglas' trial for sedition and acquittal of importance and the finding of eighty-eight bills for high treason, involving three executions and twenty-two transportations for life not of "sufficient importance". The reason for the disappearance of the records, the lack of mention in the State Trials volume, indeed, the general lack of knowledge of the 1820 uprising is certainly a matter for interesting speculation but it is not within the scope of this volume to comment further.

SEVENTEEN

"MURDER! MURDER! MURDER!"

From the outset it had been made clear that Baird and Hardie were to be executed as an example by which the authorities hoped once and for all to crush the disaffection in Scotland. Lord President Hope had been adamant in stating: "To Baird and Hardie I can hold out no hope of mercy in this world; they were the leaders and I am afraid they must suffer." In the case of Wilson, however, it was generally accepted that he would be reprieved along with the nineteen other condemned men whose sentences had been commuted to transportation for life. The jury had unanimously recommended him to mercy and public sympathy was outspokenly on his side. A movement for Royal Mercy was started by Hardie's cousin, Robert Goodwin, who managed to enlist the support of such important figures as Lord Keith, Rev. Dr Chalmers, Rev. Dr Ewing, Admiral Fleming and Robert Graham of Whitehall, and a petition was drawn up. Armed with this petition, Goodwin went to see the Lord Provost of Glasgow to plead with him, as a Member of Parliament for Lanark, to present the petition at Westminster. Despite the number of signatures on the petition, Henry Montieth refused to accept it, dismissing Goodwin by saying he "would let the law take its course"; he added that Hardie "justly merited its severest sentence". At this Goodwin became angry and protested at the Government espionage system which had been employed to snare the unwary Radicals. Montieth, without more ado, called his servants and had Goodwin ejected from his house. Goodwin and Robert Graham contacted several other Members of Parliament but they all had decided that the law should "take its course". In a desperate last attempt to raise the matter of clemency in Westminster, Robert Graham rode to London himself with the petition which he delivered to Lord Sidmouth via a friendly English Whig M.P. But Sidmouth did not even bother to acknowledge its receipt. Montieth commented that Wilson, and his Radical colleagues, were not "fit objects for Royal Mercy".

Wilson, however, was a very popular figure and the authorities were apprehensive at the growing public sympathy for the 63-year-old weaver. Although Wilson had been guilty in accordance with the law it was felt that something must be done to discredit him in the eyes of the general public in order to turn their sympathy away from him. A rumour was circulated that Wilson had burnt his Bible and denounced the Christian religion. The lie was a common enough ruse and used by the authorities on many occasions to discredit their enemies . . . atheism had the same connotation in those days as communism during the McCarthy era in the U.S.A. Accusations of atheism were levelled against the United Irishmen, despite the fact that a great number of members were Catholic priests. The rumour, in Wilson's case, did not decrease his popularity. So far the authorities had not succeeded in breaking Wilson's spirit and his belief that he was dying a martyr for freedom; if Wilson could be made to confess the "enormity of his guilt", the authorities reasoned, public sympathy would turn away from him. Wilson was a deeply religious man and the authorities felt that this would be the medium by which to force a written confession out of the weaver. On Sunday, August 20, the Rev. Dr Greville Ewing conducted a service in Glasgow Jail which Wilson, conspicuously carrying a Bible, was allowed to attend. Ewing based his sermon on Paul's Epistle to the Galatians, Chapter Six, verses 7 and 8:

Be not deceived; God is not mocked; for whatsoever a man soweth that he shall also reap.
For he that soweth to his flesh shall of the flesh reap corruption; but he that soweth to the Spirit shall of the Spirit reap life everlasting.

During the course of a tirade, which Ewing directed solely at Wilson, the Reverend Doctor sneered that Wilson need have no thoughts that he was a political martyr, or a martyr for liberty; he was a base, convicted criminal, damned in the sight of God. Following this sermon, Psalm 25 was sung and, at verse 11,

For thy name's sake, O Lord,
Pardon mine iniquity; for it is great,

observers noted with smug satisfaction that "tears swum into his [Wilson] eyes and his lip quivered".

The authorites decided to follow up this psychological attack by sending the Rev. James Lapslie of Campsie to visit Wilson in his cell, ostensibly to comfort the condemned man in his last days. Lapslie, a former member of the Friends of the People had turned Government informer on the nationalist-reformers and had been financially rewarded for his betrayals by a grateful government. As Wilson was practically a founder member of the Friends of the People, one would assume that he would have known Lapslie, or about Lapslie's betrayals, and therefore the wisdom of the authorities in sending this man to obtain Wilson's confession seems questionable. This aside, Lapslie also lacked the diplomacy to follow up the psychological advantage over Wilson and, on entering his cell, immediately launched into a tirade against Radicalism. He demanded, with little preamble, a confession of guilt of the "heinous crime" and threatened Wilson with eternal damnation if he refused. Wilson's reaction was to almost throw the man from his cell. He gave orders to the turnkeys not to allow Lapslie or "any of his ilk" to disturb his last few days on earth again.

The date of Wilson's execution was fixed for Wednesday, August 30, and, in the evening of Tuesday, he was allowed to see his wife, his daughter Mrs Walters, and his grandchildren for the last time. This was the day that Wilson was supposed to have written his "dying declaration" which was published fifteen years later by Peter MacKenzie. This declaration, which—it is alleged—first came to light in the shop of James Robertson, the Lennoxton librarian in 1834, was immediately denounced as a forgery by Wilson's former Radical friend from Strathaven, John Stevenson. The declaration is certainly a peculiar vindication of Wilson. The weaver is purported to state in one paragraph:

I acknowledge that I die a true patriot for the cause of freedom for my poor country, and I hope that my countrymen will still continue to see the necessity of a reform in the way of the country being represented [in Westminster] . . .

But, while giving this stirring message, Wilson is alleged to plead his innocence because when the news of the rising reached

Strathaven "I refused to go; but they [the Radicals] threatened to blow my brains out if I did not accompany them." While Wilson's friend, Stevenson, thinks "it was not Mr MacKenzie that forged this dying declaration", MacKenzie did try to vindicate the Radicals in such a way as to make them seem like stupid sheep led into the path of folly by evil designing people. The picture which MacKenzie presents of Wilson, Baird and Hardie is of ignorant men, forced into acts of rebellion without any understanding of events. As Wilson had been a nationalist-reformer since the days of the Friends of the People, such an idea seems incredible. Stevenson comments that MacKenzie "not content with robbing Wilson of his fair reputation . . . actually hung the good old man in chains . . .". Could it be that MacKenzie produced the declaration in order to add weight to his version of the rising? MacKenzie claimed that it was Wilson's family who gave him the document. Wilson's family denied this. MacKenzie also claims that as Wilson "was on the brink of eternity, he put into his wife's hand the . . . solemn and interesting document . . .". The date of the document is "Glasgow Jail, Iron-room, 29th August, 1820", and Mac-Kenzie says the declaration was given to Mrs Wilson during that last interview on Tuesday evening.

But [says Stevenson] John Walters, Wilson's grandson, who was present at this interview, is positive that his grandmother got no such paper, there was a grated door or window between the parties, the turnkey was also present to watch the proceedings. Wilson told his grandson, John Walters, that in his present situation he had nothing to give him except his tobacco speuchan, and said that he hoped he would keep it for the sake of his unfortunate grandfather, and after a pause, he added, "I hope that my countrymen will at least do my memory justice." Walters is certain that if his grandmother had got a dying declaration, she would have told him, and put the matter fairly at rest. When the old woman died, Walters came into possession of her papers, and there was no such document to be found among them; he assured me that he had never heard of it till Mr MacKenzie's account reached him at Strathaven.

After his wife and relatives left him, it is recorded that twelve "pious persons" remained with Wilson in his cell during the night.

Wednesday was a bright summers day, according to the

correspondent of the *Glasgow Herald*. The gallows had been erected towards the south angle of the Justiciary Hall, near the River Clyde, and—from early morning—crowds had been gathering in the streets and on the execution ground. It was noted that the crowd was sullen and silent and this was indeed a bad sign. Usually at a public execution, a fair-day atmosphere prevailed, stalls and entertainments were set up close to the scaffold and tradesmen did a roaring business. There were none of these festive signs that Wednesday ... just quiet groups of people watching and waiting. By midday the crowd was estimated at 20,000 strong and a feeling of apprehension gripped Major-General Reynell, charged with the safety of the area. Usually he would have designated a company of the local Yeomanry to guard the gallows but the atmosphere was electric and Reynell felt it needed only a small spark for the crowd to get out of hand for the situation to be turned into a nasty riot, perhaps into a full scale insurrection ... were the disaffected planning just such an event? His fears were doubled when it was discovered that posters were being circulated among the people:

May the ghost of the butchered Wilson, haunt the pillows of his relentless jurors—Murder! Murder! Murder!

Reynell ordered Lt.-Colonel Northcott to mobilise his 1st Battalion of the Rifle Brigade and stationed them through the streets of Glasgow. He then despatched Colonel, the Hon. William Keith Elphinstone's 33rd Regiment of Foot to the execution ground to join the newly arrived 3rd Dragoon Guards in guarding the area. It was the greatest display of military force used at an execution in Scotland before or since.

At precisely 2.5 p.m. that day, the Lord Provost, Hon. Henry Monteith, the Glasgow magistrates and the Sheriff, entered the South Justiciary Hall of the County Court Buildings, and took their seats on a bench facing the public galleries which were crowded with silent spectators. Immediately in front of the magistrates and officials was a single chair where the condemned man was to sit through the last religious service of his life. As the magistrates took their seats an unnecessary appeal was made to the public galleries that the crowd should remain absolutely silent during the service. Then Wilson himself entered with a "firm step and undaunted countenance". He was dressed in a white suit trimmed with black. He walked firmly down the hall, eyes straight ahead, and took his place before the magistrates. The Rev. Dr Greville Ewing rose and told the public to compose themselves so that the unfortunate prisoner might not be disturbed on this solemn occasion. He added that Wilson's execution was intended to be an object lesson to the evil designing people in Scotland. Looking at the weaver, he said:

. . . And now, James Wilson, although we are destitute of merit in ourselves, this is no obstacle in our salvation, for God gave His only Son to save sinners, and, oh, I beseech you to believe in Him who was taken from prison to judgement and who numbered sinners as a trophy of His victory when expiring on the cross, and ardently do I trust His holy spirit may be sent to enlighten your benighted mind, look to Him, I entreat you, cleave to Him, for whoso calleth on the name of the Lord, calleth not in vain. We have prayed for you in secret as well as in public, and, oh!, I now conjure you to join sincerely with us in singing the praises of the Almighty.

The first part of Psalm 51 was then sung and Wilson joined in:

Have mercy upon me, O God, according to thy loving kindness . . .

The Rev. Dr Daniel Dewar of the Tron Church then delivered a prayer for Wilson from which it was gathered that Wilson's spirit had not been broken and that he still adhered to his nationalist-reformer principles and believed he was a martyr in the cause of Scottish freedom. Following the prayer Wilson took the customary glass of wine. Dewar then read a passage from the Bible and beseeched Wilson to ask God to forgive him. Psalm 51 was sung again beginning at verse 7:

Purge me with hyssop, and I shall be clean . . .

and ending at verse 12. Again, Wilson joined in, inclining his head in emphasis on certain phrases with which he agreed.

The service at an end, Wilson remained seated while the hall was cleared. Then he was led to the south door of the hall where the company waited a few minutes before the executioner arrived from Glasgow Jail by the passage used to transport prisoners from the court to the prison. The executioner was dressed in a grey coat and fur hat with a piece of black crepe masking his face. He carried a large headsman's axe in his right hand and a knife in his left. The man who had volunteered for this gruesome task was a 20-year-old medical student from Bridgegate, Glasgow, named Thomas Moore. Soon after the executions he left Scotland and was last heard of living in Mayroe, County Derry, Ireland. At the south gate the hurdle, which was to transport Wilson on his last journey to the scaffold, was waiting. This was a box on wheels painted black with seats placed at each end—instead of the usual iron railing. Wilson's arms were firmly pinioned behind him and, assisted by the executioner and officers, he was made to sit in the rear seat of the box. The executioner took his seat facing Wilson, with the sharpened blade of his axe pointing towards the condemned man. Drawn by horses, the hurdle lurched forward, surrounded by a strong body of the 3rd Dragoon Guards, their swords resting lightly upon their shoulders. Behind them came the Lord Provost, the Sheriff and other high officials of Glasgow.

Murmurs of sympathy began to sweep through the crowd lining the route but Wilson remained stoical.

"Did y'ever see sic a crowd, Tammas?" he was heard to remark to the executioner.

At 2.55 p.m. the party mounted the scaffold. A tremendous shout mingled with hisses and cries of "Murder!" rose from thousands of throats as Wilson was placed under the gallows. A stocking cap was drawn over Wilson's head and the ordinary hangman speedily adjusted the rope around his neck. As Wilson dropped his handkerchief to show that he was prepared to die, the drop fell. The angry cries and hisses became an ominous rumble like thunder and, from one section of the crowd discordant screams were heard and the outer part of the crowd was seen running towards Calton, crying "the cavalry are coming!" There was great confusion and many people were injured. The correspondent of the *Glasgow Herald* dismissed it as a feint of some pickpockets who hoped, in the ensuing confusion, to put their talents to use. However, it transpired that an officer of the 3rd Dragoon Guards, observing the revulsion of the crowd and thinking a rescue attempt was about to be made, charged into a section of the people with his men in an attempt to disperse them. Three minutes later quiet had returned.

Wilson's body was convulsed with agitated jerks for five minutes. "Some blood appeared through the cap opposite the ears, but upon the whole he appeared to die very easily."

The body hung for half an hour until 3.30 p.m. when the officials took it down and lowered it on to three short spokes laid across the mouth of a waiting coffin, the head was placed on a block at the top of the coffin. The cap was taken off and, with the crowd yelling their disapproval and anger, the executioner severed the head with one stroke. The *Glasgow Herald* correspondent reported that the young man executed his task "with most determined coolness". Picking up the bloody head of Wilson, the executioner stepped forward and raised it for the crowd to see, shouting the customery formula: "This is the head of a traitor!" It was reported that even several of the soldiers fainted at the gory sight. Again the crowd thundered its disapproval and cries of: "He is a murdered man!"; "He bled for his country!" and "He is a martyr!" were hurled at the scaffold.

The *Glasgow Herald* reported: "The whole ceremony of decapitation did not occupy above a minute, and at four o'clock the ground was clear, without any material accident having happened."

The mangled remains of Wilson were then secured in a coffin and, under the direction of Alexander Calder, the Sheriff's officer, were taken to the "pauper's ground" near Glasgow High Church where they were buried without ceremony. This was a great shock to Wilson's relatives who had been led to believe that, in accordance with Wilson's last wishes, his body would be handed over to them for burial in his home village of Strathaven. The authorities turned a deaf ear to their pleas. Wilson's daughter, Mrs Walters, and his niece, Mrs Ritchie, who had come to supervise the transportation of Wilson's remains back to Strathaven, refused to let the matter lie there. At midnight on the same day, with a coach and a couple of loyal helpers, they went to the "pauper's ground" and dug up the newly filled in grave. In a short while the remains of James Wilson were being borne back to his native Strathaven for an honoured, but secret, burial in the parish churchyard only a few yards from his own house. While the authorities were displeased by this turn of events they did not cause any action to be taken against Wilson's relatives or the local clergyman.

With the execution of Wilson, Baird and Hardie seemed to resign themselves to death. The date of their execution had been fixed for Friday, September 8, at Stirling. Two weeks before the date fixed for their execution the two men were placed in the same cell in Stirling Castle. From their cell they wrote innumerable letters to friends and relatives. On September 4 John Baird wrote to his friend Daniel Kilsyth, whom he and Hardie requested to write a dirge over their grave, and said that he was "a martyr to the cause of liberty". Their letters were full of religious references but in one letter to his cousins, Andrew Hardie referred to the perjury of James Hardie and Private Nicol Baird saying: "I freely forgive them and I hope you will keep no ill will at them." The most moving letter that Andrew Hardie wrote from his cell the day before his execution was addressed to his fiancée, Margaret McKeigh, in which he tried to comfort her.

My dear Margaret, I hope you will not take it as a dishonour that your unfortunate lover died for his distressed, wronged, suffering and insulted country; no, my dear Margaret, I know you are possessed of nobler ideas than that, and well do I know that no person of feeling or humanity will insult you with it—I have every reason to believe that it will be the contrary. I shall die firm to the cause in which I embarked, and although we were outwitted and betrayed, yet I protest, as a dying man, it was done with good intention on my part. But well did you know my sentiments on that subject long before I was taken prisoner. No person could have induced me to take up arms to rob or plunder; no, my dear Margaret, I took them for the restoration of those rights for which our forefathers bled, and which we have allowed shamefully to be wrested from us; but I trust the innocent blood which will be shed tomorrow, in place of being a terror, will awaken my countrymen—my poor, suffering, countrymen, from that lethargy which has so overclouded them!

Paying his last farewell to the girl he had hoped to marry, Andrew Hardie wrote:

Farewell—a long farewell to you and all worldly cares, for I have done with them. I hope you will call frequently on my distressed and afflicted Mother. At the expense of some tears I destroyed your letters. Again farewell, my dear Margaret, may God attend you still, and all your soul with consolation fill, is the sincere prayer of your most affectionate and constant lover while on earth.

The last letter that Hardie wrote, at 10 p.m. that Thursday night, was to his "dear young friend" Isobella Condy of Stirling, a young woman who had nursed the wounded prisoners in Stirling Castle. The letter dwelt on Hardie's religious beliefs and his hope that Isobella would also receive comfort through religion. Hardie addressed the letter "as a token of gratitude for her kind attention to him while a prisoner in Stirling Castle, who fell a martyr to the cause of truth and justice on the 8th of September, 1820".

That Thursday the friends and relatives of the condemned man were granted their last meeting. Baird's family, his 80-year-old father, three sisters, two brothers and two brothers-in-law arrived with a friend named Mr Bruce. Baird is reported to have spoken to them on his hopes and feelings for Scotland, telling them not to mourn for him but to thank God for sustaining him throughout his trial. When the time came for his aged father (who he had not seen since before Bonnymuir) Baird took out a home-made snuff box with a silver mounting and said: "Oh, dear father, please accept this from me. You will perhaps look at it when you can no longer look at me in this world."

The last night was spent in prayer and the deputy governor of Stirling Castle, General Graham, gave permission for some relations, Rev. Dr Wright, Rev. Dr Small and Messrs. Smart, Bruce and Sheriff, to spend the night with them, reading portions of the scriptures, praying and in conversation. Throughout the night, said an observer, Baird and Hardie showed great calm. At four o'clock they fell asleep but were up again at 6 a.m., washed and dressed. They sang Psalm 51 and Baird read the 15th Chapter of Corinthians 1 . . . The Resurrection of the Dead. Then the two men were allowed into the castle's courtyard, under the supervision of the Fort Major, W. Peddie, to pay farewell to the rest of the Bonnymuir prisoners. Baird and Hardie told them "that although they were condemned, right was on their side and that the cause which they championed would in the end prevail". They were allowed to embrace their former comrades and were then led back to their cells to await the arrival of their escort to the place of execution.

The scaffold had been erected in front of Stirling Jail in

Broad Street and two coffins had been placed on the platform next to the headsman's block. At twelve noon two troops of the 8th Dragoon Guards arrived from Falkirk and formed up in the square in front of Stirling Castle. The 13th Regiment had been detailed to guard the area and, at 1 p.m., a troop of the regiment accompanied the Sheriff, Ranald MacDonald of Staffa and magistrates of Stirling to the castle. Baird and Hardie, dressed in black suits and white gloves, were seated in a similar hurdle to the one which escorted Wilson to the scaffold. Opposite them sat Moore, the medical student, in his executioner's garb, holding his axe before him. Baird and Hardie each clutched a New Testament in their hands while around the hurdle were grouped Rev. Dr Wright, Rev Dr Small, Mr Bruce, two sheriff's officers and relatives. With a group of dragoons in front, clearing a path through the crowds, and a group at the rear, the party set off from the castle. Baird, it was observed, was mournful while Hardie smiled and seemed cheerful. As the procession moved off both men began to sing a hymn "The hour of my departure comes". After they had finished, Hardie smiled and bowed, calling out "God Bless you" to the weeping women, on the quarter-mile route to the place of execution. As at Wilson's execution, the crowd was sullen and silent, and the authorities were uneasy.

The procession reached the jail and Baird and Hardie were escorted into the Court Hall, where the Rev. Dr Wright began the service with the 51st Psalm, verses 7 to 13 and Hardie led the people, two lines at a time, in singing it. Rev. Dr Small then prayed for their souls and Mr Bruce led the people in the 130th Psalm: "Out of the depth have I cried unto thee, O Lord". Rev. Dr Wright conducted the last prayers and the prisoners were given the customary glass of wine before their arms were pinioned. Hardie requested that his grateful thanks be given to General Graham and Major Peddie for the humanity they had shown him. At 2.45 p.m. Baird and Hardie were led out on to the scaffold.

The crowd, estimated at 2,000, set up a cheer. Hardie looked up at the swinging noose of the gallows exclaiming: "Hail, harbinger of everlasting peace." Baird stepped forward and addressed the people: "Friends and countrymen, I dare say you well expect me to say something to you of the cause which has brought me here; but on that I do not mean to say much, only that what I have hitherto done, and which brought me here, was for the cause of truth and justice. I declare I never gave my consent to anything inconsistent with truth and justice." He then declared he was not afraid to confront God and he exhorted the crowd to believe in God, to love and venerate the Bible. Hardie addressed the crowd in the same vein and urged them not to go into a public house to drink to the memory of Baird and Hardie but to go home and think of God. Then he added in a firmer voice: "I die a martyr to the cause of truth and justice . . .."

A roar of applause rose from the crowd and a nervous officer snapped out an order to "present arms!" The crowd panicked and for a moment it became a screaming mass of people but, as the soldiers made no further move calm was soon restored. Sheriff Ranald MacDonald of Staffa, however, told Hardie that he could not permit him to continue a speech in this way. Hardie bowed and called out: "My friends, I hope none of you have been hurt. Please, after this is over, go quietly to your homes and read your Bibles, remembering the fate of Baird and Hardie."

While the execution cap was being placed over Baird's head, Hardie knelt by his coffin and sang a hymn, followed by a short prayer. Then he, too, had a cap placed over his head. Mr Bruce said a prayer and the two men bade farewell to each other. With the noose secure round their necks, Hardie gave the signal. Both men died without a struggle. Baird's New Testament, which he had held in his hand until now, fell from his convulsed fingers to the feet of the silent crowd below. After half an hour, the Sheriff's officers cut down the bodies and laid them on the spokes over their respective coffins. Then the young executioner came forward and was greeted with yells, hisses and cries of "Murderer!" from the crowd. The young Medical student seemed to have "lost his firmness and dexterity". He felt the neck of Hardie's corpse with his right hand, raised the axe, paused, and lowered it, hesitated and adjusted his mask. The axe was raised again and the executioner aimed two powerful strokes at the neck but a third was needed to sever the head. This he held up to the crowd crying: "This is the head of a traitor!" Turning to Baird his first stroke cut the neck slightly and stuck into the wood. Prising loose the axe, the executioner again hacked at the neck and finally, holding the terrifying object out before him, he repeated the ritual: "This is the head of a traitor!"

Again the crowd yelled their disapproval, again a nervous officer brought the soldiers to the "present arms" position, and so—muttering its disapproval—the crowd began to disperse. The coffins were quickly sealed and escorted to the "pauper's graveyard" near by.

"And that, gentlemen," remarked Ranald MacDonald of Staffa, "completes the business."

He spoke too soon. That night attempts were made on the lives of some of the prominent witnesses who gave evidence at the Radical trials. Late at night a group of armed men burst into the house of James Hardie, the Glasgow justice of the peace, and demanded to know his whereabouts. The frightened servants told them that he was away from the house that night, staying with friends. The men, "brandishing all manner of weapons", contented themselves with ransacking James Hardie's house. A similar raid took place on the homes of other witnesses at Stirling, between 10 p.m. and 11 p.m., and shots were fired. On the following two days, September 9 and 10, attacks were made on the Usherwood Cotton Mills and on September 11 the labourers stopped work at Milngarvie Mill. Between 1 a.m. and 2 a.m. a group of Radicals, fully armed, attempted to fire the mill and the military were called out. One man, Malcolm Bowie, was arrested. Unrest flared up again throughout the industrial belt. The lesson, which the authorities had hoped the public executions would teach the populace, did not appear to have been learned.

Francis Jeffrey, the advocate, summed up the general situation in a letter to John Allen: "I am very much ashamed of the Commons, and have little now to say against the Radical Reformers; if any reform is worth the risk of such an experiment. The practical question upon which every man should be making up his mind, is, whether he is for tyranny or revolution."

EIGHTEEN

"REVOLUTION OR TYRANNY?"

THE EVENTS OF the 1820 rising in Scotland were almost completely overshadowed for the majority of the people in the United Kingdom by the trial of Queen Caroline. George IV had married Caroline, Princess of Brunswick, on April 8, 1795, only because of his sense of duty to the Crown. That evening their wedding was consummated for the first and last time providing, nine months later, a daughter named Charlotte. By that time, however, Caroline and George had parted for ever. In 1814 Princess Caroline had drifted abroad, travelling through numerous countries and lovers before settling down in vulgar ostentation with an Italian adventurer named Pergami. When George III died, in January, 1820, Caroline found herself Queen of England. George IV immediately offered her an annuity of £50,000 to renounce her claim to the throne. Caroline refused and immediately proceeded to England making a triumphant entry into London with the crowds cheering themselves into a state of riot.

The bitterness and intense dislike that the people felt for the libertine George IV, polarised itself into support for Queen Caroline on the simple reasoning that anything George IV was against, they were for. In a rage, George IV persuaded the House of Lords to accuse her of adultery and scandalous behaviour, although compared with the misdeeds of the King the Queen's behaviour faded into insignificance. A Divorce Bill was threatened and Henry Brougham, Francis Jeffrey's old friend who had helped him found the *Edinburgh Review*, became the counsel for Caroline's defence. Brougham had qualified at the Scottish Bar in 1800 but he moved to London and qualified at the English Bar eight years later. An ardent Whig Reformer, he was also elected as Member of Parliament for Winchelsea. At the peak of his form, Brougham tore the evidence of Caroline's adultery to shreds with devastating skill.

The temper of the public—whose hatred of the monarchy as the symbol of wanton extravagance opposed to their poverty and degradation, began to frighten the Government. George IV remained in hiding at Windsor, suffering from nervous prostration. Many peers began a discreet withdrawal from the House of Lords so that the Government majority against Caroline fell. On November 10, 1820, with only a majority of nine, the premier, Lord Liverpool, stopped the hearing and the Divorce Bill was withdrawn. London gave itself up to three days and nights of riot and celebrations, reflected all over the country and even in Scotland. George IV's mortification was complete. However, two months after his coronation, on August 7, 1821, Queen Caroline died.

The coronation of George IV took place on July 19, 1821, with parliament voting a sum of £150,000 to cover the costs. As a gesture of goodwill the Government issued pardons to all those Scottish Radicals who had fled the country in 1820, following the insurrection, and who had been declared outlaws. Few of the Radicals decided to take advantage of the pardon to return to the poverty and misery which existed in Scotland. One man who did, however, was the Commissary General of the Paisley Radicals, John Parkhill. Parkhill, who had fled from his home a few days after the start of the insurrection, had sailed for Montreal, Canada. He remained fourteen months wandering around the U.S.A. and Canada before hearing of the pardon. He sailed from New York on August 20, 1821, and arrived in Liverpool three weeks later. Returning to Paisley, where he was re-united with his wife and family, Parkhill settled down in New Sneddon Street, in the house of a man named Arthur Smith. He joined the two names together and wrote an account of the insurrection as he saw it under the title *Autobiography of Arthur Sneddon*. Later, he wrote a *History of Paisley* under his own name. MacKenzie, the historian, in an appraisal of Parkhill's work, says "the aim of his narrative is to throw ridicule, to some extent, on the actings of the Radicals. He also wishes his readers to believe that their proceedings were foolish, and that he told them so, and therefore kept aloof from them. If he had done no more than what he informs us, there would have been no occasion for him to fly the country." But, of course, Parkhill wrote his *Autobiography* while the Tories were still in power and before the passing of the Reform Bill. One cannot help getting the impression that the work was written as a mere apology for the Radicals' daring to defy a "munificent" Tory Government, rather than as a truthful account of the affair.

Francis Jeffrey, feeling "very much ashamed with the Commons", launched himself more vehemently into reform politics. On December 19, 1820, he helped to organise a public meeting in Edinburgh which became known from the building where it was held as The Pantheon Meeting. Moncrieff presided and Jeffrey addressed the people, after which a series of resolutions were drawn up calling upon the King to dismiss the Government "and were not merely political," recalls Henry Cockburn, "but directly hostile to the existing power, being the first open and respectable assemblage that had been convened in this place for such a purpose for about 25 years". Nine days later Jeffrey was elected Lord Rector of Glasgow University by the strong pro-Radical students. Jeffrey continued to follow the Whig Reformist line becoming Member of Parliament for Perth in Lord Grey's administration of 1830, when the Whig Party finally disposed of the Tory rule. In 1832 he was returned for Edinburgh and retained the seat until 1834 when he became a judge of the Court of Session. Before he died in 1850 he was given a peerage and became Lord Jeffrey. His close friend, Henry Cockburn, became Solicitor-General for Scotland under the Whig Government and had a chief hand in drafting some of the clauses of the Reform Bill. In 1834 he became Lord Cockburn, a judge of the Court of Session and three years later a lord of the justiciary.

Alexander Boswell, commander of the Ayrshire Yeomanry, found that he had served his Government well, even though he had failed to "ride in Radical blood up to his bridle reins". In November, 1820, he wrote several letters to Lord Sidmouth, pointing out how loyal he was and how he had to pay £600 out of his own pocket to equip his Yeomanry that year. With the allowances that he was making to the members of his family, Alexander Boswell told Sidmouth that he could not afford to continue to be a Member of Parliament. Sidmouth promptly rewarded Boswell with a baronetcy in 1921. Boswell is best remembered in Scotland as the author of such songs as "Good night and joy be wi' ye a' "; "Jenny's bawbee" and "Jenny dang the weaver". His only parliamentary endeavour was to change the act which abolished two old Scottish statutes making duelling illegal (59 Geo. III, cap. 70); it is ironic, then, that this man should die, on March 27, 1822, as a result of a duel which he had made legal. The duel was with his kinsman James Stuart of Dunearn, who challenged him as being the author of some anonymous political pasquinades attacking him. The duel took place on March 22, at Auchtertool, Fife, and Boswell was wounded, dying in the house of Lord Balmuto some days later. His friend, Sir Walter Scott, was moved to write:

> Alas! vindictive was the wrath
> And fatal was the blow,
> Thou pride of Scotia's chivalry
> In death that laid thee low.

James Stuart was arrested but, thanks to Boswell's own hand, could not be convicted of any criminal charge.

Another poet of the rising, William Motherwell, continued in his post as Sheriff Deputy of Paisley, contributing such volumes to Anglo-Scottish literature as *Ministrelsy Ancient and Modern* and *Poetical Remains*. Motherwell was to die, in 1835, at the early age of 38.

Samuel Hunter, the colonel of the Glasgow Yeomanry, remained editor of the *Glasgow Herald* until 1835, remaining true to his Tory and anti-reform principles to the last. Commenting on the passing of the Reform Bill in the *Glasgow Herald* on May 14, 1832, he said: ". . . sorry are we to say that our feelings on this occasion are not of the most pleasant description." Hunter died at the home of his nephew, Rev. Archibald Blair Campbell, minister of Kilwinning, on June 9, 1839, aged 70. His salary of £100 per annum was paid right up to his death and his profits in the newspaper realised £12,000. Samuel Hunter's name is still immortalised in the diary column of the *Glasgow Herald* today.

Mr Serjeant Hullock was knighted on April 21, 1823, becoming Sir John Hullock, in reward for his conduct of the treason trials. There is evidence that, despite the £2,000 fee he had received, Hullock petitioned the Treasury and claimed that he had lost money in appearing for the Crown. It was rumoured that Hullock, a gourmet, died from a surfeit of his favourite dish.

Major-General Sir Thomas Bradford remained in Scotland until 1825 when he was promoted to Lieutenant-General and commander of the military district of Bombay. In 1841 he was promoted to full general and eventually died in London, on November 28, 1853, aged 75. His colleague, Major-General Sir Richard Hussey Vivian, sat in the House of Commons from 1820 representing Truro, his home town. He held several Government offices including Irish Privy Councillor and English Privy Councillor until, in 1841, he was created the 1st Baron Vivian. He died in Baden-Baden on August 20, 1842, and his body was returned for burial at Truro. As for the leading members of the Government of the time, Lord Castlereagh, the Foreign Minister, committed suicide at his Kent home in 1822; Lord Sidmouth lived on to the ripe old age of 87, dying on February 15, 1844; and the Prime Minister, Lord Liverpool, left office in 1827, being succeeded by the more liberal Tory, George Canning.

Five years after the insurrection Marshal MacDonald, Duke of Taranto, who it had been rumoured was encamped on Cathkin Braes with 5,000 expatriate Scots in the early days of April, 1820, did pay a visit to the land from which his father, Neil MacEachain, had fled with Prince Charles Edward in 1746. But the 60-year-old Marshal of France did not come at the head of an army but simply as a tourist, receiving a tremendous reception in Edinburgh and Inverness. The Government placed a revenue cutter at his disposal and with Ranald MacDonald, an Edinburgh writer, the Marshal paid a visit to the Western Isles to visit his relatives. Alexander Carmichael, of Edinburgh, recalled that the Marshal addressed his relatives in Gáidhlig, with a slight French accent, and they answered him in Gáidhlig "for," says Carmichael in wonderment, "neither they nor the Marshal spoke English".

In 1830 the despotic George IV died and the country felt it high time for a complete change of leadership. That year the Tory party was swept from office and Lord Grey headed a Whig administration . . . the first Whig Government in almost seventy years. A Reform Bill was duly placed in the Commons, though it was not until 1832 that it was passed. The Scottish

Reform movement, now feeling secure, began to question more closely the events of 1820 and, in October, 1831, a Mr Wallace of Kelly, speaking at a meeting of the Renfrewshire Political Union, accused the authorities of creating the rising artificially. On October 13, Sheriff Dunlop of Paisley demanded what authority Wallace had for stating this. The next day Wallace wrote in reply:

I believe that persons in the confidence and employment pay of the Government were sent among the people to stir them up to mischief, and did stir them up in the years 1818 and 1819; and that troops were poured into all parts of the country at the request of the authorities—none of whom ever contradicted the allegation, although a thousand times advanced, of hired spies and informers, having betrayed the people into acts of insubordination.

Wallace then asked Dunlop some direct questions as to the employment of spies in that year and whether he knew about a man named Richmond. Dunlop replied on October 19 denying all the allegations Wallace had made, but the allegations of Wallace led to a young historian named Peter MacKenzie, who had become editor of the *Reformer's Gazette*, writing two accounts of the 1820 rising. MacKenzie had been 20 years old when the rising had taken place and had served against the Radicals in the 6th Centre Company of the Glasgow Yeomanry but he later became a Whig Reformist. When his books, *An Exposure of the Spy System Pursued in Glasgow During the Years 1816–20* and *The Trial of James Wilson for High Treason* were published in 1832, the year the Reform Bill was passed, they caused a furore. They were, at the same time, unpopular with both the Tories and the Radicals. Their unpopularity with the Tories was due, of course, to the fact that they revealed part of the fantastic spy system which had been organised to ensnare the Radicals. To the Radicals, however, they were unpopular because MacKenzie, in stressing that the rising was instigated by Government agents, made the Radicals out to be a bunch of half-witted illiterates who were incapable of forming ideas or plans. It was MacKenzie's histories that provoked the publication of John Stevenson's *Radical Rising at Strathaven*, in which Stevenson accused MacKenzie of writing a history of an affair of which he was "deplorably ignorant" and "under the mask of friendship, he has stigmatised and insulted the poor fellows that left Strathaven along with Wilson, with such virulent perseverance that one would almost think he was actuated by personal motives".

The facts of the spy system were unsavoury and the Tories leaned over backwards in order to cover up the matter. Many documents and letters concerning the affair disappeared and, as shown in previous chapters, records and documents, especially those appertaining to the trial, have completely vanished. As part of the denial, Alexander B. Richmond, still living in Scotland, decided to sue for libel damages. Instead of making out a case against MacKenzie, or his publishers in Scotland, Richmond sued Simpkin and Marshall, the London distributors of MacKenzie's work for the sum of £5,000. The case was heard at the Court of Exchequer, Guildhall, London, from Saturday, December 20, to Monday, December 22, 1834, before the Hon. Baron Parke and a special jury. Richmond conducted his own case with the aid of Thomas Brown, a solicitor, and Mr Steer, a barrister. Richmond presented MacKenzie's work to the court and, quoting extracts, claimed the whole thing to be a "base fabrication". The defendants, represented by Mr Serjeant Talfourd, pleaded justification and, in his opening defence speech, Talfourd posed the question why Richmond, a Scot living in Scotland, should bring this case to London when the matter concerned a book written and published in Scotland and concerning a Scottish event.

I ask, gentlemen, how can the plaintiff explain, for his own sake, the trial of the question here, which he might and ought to have tried in Scotland? Ah, gentlemen, he thinks to impose upon you, an English jury, strangers to him, but I shall soon tear the veil which covers him from your knowledge: I shall unmask him to you in a way which even his audacity, of which you have this day had a small specimen, never, I doubt, contemplated.

Talfourd proceeded to quote passages from Richmond's own memoirs, in which Richmond openly admitted becoming a Government agent. To prove Richmond had tried to instigate a rising, Talfourd called a number of former Radicals to whom Richmond had administered, or tried to administer, his notorious oath and whom he had advised to organise armed associations or workers as nothing could be achieved by constitutional methods. William MacKemmie, Stewart Buchan, Robert

Craig, John Miller and William Wotherspoon were among those called and even Robert Owen of New Lanark came as a witness for the defence. MacKenzie's own evidence was given by deposition which he made out on October 6, 1834, at the Eagle Inn in the presence of Richmond and his solicitor, and John Kerr, writer for the defence. During the taking of MacKenzie's deposition, he and Richmond nearly came to blows.

"I shall make you smart, sir, for this!" Richmond exploded.

"Will you, indeed?" replied MacKenzie.

"Yes sir," cried Richmond. "I shall punish you for your lies against me and I would chastise you if I had you now out of the room."

"You! You blackguard!" yelled MacKenzie. "Take care of your hand, Mr Spy! The respect I have for the court makes me quiet: but if you give me any more of your insolence I shall make your outside as black as your in!"

The trial wound up on Monday afternoon and the jury found that the defendants were fully justified in the publication and distribution of MacKenzie's book. The Government now took note of the revelations and a pardon was granted to all the 1820 Radicals who had been transported.

The absolute pardons granted to the 1820 insurgents on August 10, 1835, were reported in *The Australian* of February 9, 1836, on page 4. *The Australian* gave a list of the "Bonnymuir" men who had arrived in Australia on May 18, 1821, in the convict ship *Speke*, which had left England on December 22, 1820. Of the eighteen "Bonnymuir" prisoners, only nine were listed as still living in Sydney in the 1828 Census. What became of them after this date, and what became of their nine colleagues (who, it is recorded had arrived in the settlement), nothing is known.

James Cleland, who Australian records show was serving in the 7th Dragoon Guards at the time of "Bonnymuir", and was reprieved only a few days before he was due to be executed, was 38 years old in 1828. He was working as a locksmith and was lodging in the home of his old comrade-in-arms Alex Johnston, in Clarence Street, Sydney. Johnston was working as a carpenter and living with his wife, Mary, who had been born in the colony. Thomas McCulloch was also living in Clarence Street in 1828 and working as a labourer. He was 40 years old at this time.

His wife Sarah had joined him in 1823, arriving in the *Jupiter*. with sons Thomas and Andrew (aged 13 and 8, in 1828). McCulloch's daughter, Mary, then aged 4, was born in the colony. John Barr, aged 35, was working as a woollen man in the firm of William Holden, Pitt Street, Sidney. Benjamin Moir is not listed in the Census but there is a note made in Governor Brisbane's despatches that he applied for his wife Jane, of Green Street, St John's, Glasgow, and his two children, to be allowed to join him in the colony.

Allan Murchie, 31 years old, was working as a tailor in York Street, Sydney, with his 26-year-old wife Elizabeth, who arrived in the colony on *Jupiter* in 1823.

William Murchie, his father, had written to Lord Sidmouth, on September 2, 1820, and requested permission for Elizabeth Marshall, Allan Murchie's fiancèe, to travel to Australia and to be allowed to marry him; also, he asked for permission to let Murchie take a box of tools, donated by his friends, and several books. She had married Murchie at St James' Church, Sydney, on March 22, 1824. They had one son, William, born April 7, 1826, and two daughters, Jane Oxley, born October 13, 1824, and Elizabeth, born April 24, 1828.

William Clackson, or Clarkson, 29 years old, was working as a shoemaker in Philip Street, Sydney, living with his wife Margaret, aged 28, who had arrived in the colony on the *Orpheus* in 1826. Thomas Pike, or Pink, aged 35 years, was working as miller to F. Gerard of Sydney. Alexander Hart, aged 34 years, was working as a cabinet-maker in MacQuarie Street, Sydney.

Only one other man appears to have been traced—John MacMillan, the Camelon nailer, who had been sentenced at Stirling. He was found living in Van Dieman's Land in 1835.

Directly following the publication of MacKenzie's works, a memorial was erected to the memory of Baird and Hardie on November 10, 1832, in the grounds of James Turner of Thrushgrove. The monument, which was erected by Messrs. Nelson and Galbraith, was paid for by the former Radicals and the Whig Reformists. All the proceeds from MacKenzie's works were donated for its erection. At first it had been decided to raise the memorial at Stirling and the Kirk Session gave its approval. However, the Provost of Stirling, a man named

Foreman, refused permission. The Glasgow authorities also refused permission for the memorial to be erected near to the place of Wilson's execution. Finally, James Turner allowed the memorial to be raised on his grounds at Thrushgrove where, in 1816, the first mass Radical meeting had been held. The memorial read:

> This Monument Erected
> 10th November, 1832
> on the lands of Thrushgrove
> the property of
> James Turner Esq.

Where, on the 29th of Oct., 1816, and in spite of every opposition 40,000 inhabitants of Glasgow first bravely met and petitioned the legislature for a redress of grievances, and for a Reform of the Representation of the People in the Commons House of Parliament.

> Sacred
> to the memory of
> Andrew Hardie, Aged 28
> and John Baird, Aged 32
> who
> were betrayed by infamous spies and informers
> and
> suffered death at Stirling
> 8th September, 1820
> for the cause of Reform now triumphant
> 1832

Following the erection of the memorial, a dinner was given for 120 prominent reformers at the Argyll Hotel with Peter MacKenzie in the chair. Toasts to the memory of Baird and Hardie were drunk. MacKenzie recalled that the Strathaven Radicals carried a banner "Scotland Free—Or A Desert!" What Scotsman would hesitate for one moment to echo those words again and again, he demanded? Proposing a toast to the memory of Sir William Wallace, who in 1296 began the Scottish War of Independence against England, MacKenzie added: "I hope that the monument now erected would have the effect of shaming Scotsmen, if nothing else will do, into the erection of a monument to that first and greatest of Scotland's patriots. See the thousands of pounds that they are now collecting for a monument to Sir Walter Scott, and will they, after this, basely forget Sir William Wallace?" The memory of James Wilson was toasted and Robert Goodwin, Hardie's cousin, proposed a toast to Robert Graham of Whitehall, and Andrew Mitchell, who had defended "the victims of 1820" and spent £300 in bringing Mr Harmer, the English solicitor, to attend the trials. Robert Baird, Baird's brother, toasted Admiral Fleming who had warned several Radicals of their impending arrest and had given them time to flee the country.

During 1847 the Scottish Chartist movement decided to pay homage to the memory of Baird and Hardie by erecting another memorial, the one erected in 1832 seems to have been destroyed. A public subscription was raised under the Hardie and Baird Martyrs Stone Committee and a correspondence was conducted with the Home Office seeking permission to remove the remains of the two Radicals to Sighthill Cemetery, Glasgow. On May 5, 1847, the committee received a letter from Andrew Rutherford, the Lord Advocate, from his office at Gwyder House, Whitehall:

Sir, I have laid the memorial from the relatives of Andrew Hardie and John Baird before the Secretary, Sir George Gray, and I have the satisfaction of informing you that if the Kirk Session of Stirling see no objections upon other ground, opposition will not be made on the part of the Government to the removal of the remains of these unfortunate men from their present place of internment, but the permission is given under the express condition that the removal shall take place without any public notice or intimation, and without any procession, or concourse, or attendance of people, but in the presence of a few friends only.

Andrew Rutherford

In the early hours of July 20, 1847, the exhumations took place according to the Lord Advocate's instructions, and the remains of Baird and Hardie were re-interred in front of the large stone monument raised in their honour. The inscription read:

Erected by Public Subscription
July, 1847
To the Memory of
John Baird, aged 32
and
Andrew Hardie, aged 28
Who, for the Cause of Freedom, suffered Death
at Stirling, 8th September, 1820

A poem on the memorial reads:

> Here lies the slain and mutilated forms
> Of those who fell, and fell like martyrs true,
> Faithful to freedom through a time of storms,
> They met their fate as patriots always do.
>
> Calmly they view'd Death's dread and dank array,
> Serene in hope, they triumphed o'er dismay;
> Their country's wrongs alone drew forth their sighs,
> And those to them endeared by Nature's holiest ties.
>
> But truth and right have better times brought round,
> Now no more traitors scorn by passing breath,
> For weeping Scotland hails this spot of ground
> And shrines, with all who fell for Freedom's faith,
> Those sons of her's now fam'd made glorious by their death.

The monument was repaired in 1865 by a few people who remembered the affair and under the superintendence of the original members of the Hardie and Baird Martyrs Stone Committee. Again the memorial fell into disrepair and in 1885 another public subscription was raised to repair it. Now, 150 years after the abortive rising, the memorial stone is once again to be repaired.

The memory of the 1820 insurrection began to grow dim, and the folk memory of it was soon lost. References to it in records became obscure and soon no mention of it at all was made in history books. Spa Fields, Peterloo, the Cato Street Conspiracy, have all had mention in history, but of the events in Scotland during April, 1820, nothing is recalled, for certainly, on the evidence, the Scottish rising far outweighed Peterloo in importance and historical significance. The finding of eighty-eight bills of high treason is surely an event unparalleled in Radical history. Could this preoccupation with English Radicalism and dismissal of Scottish Radicalism have anything to do with the nationalist orientation of the Radical movement in Scotland and their wish to dissolve the Union of 1707?

Apart from its profound effect on Scottish history, which will be shown presently, the 1820 insurrection also had a profound effect on Canadian politics for the Radical ideals were taken to the American continent by many young Scottish Radicals who fled the country to escape Sidmouth's net. Among the

Radicals that fled in those early weeks of April, 1820, as soon as it was seen that the insurrection was doomed to failure, was 26-year-old William Lyon MacKenzie, from Springfield, Dundee. MacKenzie, whose grandfather Calum Dubh had followed Prince Charles Edward into exile in France, was an accountant. In May, 1817, he had gone to England to find work and in 1819 had spent two months in France. Early in 1820, MacKenzie was travelling regularly between York and Glasgow, keeping the English and Scottish Radicals in touch with each other. In April, 1820, like hundreds of other young Radicals, MacKenzie fled on the *Psyche* bound for Canada. After settling in that country he founded a Radical newspaper called the *Colonial Advocate* (which ran from 1824–34) and in 1836 founded the *Constitution* as the journal of his Reform Party. In 1828 he was elected to the provincial parliament for York but expelled in 1830.

MacKenzie was angered by the policies of the Canadian Government, which were similar to the policies of the English Government he had fought against in 1820, and so finding his Reform Party could not move constitutionally, he led a Radical rising and attempted to seize Toronto in 1837. This rising was quickly suppressed and MacKenzie escaped to the United States where he set up a Provisional Government of Canada on Navy Isle in the Niagara River. While the Americans officially took no notice of internal Canadian politics, unofficially they pursued a policy of partisan neutrality. In 1837 a small steamer named the *Caroline*, owned by U.S. citizens, was fitted out with men and supplies and sailed to aid MacKenzie and his men on Navy Isle. On December 29, 1837, English troops set fire to the ship and sent her over the Niagara Falls. One American was killed and the affair did nothing to smooth the English–American tension which, since the War of Independence and the War of 1812–15, had never ceased to be near boiling point. MacKenzie was finally captured and imprisoned but continued his Radical agitation. He was again elected to the Canadian Parliament in 1850 and remained in parliament until 1858 when he died in Toronto. MacKenzie left a tradition in Canadian politics which was carried on by his grandson, William Lyon MacKenzie King (1874–1950). King became leader of the Canadian Liberal Party in 1919 and

Prime Minister of Canada from 1921–30, except for a brief interval in 1926. After a five-year lapse he again became premier in 1935–48 and represented Canada at the important post-World War II international conferences.

The 1820 rising also had a profound effect on 9-year-old Alexander Somerville, living at Thriepland Hill, in the south-west of Scotland. Somerville, in his *Autobiography of a Working Man*, published in 1848 and claimed to be the first "working class" biography, recalls that the Radical rising influenced the childhood games of the day.

It was suggested one day by some of them [his schoolfriends] that an excellent play might be got up in the Eel Yard, a meadow with some large trees in it, if the scholars divided themselves into soldiers and Radicals. As the soldiers were the more respectable in the eyes of the better dressed sons of farmers and tradesmen, and as they took a lead in everything, they made themselves soldiers; and, in addition to that, took upon themselves to pick out those who were to be Radicals.

When Somerville grew up, he enlisted in the Scots Greys, because work was scarce, but he was soon involved in Radical reform. He wrote a poem to a newspaper and was immediately sentenced to 200 lashes by the military authorities. When this became known it caused a public outcry and a campaign against field punishment was started but it was not until the twentieth century that such floggings were abolished in the army. Leaving the Scots Greys, Somerville became a journalist and wrote a book, *On Street Warfare*. Somerville recalls the publication of the book caused him to be approached by a man called Frost who said he was organising a workers' insurrection in Wales and asked Somerville if he would become their military adviser. Bearing in mind the events of 1820, particularly the spy system, Somerville refused. Nevertheless, in March, 1831, a strike at Crawshay's Iron Works in Merthyr Tydfil led to a demonstration and the military were called out; they fired on a crowd of men and women, killing sixteen and wounding over 100. The strikers, led by Dick Penderyn and Lewsyn yr Heliwr, organised the workers into militant action, and the whole of mid-Glamorgan was placed under martial law. It was not until July, 1831, that the insurgents were finally put down and Penderyn and Lewsyn yr Heliwr arrested. The two Welsh leaders stood trial in Cardiff on a charge of killing a soldier, Donald Black, with a bayonet. On Saturday, August 13, Penderyn walked to his execution with the words: "O! Argl-wydd dyma gamwedd!" (Oh, Lord God, here is iniquity!). Lewsyn yr Heliwr was transported for life. Some years later, in Pennsylvania, a clergyman named Ifan Ifans, born at Nant-y-Glo, was called to the death-bed of another Welsh exile, Ieuan Parker of Cwmfan. Parker confessed that it was he who had killed Donald Black and Penderyn had not even been present when Black died.

Following the vicious sentences of 1820, Radical agitation did die down for a time but then it started up again. It continued until the Whig Party took power in 1830 under Lord Grey and the Reform Bill was finally passed in 1832. But a few years afterwards it was found that conditions had not altered to any great degree and, in 1838, the Chartist movement took root in Scotland. Again, as with the Radical movement, the Chartists had a peculiarly nationalist outlook, considering that the union of England and Scotland, and the government of Scotland from London, a city far removed from the country, was a prime cause of distress. It was the Johnstone schoolmaster, John Fraser, who had been imprisoned on a charge of high treason in 1820, who founded the newspaper of the Scottish Chartist movement . . . *The True Scotsman*. Monday, May 21, 1840, saw 200,000 people demonstrating in Glasgow, with all the public works stopped and a mass strike spreading across the country. Rev. Patrick Brewster of Paisley, Rev. Abraham Duncan of Arbroath and John Fraser, led the constitutionalist side of the movement while a man named John Duncan headed a physical force wing. Fraser and his colleagues feared that an organised insurrection would lead to a disaster like that of 1820, and tried to prevent physical force being considered at all. On August 12, 1839, the Whig Government, following the Tory tradition, swooped on the leading Chartists, flung them into prison, and a period of repression followed. With the Scottish leaders arrested, imprisoned and transported, people again turned to the idea of pikes and guns.

The movement, held back for a time by the Whig suppression, started to gather strength again. Julian Harvey is reported to have travelled in A' Ghàidhealtachd organising remote villages and moving on foot to elude the authorities. In 1848 came the news of another revolution in France, and, at the same time, the Young Ireland movement arose to try to secure an Irish Republic. This was the moment the Scottish Chartists had been waiting for. One leader, John Dalry, told the people that "prayers and petitions were the weapons of slaves and cowards, arms were the weapons used by the free and the brave. We can best help Ireland by keeping the army in Scotland." A tailor named Hamilton urged the people to purchase muskets and pikes. Another leader, Samuel MacDonald, said the people of Ireland were justified in resisting the English "to the death" and called upon the Scottish people to do the same. The people began to chant a new ditty:

> The Lion of Scotland
> has risen from his lair
> Beware, Whigs! Beware!

Dragoons were called into Edinburgh and Glasgow to put down the rioting crowds. Some 150 prisoners were taken, many armed with guns ready for a full-scale rising. Cavalry attacked unarmed workers at Bridgeton, killing two and seriously wounding many more. A mass gathering in Glasgow Green was surrounded by the military and charged. Two leaders, Smith and Crossan, were arrested. A Scottish National Guard was formed by the people (it is reported that the Aberdeen branch numbered 1,000 alone) but the Government struck before an organised attempt at a rising could be made. Many were arrested and imprisoned, many more were transported for life. The Whig Government had shown themselves no better than the Tories in using military violence against the masses.

The Scottish Radical tradition has always gone hand in hand with Scottish nationalism, a belief that the Union with England, the removal of government from Scottish soil, and Scotland's future placed subject to the majority of English representatives in the House of Commons, was the major source of Scottish ills. That feeling has existed in an unbroken thread from the very date of the Union of 1707, which had been passed without the approval of the people of Scotland. We have seen that when the Scottish representatives at Westminster saw the futility of the Union, how impracticable and unworkable it was, they tried to revoke it by constitutional means in 1714 but were outvoted by the English majority. We have seen that they then resorted to arms to retrieve Scottish independence and that they failed. The feeling that the Union is the prime cause of Scottish ills has manifested itself in many different forms, sometimes making its real purpose obscure; the Scottish attempts to restore the Stuart monarchy because the Stuarts promised the dissolution of the Union; the attempts to set up a Scottish Republic with French aid at the close of the eighteenth century; the Radical rising of 1820 with its emphasis on nationhood and its original intent to re-establish a parliament on Scottish soil; and the nationalist-orientated Scottish Chartist movement.

A few years after the suppression of the Chartist movement, the feeling again revealed itself when the National Association for the Vindication of Scottish Rights was formed at a meeting in Edinburgh in 1853 with Lord Eglington as chairman. The Association stated, "we must demand a Scottish Parliament meeting on Scottish soil". From this movement grew the Scottish Home Rule Association, founded in 1886, and supported by *The Scotsman* who, in 1887, published a Charter of Scottish Home Rule. This agitation led to the first Scottish Home Rule motion since 1714 being presented in the House of Commons on April 9, 1889. From 1889 until the present day no less than twenty-three Scottish self-government motions and bills have been proposed. The movement for Home Rule was taken over by the Liberal Party (which grew out of the old Whig Party) and dropped when the party assumed power; it was also the premier aim of the Labour Party who also dropped it when it came to power. Whenever the majority of Scottish M.P.s have voted in favour of self-government bills, the majority English vote has always defeated them.

The Scottish national movement in the late nineteenth century and early twentieth century became extremely fragmented, the various groups ranging from extreme right wing to extreme left wing. As a nationalist umbrella covers all forms of political opinion, the diversity was, of course, a natural one. But, unlike other countries where the nationalists of all political opinion sank their differences until the premier aim of self-government was obtained, the Scots seem never to have found any basis of unity in their national movement. This diversity led to the betrayal of the self-government pledges made by both Liberals and Labour parties when in power.

Of the national movements in the late nineteenth century, Comunn an Fhearainn, the Highland Land League, was the one that kept closest to the aims of the 1820 Radicals. The Land League, modelled fairly closely on the Irish Land League, was active between 1883 and 1895. When it was re-established in the twentieth century it sought the re-establishment of the Scottish state, and aimed at the restoration of the national language (Gàidhlig) over the whole of the Scottish territory. It was the Hon. Ruaraidh Erskine of Marr, founder of the periodical *Guth na Bliadhna* (Voice of the Year) who helped to restart the Land League with the aim "that Scotland may become again an independent nation, and that all lands, mines and fisheries be restored to the Scottish commonwealth". Erskine of Marr found considerable difficulties in propagating his policies, especially that of the language restoration, for the "Highland"–"Lowland" myth had been propagated for too long for the people to accept the truth overnight. His clear socialist policies brought in many supporters, however. Writing in the *Scottish Review* in 1919, Erskine said:

Until the people reign—until the Proletariat is everywhere in undisputed power—it were folly to expect enduring Peace, drastic retrenchment, or honest and searching reform. . . . It is possible, of course, that the Proletarian rule may disappoint in practice the glowing expectations formed of it by its friends, and may show itself to be as little dependable as medicina anini as Monarchy, Aristocracy and government by the Capitalist class have proved themselves to be so . . . but . . . apart from the fact that real popular rule is as yet a practically unknown and untried force in political Europe, the Dictatorship of the Proletariat, how dismally so ever it might fall, could not possibly sin against humanity more deeply and unforgivably than the other systems of government have done.

The unadulterated Radical-nationalist tradition was carried on by John MacLean, who formed the Scottish Workers Party in 1920, and stood as a parliamentary candidate in the Gorbals division of Glasgow in 1922, stating:

I . . . stand out as a Scottish Republican candidate feeling sure that if Scotland had to elect a Parliament to sit in Glasgow it would vote

for a working class Parliament . . . the social revolution is possible
sooner in Scotland than in England . . . Scottish separation is part
of the process of England's Imperial disintegration. . . . This policy
of a Workers' Republic in Scotland debars me from going to John
Bull's London Parliament . . . had the Labour men stayed in Glasgow and started a Scottish Parliament as did the genuine Irish in
Dublin in 1918, England would have sat up and made concessions
to Scotland just to keep her ramshackle Empire intact to bluff
other countries.

In 1928 the Scottish national movements tried to submerge
their differences and to join together under one nationalist
umbrella—the Scottish National Party. But, within a few years,
fragmentation had again occurred. Today, the Scottish
National Party is rising to prominence in Scottish affairs and
still encompasses within its membership many shades of political
opinion. But Professor H. J. Hanham (*Scottish Nationalism*)
comments that the independent Scotland "envisaged by S.N.P.
would be very like the present Scotland, except that it would
be better governed and have a focus of national loyalty. In this
sense the S.N.P. must be regarded as a much more conservative body than its critics on the left and the right are inclined
to make out." In the more extreme Radical tradition, however,
comes the Workers' Party of Scotland, whose main aim is a
"Socialist Republic of Scotland" in the old tradition of
MacLean. The tradition of nationalist radicalism is still very
much alive in present-day Scotland.

The Scottish insurrection of 1820, even though it was induced
by agent provocateurs a year or two before the Radicals were
really ready, is a highly important piece of Scottish history; in
fact, of world labour history. It was not an isolated historical
incident, nor were the Scottish Radicals a regional branch of the
English Radical movement. The Scottish Radical movement
was a logical progression of what had gone before. The Radicals
not only reacted against the appalling social conditions but
against their country's union with England which they considered the main reason for all their ills. As Lord Daer, writing
in 1793, commented: "Scotland has long groaned under the
chains of England and knows its connections there have been
the cause of its greatest misfortunes . . . thinking we have been
the worse of every connection hitherto with you, the Friends of

Liberty in Scotland have almost universally been enemies to the Union with England." This book, therefore, has tried not only to describe the 1820 uprising in Scotland's industrial belt, a rising which has until now been totally ignored, but has tried to put that rising in its historical context.

APPENDIX ONE

*The Letters of John Baird and
Andrew Hardie from
Edinburgh Castle
and
Stirling Castle*

THE LETTERS OF JOHN BAIRD

Edinburgh Castle, May 9, 1820

Dear Brother,

I send you these few lines to let you know that I am in good health at present, thanks be to God for it; I hope they will find you and yours in the same. I am very well used in this place. The Captain of the Jail is a very fine man; he gives us every indulgence that is in his power; he has got a very humane lady: she gets our linen washed, and charges nothing. The Colonel of the 80th Regiment is one of the best of men; he has given each of us a fine shirt as a present. Our precognitions are not yet closed. Until then no one can see any of us. I hope that none of you will come here until I send you word, and I will let you know what things I stand in need of. I hope you will bear with my situation as well as possible, for you can neither add to, nor take away from it. I hope you will look to your own state, and leave me to mine and God, who is both able and willing to save to the very uttermost all that put their trust in him. He is my rock, and my strong tower, and my sure defence; to redeem me from sin; I will not fear what flesh can do to me. I hope you will be steadfast in the faith, studying to have your conscience void of offence towards God and towards man. Being justified by faith we are at peace with God. When God is with us, who can be against us? Go and prosper. Give my kind love to all inquiring friends. No more at present, but remain your affectionate brother,

John Baird

Edinburgh, June 1, 1820

Dear Brother,

I have nothing new to inform you of at present. We are very well provided for here; we want for nothing that our situation will admit us to receive. I am taking very well with my confinement, I pass my time more cheerfully than you would imagine. I am come to this of it now, when courage must face danger—conscience support pain —patience possess itself in the midst of discouragements. No more at present, but remain yours until death,

John Baird

Edinburgh, June 5

Dear Brother,

I received your kind and welcome letter dated the 9th of May and I wrote you shortly after, but I understand by Thomas Cowie's letter that it has not come to your hand; so I have wrote you again. You wished to know if I was in possession of a Bible; I got one as soon as I was admitted to the Castle, and I spend a good deal of my time in scanning its pages. I hope you will all study as much as possible against grieving on my account, for you can do no good by sorrow for me, but ill for yourself. I am well looked after; I am visited eight times a day, and sometimes oftener; I am in a cell by myself; the precognitions are not yet closed; I will let you know as soon as you can see me. I am very sorry that you did not get the last letter that I sent off on purposes for you; there was something in it that I wished an answer to; but it has gone out of the way. I imagine, on that account. It can do little good to them that kept it, and it can do little ill to me that lost it: but it is keeping you out of an answer to your letter; however, we must put up with disappointments; there is no certainty in the things of this world. I wrote, my brother, Robert, but I have never got an answer from him. You may let my father and my friends know that I am well. No more at present from,
Your affectionate friend,

John Baird

N.B. I took it very kind in your franking your letter—when I came here I could not have paid for one; my money was all taken from me in Stirling and kept up. The high powers do as they please, and I dare not say what doest thou.
Yours,

John Baird

Stirling Castle, August 14, 1820

Dear Brother,

I take this opportunity of letting you know my mind; it is not in so good a state as I would wish it, but I humbly thank God that it is not worse than it is, when I consider my former ways. But the Lord Jesus is offered first to the chief of sinners, as they have most need of him; and he does not say to me, what wast thou once? But what dost thou now think of Christ? He is my all—I ask no more—he is all and in all blessed for evermore. They that wait on him, shall still increase in strength and their hearts shall rise on the wings of faith and love; until they pass all the cloudy regions of doubts and fears in this world, and mount to heaven, where they shall see him face to face—where they shall be filled with light, love and praises.

I need not make any excuse to you for not writing you before this time, as I am well aware you know more reasons for it than I will mention here. I hope you will look to yourself, and not cast yourself down so much about me. If you knew the state of my kind, you would envy my situation. My hopes are not in this world—I look for a better. The sentence of death had as little impression on me as if the Lord President had read an old ballad. As this is an unpleasant subject to you, I will say no more about it; but, oh! God prepare me for thy will and my duty.

Your affectionate brother,

John Baird

Stirling Castle, 28th July 1820

My dear Sister,

I now write a few words to you. My situation is no doubt painful to you, but you must not grieve for me as one that hath no hope, for I have found more comfort in the dungeon than ever I have found in this world. Although I am under the rod of affliction, God in his mercy has sent grace to support me. Although man be the instrument that afflicts me, it has a twofold meaning; man for his pleasure and God for his justice and my good. Man will be brought to judgement for what he does to me. I pray God enable me to forgive them freely. Ah! My beloved sister, why all this care for me? To a life so lost, so totally undone, yet not doubting from mercy from His Grace, who bled on the cross for all those who seek Him with their whole hearts. Oh! May each breath, while God that breath shall spare to me, be instant in prayer, Mankind shall learn by my story, your kind concern for me. May the Lord Jesus inspire us all with the sacred fire of his grace; in the arms of his free grace and mercy may we trust our souls and our bodies, for he above is able to keep them. Glory be to His name for ever and ever Amen. My kind love to all enquiring friends.

Your affectionate brother,

John Baird

Mrs Leisham.

Stirling Castle, 28th July, 1820

Dear Brother,

I have to inform you that I am in good health at present, thanks be to the giver of all good, for it. I hope this will find you and yours in the same. I am tried and the verdict of guilty pronounced against me; but I will not get the sentence passed on me for some time. You will be well aware of what it will be. I hope when I am cast out from the presence of men, that the Lord Jesus, through his blood will prepare me for joining with the angels, and the spirits of those whom he has made perfect. I hope you will be making it your daily employment to approach your God in prayer, and when you do this, I would warn you to take a great care of how you approach him. You must know that you are approaching one who knows your heart and thoughts and your imagination. You are now the father of a family. You must keep in mind that you have a great charge—see that you spare not the rod when needful and take care that you do not make use of it in the fury of passion, but let your mind be settled when you use it. You cannot expect me to write you on these very important subjects when you consider my situation, but I hope that what I have said will not be lost. I hope that you will not read it and then forget it, but that you will lay it to heart, remembering that you have it from an affectionate brother that looks death in the face. Although my race is run, and my sun about to set, and never more to rise in this world, yet I look forward to the son of righteousness, who shall arise with healing under his wings and conduct me to his rest. Give my kind compliments to all enquiring friends. I remain yours until death,

John Baird

To. Robert Baird Esq.,
Condorrat.

Stirling Castle, September 4, 1820

Dear Friend,

I take this opportunity of sending you my long and last farewell. On Friday I am to be made immortal. Although man may mangle this body, yet blessed be God, he has kept the most noble part in his own hand. I do not mean to say anything about them who have been so sore against me, for I have made it my study to forget and forgive all men any wrong that they have done to me. I received your kind and welcome letter. It cheered my very heart to think you will go so far as to see my grave; and it gave me some consolation to hear you say, you will write my dirge. All this, you have said, I hope you will do. It gives me no small concern to think that any person blames you concerning me; that I never could do; I look on you still as my trusty friend; but you know men oft are blamed, when they are not worthy of it. I hope that you will let all animosity cease, and let love and harmony abound, is the sincere wish of your dying friend.

Let troubles rise and tyrants rage,
And days of darkness fall;
But those that wait upon the Lord,
Shall more than conquer all.

"If God be for us, who can stand against us?" "It is God that justifieth, who is he that can condemn?" No more from your dying friend, a martyr to the cause of liberty. May the grace of God protect you and yours. Give my kind love to all friends of liberty.

John Baird

[written on the same letter]

Dear Sir,

This comes from a hand you never saw, to the best of my knowledge—from a hand that in a few days must mingle with its native dust. Hard is our fate, my dear unknown friend; yet, I resign my life without the least reluctance, knowing that it is for the cause of truth and justice; and to the which I remain under conviction. I die a martyr—

"I die firm to the cause, like a magnet to its pole,
With undaunted spirit and unshaken soul."

My dear friend, I must bid you farewell; and I hope you will keep in your remembrance the cause for which Baird, Hardie, and Cleland died on the scaffold. No more, farewell.

I am, sir, your most obedient servant,

Andrew Hardie

PS. Since writing this, I am happy to announce that Cleland has got a respite.

To: Daniel Taylor of Kilsyth.

THE LETTERS OF ANDREW HARDIE

Edinburgh Castle, April 22, 1820

Dear Mother, Sisters and Brothers,

This is the second letter I have written to you; to the first, dated the 9th instant, I have received no answer, which surprised me much, for I expected an answer by the first post. I received a parcel, containing some articles, all which I stood in great need of. I informed you in my first letter how we were situated, and how we had been deluded away. We are now in the Castle, and are used with the utmost civility, far beyond my expectation. I have a Bible, which I use with attention, a good bed and fire, with an allowance of a shilling a day to keep me; and for these favours I give the civil authorities of Edinburgh my sincere thanks. I wrote to you for a little money, which I knew you could ill spare, but you need not send any, for the allowance I have is quite sufficient. I have plenty of time to reflect upon my past conduct, which I hope will be forgiven me, through the merits of our blessed Saviour, who suffered death that our sins might be forgiven us. I know that you will be concerned about my unfortunate situation, as I observed in my first letter, but I hope God will strengthen your hearts to bear with patience whatever is His holy will; as for me, I am bearing it with great fortitude. I sent my compliments (in my first letter) to Margaret MacKeigh and Mrs Connell, which I hope you have delivered; you will be so kind as to do the same again, and tell Margaret to give my best respects to her brother and sister. My dear friends, I hope you will not delay writing to me, as soon as this comes to hand; I have been in great anxiety, day after day, to hear from you; I expected to have got a few lines with the bundle you sent me, but, to my great disappointment, there was none. Give my kind compliments to my shopmates; I know they will miss me—I hope they take care of my poor bird, which you may allow to remain with them if you please. I hope you have got a journeyman to my web. Give my kind compliments to all my acquaintances and my comrade, Walter. I heard there was a man from Glasgow in Stirling, who was inquiring for me—I suppose it was him. Let me know if he had an interview with Jean MacKechnie. I saw her at the door as we passed through Queen Street, Stirling, on our way to the steam-boat. Give also my kind compliments to all my relations, and let them know that I am in good health, for which I thank God. I again entreat you to write immediately. May God bless you, is the sincerest wish of

Your unfortunate son and brother

Andrew Hardie

My unfortunate companions, Pink, White, Johnston and Thompson, are all in good health, as far as I know, we being in separate apartments; all the others are strangers to me.

Direct to me—

Prisoner, Edinburgh Castle, to the care of Mr Sibbald, New Jail, Edinburgh

Edinburgh Castle, May 5, 1820

Dear Cousins and Relations,

I received your kind and welcome letters, one dated the 7th, the other the 21st April, also my mother's dated May 1; and was truly happy to hear that you were all well, as this leaves me, thank God for his kindness to us. I am truly sorry that you did not receive my letter, dated April 9th. I cannot understand how you did not receive it, for the gentlemen told me that it would be sent away, and I thanked them for their kindness, and said, "I hoped there was nothing offensive in it"; and they said, "By no means." I think it will be mislaid in the Post Office; it was directed to my mother care of James MacKechnie. Dear cousin, I am truly sorry that you came to Edinburgh on my account; I should have been very happy to have seen you, no doubt, but it was a great neglect in me not to let you know that no person could be admitted; but I thought you would have understood that. Dear cousin, you will accept my sincere thanks for your trouble—it is all I can give you, for I am well assured that I shall never have it in my power to do as much for you. Dear cousin, you was perfectly right in your conjecture with regard to my wishing that I had been killed, I really did wish so. When I got to Stirling, and took into proper consideration what a rash and foolish, and unlawful action I had been guilty of, I wished I had been shot; but I sincerely repent of that rash wish, and hope it will be forgiven me, and I thank my God that he did not hurry me into his presence in such an unprepared state. Cousin John, I am bound in gratitude to you for your excellent letter, which I have studied with great diligence. With the assistance of God, I have got a pretty good knowledge of the Scriptures, which I was far deficient in before I came here; and I do greatly admire the wonderful works of God, seeing how just he is in all his ways—long suffering and slow to anger. How beautiful is the language of the Psalmist, on his goodness to mankind—"When I consider thy heavens, the work of thy fingers, the moon and the stars which thou hast ordained; what is man, that thou art mindful of him? And the son of man, that thou visitest him? For thou hast made him a little lower than the angels, and hast crowned him with glory and honour." Ps. VIII. And above all, to send his only begotten son into this world, who took upon himself our infirmities, and suffered death for our salvation; upon this belief, I build my faith, and by this faith I hope to be saved. I could furnish you with many more proofs of my belief, which I shall reserve for some other time, for I see the limits of my letter will not contain them. My dear friends, I cannot refrain from shedding my tears when I think on the kindness you have shown to me in my hopeless situation, with your offer to adminster to my wants; but, thank God, I have none. I received 5s. from Mr Sibbald, the Governor of the prison, a silk handkerchief, and a dickie; I bought a pair of rund shoes, for which I paid 2s. 10d. my shoes being entirely done before I got to Stirling; the remainder of the money I have lying beside me. I received a shirt, handkerchief, and stockings from Stirling but the money, I hope, will be returned to you, as I have not the least need for it. You will give my grateful acknowledgements to my comrade for his trouble and kindness. We are visited every day by the Colonel of the 80th Regiment, and other officers, who ask if we have any complaints, and if we are comfortable etc. That gentleman has been so kind as to give those men shirts who had not a change, which, you know, I had no need of; but I gave him my thanks the same as if I had gotten one. You need not send any clothes; I will let you know if I want any. Give my compliments to my grandfather, and all my relations and acquaintances that I mentioned in my former letter. Give my compliments to Margaret MacKeigh; let her know that I expect a letter from her shortly. This is my birthday, my dear friends; I little expected to pass it as a prisoner in Edinburgh Castle or any where else. I am 27 years of age, this 5th day of May. I would take it as a particular favour if any of my friends would send me some religious books; I will take good care of them, and return them back again, whatever is to be my fate; I have need of nothing else. You may let White's mother know he is well, and the rest of them as far as I know. I delivered her message to our keeper, to tell him. I hope some of you will not be long in writing to me. I have nothing more to add, but remain,

Your unfortunate cousin,

Andrew Hardie

[on the back of the letter]

> In these sad moments of severe distress,
> When sorrows threaten, and when dangers press,
> For my defence, behold what arms are given—
> Firmness of soul, and confidence in Heaven.

Edinburgh Castle, May 16, 1820

Dear Mother, Sister, Brothers and Relations all,

I received your kind and welcome letter, of date May 1, at which I was happy, the more so, as it informed me you were all in good health. I have received a letter from my cousin, of date the 9th instant, containing the articles mentioned therein. I can give you no news, my dear friends, neither am I desirous of any, as I am shut up from this busy world. I am preparing myself, with all possible speed, to go to that land where all is love and harmony, and, by faith in Jesus Christ, I hope to be admitted—and to him in God, and God in him, I offer up my prayers with a penitent and contrite heart. David saith, "If thou shouldest mark iniquity, O Lord, who shall stand? But there is forgiveness with thee, that thou mayest be feared." Do not concern yourselves about me, dear friends; I am waiting with great patience, and quite willing to resign, whenever it is the will of God to call upon me. He who gave me life can take it away at any time, and in such manner as seemeth good to him. But his arm is not shortened that it cannot save—all things are possible with God; and if it is his will to lengthen my span a little longer, I shall be very thankful. My cousin takes his excuse for holding so dark a prospect to me, but I would be truly sorry if you were of any other opinion, as it exactly agrees with mine. Dear Brothers and sisters. I hope you will be kind to your and my afflicted mother, as I know my melancholy affair will sink deep in her tender heart, which has already been almost broke by the loss of our dear father, sisters and brothers, who were hurried from this world and, by all appearance, your brother is going to be hurried away likewise, in the bloom of his youth: therefore, I hope you will lead a sober, honest, and industrious life, serving God with all your heart and all your strength, and love your neighbour as you love yourself.— "Upon these hang all the commandments." Although I have done nothing in my past life that merited public censure, until this melancholy catastrophe, yet I have come far short of the love of God, which surpasses all knowledge. "Call upon him while he is near, seek him while he may be found."—"At such an hour as ye think not, the Son of Man cometh." Think upon these things, and see if you can take an example from my misfortune; and when you come to a death bed, what a pleasure will it be to you when you take a review of your past life, if it has been well spent. I have a great deal more to say to you, but I will reserve it to a future period. The shoes you have sent fit me exactly. I was surprised when I saw them, as I had no need for them. The books you sent me are well adapted for my present situation; you could not have sent better, and, I assure you, they were a welcome sight to me. I think, dear cousins, Providence directed you in sending the hymn book, as I regretted much, after I had sent away my letter, that I had forgot to bid my mother send an old one that is in our house, as the Bible I have, though an excellent one, has neither psalms nor hymns in it.

I make worship morning and evening, and whenever I find my mind the least disturbed, I have recourse to prayer, with a penitent and contrite heart. Thus employed, reading your books and my Bible occasionally, I pass my time with great pleasure. You will give my compliments to my aged grandfather, and desire him to remember me in his prayers; I sent this notice to him in my first letter, which I was sorry you did not receive. Dr Lockhart has not called upon me yet; I do not think he would be admitted, as no person is allowed to see us. I would have been very happy to have seen that pious and charitable gentleman. Dear friends, I again return you my grateful acknowledgements for your kindness to me; and I hope God will reward you kindness. I send my compliments to all my acquaintances. I need not distinguish you by your names, my dear friends, but may God bless you all, is the earnest prayer of

Your afflicted and unfortunate friend,

Andrew Hardie

PS.—Give my compliments to my friend in Taylor Street; she may expect a letter from me in a few days. I hope you will not be long in writing to me, as it all the consolation I get, my Bible excepted, which is great comfort to me. A.H.

Edinburgh Castle, June 10, 1820

Dear Mother and Relatives,

I have to inform you that my Trial is to take place on the 23rd of this present month, at Stirling; therefore, I hope you will make no delay in getting testimonials of my character; and likewise, I have to inform you, that I shall be allowed counsel by the county, I suppose, but I am wholly ignorant of these matters; and, therefore, I wish you would make inquiry, and let me know how to proceed. I would be very happy if any of you would come to Edinburgh, and see me, this next week, as probably liberty will be given now. I have nothing more particular. I am in perfect good health, for which I return my sincere thanks to God, who has preserved my health and understanding complete. I hope this will find you in good health. I am yours and etc.

Andrew Hardie

PS. If permission cannot be granted for you to see me, I hope the gentleman who examines this letter will give you notice, by writing in this letter. Since writing the above, I have got notice that no permission can be granted to visit us in Edinburgh. I will write to you when I get to Stirling. Permission will be granted there. A.H.

To: Widow Hardie,
26 Kirk Street, Townhead, Glasgow.

Edinburgh Castle, June 6, 1820

My dear Mother,

I received your long expected letter of date May 25 on Saturday, the 3rd instant, being nine days after date; I suppose it had been detained by the carrier; I also received four books & etc. My brother informs me, in your letter, that you are in a poor state of health, which I am truly sorry to hear; and the more so, as I have been the occasion of it; but you must put your trust in divine Providence who, I hope will enable you to abide with patient submission whatever is to be the result. I have had some severe attacks of toothache lately, it began with me about the time I left Stirling, where I had been confined in a damp cell, and our meat was cold, which, I think, have been the causes of it; however, I bear it with great fortitude. My health otherwise remains unimpaired, for which I return my sincere thanks to the Sovereign Dispenser of all our human comforts, for his great mercies. I am still in solitary confinement there has not the least alteration taken place since I wrote you last, and we are still treated with the same civility as I informed you of before. I have nothing more particular to inform you of at present, only I am still prosecuting my laudable and needle design, that is, making my peace with God, and through all the merits of a blessed Saviour, I hope he will accept me as a labourer at the eleventh hour, or as a prodigal son. I am greatly assisted by the most excellent books you have sent, as also by your excellent letters, which I pay great attention to. You will give my undissembled love to that gentleman who has so kindly interested himself in my welfare, and has kindly offered to send me more books, but as I have a bad memory, I will be content with those I have, as I read them oftener than once. I have profited much by them, and when I turn to them again, I always find some passage that had escaped my memory. My dear friends, I again entreat you to put yourselves to as little concern about me as possible. But alas! I know your tender hearts

are alive to every feeling. I would not have believed three months ago, if any person had told me that I would be in solitary confinement so long, and that I could have stood it so well, even suppose it had been without crime, for being formerly of a cheerful temper, to be confined was, above all things, what I never expected; who was supported me under such a trial. Dear brothers and sisters, I hope you will pay attention to the advice I have already give you in my former letter. I suppose you would hear the letter that I received last, read before it came to me, and I hope you will profit by it as well as me; and I would have you keep in your remembrance, that you are under the immediate eye of God, who sees and knows all our actions; and that we shall all have to give an account of our stewardship some day, sooner or later; and, likewise, that you have a blessed Saviour, that is always ready to take you by the hand;— he has no pleasure in the death of a sinner, but is willing that we should come to him, and inherit eternal life. I can add little more at present, only I hope you will reconcile yourselves as well as possible. Give my kind compliments to my grandfather, and his family, and all my inquiring friends; likewise to Margaret MacKeigh; let her know that I expect a letter from her shortly. I remain, dear mother,
Your unfortunate son,
Andrew Hardie

PS. Do not be so long in writing, as your letters are, in general, five days after date before I get them; you know they have to lie for inspection. A.H.

Stirling Castle, 1st August, 1820

My dear friends,

The following is an account of the whole of our proceedings to, and at the Battle of Bonnymuir & etc. I hope you will look over any repetition of sentiment, and the ungrammatical manner and style in which it is written, when you consider that while I was writing it, I was always in fear of being discovered, as it is against orders. I would very willingly write another copy, as I could make some improvements in it, both the subject and writing, but I am afraid that they will suspect me by getting so much paper, and for these reasons, I hope you will not look upon it with the eye of a critic. Let it suffice to say, that it contains nothing but the truth. I could have dwelt much longer upon it, but for the above reasons, I made it as short and comprehensive as my weak ideas would permit. You will see by the ending of this, that I intend a continuation of it, as soon as I get paper and an opportunity.
I am, my dear friends, yours & etc.,
A. Hardie

To: Mr Robert Goodwin, Glasgow,
  Care of Mr John Fallon, Roploch, Stirling.

On the 4th of April, 1820 (the night I left Glasgow with two men, whose names I forbear to mention), we arrived at Germiston, where we found, as was expected, a number of men in arms, whom I immediately joined, and after some delay, expecting some more, as we were told, from Anderston and other places (but which did not come forward), we got notice where we were to go, and received a very encouraging address from a man I did not know. I was made to understand the nature of our affair by the two men, and, likewise, that the whole city would be in arms in the course of an hour afterwards, which he who addressed us told us likewise; and that the coach would not be in the following morning; and that England was all in arms, from London downwards, and everything was going on beyond our most sanguine expectations; and declared that there were no soldiers to oppose us betwixt that and Edinburgh; and further that the whole was ready to receive us, and well armed, and those that wanted get arms by the road, refreshments and every thing necessary. I heard likewise through the course of the day, or early in the evening that there was going to be a turn-out, but I did not get information of the nature of it before our departure. I asked if there was no person going alone with us who had instructions how to proceed, or take the charge of us. There was one Kean told me that there was a person with us who would give us every satisfaction, and had every necessary instruction for our proceedings, but that I might take the command until we came to Condorrat, where we would be joined by a party of fifty or sixty men, and get one there to take command of the whole; but this I did not assume until we came within a mile of Condorrat, when we halted, and proposed to form ourselves in regular order, and I was appointed by the men themselves to do this, which I did by forming and front and rear rank, and sized them accordingly, and likewise numbered them the same as a guard; my reason for doing was because we were all strangers to one another, and did not know our names, that if anything was wanted, we might answer to our numbers. After this was done, I left the party and went before them (with Kean) to find out Mr Baird, and when we found him, there was one King had been waiting with him, upon us coming forward. This King belongs to Glasgow, but what he is I do not know, but this I know, that he acted a very unbecoming part with us. King had told Baird that there was a part of two hundred well armed men coming out, and that they were all old soldiers. When I arrived at Condorrat with Kean, I did not stop with him and Mr Baird, but joined the party, and went to a public house to get a refreshment, which consisted of one glass of whisky, and a bit of bread. Now, during the time we (the party) were in the public house, one of them told Mr Baird a quite different story than that which we were made to believe, and apologised for the smallness of our party, by saying, that the Anderston party & etc. had mistaken the road, and had gone by Airdrie; he likewise said that there was a party gone to Hamilton to stop the coach there. But to proceed, after some time was spent in fixing pike heads & etc. we proceeded on, but in place of being joined by fifty or sixty men, I think we only got six, but had a sufficient force from Glasgow, it would have been far otherwise; yet it was quite reasonable for people to decline from coming out, when such a small force could only be brought from Glasgow. Yet, in consequence of this great disappointment, we were not at all discouraged, but proceeded on in the most orderly manner. After we left Condorrat, our first halt was at Castlecarry Bridge, where we received half a bottle of porter, and a penny worth of bread each man, which was paid for, and a receipt obtained for the same. We again proceeded, but I should have observed before this that King left us at Condorrat, and went before us on the pretext of getting the Camelon and Falkirk people ready by the time we should be forward, and in case we should miss them, or the party that was to meet us, I, with other four or five stout men, went by the road and the main party went by the canal bank. The first we met, after leaving the main party, was a gentleman on horseback, whom we, in a very civil manner, asked if he was going to Glasgow—he answered in the affirmative; we then told him (as we were made to believe ourselves) that there was sad work going on there, and advised him to turn, but he did not turn at that time; however, in a short time he came past us, and told us he would take our advice. We went into a house, a little way off the road, and got a fowling piece, for which we offered a receipt, but it was not accepted; the gentleman to whom it belonged was very civil, and did not say much against us taking it away, and asked when he should get it back. Soon after we came upon the road again we saw a Hussar at a little distance; upon this we drew ourselves upon the road, and called to him to halt, which he did immediately; we then agreed that we should do him no harm, and desired him to come forward which he did, and stopped when he came up to us, and told a very good story that he was a friend to our cause, that he was a weaver, and had a wife and five children & etc. I told him it was no matter what he was, we should do him no harm; he answered every question we put to him very correctly; said he was going to Kilsyth, and that he had fallen behind his detachment. Henderson then gave him one of the addresses, and some conversation passed, which I do not remember, and we let him pass. We proceeded along the road about a mile and a half past Bonnybridge, where we got a signal from the party on the bank to join them, for King had come to them and said, that we should have to go up on the moor and wait there until we got a reinforcement from Camelon; the whole of us turned and went through an aqueduct bridge, and went up about a mile into the moor, and sat down on the top of a hill, and rested (I think) about an hour, when the cavalry made their appearance; upon this we started upon our feet, and at once resolved to meet them. I proposed forming a square where we were, but Mr Baird said it would be much better to go under cover of a dyke, which was not far distant; we then immediately ran down the hill, cheering, and took up our position. There was a slap in the dyke, which we filled with pikemen. The cavalry took a circular course through the moor, and came under the cover of a wood at our right flank. As soon as they made their appearance past the end of the wood, firing commenced immediately—I cannot say who commenced firing; I think the cavalry had fired a shot or two before they came to the wood, with the intention, probably, to frighten us, for they afterwards told us they did not expect we would face them. However, this is a matter of no importance. They came up right to the dyke—the Hussars in front, led by their officer, who called out to us to lay down our arms, but this was not agreed to. After firing some shots at us, they made an attack at the slap, and got through, but were repulsed and driven back. They, in general, stood a little distance from the dyke, so that our pikes were rendered unserviceable. One of the Hussars came close up to the dyke, a little to the right of where I stood, and one of our party made a stab at him. The Hussar fired at him in return, and he fell forward on his face. They made a second attack at the slap, and got through, but were kept at bay in the inside and the officer again called out to us to surrender, and he would do us no harm, which most of our men took for granted, and threw down their arms and ran. (It will be here necessary to observe, that some of our men never came into action at all, but made their way into a wood at some distance.) But those that tried to make their escape after our surrender, (viz. after the officer had called out the second time, and by this time was in the inside, on our side of the dyke), were instantly pursued, but were not all taken, and some of them wounded in a most shocking manner; and it was truly unbecoming the character of a British soldier to wound, or try to kill any man, when he had it in his power to take him prisoner, and when they had no arms to make any defence. One of the Yeomanry was so inhuman, after he had sabred one of the men sufficient, as he thought, to deprive him of life, as to try and trample him under his horse's feet; but here, my friends, the horse had more humanity than his master, and would not do as he wished, but jumped over him, in place of trampling upon his wounded and mangled body; and after he had returned from doing so, he called out (speaking very broad) that he had left him lying wi' his head cloven like a pot. There were several others wounded, but I will not say any more about them, as I suppose you have heard all particulars long before this. Mr Baird defended himself in a most gallant manner: after discharging his piece, he presented it at the officer empty, and told him he would do for him if he did not stand off. The officer presented his pistol at him, but it flashed and did not go off. Mr Baird then took the butt end of his piece and struck a private on the left thigh, where-upon the sergeant of the Hussars fired at him; Mr Baird then threw his musket from him, and seized a pike, and, while the sergeant was in the act of drawing his sword, wounded him in the right arm and side. Before this, the officer was wounded in the right hand, and his horse was also wounded; yet notwithstanding, he would not allow one of his men to do us any harm, and actually kept off, with his own sword some of the strokes that were aimed against us. One of the Hussars recognised one of our party who, he said, had wounded this officer, and would have instantly sabred him, had not the officer speedily interfered, and told him there was too much done already. Although my enemy, I do him nothing but justice by saying that he is a brave and generous man; he came up in front of his men, and I am truly happy (but surprised) that he was not killed, as I know there were several shots fired at him. After the wounded men, and those who tried to make their escape, were all brought together, we were taken off the moor. Mr Baird and I assisted one of the wounded men, until we got a cart and were put into it; one of them was dreadfully wounded in the head, I think in four places, and shot through the arm. Another old man, with a frightful looking wound in his face, so much so that his jaw bone was seen perfectly distinct; and the third, with a sabre wound on his head; and two or more left on the field for dead; but I was truly happy to hear afterwards that it was not so, but that they had recovered and got safe off. The officer of the Hussars asked who was our captain and if his name was Baird, which made it evident, that some person who knew him, had given them information. We were all very fatigued by being up all night, and having got no victuals but what is before mentioned, viz. a penny loaf and a drink of porter, we made application to the officer of the Yeomanry to let us halt and get a drink of water, but alas! That small favour could not be granted,—you must observe that the officer of the Hussars was at this time absent, getting another horse, as his was so wounded that it could carry him no farther; when he came up to us he granted our request immediately.

After we arrived at Stirling, we were all put into one room, and being uncommon tired, it was not long before the most of us buried all our cares in a sound sleep, having previously obtained some bread and water. Mr Baird and I went to bed together, but he was taken away from us shortly after, and put into a dungeon, and had about four or five stones or irons put upon him. After being in Stirling Castle a day or two, we were all examined, and on being asked the reason why I was in arms, I told them I went out with the intention to recover my rights; they then asked me what rights I wanted? I said annual parliaments and elections by ballot. Question—what reason had you to expect those rights? Answer—because I think Government ought to grant whatever the majority of the nation requested, and if they had paid attention to the people's lawful petitions, the nation would not have been in the state that it at present was, or words to this purpose; but this last part of my answer they did not think proper to put down; when I told them so, they looked at one another, but said nothing. A number of other questions were put to me, which are not worth notice. Concerning our proceedings on the road & etc. I was examined time after time; after we were taken to Edinburgh, and everything that took place on the road was put to me precisely as they had happened, which at once let me understand that . . . had told all that was transacted; he had made no less than fourteen pages of declaration before we left Stirling, beside what he gave in Edinburgh, which I suppose was much more. I knew well that he told all he could concerning me, but the questions asked me at my examinations, and I was told by a soldier on sentry in the new jail that one of us had turned King's evidence, and well I knew who it was; but after they had made him their tool, and got all they wanted out of him, they have, to all appearances turned him over with the rest, which was not what he expected for he told since he came to this Castle, a few days before our trial, that Captain Sibbald was to get him work in Edinburgh. I allowed that we were very justly examined, as they told us not to answer any questions but as we choosed ourselves; but, on the other hand, I was plied with unwearied importunity by Captain Sibbald, which was not his duty to do, but he might as well have saved himself the trouble, for I would not tell him a word, although he foretold me my fate; neither did I in my declaration but what passed on the road, because I knew it was all told before they asked me. I will not trouble you with an account of my imprisonment, but shall close this long letter with a few observations on my trial and witnesses. The first in order is Mr Hardie; it is not at all necessary that I should give you the sum of his evidence, and I do not deny preventing him from taking down the bill and asking him his authority for doing so; neither shall I mention the abusive language he gave to me, nor what I said to him. But as I have a good and just God to answer, and to whom I must give account of my actions, in a very short time, I hope you will form a more favourable opinion of me than to think I would tell you any lies. He said that I seized him by the collar and drove him off the pavement twice, but it is very strange that I mind all that passed and cannot charge my memory with doing so, and yet two other witnesses corroborated his evidence. I remember perfectly well of telling Mr Stirling that I knew his principles, and that he was taking up arms against those from whom he had his bread, or words to that effect. And likewise of Mr Anderson, that he had said in a certain house that the Radicals were going to plunder and divide property and etc. and that he was supported by the Government, or perhaps his opinions would be the same as mine. But driving Mr Hardie off the pavement is entirely out of the question; but according to his own statement, there were about thirty persons there, and I trust some of them will have in their remembrance all that passed. The next that I shall mention is Nicol Hugh Baird, of the Kilsyth Yeomanry Cavalry, who actually swore that he met ten or twelve of us on the road, and that we demanded his arms, and he, in return, presented his pistol at us, and said that he would give us the contents of it before he would do so. In the name of common sense, what could tempt this coxcomb to swear a notorious lie as this—to face and frighten ten or twelve well armed men; he is worthy of being classed with Sir William Wallace. I am astonished that, after such a feat, he did not petition the officer of the Hussars to fight the whole of us on the moor himself; but he had done enough for one day. But the truth of the matter is this, we never saw him on the road at all. He had got notice of our approach and putting more confidence in the swiftness of his horse than his own valour, had either turned or hid himself until we passed; and I understand that there are about twenty people who could testify that he did not pass until we were off the road altogether. How different was the evidence of the Hussar from this Don Quixote, who told the truth and stated our number to be five or six, yet he had more policy than to offer to attack us, and very prudently capitulated with us, and told us, after we were taken prisoners, that he thought we were a set of damned dangerous looking fellows; and yet this imaginary hero, i.e. the Yeoman, identified me, the prisoner at the bar, as one of the party! I was more than astonished when I saw him come forward and assert such falsehoods, and went immediately and told one of my counsel that it was altogether lies. I saw the newspapers (when I was in the steam boat going to Edinburgh) an exaggerated account of the battle, stating our numbers to have been about 100; but if there had been that number, I am of the opinion that I should not be sitting here, this day, a solitary prisoner, under sentence of death. But the truth is, there were only 24 or 26 of us, and there were three or four who never came forward at all, so by that means our numbers were reduced to about 20; and although those men had come forward, they would have been of little service, as I believe they had no arms, for I remember there were two or three without arms, and in all probability it was these that did not come forward. The numbers of the Hussars and Yeomanry cavalry were, I think, according to the officer's own statement, 32; yet they found some difficulty in subduing us. The paper gave an account of us meeting a yeoman on the road, and likewise the Hussar, which made me think that the gentleman whom we had first met had been him, as he had a tartan cover on, and saddle bags, and I thought he might have been armed and in regimentals, although unseen to us, as his tartan cloak was sufficient to conceal them; yet I am certain it was not so, for that gentleman was a lusty, stout man—but the Kilsyth hero was quite the contrary; so I shall now leave this son of Mars. You will observe that I promised to give you some observations on my Trial, but this I think unnecessary, as no doubt, it will be handled by an abler pen than mine; and as the short time allowed me is drawing to a close, and as I have matter of much greater importance to take up my attention, I shall now confine myself to a few observations. You will be curious no doubt, to know what views I now entertain of those principles which induced me to take up arms.

My suffering countrymen! As I am within view of being hurried into the presence of my Almighty Judge, I remain under the firm conviction that I die a Martyr in the Cause of Truth and Justice, and in the hope that you will soon succeed in the cause which I took up arms to defend; and I protest, as a dying man, that although we were outwitted and betrayed, it was done with a good intention on my part, and I may safely speak for the whole of those that are here in the Castle, that they are in the same mind; I have had several interviews with them, and I was happy to find them all firm to the cause. I intended to speak at some length on the scaffold, but I have changed my opinion on that point, as I am a little quick in temper, and more particularly when I enter upon that subject; I have found by experience, when I entered upon politics with some of the clergymen who visited me, particularly one who introduced the subject of the French Revolution, and tried to point out the fatal effects arising from it, I was completely nettled at this, and was much the worse of his visit; as it took me some pains to get it erased from my mind; neither do I think it proper for a person so near to eternity to

L

enter upon these matters. However, I may speak a few words.—
Farewell, my suffering countrymen: may God send you a speedy
deliverance from your oppressors, is the earnest prayer of yours,

Andrew Hardie

Stirling Castle, August 10th, 1820

My dear Grandfather,

I received your letter of date 10th June, and you will have heard
of the result of my unfortunate affair, but there is no help for it now
and therefore it becomes me to submit to the will of God; permit me
therefore to lay before you a few reflections on this most important
point, viz. our submission to the will of Providence; and although I
am a young man and have had but little experience in this world
compared with you, I hope you will excuse my presumption for
doing so. You have seen much of the vicissitudes of life. You have
seen your wife, sons and daughters and other relations and acquaintances drop off like the ripe leaf in autumn, others, as it were by a
sudden gust of wind blown from the tree before they arrived at
maturity; nay some of them in very bud. You see what a wide
contrast there is between you and me, yet to all human appearances
I shall be away before you. Dear grandfather, as I am standing on
the verge of eternity and according to the course of nature, you
cannot be long in this world, this land of misery and as we are all
poor, needy, sinful creatures, let us throw ourselves upon Him who is
both able and willing to save. My earnest prayer is that he might put
upon us for that society whose business is perfect love. My health continues, with a calm and tranquil mind, and I trust God, who has been
so kind to me, will continue with me to the end. I hope and pray for
my distressed mother and give her all the consolation in your power.

Andrew Hardie

Mr Hardie, Glasgow

Stirling Castle, 19th August, 1820

My dear relations,

According to promise, I embrace this opportunity of writing a few
lines letting you know that I enjoy a good state of health: thank God
for the multiplying of his tender mercies to usward, for although he
visits his feeble sons with allifications, he still remembers them with
his unbounded love. In addition to my good health, I enjoy a calm
and composed mind, which is one of the greatest blessings the
Almighty bestows on the human race, and with these excellent
advantages, I am labouring in his vineyard with diligence. And
although I find myself altogether an unworthy, and unprofitable

servant, and my sun nigh about set, yet under the consolatory promise and assurances, that are set before us, and through the merits of a blessed Saviour, I trust the short labour I give will be acceptable, and I hope I shall receive my penny, with those that went in at the eleventh hour. My dear friends, although I am to be taken away in the bloom of life, and to suffer an unnatural death, this gives me a very little concern knowing that he who gave me life, can take it when it seemeth good for him to do so; and ever blessed be his holy name, he takes but what he gave. The time and manner is of no importance to us. Our immediate duty is, to be ready. What are all our sufferings in this land of shadows—in this vale of misery? They are only for a moment. This is not our resting place. We are only sojourners here. When we take it into our serious consideration, what a blessed and innocent Saviour suffered to purchase rest for us, we ought to remain silent, and contemplate at a humble distance his great and unbounded love for us, by taking upon himself our nature, and suffering a most cruel death, to extricate us poor, miserable, lost sinners, from a gulf of sin and misery, into which we have fallen, and from which we were wholly unable to extricate ourselves by any means whatever. My dear friends, we ought to bear all our trials and sufferings in this world with patient submission. See Hebrews chapter XIII verse 11. "Now, no chastening for the present seemeth to be joyous, but grievous: nevertheless, afterward it yieldeth the peaceable fruit of righteousness unto them which are exercised thereby." My dear friends, I hope you will excuse my presumption for laying these things before you, as I am well aware you are not ignorant of these important matters: my reason for so doing is only to show you the state of mind into which the Lord has brought me. I have profited much by contemplating on these and other important matters. Indeed, God has brought my mind to a state of happiness, which I never experienced in all my past life. And how ought we to bless that God, who is able to give support under every dispensation of his Providence. I have been visited several times by Mr Heugh, to my great satisfaction, and have profited much by his instructions. I have little more to inform you of at present. I take my victuals regularly, and sleep as well as ever I did in my life. I hope you will write when this comes to hand, and let me know all particulars. I trust you will put yourselves to as little concern about me as possible, seeing that I am perfectly resigned to the will of God, and may he, who has been so particularly favourable to me, support you under every dispensation of his Providence, is the earnest prayer of your affectionate relative,

Andrew Hardie

PS. I earnestly hope this will find you all in good health and I again request that you will write immediately, as the little time I am to remain in this world is drawing near a close.

Andrew Hardie

Mr James Danskin, Weaver,
Cumbernauld.

Stirling Castle, August 28, 1820

My dear friends,

I take this opportunity of transmitting a few lines. I was much surprised at being visited by my grandfather, as I did not expect him; I was truly happy to see him, and I earnestly hope, that our next meeting will be in that happy land, where sorrow never enters—where all is love and harmony. You would understand by my brother and cousin, that Mr Baird and me were advised to send petitions to the Lord Advocate, signed by the Provost and two Baillies of this town, several clergymen, and other respectable gentlemen, but we have not got an answer yet. However, we expect nothing favourable. The petition was drawn out according to your request, but I hope you are putting no dependence upon it, as I am fully persuaded that it will be of no service. Our time is drawing apace, and I earnestly entreat you to shift your mind off me as much as possible; you ought rather to bless God, that I am going to be separated from an evil world. It is my earnest prayer, that you may be supported in this trying circumstance. My uncle wishes me to write to him, concerning my eternal concerns, but I intend to draw up a few remarks to my brothers and sister, which I hope will be useful to them and at the same time shew you my belief. I have little more particular at present. I earnestly hope you are all in good health.

I remain your sincere friend, and well wishes,

Andrew Hardie

PS. You will give my kind compliments to Mr and Mrs Ferguson and all other who may inquire after me: I am sure they are numerous, A. Hardie.

Directed to Mrs Hardie.

Stirling Castle, Sept. 1, 1820

Dear Sir,

I take this opportunity of transmitting a few lines, to let you know that I am in good health and spirits, thank God for his great mercies to me, in this last and closing period of my life. And although I am within a few days of being separated from this world, it gives me very little uneasiness, as I trust I am going to make a good change: and with faith in a blessed Saviour, I hope, I shall be transported from a state of warfare into a state of peace—from a miserable, transient world, to a state of happiness: and with this in view, I am waiting with patience till my change comes. And although I am altogether a poor miserable sinner, yet I have this consoling assurance, that our blessed Saviour is both able and willing to save to the uttermost, if we look unto him with a steady eye of faith. "Come unto me, all ye that are weary and heavy laden, and I will give you rest. Look unto me, all ye ends of the earth, and be saved." What a consolation is this to me, to think, that our blessed Saviour will reward those that went in at the eleventh hour, the same as those that went in at the first, and that there is more joy in heaven at one returning sinner, than for ninety and nine just persons that needed no repentence. "I will go to my Father, and will say unto him, Father I have sinned against heaven and before thee, and am no more worthy to be called thy son, make me as one of thy hired servants", Luke, chapter XV, see the chapter throughout. My dear friend, we have nothing to tempt us to stay here. This is not our resting place. We are only sojourning here, as it were in a strange land, and why should we place our affections on it, knowing that we have a rest provided for us, "eternal in the heavens"? And what ought we to render for this? How ought we to adore a blessed Saviour, who purchased this precious rest for us with his blood— who died out of his own free love, offered himself up a ransom to satisfy offended justice, and reconcile to himself a guilty and justly condemned world. How ought we to repay all this love? To think that he would leave the bosom of his father, and take upon himself our infirmities, and suffer a cruel and ignominious death, for the sins not his own! My dear friend, I hope you will take what I have stated into your serious consideration, while it is called to-day, for we do not know what an hour may bring forth. We are at all times under sentence of death. We have not a moment to call our own. We have examples every day before our eyes. "Death's shafts fly thick." The cup goes round, you cannot put it past, you cannot hand it to your neighbour. High and low, rich and poor, all must take their drink. "Be ye therefore ready, for at such an hour as ye think not, the call cometh." I hope that these few observations will not be offensive, as they are nothing but truth, and I earnestly beg that you will take them into your serious consideration. Remember that you have a young family, and therefore have a great charge on your head, and it becomes you as a parent to instruct them early in the principles of Christianity. I have little more particulars to let you know. I hope you will put yourself to no concern about me, as I am perfectly resigned to my fate, hard as it is. Give my kind compliments to Mr. Watson; you may, if you please, give him a perusal of this letter. Give my compliments also to Helen, and let her know that she may expect a letter from me in a few days. I am, my dear friend, your unfortunate friend,

                                                    Andrew Hardie

PS. I hope you will look over any inaccuracies, and the manner that this is written, as I had but little time, and my friends who are to carry this letter are upon the eve of going away. A. Hardie

Mr Robert Young,
New Vennal,
Glasgow.

[added on the letter]

   This alludes to an interview with my friends on the 31st of August; I borrowed it from Dr Dodd. A.H.

                "Cheerfuly, my friend, oh! look not thus
                With Pity's melting softness! That alone
                Can shake my fortitude. All is not lost.
                Lo! I have gain'd, on this important day,
                A victory consummate o'er myself,
                And o'er this life a victory. On this my
                Birthright to eternity—I've gained
                Dismission from a world, where for a while,
                Like you, like all, a pilgrim passing poor,
                A traveller, a stranger, I have met
                (But stranger) treatment rude and havoc!—so much
                The dearer,—more desir'd, the home I seek,
                Eternal of my Father and my God!
                Ah! little thought the prosecutors prompt,
                To do me good like this! Little thought
                The surely, ——****, —— our name's disgrace,
                Who voluntar'ly came to prove my ruin;
                Ah! little thought the other perfidious crimson'd,
                Perjur'd ****, that they were doing dood,
                For earthly poverty, to give th' exchange
                Of wealth eternal. Freely, triumphantly,
                My soul forgives each inj'ry, each evil
                They have wrought, each fear they've
                Drawn, each groan they've cost my heart.
                Hapless men! Down do I look with pity,
                Feverent beg, and unremitting, from all gracious

Heaven, eternal blessing on you! Be your lives
Like mine, true convertites to grace, to God!
And be our deaths—ah, there all difference ends!
Then be our deaths like this, th' atoning just;
Like his, the only righteous. Our last end!

[Among Hardie's papers in Stirling was found, after his execution, several quotations from Dr Dodd's *Thoughts in Prison*, written in Hardie's own handwriting.]

Stirling Castle, September 5, 1820

My dear Relations,

I now write you my long and last farewell letter, as I am, in a short time, to fall a victim beneath the stroke of the tyrant for seeking those rights for which our forefathers bled, and for which I shall lay down my life without the least reluctance, knowing it for the cause of truth and justice. I have wronged no person, I have hurt no person, and although I have formerly been of a very easy temper, I bless God, who has the hearts of all men in his hand, that it never entered mine to hurt my fellow creatures—no person could have induced me to take up arms in the same manner to rob and plunder; no, my dear friends, I took them up for the good of my suffering country and although we were outwitted, yet, I protest, as a dying man, that it was with a good intention on my part. But, dear friends, it becomes me, as a dying Christian, to look over all these matters, which bless God, I can do with pleasure. If I can't forgive my enemies, or those that have injured me, how can I expect my blessed Saviour to make intercession for me? Who so freely forgave his, even when expiring on the cross he prayed for his enemies: "Father, forgive them, they know not what they do." I could take the greatest enemy I have into my bosom, even the perjured Baird, who, in the presence of Almighty God, and a large assembly, stained and imbrued his hands in my innocent blood; even also the unrelenting Hardie . . . who voluntarily came to prove my ruin. Yes, my friends, my earnest prayer to God, is that he may forgive them. My dear friends, I again hope you will put yourselves to as little concern about me as possible. It becomes us to submit to the will of God and to every dispensation of his Providence. He is infinitely pure, He can do nothing wrong. He Chasteneth whom he loveth. And I earnestly hope and pray that he will sanctify this dispensation of his Providence to me and all of us.

I remain, your unfortunate nephew, while on earth,

Andrew Hardie

PS.—Hardie and Baird, alluded to in this letter is Mr Hardie,

Justice of the Peace, from Glasgow, and Mr Nicol Baird, Civil Engineer at Kelvinhead, and private in the Kilsyth Yeomanry Cavalry. These two were the principal witnesses against me. *** But I freely forgive them, and I hope you will keep no ill-will at them, and as my prayers on this earth will soon be ended, I earnestly beg of you to mind them in yours. Again farewell, till, I hope, we meet in glory.

A. Hardie

Stirling Castle, September 5, 1820

My dear young Cousins,

I now address a few lines unto you. You are all young and no doubt looking forward for long life, and placing your affections on this vain and transient world, and, as it were, trying to make it a place of rest, as I also too long did. But we have no resting place here. We are only sojourning in a strange land; and, let me remind you, if you try to make this your resting place, you will not only be miserably disappointed, but will lose your rest in that heavenly Jersusalem, the place appointed for all living. I hope you will keep your unfortunate Cousin's death in your remembrance, as one that was snatched away in the blood of youth; and although I fall by the hand of man, you know that a sparrow falleth not to the ground without the knowledge of Almighty God; and remember, what he saith to one so he saith to all, "Be ye therefore ready, for at such an hour as ye think not, the Son of Man cometh." I earnestly entreat you, as a dying friend, to be kind and obey your parents, agreeable to the commandment, and to attend church regularly. I shall close this short advice (and I hope you will attend to it) with a very important passage, which contains a great deal of matter, and, I may say, the whole duty of man. "Finally, brethren, whatsoever things are true, whasoever things are honest, whatsoever things are just, whatsoever things are pure, whatsoever things are lovely, whatsoever things are good report, if there be any virtue, if there be any praise, think on these things." Let me again remind you of this important commandment, "Be ye therefore ready, for at such a time as ye think not, the call cometh."

> O may God's grace your life direct,
>   From evil guard your way;
> And in temptation's fatal path
>   Permit you not to stray.
> So, fare you well, may God attend you still;
> And all your souls with consolation fill.

I am, dear Cousins, with respect, yours & etc.

Andrew Hardie

Stirling Castle, September 7, 1820

My dear and loving Margaret,

Before this arrives at your hand I will be made immortal, and will be, I trust, singing praises to God and the Lamb, amongst the spirits of just men made perfect, through the atoning blood of our Lord and Saviour, Jesus Christ, whose all-sufficient merits are infinitely unbounded, then even all the sins of a sinful world—and he is able and willing to save to the uttermost all those that are enabled to come to him by faith in his blood. What consolation does this render to me, who, while writing this, and within a few short hours of launching into an eternity, where I am not afraid to enter, although a poor, unworthy, miserable sinner, and not worthy of the least of this notice. Yet I trust he will put on his unspotted robe of righteousness, and present my poor and unworthy soul to his Father, redeemed with his most precious blood. Think, my dear Margaret, on the goodness of Almighty God to me in the last and closing period of my life. O think on it, and draw consolation from that source from whence I obtained it, and from whence consolation and real fortitude can alone be obtained. Could you have thought that I was sufficient to withstand such a shock, which at once burst upon me like an earthquake, and buried all my vain earthly hopes beneath its ruins, and at once left me a poor shipwrecked mariner on this bleak shore, separated from thee, in whom all my hopes were centred? But, alas, how vain are all the earthly hopes of us weak sighted mortals. How soon are they all buried in oblivion. My dear Margaret, put yourself to no concern about me—O may that good and gracious God who has supported me so peculiarly support you in every gracious dispensation of his Providence that he is pleased to visit you with. O that he may send his ministering angels and soothe you with the balm of comfort. O may they approach the beauteous mourner and tell you that your lover lives—triumphs— lives—though condemned, lives to a nobler life. My dear Margaret, I hope you will not take it as a dishonour that your unfortunate lover died for his distressed, wronged, suffering and insulted country; no, my dear Margaret, I know you are possessed of nobler ideas than that, and well do I know that no person of feeling or humanity will insult you with it—I have every reason to believe that it will be the contrary. I shall die firm to the cause in which I embarked, and although we were outwitted and betrayed, yet I protest as a dying man, it was done with good intention on my part. But well did you know my sentiments on that subject long before I was taken prisoner. No person could have induced me to take up arms to rob or plunder; no, my dear Margaret, I took them for the restorations of those rights for which our forefathers bled, and which we have allowed shamefully to be wrested from us; but I trust the innocent blood which will be shed tomorrow, in place of being a terror, will awaken my countrymen—my poor, suffering countrymen, from that lethargy which has so overclouded them! But, my dear Margaret, this is not a very pleasing subject to you, so I will leave it, and direct your attention to matters of more importance—to the one thing needful. Recollect, my dear Margaret, that we are, one and all of us, lost and miserable sinners, and that you have, as well as me, to stand before a great and just God, who is infinite and pure, and who cannot look upon sin but with the utmost abhorrence, and that it is only through the blood of a crucified Saviour that we can expect mercy at this awful tribunal, my dear Margaret, I will be under the necessity of laying down my pen, as this will have to go out immediately.

> "O may God's grace your life direct,
>   From evil guard your way;
> And in temptation's fatal paths
>   Permit you not to stray."

You will give my dying love to your Father and Mother, James and Agnes, Mrs Connell and Jean Buchanan, and I exhort you all to a close walk with God, through our Lord and Saviour, Jesus Christ; and when you have fulfilled a course of life agreeable to his word, that we may be united together in the mansions of peace, where there is no sorrow—Farewell—a long farewell to you and all worldly cares, for I have done with them. I hope you will call frequently on my distressed and afflicted mother. At the expense of some tears I destroyed your letters. Again, farewell my dear Margaret, may God attend you still, and all your soul with consolation fill, is the sincere prayer of your most affectionate and constant lover while on earth.

Andrew Hardie

Miss Margaret MacKeigh

Stirling Castle, September 7, 1820

Dear Friend,

Before this reaches your hand I will be immortal, and, I trust singing to the glory of God and the Lamb among the spirits of those who have washed their robes in the precious innocent blood of our Lord and Saviour, Jesus Christ, whose all-sufficient merits are infinitely unbounded to save a whole sinful world through his blood. My dear young friend, I hope you will not put yourself to concern about me, if you would allow yourself to contemplate a little on the wisdom and goodness of God in all his procedure with us, the weak children of his hand. He gave us our being; we are subject unto him; and he can call us to his glorious presence whenever he sees it meet. He is pure and infinite; he can do nothing wrong; and however painful our trials and afflictions may be to us poor, feeble, weak mortals, yet we are assured that he worketh to reconcile those whom he loveth to himself, as it is written "The Lord chasteneth whom he loveth." What will it avail me tomorrow at this same hour if I be found in Christ? Although I had lived a thousand years in this miserable and transient world mattereth nothing to us, if we are ready; "Be ye therefore ready, for at such an hour as ye think not the call cometh." My dear friend, this is a command of great importance, and I earnestly entreat you will never forget it. My dear friend, although my past life never merited public censure, yet upon serious self examination I found myself far deficient in my duty towards God, I found myself a poor, lost, miserable sinner, and utterly unable by any means whatever to extricate myself from a gulf of sin and misery into which I and the whole race of mankind were plunged, and I found also, that I had greatly aggravated my charge, by actual transgressions innumerable. I found also, by reading my Bible, which I had often done before this affair happened, but not with that serious attention which, with the assistance of God, I performed after I was taken prisoner—I found that God was just and pure, and could not look upon sin but with abhorrence, and that sin merits eternal death. Now, my dear friend, I was forced to call out, like the jailor at Phillippi, who, when he saw Paul and Silas out of the stocks, or irons, which he had previously locked them into, he doubtless was convinced at once that this could not be done but by the interposition of some supernatural power—he was convinced that the god or gods which he worshipped (being a heathen) could work no such miracles as this, and trembling, fell down before Paul and Silas, and said "Sirs, what must I do to be saved?" which brought forth that joyful and important answer from the blessed apostle, "Believe in the Lord Jesus Christ, and thou shalt be saved." O joyful sound! O joyful words!! How comprehensive—how important—how complete. "Believe in the Lord Jesus Christ, and thou shalt be saved." Lord, I believe, help thou mine unbelief. This is the balm that heals every wound—this the cure for a wounded conscience. "As Moses lifted up the serpent in the wilderness, so shall the Son of Man be lifted up." So, my dear young friend, if we look unto the Lord Jesus Christ with a steady eye of faith, we shall find a balm for every wound. My dear friend, I hope you will keep a steady walk with God, through our Lord and Saviour Jesus Christ; but I hope you are not ignorant of the nature of these matters. However, I trust you will excuse me for laying them before you; you will be nothing the worse by being put in mind of them, and I earnestly hope that you will keep them in your remembrance, particularly as they are from a poor, unfortunate young man, who was cut off in the bloom of his prime, just as it were entering into life, and who had built, as he thought, for ages, his earthly hopes; but, alas! how vain are all the hopes of man "He cometh forth like a flower and is cut down, he appears also like a shadow, but continueth not." Farewell! Farwell my dear young friend! Farewell all the fond boasted pleasures, of a vain world, I have done with them.

> "A brother the Heavens hath gained,
>   Out flying the tempest and wind;
> His rest he hath sooner obtain'd,
>   And left his companions behind."

I hope you will excuse any inaccuracies in this letter, as my time is drawing very close. Again farewell, my young friend; I hope our next meeting will be in glory.

Addressed by him thus: From Andrew Hardie to Isabella Condy, as a token of gratitude for her kind attention to him while a prisoner in Stirling Castle, who fell a Martyr to the cause of Truth and Justice on the 8th of September, 1820.

Stirling Castle, Thursday night, at 10 o'clock, 7th September, 1820.

To Isabella Condy, Stirling.

Stirling Castle, September 8, 1820
My dear Brothers and Sister,
    As I am in a few short hours to take my leave of this vain and transient world, I think it a duty incumbent upon me to lay before you a few observations, and however weak they may, or seem to be, yet upon consideration that they are from your dying brother, and as the words or advice of dying friends generally attract the attention, such as they are, I shall transmit them; and may the Lord illumine every dark ray of my mind, and enable me to impress your minds with a serious awe and resignation to his divine will. You will remember, in a letter from our dear distressed mother, of date 2nd [sic] August, in which you express your deep concern for me, which has been a great source of grief to me. But I beg your serious attention while I state something of more importance. In the same paragraph you remind me of "Eternity" and that it is an awful word, and so it is my dear brothers and sister, and I hope you will take it into serious consideration. And let me remind you, that you have a

dear father and six brothers and sisters already dropt into eternity and while writing this, I am standing on the very brink of eternity. Indeed we are at all times under sentences of death; and remember, that what God saith to one, he saith to all. "Dust we are, and unto dust we must return." From every age and condition of life—from every spot of ground—every moment of time, there are short and sudden ways of descent into the grave. He regards not the strength of the vigorous—the beauty of the comely—nor the arts of the wise; alas! neither can the sighs of the poor widow, nor the cries of the helpless orphan, melt him into compassion; but, like a rapid torrent, he carries down all, without distinction, before him. Grey hairs are his ripe harvest! Yea, like the raging storm, he crushed down the tender flower in its very bud. Now, my dear brothers and sister, I think I have said enough on the uncertainty of time. In sojourning in this valley of tears, we have no resting place here, but let us seek that eternal rest which is to be found through the merits of Jesus Christ, in that celestial city made without hands, in that heavenly Jerusalem, whose builder and maker is God, where there is no created sun, moon, nor stars, but the glory of the Lamb is the light thereof. I earnestly entreat you, dear brothers and sister, to take my former advice into your serious consideration. Remember that you are baptized unto the Lord Jesus Christ, and that you are in a country where his gospel is preached in its purity. And I warn you, as a dying brother, who is deeply interested in your welfare, to fly immediately to the protection of that blessed Saviour, who is stretching forth his hand ready to receive you. Do not delay. Remember what he saith to one, he saith to all. "Be ye therefore ready, for at such an hour as you think not, the call cometh." He willeth not the death of a sinner, he wishes all to come unto him and inherit life. "Come unto me all ye that are weary and heavy laden, and I will give you a rest. Take my yoke upon you and learn of me, for I am meek and lowly in heart, and ye shall find rest unto your souls, for my yoke is easy and my burden light." Now, dear brothers, if you do not accept of his invitations it will be better for you—you never had been born. It will be more tolerably for the sun burnt African, or the shivering Greenlander, on the day of judgment, than for you. They have not the least knowledge of revelation and consequently worship any thing which their imaginations suggest. The word of God has not yet been revealed to them. I was going to say much more on this subject, and I intended to give you some moral instruction; but alas! my dear brothers and sister, my dissolution is at hand, I am within a few short hours of flying into the arms of my dear Lord and Saviour Jesus Christ. O how beautiful is my prospect, to be admitted into the arms of that lovely Redeemer whom I had hitherto neglected! Do not mourn for me, my dear relatives, friends and acquaintances. While you are reading this I will be singing the glory of God amongst angels, and those who have washed their robes in the blood of that innocent Lamb who sitteth at the right hand of God. I am not afraid to die; I shall hail the scaffold as the harbinger of my salvation. O, my dear brothers and sister, I earnestly entreat you for the love of God, to be kind to my dear and distressed and affectionate and loving mother; and remember, when you do so, that you are only doing your duty. O do! my dear brothers and sister, O remember her, I earnestly entreat you: and also do attend the church regularly. O my dear brothers and sister, I must now lay down my pen. May the Lord of his infinite mercy, guide, protect, and lead you through the paths of this wilderness where you are residing, and after you have filled a course of life agreeable to his commandments, enable me to hail you as happy and immortal spirits in glory. Remember my dear mother. Farewell! my dear friends, farewell! A long farewell to this vain world and all its boasted pleasures. When James Goodwin calls on you, I hope you will read this to him, and I trust that all my dear young cousins will pay attention to it. Do not weep for me, my dear friends, weep for yourselves and for your sins. Again farewell!

I am, my dear friends, your dying brother in Christ,

Andrew Hardie

APPENDIX TWO

Alleged Declaration of
James Wilson
in the Death Cell

The forged "Dying Declaration of James Wilson" which was used by Peter MacKenzie to support his argument that Wilson was forced out by the insurgents. Stevenson, however, says that he did not think that MacKenzie forged the document himself but that someone else wrote the document and duped MacKenzie into thinking it was genuine.

DYING DECLARATION OF JAMES WILSON

(Written by himself)

Being desirous that a correct account of my conduct in the matter for which I am to suffer should go to the public, I have to submit the following short narrative, which neither conceals nor misrepresents the truth.—I am just entering the sixtieth year of my age; was born in the village of Strathaven, of respectable parents; was bred a hosier; was married about thirty years ago, and never once left the house in which I was born till I lately was confined to a prison; I will readily be believed, therefore, when I mention that my life was peaceable, and harmlessly passed away; and indeed I know no one in my neighbourhood that can say that I ever injured or offended them. It was not till Thursday the sixth of April last that this in-offensive life was interrupted by an occurrence which, in the little I had to do in it, I will now detail.

In the morning of that day, about twenty men, mostly belonging to Strathaven, came to my house, and said that a person of the name of Shields had brought some news from Glasgow, which had in-clined them to set off immediately for that place: and they added, they were determined I should go along with them. I never heard of this person Shields before. I refused to go; but they threatened to blow my brains out if I did not accompany them. I said I had no arms; when the persons noticed the blade of a sword, which had no hilt, and was broken at the point, and which I used as a bow for my stocking frame, and they observed, I might take it. At length, carrying this useless blade with me, we left my house for Glasgow; but when near to Kilbride, which is half way, we heard that we were deceived by the Glasgow committee having turned all traitors. I then left these persons, and, after stopping a short time at a friend's house by the way, I returned home, where I had scarce arrived when

I was secured by the officers of the law, and conveyed to Hamilton Barracks, where I lay till Sunday, when I was taken to Glasgow prison. I was now charged with taking up arms, and levying war against the king, and am doomed to suffer the extremist punishment of the law, as one who has committed high treason. My trial is before the world; the facts of my case are already public, and I refrain, in present situation, from making any observations on those singular proceedings. I meet my fate in the calmness and tranquillity of a man who is decidedly conscious of suffering innocently. I most solemnly deny that I took up arms to levy war against the king. I indignantly reject the imputation that I committed or intended to commit high treason. Of that crime, or of any offence done or meditated against the lives or properties of my fellow creatures, my heart does not accuse me; and the humane and discerning will, I am sure, with difficulty persuade themselves that the facts above detailed merited the name and the punishment of treason. I acknowledge that I die a true patriot for the cause of freedom for my poor country, and I hope that my countrymen will still continue to see the necessity of a Reform in the way of the country being represented; and I am convinced that nothing short of universal suffrage and annual parliaments will be of any service to put a stop to the present corrupted state of the House of Commons; therefore, I hope my dear countrymen will unite and stand firm for their whole rights.

In order to confute a most scandalous falsehood that has been circulated by two men of but very indifferent characters, viz. of my having burnt a Bible, as a dying man I solemnly deny that ever I did any thing of the kind, and I do solemnly declare it to be false. I therefore do declare and firmly believe the Bible to be the word of God; and I do believe that Jesus Christ is the Son of God and the Saviour of the world, and I do place all my hopes and confidence in the mercy of God the Father, and in the merits and meditation of Jesus Christ, my Lord and Saviour. Amen.

(Signed) James Wilson

Glasgow Jail, Iron-room. 20th August, 1820.

APPENDIX THREE

Songs of the 1820 Rising

BONNYMUIR

Written by Andrew Hardie while waiting execution

Your wish is granted, I did say,
Then steered our course along the way,
But when we came near Camelon town,
We saw no men of great renown,
Him* we saw who had us sent
And on the cause he still was bent,
In one short hour I will you meet—
With twenty men, equipped, complete.

You'll speed your way up on the moor:
You and your men may rest secure,
For all is going on so well—
Yes, more than mortal tongue can tell.
Then to the moor we went with speed
And on the heather laid our head:
But here we did not long remain
Until we saw a dreadful train.

Men and horses in armour bright,
Advancing speedy in our sight.
Up we sprang, to arms we flew
And this we then designed to do,
Close to the dyke to run with speed
And then to face the prancing steed,
To keep them back as long's we could
Or in the cause to shed our blood.

With anxious eye, we looked in vain
To see this hero and his train
To help us in the time of need
Against the rider and his steed.
Firing commenced on every side,
Swords and pikes did next succeed,
Thro' the dyke a few advanced,
But back we drove them with the lance.

* Hardie refers to King, the Government agent.

BONNYMUIR

Written by Allan Murchie while waiting to be transported for life

Although our lives were ventured fair
To free our friends from toil and care,
The English troops we dint to dare,
And wish'd them a' good mornin'.

It's with three cheers we welcom'd them
Upon the Muir of Bonny Plain,
It was our rights from them to gain
Caused us to fight that mornin'.

With pikes and guns we did engage;
With lion's courage did we rage—
For liberty or slavery's badge
Caused us to fight that mornin'.

But some of us did not stand true,
Which caus'd the troops them to pursue,
And still it makes us here to rue
That e'er we fought that mornin'.

We're a' condemned for to dee,
And weel ye ken that's no a lee,
Or banish'd far across the sea
For fightin' on that mornin'.

But happy we a' ha'e been
Since ever that we left the Green,
Although strong prisons we ha'e seen,
Since we fought that mornin'.

If mercy to us all shall be shown
From Royal George's kingly crown,
We will receive't without a frown,
And sail the seas some mornin'.

Mercy to us has now been shown
From Royal George's noble crown,
And we're prepared, without a frown,
To see South Wales some mornin'.

THE RISING

Written by the Radical poet Alexander (Sandy) Rodger, cleared of High Treason

What howlings are these from the high lofty dwellings,*
    As if some fell sorc'ress were struggling with death?
'Tis bedlam, corruption, lies cursing and yelling,
    And tainting the air with her putrified breath.

She curses the fate of her Spies and Informers—
    She wails o'er the efforts so fruitlessly made,
When they prowl'd through the land for the blood of Reformers
    Seduced the unwary—then basely betrayed.

She called on her Reynolds, so famous for murder,
    Her Oliver, Castle, and Richmond, most dear:
And dubbing them knight of the Spy's noble order,
    Bestowed the insignia they henceforth should wear.

Hence, nothing was heard of but plots and sedition,
    High Treason, rebellion, and blasphemy wild,
Because that the people had dared to petition
    In plain honest language, firm, manly and mild.

The laws were suspended—the prisons were glutted,
    Indictments preferred, and Juries enclosed;
But mark! In her own wicked efforts outwitted—
    Corruption at once is defeated—exposed!

For truth must prevail over falsehood and error,
    In spite of the Devil, Corruption and Spies;
Who down to their dens shall be driven in terror,
    While man to his scale in creation will rise.

ON A RADICAL DEMONSTRATION

Written by Alexander (Sandy) Rodger

Vile, "sooty rabble", what d'ye mean
By raising a' this dreadful din?
Do ye no ken what horrid sin

* Glasgow's Bridewell.

Ye are committing
By handin' up your chafts sae thin
    For sic a meeting?

Vile Black-nebs! doomed through life to drudge
And hawk among your native sludge
Wha' is't gives you the right to judge
    O' siccan matters,
That ye maun grumble, grint an' grudge
    At us, your betters?

Base Rads! Whose ignorance surpasses
The dull stupidity of asses,
Think ye the privileged classes
    Care aught aboot ye?
If only mair ye dour to fash us,
    By George! we'll shoot ye!

We've wealth o' sodgers in the toun
To keep sic ragamuffins doun;
So gin ye dina settle soon,
    By a' that's guid!
We'll giv' the commons sewers rin
    Wi' your base bluid!

Tak', therefore, this kind admonition:
Recant, represent, be a' submission!
And, as a proof that your contrition
    Is frae the heart,
In Gude's name burn that vile Petition
    Before ye part!

THE RISING AT PAISLEY
Written by an anti-Radical poet John Goldie

What think ye o' our Paisley wabsters sae smart
Wha bauldly resolv'd their shuttles to part
    For a sharp pike and a Radical cleg;
Wha vow'd that the patriots should be crusht,
An' the altar o' loyalty levell'd in dust;
That nae mair wi' their heddles an' treddles they'd toll,
But salute a' their faes, on the first o' April,
    Wi' a sharp pike an' a Radical cleg.

A foragin' party ae e'ning was sent
On murder an' plunder an' robbery bent.
   With their sharp pikes and Radical clegs.
Some two-three auld pistols an' guns they had got,
But the Radicals wanted baith pouther and shot;
For without them they cou'dna keep up the war
But, gude faith, they got plenty o' baith at Foxbar,
   With their sharp pikes and Radical clegs.

At length the lang leukit for morning cam' roun',
When their hosts should assemble in country an' toun,
   With their sharp pikes and Radical clegs,
When they vow'd that such valorous deeds should be done,
What battles they'd fight, an' what fiel's they wad win;
But they countit their chickens afore they were hatch'd,
An' they gutit their haddocks afore they were catch'd,
   With their sharp pikes and Radical clegs.

For their courage grew cauld when it cam' to the bit,
An' the puir bodies thocht it was time to flit,
   Wi' their sharp pikes and Radical clegs,
Their orator leaders turn'd out rather shy,
An' they thocht it was best to let sleepin' dogs lie;
For they dina' much relish the leuks o' the chiels
Wha were ready to scatter some Wellington pills,
   'Mang their sharp pikes and Radical clegs.

Success to each Briton who fearlessly rose
To defend Freedom's birthplace frae rebels an' foes,
   With their sharp pikes and Radical clegs;
May they ne'er lose the freedom they rose to defend,
May peace and content spread their wings o'er the land,
An' may ilk trait'rous chiel wha rebellion wad breed
Get a prog in the guts an' a skelp on the head
   With a sharp pike an' a Radical cleg.

RADICAL BODIES, GAE HAME

Written by the yeomanry soldier John Goldie

Ye Radical set, that in bodies hae met,
I redd ye to part and gang hame, gang hame,
Or faith ye will fin' that it's nae pleasant thing,
For bullets to riddle your wame, your wame.

The cavalry's comin', gae hame, gae hame,
Wi' riflemen runnin', gae hame, gae hame,
The cavalry's comin', wi' riflemen runnin',
Sae, Radical bodies, gae hame, gae hame.

Ilk delegate chiel has been playin' the deil,
Wi' your purses, your causes, and your fame, your fame,
Your pikes and your clegs are o'er short in the legs,
For a rifleman's bullet, gae hame, gae hame.

The cavalry's comin', gae hame, gae hame,
Wi' riflemen runnin', gae hame, gae hame,
An' if ance they begin, they'll gar a' your troops rin,
Tho' ye were a dizen to ane, to ane.

The night it was set, when your troops should hae met,
To conquer or die for your claim, your claim,
But at bugle or drum, deil a out ye wad come,
For ye thought ye were safer at hame, at hame.

The cavalry's comin', gae hame, gae hame,
Wi' riflemen runnin', gae hame, gae hame,
When cavalry's comin', and riflemen runnin',
A Radical's safest at hame, at hame.

On Cathkin your camp was nae doubt rather damp,
An' when it began to rain, to rain,
To keep yousel' warm frae the weet and the storm,
Ye were wise just to step awa hame awa hame.

The cavalry's comin', gae hame, gae hame,
In case you should get yoursel' lame, lame, lame,
For I wad ye a groat, if ye slocken a shot,
Ye'll think ye bin better at hame, at hame.

Ye expeckit, nae doubt, at your first turn out,
That your foes would a' shrink at your name, your name,
That our sodgers would join, for to strengthen your line,
But, my conscience! you're rather mista'en, mista'en.

The cavalry's comin, gae hame, gae hame.
An' a riflemen takes a guide aim, guid aim,
An' if ance he should mak' a bull's eye o' your back,
Ye needna care muckle for hame, for hame.

THE DIRGE TO BAIRD AND HARDIE

Written by Daniel Taylor of Kilsyth at the dying request of Baird and Hardie and read at their graveside

Though I can boast no animinating song
To meet the lover or inspire the brave
Yet friendship bids me leave the busy throng
To pour my sorrows o'er the bloody grave.

Not only friendship but their dying charge
My promise made, how base were it forgot?
Then on this grave to write this funeral dirge
And mourn their fate, since here I find the spot.

Thou gracious power who through the shepherds
Used to sing the glory of Emmanuel's birth,
Teach me in friendship, pious humble strains
To mourn a friend—a brother of the earth.

Teach those who weep o'er this revered grave,
To bless thy name, thou everlasting Hope,
Who Baird and Hardie such assurance gave
As made them hail with joy "the fatal rope".

For hear the brave, the generous youth exclaim,
When the degrading hurdle ceased to move,
And from his car the bloody axeman came
With terrors more than human strength to prove.

Hail, harbinger of everlasting peace!
In manly accents they addressed the stage,
Where soon the sorrows of their souls would cease
To join the saints of every former age.

But o'er this grave, the children yet unborn,
May shed a tear, when told by history's page
How they from friends and aged parents torn,
Braved all the horrors of the bloody stage.

Surprised, perhaps, to read the mournful tale
The rising youths may asked their aged sire—
"Was Scotia conquered? Did her foes prevail?
Oh where was then your patriotic fire?

Or did her Laws such sacrifice require?"
"No foreign foe that ever ploughed the wave
Or crossed the Tweed," methinks the sire replied
"Could leave us weeping o'er so sad a grave.

"No, Scotia every foreign foe defies,
But, oh, my son, excite me not to tell
What I have known of Hardie and of Baird,
So strong of Freedom did their hearts excel.

But let those tears express my fond regard."
Yet why should fancy fly the present grief,
And point our hopes to some more distant date?
Thus fate decreed for us there's no relief?

And must we sink beneath oppression's weight?
Forbid it Heaven—Oh, may thy mighty arm
Protect the humble and the friendless poor,
Oh let thy grace, their sinking spirits charm,
Be thou their stay, their refuge most secure.

However dark the present may appear,
Though those in power our dearest rights deny,
Yet Truth and Justice shall our bosoms cheer,
And Freedom's sun shall blaze o'er Europe's sky.

But night returns, with all her sable train,
And I must bid the lone churchyard "Adieu",
Yet never shall this dreary spot contain
Two hearts more faithful, honest, kind and true.

It may be said, we have patriots resting here,
Who gave their life to heal their country's woes,
For Baird and Hardie loved their country dear,
And only fell before their guilty foes.

Here pity weeps o'er a friend,
They too, were pious as their letters tell;
Say ye who saw them to their bitter end,
Could stronger faith in human bosoms dwell?

Though near this place no marble statue stand,
Nor weeping angel pointing to the spot,
Their fame is known all through their native land,
And never, never, shall they be forgot.

IN MEMORIUM

Lines composed for the Baird and Hardie Memorial of 1832

Here lie their slaughter'd mutilated frame,
    Who fell to Liberty like martyrs true,
Who keenly felt the Patriot's purest flame,
    And met their fate, as martyrs always do—
    Despising death, which ne'er can Patriot's souls subdue.

Calmly they death's apparatus view'd,
    Then upward turned their heaven directed eye,
Serene, collected, firm and unsubdued,
    Their county's wrongs alone, drew forth their sigh—
    And those to them endeared by nature's holiest tie.

Though falsely styled "low traitors" when they fell,
    Yet shall their names revered, soon rank with those,
of Hampden, Sidney, Wallace, Bruce and Tell,
    Who nobly bled to heal their countyr's woes—
    Whose enemies were men's, were Freedom's, deadliest foes.

Selected Bibliography
and
Index

SELECTED BIBLIOGRAPHY

It is, of course, impossible to list all the sources of the material contained in the background chapters 2–4; where it is relevant, the source is mentioned in the text. The following is a selected bibliography of material directly appertaining to 1820.

GENERAL

Annual Register, Vol. LXII. 1820
BARRET, C. R. B. *The 7th (Queen's Own) Hussars*, Vol. 11. 1914
BELLASIS, M. *Canadians Rise*. 1955
BELLESHEIM'S *History of the Catholic Church in Scotland* (Hunter Blair's translation)
BROWNLIE, MAJOR W. STEEL. *The Proud Trooper, a history of the Ayrshire Yeomanry*. 1964
CAMPBELL, JOHN. *Recollections of radical times, descriptive of the last hours of Baird and Hardie*. 1880
COCKBURN, LORD. *Trials for Sedition in Scotland*. 1888
Dictionary of National Biography
HANDLEY, JAMES E. *The Irish in Scotland 1798–1845*. 1943
JOHNSTON, THOMAS. *The History of the Working Classes in Scotland*. 1920
LIDDELL, COLONEL R. S. *The Memoirs of the 10th Royal Hussars*. 1891
MACKENZIE, PETER. *An exposure of the spy system pursued in Glasgow during the years 1816–30 with copies of the original letters of Andrew Hardie*. 1832
MACKENZIE, PETER. *Old Reminiscences of Glasgow and the West of Scotland*, Vol. 1. 1890
MACKENZIE, PETER. *Some Curious and Remarkable Glasgow Characters*. 1891
MACKENZIE, PETER. *The trial of James Wilson for high treason with an account of his execution at Glasgow, September 1820*. 1832
MARWICK, W. H. *Labour in Scotland. A short history of the Scottish working class movement*. 1945
MATHIESON, W. L. *The Awakening of Scotland 1747–97*. Glasgow, 1910
MEIKLE, H. W. *Scotland and the French Revolution*. 1912
Report of the State Trials

Report of the Trials for High Treason in Scotland
The Statistical Account of Scotland. Edinburgh. 1841

BIOGRAPHICAL WORKS

COCKBURN. *Life of Francis Jeffrey.* 1852 (2 vols)
COCKBURN. *Memorials of his Time.* 1856
FRASER, J. R. *Memoir of John Fraser of Newfield.* 1879
GREIG, W. A. *Life of Francis Jeffrey.* 1949
LINDSAY, CHARLES. *Life of William Lyon MacKenzie.* 1862
MACDONALD, MARSHAL. *Souvenirs.* 1898
PARKHILL, JOHN. *Autobiography of Arthur Sneddon.* 1825
RICHMOND, ALEXANDER B. *Narrative of the condition of the Manufacturing Population and the Proceedings of Government which led to the State Trials in Scotland.* 1824
SOMERVILLE, ALEXANDER. *The Autobiography of a Working Man.* 1848
TURNER, JAMES. Reminiscences. 1854

LOCAL HISTORIES

BROWN, ROBERT. *The History of Paisley from the Roman period down to 1884*, Vol. 2. Paisley. 1881
BRYSON, J. M. *Handbook of Strathaven and vicinity.* Strathaven. 1900
BUCHAN, JAMES WALTER. *A History of Peebleshire.* 1925
DRYSDALE. *William Auld Biggins of Stirling.* Stirling. 1904
GEBBIE MARY. Sketches of Strathavon and Avondale. 1880
HOWIE, JAMES. *An historical account of the town of Ayr for the last fifty years.* Kilmarnock. 1861
KNOX, JAMES. *Aidrie, and historical sketch.* 1921
MACLEOD, D. *The Clyde District of Dumbartonshire.* Dumbarton. 1886
MACLEOD, D. *History of the castle and town of Dumbarton.* 1886
MACNEIL, P. *History of Tranent.*
MACPHAIL, I. M. *A Short History of Dunbartonshire.* Dumbarton. 1962
METCALFE, W. M. *A History of Paisley 600–1908.* Paisley. 1909
NIMMO, WILLIAM. *The History of Stirlingshire*, Vol. 1. Hamilton. 1880
PARKHILL, JOHN. *A History of Paisley.* 1850

MANUSCRIPTS

National Library of Scotland
Devon Record Office
Letters concerning disturbances 1819–20 MS 2836 (Papers of General Sir George Brown)
Letters of Lord President Hope (1817–19) MS 10 (Melville Papers)

Letters on disaffection in Glasgow (17–19) MS 1054 (Melville Papers)
Orders issued to Royal Edinburgh Volunteers during Radical troubles. 1819. MS 3581
Reminiscences of a sergeant of the Glasgow Yeomanry, classified as "Notes on Radicalism in the West of Scotland". MS 2773 ff 2r. 32v
Devon Record Office
The Sidmouth Papers, 1820
Public Records Office, London
Baga de Secretis (K.B.8.)
Correspondence (Disturbances) 40/11 and 13
Correspondence and Papers (Disturbances) H.O. series 102 and H.O. series 104
Entry Books, Disturbances H.O. 41/6 p. 260
Treasury In-Letters (T.L.)

PAMPHLETS

A full account of the sentences of 22 Radicals at Stirling for High Treason. Stirling. 1820
Hints to Radical Reformers. Anon. London. 1817
A Letter to the Duke of Hamilton detailing the events of the late Rebellion in the West of Scotland by a British subject. Glasgow, April 28, 1820
The proceedings of a meeting that took place at Linktown of Kirkcaldy on the Third of November, 1819, to take into consideration the proceedings at Manchester.
The Radical Rising at Strathaven by John Stevenson. 1835
Reply to the Letters of Kirkman Finlay Esq. on the Spy System. Peter MacKenzie. Glasgow. 1833
The Rising of 1820 by F. A. Sherry. Glasgow. 1968
Trial for Libel in the Court of Exchequer, Guildhall, London, Saturday and Monday, December 20—22, 1834. Richmond versus Simpkin and Marshall.
Wilsons Baird and Hardie. William C. MacDougall. Glasgow. 1947

NEWSPAPERS AND PERIODICALS (CONTEMPORARY)

London
    Courier; London Gazette; Morning Post; Observer; St James Chronicle; The Times
Scottish
    Ayr Advertiser; Edinburgh Gazette; Glasgow Chronicle; Glasgow Herald; Greenock Advertiser; The Scotsman; Stirling Journal

Magazines
  Blackwood's Magazine; Edinburgh Review; Hansard, official parliamentary report; *Scots Magazine*
Not contemporary
  Glasgow Evening Post, September 28, 1933; *Glasgow Evening Post,* April 30, 1935; *Innes Review,* Vol. XVI; *Kilmarnock Standard,* March 16, 1912

INDEX

Abbott, Joseph (Galston Radical), 232

Abercromby, Hon. George (foreman of Grand Jury), 224, 225

Abercromby, Lord, 63

Aberdeenshire, riots in, 77

Adam, Matthew, 122

Adam, W. (Lord Commissioner of the Jury Court), 220, 223

Adam, William (Ayr Radical), 136

Adamson, Andrew (Galston Radical), 232

Agricultural labourers, plight of, 87–8

Aherne, Captain, 72

Aikman (magistrate), 223

Airdrie, 20, 123, 147, 194, 212

Aiken, James (Camelon Radical), 226, 257, 262

Aitken, James (Falkirk Radical), 226, 257, 262

Alexander, Thomas, 185

Alexander, William, 226

Alien Act (1704), 41

Allan, George (Glasgow Radical), 227, 235, 253

Allan, John (Condorrat Radical), 220

Allan, Mr, of Flemington, 185

Allan, William, 182, 183

Allison, James, of Paisley, 116

Alloway, Lord, 128

Alston, Alexander, of Strathaven, 247

Alston, Robert Douglas (second-in-command, Glasgow Yeomanry), 25

American War of Independence, 36, 50, 52

Amiens, Peace of, 86

Anderson, James (member of Friends of the People), 61

Anderson, James (Radical), 226

Anderson, John, Jnr. (Glasgow Radical), 142, 193–4, 245, 263

Anderston, 167, 192

André, Citoyen J. B., 69–70

Anne, Queen, 46

Antrim, rising in, 81

Ardchattan, parliament at, 37

Armed Association (Glasgow), 147

Arnott, James (Advocate), 233, 238

Atholl, Duke of, 77, 257

Ayr, 29, 118, 137; Radical meetings in, 123, 135; trials of Radicals for theft, 206; Special Commission of Oyer and Terminer, 232, 236; treason trials, 257, 264–5

Ayr Chronicle, 213–14

Ayrshire Yeomanry ("Dandies"), 30, 129, 135, 142, 148–9, 152, 154, 181

Ayrshire Yeomanry Cavalry, 30, 209

Aytoun, Roger (Duke of Hamilton's agent), 128

Baird, John (commandant of Condorrat Radicals), 138, 268, 271, 276, 277; in action at Bonnymuir, 166–75; defeat and capture, 175–6; arraigned, 226; trial of, 243–4, 263, 264; executed, 277–80; memorials to, and reinterment of remains, 289–92; letters of, 303–7; dirge to, 347–8; memorial verses, 349

M*